PRAISE FOR MELVIN GOODMAN'S
National Insecurity: The Cost of American Militarism

"In this impassioned exposé of the astronomical costs of America's defense policy, former CIA analyst Goodman demonstrates how post–cold war neoconservatives . . . promoted a pugnacious militarism that has led to a string of foreign policy debacles and unprecedented levels of military spending. Few will finish this precisely argued polemic without the uneasy feeling that military spending is out of control." — *Publishers Weekly*

"A 25-year CIA veteran examines how recent presidents have handled the military and defense spending. Engaging reading for those interested in foreign policy and military spending." — *Kirkus Reviews*

"Melvin A. Goodwin is a damn fine author, and *National Insecurity* is a damning assessment of U.S. defense spending and covert operations." — *New York Journal of Books*

"In *National Insecurity* Mel Goodman shows how every president since Eisenhower has ceded authority to the Pentagon, to the detriment of our security and our democracy. But he doesn't just lament this dangerous condition — he provides a road map for demilitarizing our security policy at abroad and at home." — William D. Hartung, author, *Prophets of War: Lockheed Martin and the Making of the Military Industrial Complex*

NATIONAL INSECURITY

The Cost of American Militarism

Melvin A. Goodman

Open Media Series
City Lights Books | San Francisco

This book is also available as an e-edition: 978-0-87286-595-2

Library of Congress Cataloging-in-Publication Data
Goodman, Melvin A. (Melvin Allan), 1938–
   National insecurity : the cost of American militarism / Melvin A. Goodman.
      p. cm.
   Includes index.
   ISBN 978-0-87286-589-1
1. United States—Military policy. 2. Militarism—United States. 3. National
security—United States. 4. National security—United States—Decision
making—History. 5. United States—Military policy—Decision making—
History. 6. Eisenhower, Dwight D. (Dwight David), 1890–1969—Influence.
7. Weapons systems—Government policy—United States. 8. Military bases,
American—Foreign countries. 9. United States—Foreign relations. 10.
Strategy. I. Title. II. Title: Cost of American militarism.

   UA23.G734 2013
   355'.033573—dc23
                                    2012036018

City Lights Books are published at the City Lights Bookstore
261 Columbus Avenue, San Francisco, CA 94133
www.citylights.com

To Lini and our nine magical grandchildren:
Alex, James, Julia, Matthew, Willa, Quinn, Eleanor,
Eoin, and "Rango."

CONTENTS

AMERICAN MILITARISM:
COSTS AND CONSEQUENCES

*Wherever the standard of freedom and independence has been
or shall be unfurled, there will her heart, her benedictions and
her prayers be. But she goes not abroad, in search of monsters to
destroy . . . she is the champion and vindicator only of her own.*
—John Quincy Adams

*We have to recognize that no matter how great our strength, we
must deny ourselves the license to do always as we please. No one
nation . . . can or should expect any special privilege which harms
any other nation. Unless we are all willing to pay that price, no
organization for world peace can accomplish its purpose. And
what a reasonable price that is!* —President Harry S. Truman

We in the United States have created a land of illusion. We have
the world's best medical facilities, but also its highest medical
costs, and we still lack genuine universal health care coverage.
Our costs for entitlements such as Medicare and Social Security
are out of control, but we are unwilling to discuss reform. Our
corporations and the wealthy classes pay the lowest taxes in the
industrial world, but we adamantly oppose raising tax rates that
could alleviate one-quarter to one-third of our deficit problem. We have the most expensive and lethal military force in
the world, but we face no existential threat; nonetheless, liberals
and conservatives alike declare the defense budget sacrosanct.

A reasonable reduction in the amount of money we spend on defense would enable us to reduce our debt and invest in the peaceful progress and development of a civilian economy.

The United States has the most secure geopolitical environment of any major nation, but sustains a defense budget that equals the combined budgets of the rest of the world. Cuts in the defense budget over the next five years, announced in January 2012, were extremely modest, amounting to a minuscule 1 percent real cut when factoring in inflation. The cuts in Army and Marine personnel over a five-year period ending in 2017 will leave these services larger than they were in 2005. The mere lowering of recruitment quotas and the retirement of officers and noncommissioned officers will cover the modest reduction of the 92,000 troops.

Those who criticize even these modest reductions fail to recognize that, over the past two decades, the Cold War has ended and the greatest strategic threat to the United States—the Soviet Union—has dissolved. Nevertheless, we barricade ourselves behind a national missile defense, fight wars in which no vital national security interests are at stake, and post hundreds of thousands of troops overseas. U.S. nuclear forces, which have no utilitarian value, remain the same, although President Obama persistently claims to support arms control and disarmament. The United States has become that militarized nation that President Dwight D. Eisenhower presciently warned against in his farewell address more than fifty years ago.

The United States lacks a strategic vision for a world without an enemy, and it continues to spend far more on defense, homeland security, and intelligence than the rest of the world combined. We are the only nation in the world that deploys its military primarily to support foreign policy rather than to defend our borders and people. U.S. corporations dominate the sales of military equipment, selling extremely sophisticated weapons to countries such as Saudi Arabia that have the hard currency to pay for them but lack the skill to use them. We have more than 700 military bases and facilities around the world; few other countries have any. We can deploy eleven aircraft carriers; among our rivals only China even plans to deploy one—and that is a revamped Ukrainian aircraft carrier, a carryover from the ancient Soviet inventory.

U.S. militarization, reliance on the military to pursue foreign policy objectives better achieved by other means, has continued to expand since the end of the Cold War, when we might have expected and experienced a peace dividend. Military expansion during the Cold War, especially during peaks in the U.S. arms buildup against the Soviets and during the Vietnam War, at least had as its rationale the spectre of an aggressive Soviet Union. The administrations of Bill Clinton, George W. Bush, and Barack Obama, facing no existential threat, have given the Pentagon an unprecedented position of power and influence, including huge increases in defense spending and a dominant voice in the making of national security and foreign policies. The key contributions to the Pentagon's enhanced role have been President Bush's doctrine of preemptive attack and the permanent War on Terror, or the Long War; the misuse of power in Iraq; and President Obama's initial expansion of the war in Afghanistan. The Bush and Obama administrations have made sure that military figures dominate national security positions, and both administrations have failed to use the tools of diplomacy to deal effectively with foreign policy conflicts in the Middle East or with Iran or North Korea.

The roots of the militarization of U.S. foreign policy lie in the year 1947, with the beginning of the Cold War. Passage of the National Security Act in 1947 made the U.S. armed forces an inherent part of national security policy in peacetime. Previously, the Pentagon had rarely asserted itself in the policy process, even in wartime. Military influence grew over the next four decades, leading to the Defense Reorganization Act of 1986, commonly referred to as the Goldwater-Nichols Act, which made the chairman of the Joint Chiefs of Staff the "principal military adviser to the President, the National Security Council, and the Secretary of Defense."

One of the consequences of U.S. militarization and unilateralism has been an unwillingness to join international agreements and conventions designed to foster moderate actions in the global community. The United States, for example, joined the so-called "rogue states" (Algeria, China, Libya, Iran, Iraq, and Sudan) in opposing creation of the International Criminal Court (ICC), which extended the scope of international law and provided a means of bringing the world's worst human rights violators, such as Yugoslav President Slobodan Milosevic, to justice. Every member state of the European Union, including all of America's NATO allies, favored the ICC, as did President Clinton initially. Clinton ultimately deferred to the Pentagon and Senator Jesse Helms (R-NC), who argued that the Court would expose U.S. soldiers to international justice. This was a red herring, as the member states of the ICC have the right to try any of their own citizens charged with international crimes in their own courts, which is exactly what the United States has done in the past. Thus, as with the creation of the League of Nations in 1919, a major step forward in international law was taken without the endorsement and participation of the United States, which had prided itself on its support of international justice since the Nuremberg trials after World War II.

The United States has also been out of step with the global effort to ban the use of landmines, an effort that political conservatives and the Pentagon have opposed because of U.S. deployment of landmines near the border between North and South Korea. Although anti-personnel mines have killed and maimed thousands of civilians, including children, all over the world—Afghanistan, Angola, Bosnia, Cambodia, El Salvador, Mozambique, and elsewhere—the marginal advantage of their deployment in South Korea has been used to justify U.S. refusal to adhere to the convention. Not even the possibility of warmer relations between the two Koreas has led the United States to take a new position on the issue.

Since the 9/11 attacks of 2001, the United States, using the pretense of a global war on terror, has gone to war in Iraq and Afghanistan and has used military force in Pakistan, Libya, Somalia, and Yemen. It is no surprise that we now find ourselves overcommitted in the Middle East, North Africa, and Southwest Asia, which has become an "arc of crisis" for the United States. President George W. Bush helped to create this arc with his wars in Iraq and Afghanistan. Although President Obama has undertaken military disengagement in both countries, he has widened covert action throughout the area as the Pentagon and the CIA conduct assassination programs against insurgents and terrorists. The United States may be closing down the arrogantly named "Camp Victory" in Iraq, but it is building secret facilities in Ethiopia, Djibouti, the Seychelles, and the Arabia Peninsula (presumably in Yemen or the United Arab Emirates) as bases for Predator and Reaper drone aircraft. These drones have been used against targets in Afghanistan, Iraq, Libya, Pakistan, Yemen, and Somalia, according to State Department cables obtained by WikiLeaks, an anti-secrecy group.[1]

In addition to drone bases, U.S. secret facilities support special operations against dozens of countries from South America to Central Asia. Army Rangers, Navy Seals, and CIA personnel operate out of them. Military personnel are deployed throughout the Middle East and North Africa, and the Pentagon and the Department of State are training special forces from dozens of countries in the art of counterinsurgency. The *New Yorker's*

Seymour Hersh has been reporting for several years that the United States is conducting special operations in Iran, and the *Wall Street Journal* has reported that Pentagon and CIA teams are conducting covert operations to stop the smuggling of Iranian arms into Iraq.[2] Such operations contribute to the increase in anti-Americanism throughout the region.

U.S. response to the attacks of 9/11 has brought a new dimension to the national security state: the increase in largely unaccountable security contractors, such as the notorious Blackwater (now brandishing the benign corporate name of Academi LLC), and consulting agencies that act as intermediaries between the federal government and defense contractors. They operate without any apparent code of conduct, and the uncontrolled violence of Xe, another of Blackwater's incarnations, is well known. Working with these contractors has involved huge payments to consulting agencies managed by former administration officials such as Secretary of State Condoleezza Rice, national security adviser Stephen Hadley, directors of homeland security Michael Chertoff and Tom Ridge, and CIA director Michael Hayden.

More than one-third of the personnel in the intelligence community are private contractors, with the relatively new Department of Homeland Security and Office of National Intelligence relying most extensively on them. Private contracts now consume 70 percent of the intelligence budget, and private contractors represent more than half of the employees at the new National Counterterrorism Center. The overwhelming U.S. presence in Iraq is largely contractual, and in 2011, for the first time, deaths among contractors in Afghanistan exceeded fatalities of U.S. soldiers and military personnel.

The U.S. reliance on military force has damaged U.S. national interests at a time when the world is facing severe economic stress. The Iraq and Afghan Wars have been costly in terms of blood and treasure, and they have not made America more secure. The war on terror has created more terrorists than it has eliminated, and the war is expanding in the Persian Gulf and Africa, particularly in Yemen and Somalia. The United States is no longer seen as a beacon of liberty to the world, but as an imperialistic bully with little respect for international law. The economic costs of our emphasis on the military have been enormous, coming at a time of necessary constraint for U.S. expenditures and investment policy.

As the military expands, the Department of State declines, losing resources and influence; it is no longer able to provide robust diplomatic alternatives to militarization. During the crucial decision-making in 2009 to determine troop levels in Afghanistan, Secretary of State Hillary Clinton merely echoed the positions taken by Secretary of Defense Robert M. Gates, making no effort to question the strategic and geopolitical implications of a wider war in Southwest Asia. The budget of the Department of Defense, exceeding levels reached during the worst days of the Cold War, needs to be significantly constrained. The United States devotes little attention to one of the greatest losses in wartime, the civilian casualties that have taken place in Afghanistan, Iraq, Libya, and Pakistan over the past decade. As General Tommy R. Franks infamously said during the first years of the Afghan War, "We don't do body counts."[3] In view of the scale of destruction that has taken place at the hands of the U.S. military, particularly in Afghanistan and Iraq, we certainly should. The United States prefers to ignore the loss of civilian life as it does the destruction of the civilian economy, let alone schools, infrastructure, and even hospitals. The U.S. military failed to understand that the lack of security provided to civilians in Iraq led to greater success and recruitment for militias and insurgent groups. The lack of U.S. understanding of Afghan opposition to midnight raids and house-to-house searches has compromised

Washington's relations with the government of Hamid Karzai. The U.S. killing of two dozen Pakistani soldiers in November 2011 and the belated unwillingness to apologize exposed a cavalier attitude toward loss of human life and further damaged the troubled U.S.-Pakistani relationship.

It is past time to hold a national debate on the role and purpose of U.S. power in today's global environment. It is time to define a new international policy that recognizes the constraints and limitations of military power. A good start would be to heed the arguments of realists such as Dean Acheson and George Kennan, who opposed extended military involvements. Over the past four decades, the United States has deployed large numbers of forces to Vietnam, Iraq, and Afghanistan with no gains for national security and huge setbacks to U.S. interests. We must understand how the United States reached the point of willingness to expand its national security interests to all areas on the globe. There are no national security interests, let alone vital interests, in areas that we have invaded and occupied for the past fifty years: twelve years in Vietnam; eight in Iraq, where the U.S. military withdrawal is mostly complete; and more than a decade in Afghanistan, where a modest withdrawal has begun.

Nevertheless, Admiral William H. McRaven, the commander of the Special Operations Command (SOCOM), is pressing for a larger role for his elite units and more personal autonomy to position his forces in troubled areas. McRaven, who oversaw the operation that killed Osama bin Laden in May 2011, wants to deploy 12,000 special forces around the world at all times to strike terrorist targets and rescue hostages.[4] The Command has doubled in size since 2001, currently at a level of 66,000 military and civilian personnel, and its budget has more than doubled, from $4.2 billion to $10.5 billion. Greater authority for SOCOM would reduce the influence of the State

Department in dealing with difficult political situations as well as the authority of the Pentagon's regional commanders. The heightened secrecy would complicate the problem of congressional oversight.

Exaggeration of the threat has been a critical component in the militarization of national security policy. Such exaggeration fostered the huge strategic buildup during the Cold War, the unprecedented peacetime buildup by the Reagan administration, and massive increases in defense spending during the Bush II administration. In an effort to assure their own self-preservation, according to Harvard professor Daniel Yergin, nations often "push the subjective boundaries of security outward to more and more areas, to encompass more and more geography and more and more problems."[5] This often leads to a paradox—an expanded perception of threat rather than a greater sense of security. The United States has created such an environment. We now view each example of terrorist activity as an existential threat, and we are in the process of exaggerating the threat of China.

The global war on terror is the latest example of the use of unilateral and hegemonic power, described by British theorist Edmund Burke in the eighteenth century. Burke was concerned with the British exercise of such power. The sovereign state came fully into its own in the seventeenth century, signaled by the Treaty of Westphalia in 1648, which ended Europe's religious wars and saw the final breakup of a universally Catholic Europe. No longer were territories ruled by multiple jurisdictions of empire, nationality, fiefdom, church, and holy orders, united by common language and common religion. A new system was established, consisting of separate and exclusive sovereignties. Each nation had its own economy, society, laws, established borders, national church, bureaucracy—and the armed forces to protect them.

At the end of the eighteenth century, however, England, whose navy "ruled" the seas, could dream of establishing English hegemony, a Pax Britannica of English law and English economics for Indian, Hottentot, and Irishman alike. It could look to a future of English economics and an English language spoken around the world. The vision of American superiority and hegemony advocated by the proponents of unilateralism and exceptionalism in the wake of the Cold War is little different than the dreams of Englishmen over two hundred years ago.

In fact, the world has never before seen a disparity of military power comparable to that now existing between the United States and the rest of the world. According to Paul Kennedy, the author of *The Rise and Fall of the Great Powers*, Pax Britannica was "run on the cheap," particularly compared to the hugely expensive U.S. arsenal.[6] The British army in the nineteenth century was much smaller than the armies of Europe, and the Royal Navy was equal only to the next two navies combined. Today, the U.S. Navy is superior to the naval fleets of the entire global community; its aviation and power projection capabilities are beyond comparison. Kennedy observes that there has never been a military hegemony to match that of the United States. After all, he points out, "Charlemagne's empire was merely Western European in its reach." The Roman empire stretched farther afield, but it competed with a great empire in Persia and an even larger one in China.

Military Power from Bush I to Obama

In 1991, when the Soviet Union collapsed and the post–Cold War era began, the unilateralists initially lost momentum. But three leading neoconservatives at the Pentagon (Secretary of Defense Dick Cheney, his longtime aide Lewis "Scooter" Libby, and Pentagon intellectual leader Paul Wolfowitz) authored their "Defense Policy Guidance," recommending unilateralism as the guiding principle of U.S. foreign policy. These men did not want to return to the arms control and disarmament table, and they wanted no cuts in the defense budget. Along with U.S. intelligence and defense planners, they had been unprepared for the collapse of the Berlin Wall, the Warsaw Pact, and the Soviet empire, and they wanted to justify continued huge defense expenditures. Written after the extremely short and destructive Gulf War against Iraq, the "Guidance" advocated permanent U.S. dominance by preventing the rise of any potentially hostile power. It defended the preemptive use of force against states suspected of developing weapons of mass destruction, which became the ostensible justification for U.S. preemption against Iraq in 2003. Ironically, the Desert Storm war in 1991 had destroyed Iraq's capability to manufacture weapons of mass destruction, and Saddam Hussein had not restored it.

When then-Senator Joe Biden (D-DE) read the "Guidance," he was appalled, denouncing it as a prescription for a Pax Americana. The Cheney-Libby-Wolfowitz document advocated a reversal of the bipartisan moderation and multilateralism endorsed by U.S. administrations since the end of World War II. Throughout the post-war period, the United States had made numerous efforts to pioneer a system of world diplomacy, including the United Nations, that looked to increased cooperation among nations along a broad front of peacekeeping and political-economic cooperation. The United States fostered a peaceful, viable Western Europe, which helped prevent the spread of Soviet-sponsored communism and encouraged efforts to provide a democratic life for its citizens. Economic aid was used to increase the stability of such vulnerable nations as Greece and Turkey, and a rich tapestry of international law was sponsored to protect human rights. Finally, both Democratic and Republican administrations endorsed and participated in a series of arms control agreements that were designed to curb the proliferation of nuclear weapons, limit the number of nuclear powers, and create an international and verifiable arms control regime.

The objectives and policies of the neoconservatives challenged all these goals. Fortunately, the "Guidance" was leaked to the *Los Angeles Times*, provoking a backlash and prompting President George H.W. Bush, National Security Adviser Brent Scowcroft, and Secretary of State James Baker to mothball it. Various right-wing think tanks, such as the Heritage Foundation, the American Enterprise Institute, the Center for Security Policy, and the Project for the New American Century kept alive the ideological premises of unilateralism and preemptive attack, however. These groups had been impatient with the Cold War's "rules of the game," which had deterred the United States and the Soviet Union from aggressive moves that risked confrontation. With the exception of the Cuban missile crisis in 1962, the Soviet Union had avoided steps that might cause confrontation with the United States. The United States, even when it resorted to the use of military power, as in the Vietnam War, has avoided gratuitous provocations aimed at the Kremlin.

The policies and personnel of the Project for a New American Century were central to the "Bush Doctrine," which marked a departure from the practices of every post–Cold War president, including George W. Bush's own father. The neoconservatives of his administration, particularly Vice President Cheney and Department of Defense figures Wolfowitz, Douglas Feith, and Steve Cambone (along with Richard Perle from the department's advisory group), wanted the United States to exploit its political-economic-military superiority to expand its influence. While the 9/11 attacks and the false charges of weapons of mass destruction became the pretexts for the use of force in Iraq, Bush, Cheney, and Rumsfeld would have pursued the war even without terrorist attacks against the United States. The increase in military, security, and intelligence spending had begun even before 9/11: The objective was creation of unquestioned U.S. military preeminence that could not be challenged by any nation or group of nations. The group never determined how to turn military power into political influence, however. Meanwhile, the U.S. military has become a liability in the Middle East and Southwest Asia, and the influence of U.S. diplomacy has declined.

Frustration with the policies of the Clinton administration had led neoconservatives and influential members of the defense community to form the Project for a New American Century in 1997. The Project was the natural heir of the Coalition for a Democratic Majority and the Committee on the Present Danger, which were formed in the 1970s to challenge the foreign policies of the Carter administration, particularly the president's commitment to arms control, disarmament, and conflict resolution in the Third World. The Bush I administration had frustrated the neoconservatives, but the Clinton administration drove them to distraction. President Clinton and Vice President Al Gore supported international cooperation on climate change and controlling AIDS; humanitarian intervention and peacekeeping in the Balkans; nation-building; and the creation of the International Criminal Court. All of these were anathema to Cheney, Perle, and Wolfowitz. Clinton's policies were called "globaloney" for their reputed failure to deal with the new realities of power in the post–Cold War world.

The Project for a New American Century sponsored a letter to President Clinton in January 1998 declaring that "we may soon face a threat in the Middle East more serious than any we have known since the end of the Cold War. We urge you to enunciate a new strategy that would secure the interests of the United States and our allies around the world." The "threat" that the group referred to was Saddam Hussein's weapons of mass destruction, which, in fact, no longer existed. The signers of the letter included major players in the administrations of both Bush I and Bush II: Elliott Abrams, John Bolton, Perle, Rumsfeld, and Wolfowitz. A year earlier, the right-wing Center for Security Policy had drafted a statement endorsing the deployment of a national missile defense. Again, major Bush players signed the statement, including Rumsfeld and Cheney. The Center gathered politicians and defense executives together in a way that President Eisenhower had anticipated in his warning about the military-industrial complex more than fifty years earlier.

The New American Century and the Center for National Security were buttressed by a collection of right-wing groups and think tanks committed to the militarization of policy and the use of military power. The failure of the use of force in Iraq and Afghanistan over a ten-year period has done nothing to mitigate the exhortations of the American Enterprise Institute and the Heritage Foundation, whose members regularly write op-eds for major newspapers, including the *Washington Post* and the *New York Times*. Their style is coercive, dismissive, and arrogant in describing both a world where U.S. force prevails, and a United States where military power is the measure of our health and global sway. They dismiss multilateralism and international law in favor of aggressive unilateralism and U.S. economic dominance.

Even liberal organizations are attracted to these policies. The Brookings Institution and Carnegie Endowment for International Peace, and their scholars—Michael O'Hanlon and Robert Kagan, respectively—have advocated the use of military power in Iraq and Afghanistan. All are opposed to reduced defense spending. In his most recent book, Kagan argued that "when American power declines, the institutions and norms American power supports will decline too."[7] He contends that Americans have "developed a degree of satisfaction in their special role" overseas, and suggests that the silent prayer offered during the seventh-inning stretch of baseball games reflects pride in the nation's role "around the world."

The election of President George W. Bush was a welcome relief to the neoconservative community. President Bush and Vice President Cheney were unwilling to permit the facts on the ground to block their goal of overthrowing Saddam Hussein. Although Bush campaigned on the basis of moderation in foreign policy, multilateralism, and the so-called "new world order," he and Cheney moved quickly to establish a "wartime presidency." He campaigned on the basis of a modest buildup of the defense establishment, but doubled the defense budget during his presidency. Bush appointed only one moderate, Colin Powell, to a key position, but the general-statesman was thoroughly ignored by the neoconservatives who dominated Bush's presidency. While the administrations of Bush I and Bill Clinton were wary of the use of force, Bush II relished brandishing military symbols and took advantage of every opportunity to define himself as a "wartime president." His memoir notes his regret over the fulsome use of military language such as "bring 'em on," "mission accomplished," and "dead or alive," but offers no regret about the actual use of force.

Members of right-wing groups became key players in the administration of George W. Bush, occupying the positions of vice president, secretary of defense, and UN ambassador; they also were key staffers at the National Security Council and the Department of Defense. Right-wingers played key roles in the intelligence community, where ideologues such as Congressman Porter Goss became director of central intelligence. When the CIA refused to distort the intelligence to suit the conclusion the Bush administration was seeking, the Office of Special Plans was created at the Pentagon under associates of Cheney such as Douglas Feith, William Luti, and Abram Shulsky with the task of making the case for war against Iraq.

President Bush enunciated his doctrine of preemptive war in Iraq and, by declaring a counterproductive "war on terror," assured that the Pentagon would be the leading policy agency in combating terrorism around the world. His policy of unilateralism, proclaimed at West Point in 2002, marked a radical turn in U.S. foreign policy. President Bush ineffectually relied on saber-rattling against the nuclear programs of Iran and North Korea. He abrogated the Anti-Ballistic Missile Treaty, the cornerstone of deterrence since 1972, and he funded a national missile defense system that is not workable but remains the largest line item for a weapons system in the current defense budget. The Bush administration's politicization of the intelligence community reached its nadir in 2002, when the CIA prepared the specious National Intelligence Estimate that was used to justify the war against Iraq.

Even before the end of the Cold War, there had been an unfortunate tendency for U.S. presidents, in their first year in office, to use military or paramilitary power as an instrument of policy, perhaps to prove their mettle. President John F. Kennedy used the CIA against Cuba (the infamous Bay of Pigs), an operation that backfired and tarnished his administration. President Lyndon B. Johnson escalated the war in Vietnam in 1965, although, in his campaign the previous year, he had argued against sending American boys to fight an Asian war. President Nixon escalated the war in Vietnam and fought a secret war in Cambodia. President Gerald Ford used force in response to the seizure of a U.S. freighter, although the crew had already been released. There were more U.S. forces killed and wounded in that action than there were crew members of the merchant ship, the *Mayaguez*. And the intelligence community sent the rescue team to an obscure island rather than to the mainland, where the crew had been held. President Jimmy Carter actually avoided the use of military force until his last year in office. Even in the wake of 9/11, when George Bush and Dick Cheney significantly increased the defense budget, Senator Lieberman argued that the additional funds were "not nearly enough to meet the military's essential needs for procurement and transformation."[8] Senator Lieberman was the classic reincarnation of the late Senator Henry "Scoop" Jackson (D-WA), liberal on domestic social issues but far to the right on national security and defense issues. The Lieberman link to the politics of Republican Senators John McCain of Arizona and Lindsay Graham of South Carolina has been a powerful force on behalf of the military-industrial complex for two decades.

President George H.W. Bush made no one happy during his stewardship of U.S. national security policy. Liberals believed that he could have taken better advantage of the end of the Cold War to address inflated defense spending and unnecessary U.S. deployments abroad. Neoconservatives believed that he did not expand the defense budget sufficiently and was absurdly dovish in not occupying Iraq and driving Saddam Hussein from power. Secretary of Defense Cheney was sympathetic with the policies of the neoconservatives and, by the time he joined the administration of George W. Bush as vice president, he was a full-fledged war hawk supporting not only wars against Iraq and Afghanistan, but military action against the nuclear facilities of Syria and Iran.

At his last State of the Union address in 1992, Bush senior seemed to provide an endorsement of President Eisenhower's farewell address when he urged that the collapse of the Soviet Union be used to "accelerate" cuts in defense spending as well as increased domestic spending. In many ways, Bush was a traditional fiscal conservative who was not in favor of great increases in defense spending. Secretary of Defense Cheney was sympathetic with this position, but, after his employment by the defense contractor Halliburton in the 1990s, he returned to government in order to open the floodgates of defense spending. If Bush's successor, President Clinton, had followed the pace of the Bush defense cuts, defense spending would have been cut by 30 percent since George H.W. Bush took office.

ONE

PRESIDENT EISENHOWER'S LEGACY

We have met the enemy and he is us. —Pogo

Every gun that is made, every warship launched, every rocket fired, signifies in a final sense a theft from those who hunger and are not fed—those who are cold and are not clothed. This world in arms is not spending its money alone—it is spending the sweat of its laborers, the genius of its scientists, the hopes of its children. —President Dwight D. Eisenhower

I hate war as only a soldier who has lived it can, only as one who has seen its brutality, its futility, and its stupidity. —President Dwight D. Eisenhower

The United States never lost a soldier or a foot of ground during my administration. We kept the peace. People ask how it happened—by God, it didn't just happen. —Eisenhower quotation inscribed on the wall of the Eisenhower Museum, Abilene, Kansas

At a black-tie dinner in November 2011, the Panetta Institute for Public Policy, an academic center founded by Secretary of Defense Leon Panetta, gave a special award to Panetta's predecessor as defense secretary, Robert M. Gates. Lockheed Martin, the nation's largest defense contractor, has a history of donating money to causes favored by influential lawmakers and government officials. On this occasion, it donated $8,000 to the institute for the dinner and sponsored a table of guests from the defense industry. Panetta's wife, Sylvia, who is running the institute in her husband's absence, said that the institute has a policy of not accepting donations from defense contractors, but made an exception for Lockheed Martin because it has contributed to the institute for several years. "These folks have been supporters of ours before Leon became secretary of defense," Sylvia explained. "Do you really think they would give us money if they didn't think we were doing a great job? They live what we're doing."[1] It would be difficult to find a better example of President Dwight D. Eisenhower's warning about the military-industrial complex than this one.

President Eisenhower is best known for leading the Allied cross-channel invasion of Normandy in 1944, which helped to turn the tide of World War II, and for his Farewell Address to the nation in January 1961, which carried the famous warning about the military-industrial complex. Like President George Washington, in another famous Farewell Address, President Eisenhower warned about the dangers of overgrown military establishments that, in Washington's words were "inauspicious to liberty, and . . . regarded as particularly hostile to republican liberty." Like Washington, Eisenhower understood the need for limited, rational engagement to advance the nation's standing; he worried about the consequences of a militarized nation, which is what the United States has become, and understood the dangers of an alliance between the uniformed military and the nation's defense contractors.

President Eisenhower's legacy for U.S. national security is a complex one, however. On the one hand, he provided a prescient warning regarding "unwarranted influence" of the military-industrial complex; raised the concern that U.S. investment in defense would compromise important domestic requirements in education, engineering, and innovation; and sounded a clarion call about the danger that permanent war would lead to restrictions on civil liberties at home. President Eisenhower was opposed to war and was particularly skeptical of what he called "brushfire" wars. He said that the United States should avoid "little wars at great distances from the United States" that could lead to greater confrontations. Vietnam, Iraq, and Afghanistan, where U.S. forces have fought over the past five decades, would be excellent examples of such "brushfire" wars. He ended the Korean War as soon as he could, accepting compromise and proclaiming, "I will never commit our forces to battle where I cannot get to the heart of the enemy's power and support."[2]

Although Eisenhower's Farewell Address is famous for its foreign policy prescriptions, it also warned that permanent war and a "permanent arms industry" would do great harm to American rights and liberties. Fifty years later, the United States is trying to rationalize its use of secret courts and warrants, secret searches of individuals who have not been identified as terrorists, and warrantless eavesdropping in violation of the Constitution. President Obama, who taught constitutional law for a decade, has failed to reverse the transgressions of the Bush administration. He arranged for immunity for the communications companies that assisted in the secret eavesdropping program, which was a complete repudiation of a position he took during the campaign. The monitoring of U.S. citizens has increased significantly in the past decade, and Obama's administration has called for legalizing for the use of GPS devices to monitor U.S. citizens without judicial review. Obama approves of the use of secret evidence in federal and military courts when national security issues are involved. The president also signed the National Defense Authorization Act on December 31, 2011, which gave him the authority to detain citizens indefinitely in cases involving terrorism. President Eisenhower would have been shocked at these domestic restrictions, let alone the war crimes that have involved torture and abuse, extraordinary rendition, and secret prisons.[3]

On the other hand, President Eisenhower took unprecedented advantage of the secrecy and international reach of the Central Intelligence Agency to authorize assassination plots and the covert overthrow of governments, including democratically elected governments, and he made no attempt to make sure that CIA activities were known to the Department of State or to U.S. ambassadors. Unfortunately, President Eisenhower's qualms about traditional warfare did not extend to secret war and covert action. Today, we see that both aspects of his legacy remain relevant to U.S. national security policy: on the one hand, the need to challenge the military-industrial complex; on the other, the need to monitor the CIA's covert actions.

Fifty years ago, President Eisenhower also communicated a concern about the ability of the president to control the military. Several weeks before his Farewell Address, he told his senior advisers in the Oval Office of the White House, "God help this country when someone sits in this chair who doesn't know the military as well as I do." Since his presidency, most U.S. presidents have lacked military experience. As a consequence, they have been deferential to the military and have used military force to bolster their credentials. This has been a key factor in the expanded power of the military establishment.

In December 2010, the National Archives and the Eisenhower Presidential Library and Museum released a new group of documents, including a draft of a speech dated December 21, 1960. In it, President Eisenhower demonstrated that he was concerned about far more than the military implications of the military-industrial complex. He had reason to be alarmed, of course, because in the early 1950s military spending represented more than half of all federal spending as well as more than 10 percent of U.S. gross domestic product. The tremendous growth in the nonmilitary economy and the shift in government spending to nonmilitary expenditures has changed this equation significantly. He warned that the influence of the military-industrial complex was "economic, political, and even spiritual" and "felt in every city, every statehouse, every office of the federal government." As James Ledbetter noted in *Unwarranted Influence: Dwight D. Eisenhower and the Military-Industrial Complex*, the president exhorted Americans to break away from our reliance on military might as a guarantor of liberty and "use our power in the interests of world peace and human betterment."[4] President Obama issued a similar warning in his inaugural speech in January 2009, but he has failed to act.

In 1959, President Eisenhower began a dialogue with his brother, Milton, the president of Johns Hopkins University, regarding U.S. military policy. In the spring of 1961, a small group of undergraduates met with Milton Eisenhower to discuss the president's farewell address. Eisenhower informed us that he and a Johns Hopkins professor of political science, Malcolm Moos, played major roles in the drafting and editing of the farewell speech of January 1961. The key drafter of the speech, Ralph E. Williams, relied on guidance from Professor Moos. Milton Eisenhower explained that one of the drafts of the speech referred to the "military-industrial-congressional complex," with the president himself inserting the reference to the role of the Congress. When the Farewell Address was given, the reference to Congress did not appear. The president's brother said he had asked about the dropped reference, and the president had replied, "It was more than enough to take on the military and private industry. I couldn't take on the Congress as well."

In fact, an entire section was dropped from the speech, dealing with the president's concerns about the creation of a "permanent war-based industry." The draft had conveyed concern about "flag and general officers retiring at an early age [to] take positions in the war-based industrial complex, shaping its decisions, and guiding the direction of its tremendous thrust." The president warned that steps needed to be taken to "insure that the 'merchants of death' do not come to dictate national policy." He also warned against any belief that some "spectacular and costly action could become the miraculous solution to all current difficulties." President George W. Bush's war in Iraq in 2003 and President Obama's escalation of the war in Afghanistan in 2009 come to mind.

President Eisenhower worried that the demands of the Cold War might turn the United States into a "garrison state." He warned, "In the councils of government, we must guard against the acquisition of unwarranted influence, whether sought or unsought, by the military-industrial complex." This complex, according to Tom Barry of the Center for International Policy, has "morphed into a new type of public-private partnership—one that spans military, intelligence, and homeland-security contracting—that amounts to a 'national security complex.'" Over the past two decades, despite the collapse of the Berlin Wall, the dissolution of the Soviet Union, and the end of the Cold War, our presidents have done little to limit the national security complex.

Unfortunately, President Eisenhower did not appoint a national security team that shared his views. His key appointees, such as Vice President Richard M. Nixon, Secretary of State John Foster Dulles, and CIA Director Allen Dulles, favored greater defense spending and a more aggressive approach toward Moscow. Unlike the Dulles brothers, Eisenhower knew there was no such thing as absolute security, and warned against "destroying from within what you are trying to defend from without." In April 1953, soon after the death of Joseph Stalin, he told the American Society of Newspaper Editors that there were tremendous costs associated with the rivalry with the Soviet Union, including an enormous domestic price on both societies:

> This world in arms is not spending money alone. It is spending the sweat of its laborers, the genius of its scientists, the hopes of its children. The cost of one modern heavy bomber is this: a modern brick school in more than 30 cities. It is two electric power plants, each serving a town of 60,000 population. . . . We pay for a single fighter with a half-million bushels of wheat. We pay for a single destroyer with new homes that could have housed more than 8,000 people. . . . This is not a way of life at all, in any true sense. Under the cloud of threatening war, it is humanity hanging from a cross of iron."[5]

No president in recent history has had the credibility and experience with national security policy and military affairs that President Eisenhower had. No president since Eisenhower has been willing to express his concerns with the increased power and influence of the Pentagon over the foreign and national security policies of the United States. No president since Eisenhower has understood the need to monitor the Pentagon's supreme position in military and security policy. Unlike his successors, Eisenhower made sure that he could not be outmaneuvered by his national security advisers, particularly on such key issues as the Bay of Pigs and Vietnam, where Presidents John F. Kennedy and Lyndon B. Johnson mishandled the decision-making process. President Kennedy never knew that senior officers at the Pentagon anticipated the CIA's failure in Cuba in 1961 and planned to use air power to finish the job that the CIA and its Cuban émigré allies would certainly bungle. President Johnson knew that Vietnam was a fool's errand but failed to challenge the strategic views of the Rostow brothers (Walt and Eugene) and the Bundy brothers (William and McGeorge) or the pleas from the Pentagon for more force and additional troops.

Eisenhower ignored the hysteria of the bomber and missile gaps in the 1950s, claimed by Senators John F. Kennedy and Stuart Symington and key advisers such as Paul Nitze. Nitze had unnecessarily heightened concerns about U.S. security, which were recorded in NSC-68[6] in the late 1940s. He was also the chief author of the overwrought Gaither Report,[7] which called for unnecessary increases in the strategic arsenal. Eisenhower ignored these advocates for increased defense spending and even cut the military budget by 20 percent between 1953 and 1955 on the way to balancing the budget by 1956.

Eisenhower clashed with the military mindset from the beginning of his presidency. He knew that his generals were wrong in proclaiming "political will" as the major factor in military victory and would have shuddered when General David Petraeus, like so many military commanders, asserted that our political will is the key factor for success in Afghanistan. Eisenhower knew that military demands for weaponry and resources were always based on inexplicable notions of "sufficiency," and he made sure that Pentagon briefings on the Hill were countered by testimony from the national security bureaucracy. Henry A. Kissinger was one of the rare national security advisers and secretaries of state who understood Eisenhower's point of view. During the ratification process for the first Strategic Arms Limitation agreement (SALT I) in 1972, he countered conservative and military opposition to SALT and the Anti-Ballistic Missile Treaty with the kind of questions that President Eisenhower would have asked and that defense planners could never answer: What is strategic sufficiency? What would we do with strategic sufficiency if we had it?

Eisenhower warned in his Farewell Address in 1961 that

the United States should not become a "garrison state." Nearly fifty years later, however, we have developed a garrison mentality that supports unprecedented military spending, continuous military deployments, exaggerated fears with regard to "Islamo-terrorism" and cyberwars, and exaggerated reliance on counterinsurgency and nation-building. Eisenhower understood that it was the military-industrial complex that fostered an inordinate belief in the omnipotence of American military power. He often challenged the Dulles brothers, who were in command at the State Department and the CIA, as well senior officers at the Pentagon in their efforts to increase the U.S. role overseas.

Eisenhower knew the limits and constraints on the use of force and did not engage in the type of planning that led to Kennedy's Bay of Pigs, Johnson's Vietnam, Reagan's Grenada, Bush II's Iraq, and now Obama's Afghanistan. He heavily criticized the British-French-Israeli invasion of Egypt in 1956 and drew criticism for not assisting the Hungarian uprising weeks later. Eisenhower started no wars and settled for a stalemate in ending the Korean War. With the exception of one fatality in Lebanon in 1958, no U.S. forces lost their lives in non-covert combat operations during Eisenhower's two terms in office.

Eisenhower also defied the wishes of both the Army and the Air Force, which objected to his "New Look" military policy and demanded that the president reverse his budget cuts and bolster conventional forces. He understood that the Air Force had politicized intelligence on the Soviet Union in order to exaggerate the strength of Soviet missile forces and the Soviet air force. The U.S. Air Force took exception to a series of CIA National Intelligence Estimates in order to proclaim falsely that the Soviet Union was rapidly overtaking the United States in strategic power—first in bombers, later in ballistic missiles. Eisenhower defied both services as well as his secretary of state and his CIA director in reducing Army manpower by 44 percent from its 1953 level and refusing to sanction a crash program for bombers and missiles. The president had the support of the chairman of the Joint Chiefs of Staff, General Matthew Ridgeway, who was a strong personal and political ally from the Second World War.

In addition to rejecting large-scale increases in the military budget, Eisenhower rejected recommendations from Vice President Nixon and the Dulles brothers for military intervention on behalf of the French in Indochina as well as recommendations for the use of military force against China. He ignored the suggestions from the Dulles brothers regarding political ultimatums to the Soviet Union. Ridgeway played a key role in helping Eisenhower reject these positions. Eisenhower's immediate successors, Presidents Kennedy and Johnson, had their doubts about military success in Vietnam, but lacked the tools and insight for dealing with the bureaucracy on this issue, particularly the military bureaucracy and its congressional supporters. Unfortunately, nearly all of Eisenhower's successors ignored his warning about the "potential" for the "disastrous rise of misplaced power"—a reference to the need to control military influence over national security policy.

Unlike recent presidents, Eisenhower was prescient about the Middle East, perhaps due to his leadership in North Africa during World War II. He recognized the strategic importance of the Suez Canal, particularly for the transport of petroleum, but he feared the prospect of wider war in the region. He understood that violence runs like a dark thread through the Mediterranean. He questioned the utility of maintaining 80,000 British troops on a large base in the Suez Canal Zone, however. Eisenhower believed that it was "undesirable and impracticable for the British to retain sizable forces permanently in the territory of a jealous and resentful government amid an openly hostile population."[8] And when British-French-Israeli forces invaded

Egypt in 1956, he was appalled by their mismanagement of the conflict and ominously told British Prime Minister Anthony Eden that the "use of military force against Egypt under present circumstances might have consequences even more serious than causing the Arabs to support Nasser. It might cause a serious misunderstanding between our two countries."

The United States rarely has had a president who understood the military mindset and was so willing to limit the influence of the military. Democrats such as Kennedy, Johnson, and Clinton as well as Republicans such as Reagan, Bush I, and Bush II repeatedly deferred to the military, devoted far too many resources to the military, and resorted to the use of power instead of diplomacy and statecraft. On coming into office, President Obama inherited a situation in which the military wields far too much influence on Capitol Hill, controls far too much of the weak U.S. treasury, and has the leading policy voice on both security and diplomatic issues. Obama reads history and declares Reinhold Niebuhr his favorite philosopher and Abraham Lincoln his favorite president. He would do well to study the philosophy and advice of Eisenhower, to learn from a president who understood America's woeful infatuation with military power.

Eisenhower and the Origins of Covert Action
The CIA actually began to conduct covert actions in 1947 under President Truman, but these were modest efforts that required approval from officials from the State Department and the National Security Council. It was President Eisenhower who sanctioned the first misbegotten operations that involved regime change and assassination. The White House called for these operations even before the Agency received its mandate for such actions in 1954 from an executive-branch panel charged with examining covert action as an instrument of foreign policy. President Eisenhower was looking for ways to cut the defense budget,

and Secretary of State Dulles believed that covert action was a way to conduct aggressive foreign policy on the cheap. The panel, under the leadership of General Jimmy Doolittle, concluded:

> It is clear that we are facing an implacable enemy whose avowed objective is world domination by whatever means and whatever cost. *There are no rules in such a game. Hitherto acceptable norms of human conduct do not apply.* If the United States is to survive, long-standing American concepts of "fair play" must be reconsidered. We must develop effective espionage and counterespionage services and must learn to subvert, sabotage and destroy our enemies by more clever, more sophisticated means than those used against us. *It may become necessary that the American people be made acquainted with, understand and support this fundamentally repugnant philosophy.*[9] [Emphasis added]

The use of covert action, which the Doolittle panel endorsed, is questionable both morally and politically. Covert action, which became a staple of U.S. policy, contradicts core American values—including our belief that the United States functions more openly than other nations. This is particularly the case when we take actions abroad that would be neither tolerated nor legal in this country. Most covert operations raise moral and humanitarian questions and tarnish our quest for international stability. Key developing countries and leaders today, traditionally the primary targets of covert action, are less vulnerable to U.S. manipulation than in the past, and our allies in Europe and Asia have grown increasingly impatient with our intrusive operations. We must reconsider where, when, and whether covert actions are necessary, asking whether their supposed benefits outweigh their many costs.

The CIA has destroyed numerous files that would have provided information on many clandestine operations, thus depriving us of an authoritative record of U.S. activities abroad. Some proclaimed successes often have turned out to be disasters in the long run. These include the overthrow of Mohammed Mossadegh in Iran in 1953 and Jacobo Arbenz Guzmán in Guatemala in 1954. These so-called successes led to the decision to overthrow Fidel Castro in 1961, the so-called "perfect failure" at the Bay of Pigs.[10] Sympathetic accounts of CIA covert action describe the Iran and Guatemala operations as "unblemished triumphs," although the conventional wisdom in the wake of the corrupt reign of the Shah Mohammed Reza Pahlavi in Iran and the horror of the reign of terror against the indigenous population for decades in Guatemala teaches much different lessons.

War, Secret War, and Covert Action
President Eisenhower did not demonstrate the same caution and conservatism in dealing with the clandestine capabilities of the CIA as he did regarding the capabilities of the military. He fell prey to the seduction of using covert action in the Third World, believing that these actions were far less expensive and risky than military actions, and that the principle of "plausible denial" would allow the commander-in-chief to deny any involvement in U.S. chicanery. As a result, he placed the CIA on the path toward undertaking assassinations and regime change in many developing nations. These operations created immediate diplomatic problems for the Department of State and long-term strategic problems for the United States.

The term "covert action" is a peculiarly American invention; it does not appear in the lexicons of other intelligence services. Nor does the term appear in the National Security Act of 1947, which created the CIA, the Department of Defense, and the National Security Council. Covert action, in the U.S.

intelligence lexicon, refers to a secret operation to influence governments, events, organizations, or persons in support of a foreign policy, in a manner that is not attributable to the United States. These actions may include political, economic, propaganda, or paramilitary activities. Just as the Cold War was used to justify the most egregious activities in the 1950s and 1960s, the Global War on Terror has now become the justification for another wave of illegal CIA activities, particularly in the wake of U.S. wars in Afghanistan and Iraq that have lasted longer than either of the two world wars.

Currently, the Obama administration's covert use of Predator and Reaper drones in several countries outside the war zone in Afghanistan and Pakistan has never been debated in the Congress, even though one of the first civilian deaths involved a naturalized U.S. citizen in Yemen in 2001. These actions, conducted by the CIA and not the Pentagon, circumvent the Constitution's mandate for authorizing military action. A senior U.S. military officer, discussing the growing use of drones, asked, "So, who then is thinking about all this stuff?"[11]

The debate has been confined thus far to government lawyers, with very little interest displayed by the Congress, the press, and the U.S. public. It is the Pentagon's lawyers who support broad targeting anywhere in the world if there are connections to al-Qaeda, arguing that the post-9/11 covert action "finding" provides a legal basis for doing so. Meanwhile, State Department lawyers believe that targets outside of Afghanistan and Pakistan should be carefully vetted to make sure that victims are actually plotting against the United State. The president has sided with the Pentagon, which sanctions a wide use of drone activity that will rival the wide use of assassination and coup plots that President Eisenhower provided in the 1950s. The United States has conducted several hundred drone strikes in Pakistan since 2004, despite the harm being done to U.S.-Pakistani relations.

January 17, the anniversary of Eisenhower's Farewell Address, is also the anniversary of the assassination of President Patrice Lumumba, the first democratically elected president of the Congo. The assassination, which Eisenhower sanctioned, arguably opened the doors to the worst tyrant in Africa's history, an army officer by the name of Joseph Mobutu, who had the enthusiastic support of the United States. Although Eisenhower was not an ideologue, he shared the bipartisan view of the time that Lumumba's turn to the Soviet Union for economic assistance (after a rejection from the United States) threatened the colonial interests of the West. Several years earlier, the government of Gamel Abdul Nasser in Egypt also had turned to the Soviet Union for economic assistance when the Dulles brothers convinced President Eisenhower to withdraw support for the building of the Aswan Dam.

Covert Action: Iran
President Eisenhower's first experience with covert action was the 1953 overthrow of the democratically elected government of Prime Minister Mossadegh in Iran. Operation Ajax cost very little and took only several days; it had clandestine support from the British government and appeared to be an outstanding success. For all of these reasons, President Eisenhower and his successors grew too eager to sign off on other covert actions involving assassination plots in addition to the overthrow of legal governments. Nearly sixty years later, the United States is still dealing with the terrible strategic consequences and the intense anti-Americanism in Iran that exists today as a result of its illegal operations in that country.

The origins of some covert actions, such as the plot against the Congo's Lumumba, are murky. The coup d'état in Iran was fully described in a CIA secret history, however. The study documented the series of mishaps that accompanied the plans of U.S. and British intelligence to overthrow Mossadegh and install General Fazlollah Zehedi as prime minister in order to return the Shah of Iran to the throne. The CIA had to orchestrate efforts by the Shah's twin sister, Princess Ashraf Pahlavi and General H. Norman Schwarzkopf, the father of the 1991 Desert Storm commander, to convince the nervous Shah to return to Tehran from his gilded cage in Rome, where he had fled. The Shah's initial cowardice nearly killed the CIA plan; he repeatedly refused to sign a CIA-written "royal decree" to change the government.

Britain, fearful of Iran's plan to nationalize its oil industry, came up with the idea for the coup in 1952 and convinced the United States to mount a joint operation to remove Prime Minister Zehedi. Iranians were recruited by the CIA to pose as communists and to harass religious leaders and even stage the bombing of a cleric's home in a campaign to turn the country's Islamic religious community against the Mossadegh government. While President Eisenhower was reluctant to sign off on the covert action, the Dulles brothers persuaded him to approve the operation.

Business interests had a great deal to do with the U.S. discussion and endorsement of regime change in the 1950s and the 1970s. The oil industry pressed for intervention in Iran; the United Fruit Company was a major factor in the intervention in Guatemala in 1954; and U.S. mining interests lobbied for intervention against Salvadore Allende in Chile in 1971. In Iran, the United States and Britain were trying to protect the interests of Western oil companies, seemingly threatened by the nationalization schemes of Mossadegh. The fact that Mossadegh and Allende had won fair and free elections in Iran and Chile, respectively, apparently meant nothing to the Dulles brothers in the 1950s or to President Nixon and national security adviser Kissinger in the 1970s in their endorsement of these violent overthrows.

These covert actions created strategic disasters. The Shah assumed total control of Iran for the next twenty-five years, and, in the late 1970s, President Jimmy Carter hailed the Shah as "one of the world's greatest democrats." The Shah was overthrown in 1979. Chile eventually regained a democratic government in 1990, after years of state terror, violence and corruption. Guatemala waited three decades for genuine democracy to take hold, although the cycle of violence and lawlessness unleashed by the 1954 coup continues. In 2009, more civilians were murdered in Guatemala than in the war zones of Iraq. Iran is still waiting for democracy.

Covert Action: Guatemala

The ease of the operation in Iran convinced President Eisenhower to try a similar modus operandi against Jacobo Arbenz in Guatemala the following year. Eisenhower handed the baton of covert action to the CIA once again, with Frank Wisner, one of the founders of the Agency, leading the effort to overthrow the leftist government in Guatemala. This led to decades of violence, with hundreds of thousands of innocent civilians, primarily indigenous people, being slaughtered. Wisner was a complicated soul, suffering a nervous breakdown in 1956 and taking his own life in 1965.

In the case of Guatemala, key members of the Eisenhower administration, including Vice President Nixon and the Dulles brothers, argued that Arbenz, who won a landslide election in 1950, was pursuing a modernization strategy that included a land-redistribution program heatedly opposed by U.S. corporations, and that Arbenz was preparing to give the Soviets a foothold in Central America.[12] The real concern was not the threat of communist influence, let alone a takeover, but the fact that Arbenz was planning agrarian reforms in a country where the U.S.-owned United Fruit Company was the largest landowner and most powerful institution in the country. The Dulles brothers had done significant legal work for the company.

The coup, code-named Operation Success, included a "disposal list" of at least fifty-eight key Guatemalan leaders as well as plans for training assassins to kill them. The National Security Council issued the go-ahead for Operation Success in late 1953, and the planning for assassinations was discussed at the highest levels of the State Department and the CIA. There is no indication that the assassination plans were carried out, and there has never been a document that recorded the formal approval or disapproval of the plans by President Eisenhower. This is no surprise, however, in view of the CIA's emphasis on "plausible denial" of covert actions, designed to protect the White House from any hint of culpability. The documents do show the importance given to CIA relations with the Guatemalan military, which was described as the "only organized element in Guatemala" for effecting political change, a change that had to begin with the "subversion and defection of army leaders." Thus began the U.S. policy of endorsing close liaison between the CIA and the military leaders of Central and South American countries, where key military officers were placed on the CIA payroll.

In essence, President Eisenhower authorized a coup to protect the interests of United Fruit, the largest landowner in Guatemala, growing bananas on more than 500,000 acres. The coup ran from June 16 to June 27, 1954, with radio propaganda and political subversion proving to be the most effective weapons. Arbenz, a popularly elected president, was forced to resign, seeking refuge in Mexico. Colonel Carlos Castillo Armas was installed as president; one of his first acts was to return lands to United Fruit. Military strongmen ruled Guatemala for the next three decades; their violence against the Guatemalan people included a scorched-earth policy against a small communist insurgency. Hundreds of thousands of Guatemalans were killed over the following three decades, and Guatemalan military men remained on the CIA payroll during this entire period.

The CIA's operation in Guatemala was its most violent in Central America and one of the most violent in the world. Agency operatives organized a Guatamalan "K" group that carried out political assassinations in the 1950s. The work of the Guatemalan "K" group eventually became a model for the rest of Central America, where State Department and CIA officers were witting of "death squad" activities. Paramilitary groups in El Salvador, Honduras, and Nicaragua carried out assassinations, but it was not until the 1980s that a brace of U.S. ambassadors began to protest. When U.S. ambassadors Robert White (El Salvador), John Binns (Honduras), and Anthony Quainton (Nicaragua) reported these activities to the State Department, Secretary of State Alexander Haig ordered them to stop reporting on the subject. All three disobeyed Haig, and all three were replaced. Binns's successor in Honduras was John Negroponte, who was more than willing to go along with the cover-up. Negroponte eventually became the first U.S. Intelligence tsar under the reform act of 2004, and then undersecretary of state for Secretary of State Condoleezza Rice.

President Eisenhower's decision to overthrow the democratic government of Guatemala began a practice by virtually all post-war presidents to use force against disliked forces of any stripe in Central and South America. The coup in Guatemala was followed by the counterinsurgency in Cuba in 1961, the invasion of the Dominican Republic in 1965, and the covert program in Chile in 1973 against a democratically elected president. President Reagan's efforts to overthrow the Sandinista government in Nicaragua in the 1980s were more modest but cut from the same cloth. In this case, President Reagan used the argument of Sandinista support for the guerrillas in El Salvador to justify economic sanctions and then the Iran-Contra plot to assist the

Contras in bringing down the government. In every case, the CIA was used as a relatively inexpensive instrument of power that would avoid the risk and cost of full-scale military intervention that President Eisenhower and his successors hoped to avoid.

Covert Action: Indonesia
In the late 1940s, George Kennan referred to Indonesia as America's "most crucial issue" in stopping Soviet advances into Southeast Asia. At a time when Indonesia was fighting for its independence from the Netherlands, Kennan was concerned that a new Indonesian government would turn to communism, which he described as an "infection" that would make its way through South and Southwest Asia.[13] The Dulles brothers shared Kennan's concerns. In addition to their fear of socialists and communists, they had little tolerance for self-declared neutrals such as President Sukarno, who was leaning to the left. In 1955, the Eisenhower administration authorized the CIA to invest $1,000,000 to block Sukarno's election; for the most part, the money was lost or stolen. Over the next two years, the Agency spent $10 million in one inept operation after another to supply arms, ammunition, planes, and pilots to the rebel leaders in the Indonesian military.[14] One of the more bizarre CIA operations involved using Bing Crosby to make a pornographic film starring a Sukarno look-alike.[15] When Sukarno won his election, the CIA sent an "apology" in the form of $1,000,000 in arms and 37,000 tons of rice.[16]

Ten years later, General Suharto crushed a military plot against the government and used the opportunity to conduct a bloody campaign against Indonesian communists, leftists, and even small landowners. Suharto had the advantage of a list of several thousand communists and leftists that was supplied by the U.S Embassy and the CIA Station in Jakarta, which he used to conduct one of the worst mass murders of the twentieth century.

As many as one million Indonesians were killed in Suharto's assault, with no sign of U.S. criticism. In 1975, the United States supplied funds and logistical support for Indonesia's takeover of the Portuguese colony of East Timor, again in the name of anti-communism.

Covert Action: The Congo

President Eisenhower's biggest blunder may have been authorizing the assassination of Patrice Lumumba, the Congolese liberation leader and the first prime minister of Congo after its independence from Belgium in June 1960. Lumumba had frightened the United States because of his new and cozy relationship with the Soviets. In August 1960, the president directly ordered the CIA to "eliminate" Lumumba. According to the National Security Council note-taker, Robert Johnson, there was a "stunned silence" in the room "for about 15 seconds and then the meeting continued."[17] The Senate Intelligence Committee reviewed the assassination plot as part of the Church Committee investigations in 1975 and concluded that the CIA was not directly involved in the murder, although it confirmed that the CIA had conspired to kill Lumumba on President Eisenhower's orders. In order to maintain "plausible denial" for the president, there were never any paper records to be found regarding the order.

The CIA acted as if it had received an order from the president to eliminate Lumumba. CIA director Dulles cabled the CIA station chief in the Congo on August 26, 1960, and made Lumumba's removal "an urgent and prime objective." Dulles was concerned that Lumumba's leadership of the Congo would lead to "chaos and at worst pave the way to Communist takeover." He then sent one of the Agency's leading scientists, Sidney Gottlieb, to the Congo with a vial of bacterial culture of a disease indigenous to that part of Africa. Gottlieb also brought hypodermic needles, gauze masks, and rubber gloves.[18]

Lumumba was forced from office as the country's civil war deepened. Larry Devlin, the newly arrived station chief, could never get close enough to Lumumba to inject the poison into Lumumba's food, but, with the United States making it known that it wanted to "neutralize" the Congo president, it wasn't long before Belgian-backed rivals captured Lumumba, beat and tortured him, and eventually shot him to death on January 17, 1961, before CIA clandestine operatives could get to him. The U.S. Senate investigation concluded that the Belgian government ultimately engineered Lumumba's capture and execution and even helped dispose of by body, which was "cut up with a hacksaw and dissolved in sulfuric acid."

Eisenhower clearly sanctioned the murder plot against Lumumba in 1959, the first time that the CIA was instructed to carry out a political assassination. In doing so, the Eisenhower administration ignored the advice of Devlin, who believed that Lumumba was a "bit of a Tom Paine" and a "loose cannon," but not a communist.[19] The Dulles brothers, however, used the presence of several hundred Soviet "technical advisers" to argue for U.S. intervention. Lumumba's violent death foreshadowed CIA violence in Central America and elsewhere as well as the more recent practice of "extraordinary renditions," where suspected terrorists were kidnapped, sent to third countries, and tortured. A quarter of a century later, the Reagan administration used the presence of even fewer Cuban "technical advisers" to sanction U.S. military intervention and the overthrow of the government of Grenada.

Following the assassination of Lumumba, Joseph Mobutu conducted a successful coup that received enthusiastic backing from the United States; his thirty-two-year reign was helped by more than $1 billion in U.S. assistance. President George H.W. Bush called Mobutu "one of our most valued friends." Devlin, who had opposed the assassination attempt, retired from the CIA and became the go-between for Mobutu and the leading U.S. importer of Congolese diamonds and metals, Maurice Tempelsman.

Meanwhile, Gottlieb continued to experiment with drugs and hallucinogens for the CIA, although he had been directly involved in the death of a fellow CIA researcher, Frank Olson. In 1953, Gottlieb secretly slipped LSD into his colleague's glass of Cointreau. Olson later plunged (or was thrown) to his death from a room at the Statler Hotel in New York City, where he had been taken for psychiatric evaluation. Gottlieb received a mild reprimand, and his career flourished. Twenty-three years later, Olson's family received $750,000 from the U.S. government and a personal apology from President Gerald Ford. Gottlieb was also involved in other assassination attempts against foreign leaders that were sanctioned by Presidents Eisenhower and Kennedy. These efforts included toxins for poisoning Cuba's Fidel Castro as well as Iraqi military leaders.[20] When President Kennedy was assassinated in 1963, many Washington insiders, witting of U.S. attempts on the life of Fidel Castro, believed that the Cubans were directly involved, gaining revenge for the previous four years of CIA covert actions in Cuba.

Covert Action: Cuba and the Bay of Pigs

The CIA operation at the Bay of Pigs to overthrow the Castro regime was drawn up during the last years of the Eisenhower administration. It had a great deal of support from Vice President Nixon and the Dulles brothers, but it never received authorization from President Eisenhower. But early in his presidency, President Kennedy called his predecessor to get advice on the operation and, instead of saying "forget about it," President Eisenhower warned that if Kennedy didn't use the Cuban émigré force soon, then it would wither away. Eisenhower had stopped efforts within his own administration to mount the invasion, but had no qualms in urging the new Kennedy administration to launch the Cuban émigrés.

In 1998, after thirty-six years of secrecy, the CIA finally released its Inspector General's report on the Bay of Pigs, a startling and brutally honest inquest on the Agency's greatest fiasco.[21] The Agency had destroyed nearly every copy of the report except for those of the Director of Central Intelligence, the Inspector General, and the Records Center. The report put the blame squarely on what it described as "arrogance, ignorance, and incompetence" within the CIA, found that the Agency was shot through with deadly self-deception, and described its secret operations as "ludicrous or tragic or both." Since plausible denial is the sine qua non of covert action, it is noteworthy that the report concluded that in the Bay of Pigs operation "plausible denial was a pathetic illusion," and even recommended that the Pentagon should conduct future paramilitary operations. In the wake of the failure at the Bay of Pigs, Cubans who received CIA training conducted their own freelance anti-Castro operations. Several Cubans, initially trained by the CIA for covert action against their home country, were involved in the infamous break-in of the Democratic National Committee's offices in the Watergate complex ten years later.[22]

Covert Action: Vietnam
President Eisenhower resisted the efforts of those in his administration, including Vice President Nixon and the Dulles brothers, who wanted to bail out the French in Vietnam. But Eisenhower's legitimization of assassination plots and coup plots made it easier for President Kennedy to use such tactics against South Vietnam's ruling Diem brothers as well as Cuba's Castro. The plot against the Diems was particularly counterproductive and even evil. The younger brother, Ngo Dinh Nhu, was South Vietnam's most prominent non-Communist nationalist

and a former prisoner of Ho Chi Minh's; he had fled from North Vietnam in 1950 when the Communists sentenced him to death. Six years later, he canceled the elections that were stipulated by the Geneva Treaty, but in 1963 he was involved in secret negotiations with Hanoi in order to establish Saigon's neutrality. The U.S. withdrawal of force would be part of such an arrangement, according to CIA sources, which was unacceptable to the Kennedy administration. There were important opponents to the assassination plot, including Vice President Lyndon B. Johnson; Secretary of Defense Robert McNamara; chairman of the Joint Chiefs of Staff General Maxwell Taylor; and even CIA director John McCone. The CIA director correctly predicted that there were no ruling alternatives to the Diem brothers and that disaster would follow their removal. McCone, who was one of the lone wolves in believing that the Soviets had placed missiles in Cuba in 1962, was right once again. He eventually resigned due to his inability to be heard in the Kennedy White House.

President Kennedy, however, was prodded by U.S. Ambassador Henry Cabot Lodge; Secretary of State Dean Rusk; Undersecretary of State Averell Harriman; Assistant Secretary of State Roger Hilsman; and national security assistant McGeorge Bundy to give the green light for the coup against the Diems. On November 1, 1963, only three weeks before the assassination of President Kennedy, a CIA operative working as an intermediary between Ambassador Lodge and Diem's staff "swaggered into the plotters' headquarters, toting an ivory-handled .375 Magnum revolver and a valise bulging with the equivalent of $40,000, in case they needed funds."[23] As in the case of Lumumba's assassination, others got to the Diems before the CIA agents. An unstable junta followed the Diems, which marked the beginning of the end for South Vietnam and the U.S. role in Indochina. A wider war against North Vietnam replaced a covert guerrilla struggle, and twelve years of fighting ensued with huge losses of blood and treasure for the United States and for Vietnam.

Net Assessment of Covert Action

There is definite linkage between the various acts of covert action that started with the U.S.-British plot against the Mossadegh government in Iran in 1953. The success of the coup in Guatemala made it easier to plan the counterinsurgency in Cuba in 1961; the failure in Cuba should have given some pause to the consideration of the regime change in Vietnam in 1963, which was a strategic nightmare, but it didn't; Vietnam was immediately followed by the failed invasion of the Dominican Republic in 1965. All of these actions were followed by one of the most outrageous covert actions of all, the plot in Chile in 1973 against a democratically elected president, Salvadore Allende. There is probably no better example of the arrogance of power than national security adviser Kissinger's facetious justification of the covert action in Chile in order to "stop a dagger pointed at the heart of Antarctica." Kissinger added that he failed to "see why the United States should stand by and let Chile go Communist merely due to the stupidity of its own people."[24]

One of the clumsiest examples of covert actions was President Reagan's efforts to overthrow the Sandinista government in Nicaragua in the 1980s. In this case, the Reagan administration violated a series of laws that prohibited covert aid to the Contras in Nicaragua as well as the provision of military weaponry to the terrorist government of Iran. But President Reagan used the argument of Sandinista support for the guerrillas in El Salvador to justify economic sanctions and sanctioned the Iran-Contra plot to assist the Contras in bringing down the government. Once again, the CIA was used as a relatively inexpensive instrument of power to avoid the risk and cost of full-scale military intervention that Reagan's advisers hoped to avoid. Iran-Contra could have led to the impeachment of the president.

All of these covert actions were strategic failures with too many examples of capable, democratically elected leaders being replaced by authoritarian tyrants who scotched personal freedoms and political activity. In the Congo, Mobutu was particularly tyrannical. The violence that followed the CIA coup against Arbenz in 1954 raged for decades, and still has not fully subsided. It was not until 2011—six decades later—that a democratic Guatemala has promised to restore the legacy of Arbenz and treat him as a statesman. Arbenz's grandson, Dr. Erick Arbenz, who is an anesthesiologist in Boston, remarked recently that a "culture of silence created by the CIA and the perpetrators" is responsible for the fact that his generation does not even know who Arbenz was.[25] There has not been a government in Iran that could claim the democratic and moderate tendencies of Mossadegh, and anti-Americanism in Iran must be linked to the CIA's role in installing the Shah in 1953.

President Eisenhower's endorsement of covert action in Iran, Guatemala, and the Congo certainly made it more legitimate for Presidents Nixon and Carter to mount major covert initiatives in Chile in 1973 and Afghanistan in 1980, respectively. In Iran and Chile, the United States took illegal actions against democratically elected governments; in Afghanistan, the United States sponsored activities that unexpectedly led to the strengthening of anti-Soviet insurgent groups, which morphed into anti-Western terrorist organizations having sanctuary in Pakistan for attacking major regions of Afghanistan. The covert operation in Iran included the harassment of religious figures and the bombing of their homes in order to turn them against the government of Premier Mossadegh. Presidents Johnson and Clinton also resorted to covert actions but were far more suspicious of the CIA than most of their White House peers.

For nearly forty-five years, covert action captured the imagination of the CIA's political masters in the White House and Congress, and, according to former CIA director Robert M. Gates, these actions were the CIA's "heart and soul."[26] All major covert actions were conducted on orders from the White House, according to congressional investigations, included those headed by Senator Frank Church (D-ID) and Representative Otis Pike (D-NY) in the mid-1970s. These investigations followed revelations of CIA participation in assassination plots against leaders in the Third World as well as in illegal activities in the United States against the Vietnam antiwar movement.

Covert action remains a dangerously unregulated activity. There are no political and ethical guidelines delineating when to engage in covert action, although previous covert actions have harmed U.S. strategic interests. At various times, such criminals as Panama's General Manuel Noriega, Guatemala's Colonel Julio Alpírez, Peru's intelligence chief Vladimiro Montesinos, and Chile's General Manuel Contreras have been on the CIA payroll. Although President Bush, like every other president since Gerald Ford, signed an executive order banning political assassination, exceptions have been made in the covert pursuit of Iraqi President Saddam Hussein and former Afghanistan Prime Minister Gulbuddin Hekmatyar, both of whom received U.S. assistance in the 1980s.

A Legacy of the Cold War

It is possible to justify the use of covert action in wartime, but we must decide whether the capacity to conduct covert action in peacetime should continue. The House Intelligence Committee reported in 1996 that, in the clandestine services, "Hundreds of employees on a daily basis are directed to break extremely serious laws in countries around the world in the face of frequently sophisticated efforts by foreign governments to catch them."[27] It went on to state, "A safe estimate is that several hundred times every day (easily 100,000 times a year) officers from the National Clandestine Service (formerly the directorate of operations) engage in highly illegal activities (according to foreign law) that not only risk political embarrassment to the United States but also endanger the freedom if not lives of the participating foreign nationals and, more than occasionally, of the clandestine officer himself."

Recent congressional reports on intelligence reform indicate, however, that the foreign policy establishment is unwilling to tackle serious reform of clandestine operations.[28] Despite recent problems and scandals in the clandestine services, the reports introduce no new thinking on clandestine activity. In fact, they endorse increased spending for covert action and a global presence for the National Clandestine Services, formerly the directorate of operations. Despite the use of fabricated and fallacious intelligence from clandestine sources in order to make the case for war against Iraq, there is no discussion of the need to reform the clandestine collection of intelligence to guard against misinformation and disinformation in the national security process.

Covert Failure

More often than not, covert actions have not been beneficial, and even supposedly short-term policy successes have become long-term failures or liabilities. In Iran, which did not pose any challenge to U.S. national interests in the 1950s, the intense unpopularity of the Shah, whom the CIA had helped return to power in 1953, led to the Islamic revolution of 1979. Major covert actions in Laos and Vietnam failed to alter the results of fighting in Southeast Asia. Interventions in Angola and Mozambique had no beneficial effect on conflicts in southern Africa. Covert actions in Nicaragua and El Salvador in the 1980s increased the violence in Central America and brought great embarrassment to the United States. The excessive reliance on covert action by the Reagan administration in the 1980s contributed to the formation of radical Islamic terrorist groups that targeted the United States and its overseas military facilities.

As a result, it is reasonable to presume that CIA support for revolutionary and counterrevolutionary violence in developing nations contributed to the spread of revolutionary activity, including terrorism, against the interests of the United States and the West over the past ten to fifteen years. U.S. covert support for the apartheid regime in South Africa, the Contras in Nicaragua, and the anti-Soviet forces in Afghanistan certainly led to increased violence and destabilization in these regions. In Guatemala, Central America's most brutal regime was installed in 1954 with the help of a CIA-backed coup. The country was dominated by its repressive military for the next forty years. Governments documents show that in 1990, Colonel Julio Roberto Alpírez, a CIA informer, was involved in the cover-up of the murder of Michael Devine, an American citizen, and that in 1992 he helped cover up the murder of Efraín Bámaca Velásquez, a Guatemalan insurgent who was married to Jennifer Harbury, a U.S. citizen. In 1997 the CIA released a small batch of records on the 1954 military coup in Guatemala, but it has declassified almost nothing on the Guatemalan security forces, which have killed an estimated 200,000 Guatemalans since the coup. The Agency trained and supported some of these forces, along with similarly abusive internal security organizations in Nicaragua, Honduras, and El Salvador.[29] Such episodes undermined the credibility of the CIA and raised questions about its judgment and objectivity.

Former CIA director Gates termed the CIA's covert support for the Mujahideen in the 1980s against the Soviet Union the Agency's "greatest success." Many of the Mujahideen, however, are part of the Taliban insurgency that is creating misery for Afghans and taking American lives.[30] Much of the CIA weaponry went to the fundamentalist Gulbuddin Hekmatyar, one of the most anti-Western of the resistance leaders; Sheikh Omar Abdul-Rahman, who is imprisoned in the U.S. for seditious conspiracy to wage a "war of urban terrorism against the United States"; and Muhammad Shawqi Islarnbouli, the older brother of the assassin of Anwar Sadat. The worst of the Mujahideen, Jalaluddin Haqqani, now heads the Haqqani network that is the greatest threat to U.S. and other Western forces.

These armed and militant networks have targeted Saudi Arabia, Egypt, and Pakistan—Washington's pivotal Islamic allies in the region—and have claimed responsibility for the first terrorist attacks in Saudi Arabia and some of the worst attacks in Pakistan. Osama bin Laden, who led terrorist attacks against U.S. installations in the Persian Gulf and North Africa before 9/11, indirectly received CIA support that went to Afghanistan in the 1980s.

Eisenhower's Legacy

President Eisenhower ignored the critics who argued that there is a basic incompatibility between covert action and the American democratic political process. Although the initial use of covert action was designed to buttress democratic elements in post-war Europe and to serve U.S. national interests, Hodding Carter III argued in a dissenting opinion to a Twentieth Century Fund report in 1992 that "covert action is by definition outside the ambit of democracy."[31] In an age of terrorist activity, it is unlikely that the United States will entirely abandon covert action, but our democratic principles compel us to define the boundaries that should be placed around covert action, to determine what should and should not be attempted, and to insure that there is careful, continuous control over it. Unlike the 1970s, when the Senate and House intelligence committees tried to place political limits on the conduct of covert action, these committees have neglected their oversight functions since the collapse of the Soviet Union. As a general principle, covert action, like military action, should be applied as a last resort, only when vital security interests cannot be achieved in any other way.

President Eisenhower encouraged the CIA's covert action operations because he was trying to avoid the high economic and political cost of using military force and was hopeful of hiding the American hand in these actions. This use of covert action as a quick fix for U.S. foreign policy to deal with foreign leaders perceived as hostile or nation-states seen as renegades caused a series of strategic problems for the United States that are still with us today. U.S. interests probably would have been far better served if Arbenz, Mossadegh, and Allende had remained in power in Guatemala, Iran, and Chile, respectively. The U.S. signal to permit the overthrow of Ngo Dinh Diem in South Vietnam ultimately meant that there would not be a stable government in Saigon to serve as a U.S. ally. We are currently experiencing in Iraq the problem that has bedeviled U.S. interests in the Third World since the end of World War II: the use of military power and covert action without any plan for reconstruction and stabilization, which compromises U.S. interests and creates chaos in the target country. A National Intelligence Estimate in 2006, for example, concluded that the Iraq War led to easier recruitment of insurgents and terrorists, greater terrorist acts against U.S. interests, and less Allied willingness to cooperate with the United States in the global war on terrorism.

Clandestine operations continue to play the same prominent role in U.S. foreign policy. The end of the Cold War and the collapse of the Soviet Union in 1991, and the declaration of the Global War on Terror in 2001 demanded a reexamination of covert action. Covert action and even clandestine collection of intelligence can seriously damage U.S. bilateral relations and are often at odds with U.S. values. Over the past ten years, CIA officers have been embroiled in public accusations of spying by such friendly nations as France, Germany, India, Italy, and Japan, and CIA officials concede that the "tradecraft" of their agents in recent years has been less than professional. The failure to detect Indian nuclear testing in 1998 was linked to the inept performance of the CIA in New Delhi, and the U.S. bombing of a pharmaceutical factory in Sudan in the same year raised serious questions about the methodology of clandestine collection of intelligence used to justify military force. Ironically, Sudan was one of the few countries willing to help the Clinton administration arrest Osama bin Laden. European officials and politicians are calling for a major examination of their relations with the U.S. intelligence community because of the rendition of terrorism suspects from their nations to Islamic countries that routinely conduct torture as part of their interrogation techniques. German and Italian courts have subpoenaed CIA officials in connection with illegal renditions that have taken place in their countries.

In addition to resorting to heavy-handed covert actions in Iran, Guatemala, and the Congo, Eisenhower failed to show leadership on important domestic issues involving race and equal opportunity, McCarthyism, and homosexuality. At the height of the McCarthy era in the 1950s, which coincided with Eisenhower's two terms as president, the federal government discharged more suspected homosexuals from the government than suspected communists. The defeat of "don't ask, don't tell" in December 2010 culminated a struggle that the gay movement had been pursuing for more than sixty years. The exclusion of gays and lesbians from the military was the model for the exclusion of gays throughout the government and the public sector. Even when gays were allowed to serve as career military officers, they found promotions difficult to come by, and promotion to general or flag rank was virtually impossible. President Eisenhower was the first commander-in-chief to deal with the issue, and in 1963 he issued an executive order excluding homosexuals from employment in the military and civilian agencies as well. His orders required private companies with government contracts to ferret out and discharge their homosexual employees. Eisenhower's performance allowed numerous states to pursue their own anti-homosexual legislation, including prohibitions on bars and restaurants from serving homosexuals or even allowing them to gather.

Senator Joseph McCarthy bloodied the career records of two outstanding secretaries of state, Dean Acheson and George Marshall, but President Eisenhower made no attempt to silence the alcoholic senator from Wisconsin. The triumph of the communists in China led Senator McCarthy to be even more aggressive against Acheson and Marshall, but President Eisenhower remained silent. In view of McCarthy's contempt for common law and common decency, it was regrettable that Eisenhower didn't come to the defense of another soldier-statesman as well as a comrade in arms during World War II, General George Marshall. It was particularly unfortunate that President Eisenhower failed to weigh in against Senator McCarthy because there were no Americans who had greater credibility and influence than the statesman-soldier who occupied the White House from 1953 to 1961.

Although President Eisenhower did not challenge the extreme anti-communism of McCarthyism in the Cold War years, he was not part of those who tried to exploit the nation's fear of the Soviet Union, including the drafters of NSC-68 headed by Paul Nitze, which exaggerated the Soviet threat; the supporters of the Gaither Report in 1957, which also exaggerated Soviet power; and the various warnings of bomber gaps and missile gaps as well as concerns about a possible Soviet first strike, which Senator Kennedy used against Vice President Nixon in the 1960 presidential campaign. Eisenhower decried the hysteria that took over the country in 1957, when the Soviets surprised the world with the launching of their Sputnik missile. Eisenhower would never have approved the Team A/Team B exercise at the CIA that was designed to paint the Soviet bear as ten feet tall and to politicize the Agency's intelligence directorate. President Eisenhower was a moderate Republican who favored strategic arms control and disarmament; he would have opposed the efforts of the Committee on Present Danger to justify the unnecessary military buildup during the Reagan administration in the 1980s.

Eisenhower's most important contribution was turning away from the recommendations of his Vice President and others to consider the use of nuclear weapons to end the Korean War or to save the French garrison in Vietnam at Dien Bien Phu. He refused to introduce nuclear weapons to any military plans for dealing with possible Chinese aggression against Taiwan or to counter possible Soviet threats to Berlin. When the Joint Chiefs of Staff petitioned the White House for the use of "small" nuclear weapons against China because of spiraling tensions over the offshore islands of Quemoy and Matsu, he turned them down and pursued a diplomatic solution. The only time he ordered U.S. troops to invade a foreign land was in Lebanon in the summer of 1958, but these forces remained there for only several months, and U.S. forces suffered only one fatality and killed no Lebanese civilians. His brand of common sense in dealing with national security issues and the demands of the military is sorely needed in any discussion of U.S. policy.

TWO

PRESIDENT GEORGE H.W. BUSH'S
NEW WORLD ORDER

There is nothing more difficult to take in hand, more perilous to conduct, or more uncertain in its success, than to take the lead in the introduction of a new order of things. —Niccolo Machiavelli

We no longer have the luxury of having a threat to plan for. We don't know like we used to know. —General Colin Powell

Yet you never quite know with George H.W. Bush whether he is thinking. He does think, but not always. Reagan of course never did.[1] —Senator Daniel P. Moynihan

From the end of the Second World War to the collapse of the Soviet Union in 1991, the most serious foreign policy problem facing the United States was the political and military challenge of the Soviet Union. A series of crises highlighted the confrontation: the Berlin Wall in 1961; the Cuban missile crisis in 1962; Arab-Israeli wars of 1967, 1969, and 1973; and the Vietnam and Afghanistan wars. Washington's decision-making during this time was marked by debates over likely Soviet behavior and the possibility of U.S.-Soviet confrontation. The risks inherent in these crises were heightened by Moscow's huge military arsenal, especially weapons of mass destruction, and the possibility of the proliferation of WMD and conventional weaponry. U.S. decision-makers had to consider the U.S.-Soviet arms balance as well as regional arms balance, particularly in the Middle East and Southwest Asia, whenever projection of U.S. power was contemplated.

Richard M. Nixon, who had negotiated two major arms control agreements with the Soviets, understood that Russia needed to be treated with respect in the wake of the collapse of the Soviet Union, but he failed to convince President George H.W. Bush of the need for moderation. In one of his last interviews, Nixon warned that Russia was going through a terrible period of humiliation and embarrassment. The U.S. ambassador to Russia at that time, Thomas R. Pickering, similarly argued that Russia is a "country which knows it has made terrible mistakes and inflicted terrible, needless suffering on itself."[2] Nixon and Pickering were correct. In the early 1990s, the new Russia under Boris Yeltsin was looking for new answers, a new place for itself in the global community, and new relations with the major global powers, particularly the United States, in order to reduce global competition and confrontation.

President Bush had an unusual, indeed unprecedented, strategic opportunity to end the armed-to-the-teeth posture the United States adopted during the Cold War, but he would have to let go of the idea of the Cold War. A genuine detente with Russia would have provided an excellent opportunity for discussing a new post–Cold War relationship, including significant reductions in defense spending. Yeltsin's Russia simply could not afford an arms race; Bush's America lacked a strategic alternative to reliance on strong military forces.

So, in an unfortunate irony, at the very moment that the Berlin Wall and the Soviet empire collapsed, the United States inaugurated a conservative, Cold War politician. George Bush had traditional notions about American "exceptionalism" and was not prepared for significant change in American defense or national security policy. His national security adviser, Brent

Scowcroft, was a professional military officer who reinforced Bush's conservative views; his secretary of defense, Dick Cheney, was a right-wing ideologue who was skeptical of genuine change in the Soviet Union and rigidly opposed arms control and disarmament agreements. U.S. defense industries had no interest in a genuine detente.

Bush's hardline views were well established before his run for the presidency. During his congressional period from 1968 to 1974, he was a strident anti-communist; during the Vietnam War, he supported using nuclear weapons against North Vietnam.[3] As director of the Central Intelligence Agency from 1975 to 1976, he promoted hardline estimates on Soviet strategic capabilities.[4] Until the politicized estimate on Iraqi weapons of mass destruction that was published in October 2002, the estimates on Soviet strategic capabilities were the leading examples of politicization at the CIA. These estimates were influenced by hardline consultants under the leadership of Professor Richard Pipes of Harvard University, a well-known hardline anti-Soviet ideologue who had proclaimed, "Detente is dead." On many occasions Pipes had stressed that "Soviet leaders would have to choose between peacefully changing their Communist system in the direction followed by the West or going to war. There is no other alternative and it could go either way."[5]

Pipes headed a team of right-wing academics and former government officials that President Gerald Ford and his two key national security advisers, Chief of Staff Dick Cheney and Secretary of Defense Donald Rumsfeld, wanted to place in the CIA to apply worst-case thinking to national intelligence estimates on Soviet military power. When CIA director William Colby refused to accept the role of Pipes's team of neoconservatives, known as Team B, he was replaced by George Bush. Unlike Colby, Bush had no problem allowing Pipes and neoconservatives such as Paul Wolfowitz and General Danny Graham to challenge the estimates of the intelligence community. Ironically, the earlier CIA estimates were far more accurate than those prepared by Team B. Bush was not an original thinker on strategic matters and he had no difficulty accepting tough-minded estimates of Soviet power, even if they were wrong.

No president in the post–World War II era inherited the level of international stability that landed in Bush's lap in 1989. He followed an extremely popular two-term president from his own political party, the economy was stable, and there were no signs of upheaval in the geopolitical arena except for the tremors of change in the Soviet empire in Eastern Europe that presented geopolitical opportunities to the West. His predecessor, Ronald Reagan, had contributed to the stabilization of relations between the superpowers, making more progress in arms control and disarmament than any president since Nixon. In private, however, particularly after his election in 1988, Bush was harshly critical of Reagan's efforts to negotiate common constraints, arms control and disarmament, and a code of conduct for ending the geopolitical rivalry with the Soviet Union in the Third World.

President Bush merely had to follow the template that Reagan had created and take advantage of the collapsing Soviet Union to achieve greater disarmament and realize huge economic dividends. But he couldn't let go of the Cold War. On Bush's watch, the Cold War ended, the Berlin Wall came down, Germany was reunited, the Warsaw Pact dissolved, the Soviet empire disappeared, and the Soviet Union itself fell like a house of cards. But Bush was mostly a bystander to these events, failing to understand the historical opportunity presented to him.

During the campaign, Bush traveled to Fulton, Missouri, where Winston Churchill delivered his famous Iron Curtain speech, in order to proclaim that the "struggle" with the Soviet Union, the "threat" from the Soviet Union, was "not yet over.

According to Bush, the Iron Curtain was "rusting," but it wasn't lifting. He had no interest in listening to a bipartisan group of foreign policy professionals and Bush supporters, calling themselves the Annapolis Group, who used the transition period between the 1988 election and the 1989 inauguration to make the case for continuity with Reagan's policies.

In a memorandum for the newly named national security adviser, Brent Scowcroft, the group referred to Bush's "unique inheritance," including a "strategic arms reduction negotiation, which is very far advanced."[6] The Annapolis Group carefully chose a low-key messenger to deliver the memorandum to Scowcroft, Jeffrey Bergner, the former staff director for the Senate Foreign Relations Committee. Bergner made the case to Scowcroft, but was quickly shown the door. Even Secretary of State James Baker, the only genuine moderate in Bush's inner circle, told his aides upon arrival at the State Department, "Remember, this is not a friendly takeover."[7]

The new president had marveled at his predecessor's political charisma, but thought of himself as a political insider, a follower of the Nixon-Kissinger school of political realism. The new Bush White House was not interested in Reagan's parting comment on the day of the inauguration ("The Cold War is over") and did not see Reagan's legacy as a geopolitical gift. As far as Bush and Scowcroft were concerned, Reagan was a shallow "old man" who had rushed into detente with the Soviets, been far too conciliatory with Soviet President Mikhail Gorbachev, and moved too quickly to reduce strategic nuclear weapons. After all, from 1985 to 1989, Reagan and Gorbachev met on five occasions, which equaled the number of summit meetings Presidents Nixon, Ford, and Carter had with Gorbachev. Bush and Scowcroft called a time-out on relations with the Soviet Union that lasted a year before Secretary of State Baker could blow the whistle and resume play.

Contempt for Reagan's legacy within the Bush administration was so well established that presidential assistants began to joke openly to journalists about Reagan being a "dunce, out of touch, lazy, manipulated."[8] These aides went out of their way with journalists to compare Reagan's slothful habits with those of Bush, who wasn't exactly a workaholic. They pointed out "how hard Bush works, how knowledgeable he is on the issues and how much he hates being managed by the staff."[9] These comments eventually were read by former president Nixon, who contacted the White House with the message to stop belittling Reagan. Bush wisely called Reagan in California to apologize.

In addition to being disrespectful toward a popular president, Bush was demonstrating his opposition to Reagan's stunning and surprising turn toward moderation in his second term. There were few precedents for Reagan's sudden choice of a path of moderation in dealing with the Soviet Union. Reagan's secretary of state, George Shultz, like Secretary of State Baker, favored dealing directly with the Soviets, and over a period of time Shultz convinced Reagan to test the waters of detente with President Gorbachev. Baker's task, to persuade Bush to change direction from reliance on military power to acceptance of arms control, was more difficult than Shultz's task. Whereas Shultz had important supporters in the White House and the National Security Council backing the idea of disarmament and summitry with the Soviets, Baker was out there on his own hook.

Shultz's most important supporter was a senior foreign service officer, Jack Matlock, who served in the National Security Council in the mid-1980s, when there were serious debates over the direction of U.S. policy and diplomacy. He was a serious student of Russian culture and Soviet history.[10] Shultz and Matlock faced significant opposition from Secretary of Defense Caspar Weinberger, CIA director William Casey, UN Ambassador

Jeane Kirkpatrick, and hardliners such as Professor Pipes, who served on the National Security Council in Reagan's first term. They were believers in the use of military power and opponents of arms control.

When Reagan, Shultz, and Matlock produced the Intermediate Nuclear Forces (INF) Treaty in 1987, which eliminated an entire class of intermediate-range missiles based in Europe, Weinberger resigned. He was joined by his senior arms control specialist, Richard Perle, who wanted each side to retain a hundred intermediate-range missiles. Reagan seemed to be prepared to go far beyond his most dovish advisers and pursue the elimination of all nuclear weapons by the year 2000. The military-industrial-congressional complex never would have accepted such a move, and when key European allies such as Britain and France picked up indications of Reagan's preferences, they had to be reassured that the elimination of all nuclear weapons was not operational policy.

Reagan and Bush also had fundamental differences on policy toward China. In June 1989, the Chinese Communist Party brutally crushed a nascent Chinese pro-democracy movement in Tiananmen Square, authorizing the use of tanks and live ammunition to repress student protests. The Chinese army was responsible for the killing of nearly three thousand Chinese students, and two decades later the event casts a long and powerful shadow over elite politics in China. The June 4 anniversary of the event still leads to a huge show of force from the government and the pervasive Chinese security apparatus, with anyone defined as a dissident or political activist detained or confined to home. Media and Internet controls are toughened, and Tiananmen Square itself is virtually locked down by uniformed and plain-clothes police and paramilitary officers.

Such an event during the Reagan administration would have chilled Sino-U.S. relations and presumably would have led to increased U.S. military sales to Taiwan. President Bush, however, was determined to put pressure on the Soviet Union by improving relations with China and prided himself on his personal connections and affiliations with world leaders. Instead of a hardline policy response to Beijing, he opted for personal diplomacy in an attempt to remove the massacre as a possible roadblock to improved bilateral relations. Publicly, he tilted in the direction of the conservatives and neoconservatives who argued that Tiananmen Square proved that China would never be a reliable diplomatic partner for the United States. Privately, he maligned liberal and human rights activists who favored severe sanctions against the Chinese government. And secretly, he sent General Scowcroft and deputy secretary of state Larry Eagleburger to Beijing to express the president's dismay with the use of force against civilians but at the same time to signal that Sino-U.S. relations would not be affected over the long term by the violence at Tiananmen Square. The twenty-four-hour visit remained secret for an exceptionally long period of time.

President Bush had served in Beijing ten years earlier as head of the American Liaison Office and strongly believed that the Chinese government would not respond favorably to foreign pressure or the threat of isolation. In the first year of the administration, President Bush and national security adviser Scowcroft were operating under the rules and principles of the Cold War, which dictated that China was needed to balance the Soviet Union. Unlike President Reagan, who recognized the emergence of a different Soviet Union under Gorbachev and Shevardnadze, President Bush was wary of antagonizing China in any way. Bush and Scowcroft were more interested in sending a signal to the Kremlin that U.S.-Sino relations were going to be the key to the strategic triangle of the United States, the Soviet Union, and China.

Indeed, Bush was an old-fashioned Cold War warrior

whose anti-Soviet and anti-communist views were typical of his generation. Even before he became president, his speeches were larded with anti-Soviet references. In September 1983, for example, then Vice President Bush told an audience in Vienna that Soviet hegemony in Eastern Europe was a violation of the Yalta agreement at the end of World War II and the major reason for East-West tensions.[11] He made gratuitous references to the Soviet Union as being outside the European experience, having played no role in the Renaissance, the Reformation, or the Enlightenment. At the same time, he stressed the European roots of the United States. Bush even recited the canard that "Russian soldiers on the loose in Warsaw" in 1863 had hurled the late Frédéric Chopin's piano from a fourth-floor window. Bush declared that the "entire culture of Central Europe shares the fate of Chopin's piano."[12] He certainly ignored the legacy of President Eisenhower, who believed in speaking of adversaries with respect.

Bush's speech in Vienna, drafted originally by the Soviet desk of the State Department, had contained no references to the Soviet Union. The anti-Soviet rhetoric was introduced by a member of Bush's staff. Assistant secretary of state Richard Burt met with the vice president in an effort to have him excise the negative references, but he was unsuccessful and even failed to persuade Bush to remove factual errors. Bush charged, for example, that the Soviet "monopoly of intermediate-range nuclear missiles" was a "new element" in the balance of power in Europe.[13] Burt, a senior member of the U.S. delegation to the strategic arms limitation talks in the early 1970s, knew that Soviet intermediate-range missiles had been deployed since 1959, and the SS-20 was merely a modern replacement for obsolescent SS-4 and SS-5 missiles.

The end of the Cold War created an unusual opportunity for the United States, one that it had not faced since the 1930s.

For the first time in sixty years, the United States was not preoccupied with an existential threat. Focused on Nazi Germany and the Soviet Union for two generations, the United States had no geopolitical challenge to justify its superpower stance. The chairman of the Joint Chiefs of Staffs, General Colin Powell had the best description of the new uncertainty. "We no longer have the luxury," he said, "of having a threat to plan for. What we plan for is that we're a superpower. We are the major player on the world stage with responsibilities around the world with interests around the world."[14] When asked about the likelihood of having to use U.S. forces in future conflicts, Powell replied, "Haven't the foggiest. . . . That's the whole point. We don't know like we used to know."

This may be the best explanation for the United States blundering and blustering into situations in North Africa, the Middle East, and Southwest Asia, where it had no national, let alone vital interests, to defend. Unlike previous turmoil in the Third World, where the United States had to anticipate a Soviet reaction, the United States was in a position where it could act with impunity. It was particularly tragic that as secretary of state, Powell—who understood the limits of force in the Third World—was a key player in the decision-making team that made the biggest blunder of them all, the invasion of Iraq in 2003.

The White House and the Pentagon, needing to justify large defense expenditures, turned to regional conflict as the new geopolitical challenge. The Soviet Union as a superpower threat was gone, so small and insignificant states became the perceived threat to the new world order. The Bush administration focused on preventing "any hostile power from dominating a region critical to our interests." The most hardline members of the Bush administration, Wolfowitz and Lewis "Scooter" Libby, even drafted a Defense Policy Guidance in 1991 to serve as a neoconservative blueprint for post–Cold War strategy. These

two high-ranking Defense Department officials were supported by their boss, Secretary of Defense Cheney, who had been a
strong critic of detente in the 1970s and now saw an opportunity
for stealing a march on a weakened Soviet Union.

The document, which was leaked to the *Los Angeles Times*
in 1992 immediately after Desert Storm, presumably by critics
of the aggressive doctrine, called for maintaining U.S. dominance by preventing the rise of any potentially hostile power.
It defended the preemptive use of force against states suspected
of developing weapons of mass destruction—exactly the rationalization offered by then Vice President Cheney, Libby, and
Wolfowitz for the invasion of Iraq a decade later. The Guidance
made the case for unilateralism, arguing that the United States
should be prepared to act alone when "collective action cannot
be orchestrated." When he read it, then Senator Joseph Biden
(D-DE) was appalled; he immediately denounced the document
as a prescription for a Pax Americana. Nearly two decades later,
Vice President Biden led the way in convincing President Barack
Obama to reverse the escalation of force in Afghanistan.

The endorsement in the Guidance for a policy that depended on the use and threat of force had a great deal of support from
the mainstream media and from the Congress. Many congressmen praised the Defense Policy Guidance and Cheney's leadership. Representative John B. Larson (D-CT) noted, "One has
to admire, in a way, the Babe Ruth–like sureness of [Cheney's]
political work. He pointed to center field ten years ago, and now
the ball is sailing over the fence." The conservatives praised the
absence of any references to international organizations such
as the United Nations, or disarmament treaties such as the
Non-Proliferation Treaty. Even today neoconservatives such as
Wolfowitz argue that Saddam Hussein's "demise opened opportunities for governments and institutions to emerge in the Muslim world that are respectful of fundamental human dignity and

freedom." For neoconservatives, the Arab Spring of 2011 would never have taken place without the thinking behind the 1992 Defense Policy Guidance and the preemptive attack against Iraq a decade later.

President Bush and General Scowcroft were opposed to the Guidance, but the dissolution of the Soviet Union, the end of the Cold War and the sudden military success of the Desert Storm campaign against Iraq in 1991 made them vulnerable to "imperial temptations." With the absence of a Soviet threat, the military-industrial-congressional complex, led by its advocates in the Bush administration, exaggerated the regional ambitions and intentions of weak Third World nations such as Iran, Iraq, and North Korea, which became known as the "axis of evil" a decade later. These states faced enormous political and economic challenges that represented no threat to U.S. security interests, but neoconservatives cited a nuclear threat in Iraq where none existed and exaggerated the capabilities of Iran and North Korea in order to increase U.S. defense spending and military deployments.

Bush's Anti-Soviet Team

President Bush, the last U.S. president to have seen combat in World War II, had a lengthy job résumé and, unlike his successors, was very familiar with the major players in national security policy. His experience included tours as ambassador to China and to the United Nations and as director of the CIA. With the exception of James Baker, who had run Bush's presidential campaign and had been a close friend for many years, he named team members who were anti-Soviet and supporters of a strong military policy. In his memoirs, Baker observed that the foreign policy team "not only enjoyed one another's company, we trusted one another. That's not to suggest we didn't disagree. . . . But our differences never took the form of the backbiting of the

Kissinger-Rogers era, Vance-Brzezinski era, or the slugfests of our national security teams during the Reagan years."[15] Baker chose to ignore his significant policy differences with members of the National Security Council, particularly Robert M. Gates.

The president appointed a retired general, Brent Scowcroft, to be his national security adviser, and he served as the president's alter ego. In many ways, Scowcroft was the ideal national security adviser. He was soft-spoken and collegial in his approach to the national security team, and he tried to be an honest broker for the president. Scowcroft believed that the national security adviser should be a coordinator of policy and made sure that the secretaries of state and defense had opportunities to present policy recommendations to the president. Nevertheless, in dealing with the Russians, Scowcroft seemed to believe that Leonid Brezhnev, who had died in 1982, was still running the Kremlin.

The president's first choice for secretary of defense was the former senator from Texas, John Tower, a longtime crony. But Tower had serious baggage, including a reputation for womanizing and heavy drinking, which infuriated the straitlaced chairman of the Senate Armed Forces Committee, Sam Nunn (D-GA). Bush ignored high-level advice to ditch Tower, and when he didn't, Nunn's committee and the full Senate did the job for him, rejecting Tower 53-47. Bush didn't have an obvious backup, but when his vice president, Dan Quayle, and others began to lobby for Cheney, Bush paid close attention. Cheney, a classic right-winger his entire political career, was particularly well known to Bush from his days as chief of staff for President Gerald Ford. Bush, Scowcroft, and Baker also worked for Ford.

In Congress since the early 1980s, Cheney was one of the most enthusiastic supporters of increased defense spending and the use of military force. As secretary of defense, he favored waging a military invasion of Panama in 1989 to capture Manuel Noriega, and wanted retaliation for the terrorist bombing of Pan

American flight 103 over Lockerbie, particularly after learning that Libya, Syria, and Iran might have played some role in the attack. When the chairman of the Joint Chiefs of Staff, Admiral William J. Crowe, exhibited some tentative lack of support for such uses of military force, Cheney warned that the president "has got a long history of vindictive political actions."[16] Cheney made it known that if you cross Bush, you pay, and he even supplied the names of a few victims. In the 1980s, Cheney was a strong supporter of covert assistant to the Contras against the Sandinista forces in Nicaragua and had no concerns about the fact that domestic laws were broken in the process.

Although Cheney later became the key architect of the war against Iraq in 2003, he was opposed to invading Iraq in 1991 in Desert Storm. He explained, "If we'd gone to Baghdad and got rid of Saddam Hussein, we'd have to put a lot of forces in and run him to ground some place. . . . Then you've got to put a new government in his place and then you're faced with the question of what kind of government are you going to establish in Iraq?"[17] In 1991, Cheney asked all the right questions about the number of forces that would be needed in Iraq to prop up a new regime and how many casualties would be registered during the operation. He did not ask these questions in the run-up to the March 2003 invasion.

Powell was a political general who had made few false steps in his speedy rise up the career ladder. In the 1980s, he had served as a military assistant to Secretary of Defense Weinberger, as deputy national security adviser to Frank Carlucci, and as national security adviser to President Reagan. As Carlucci noted, Powell "knew when to follow orders and fall in line with the boss."[18] The appointment of Powell was nevertheless surprising, because he was a relatively new commander-in-chief and the most junior of all the fifteen eligible four-star generals for the post of chairman of the Joint Chiefs. There was resistance within the Pentagon to the Powell appointment because he had made his bones in staff and political assignments, not combat.

Another member of the Bush national security team who knew when to follow orders and fall in line with the boss was Robert M. Gates, who was named deputy national security adviser and then director of the CIA by Bush. On the basis of a strong recommendation from Scowcroft, Bush nominated Gates to be the deputy national security adviser. Both Bush and Scowcroft wanted Gates for his hardline views and were willing to ignore his role in politicizing intelligence on the Soviet Union and Central America. Bush named Gates to be CIA director in May 1991, even though Gates had had to withdraw an earlier nomination in 1987 because the Senate intelligence committee did not believe his denials of knowledge and participation in Iran-Contra. Bush had no qualms about any possible role for Gates in Iran-Contra because he too had played a role in that episode. Gates knew where the political bodies were buried, and perhaps the president was buying a certain amount of political protection.

Gates's confirmation hearings were the most contentious ever conducted for a CIA director because of his role in politicizing intelligence during his previous tours at CIA under Bill Casey. His nomination drew more negative votes (31) than all previous nominations for a CIA director combined. Bush was stunned at first to learn that the nomination of Gates was controversial within the Agency, but the White House recognized that its nominee was in trouble in the confirmation process. Bush named Kenneth Duberstein, an old Washington hand, to shape the strategy for a confirmation battle that lasted six months. As Gates observed, it took less time for the Soviet Union to dissolve than it took the Senate to confirm him as director of central intelligence.

Bush included in his national security team another conventional Cold War thinker, Vice President Daniel Quayle, who was at the table during most national security deliberations but left no substantive record behind. Other than Nixon's selection of Spiro Agnew as vice president, no more unqualified presidential partner had served in the post-WWII period than Dan Quayle. A "D" student of political science at DePauw University, he actually "majored" in golf, failed his final examination in political science, and probably would not have been admitted to the university if his parents, uncle, and grandfather had not been graduates and generous donors to the school. Qualye used his friends and family to avoid serving as a U.S. soldier in the Vietnam War, as did George W. Bush.

Quayle was an acolyte of such neoconservatives as Richard Perle and Kenneth Adelman and a major opponent of arms control. His views never changed, and not even the assumption of power of Mikhail Gorbachev at the Kremlin in 1985 fazed then Senator Quayle. "I don't think he's any different from Brezhnev or anybody else," Quayle proclaimed. And as late as 1988, he called "perestroika" "nothing more than refined Stalinism. . . . It's not changing the system."[19] CIA deputy director Gates was saying the same thing at the time to congressional committees and White House advisers.

The only member of Bush's national security team who understood that the world was shifting beneath his feet, creating an opportunities for U.S. diplomacy, was Secretary of State James Baker. He was no fan of the 1991 Defense Policy Guidance and, as early as May 1989, Baker tried to convince the president to make a far-reaching proposal on Soviet-American conventional forces in Europe, calling for a 25 percent reduction in weapons and personnel that would "generate the kind of political effect we were looking for, while not endangering us militarily."[20] Baker's proposal ran into a bureaucratic wall of resistance. Secretary of Defense Cheney believed that there was no need to be forthcoming because Gorbachev had to move in our direction anyway. The chairman of the Joint Chiefs, Admiral Crowe, "fought virtually every proposal tooth and nail."[21]

Baker lacked the sophistication and gravitas of Dean Acheson, the ideological fervor of John Foster Dulles, and the intellectual firepower of Henry Kissinger, but he became a force in his own right. His advice to President Bush was persistent and spot-on and, as a result, he became increasingly influential. He deserves the major share of credit for moving Bush toward a policy of interaction and conciliation, just as Secretary of State Shultz had moved President Reagan away from the "evil empire" narrative toward summitry, arms control, and disarmament. It took Baker a full year to get the White House to return to summitry with Moscow, however. The opportunity for Secretary of State Baker took place in December 1989, when President Bush and Soviet President Gorbachev met at the Malta Summit, a meeting that Baker had promoted and Scowcroft and Gates had resisted. The summit provided a breakthrough in state and personal relations, which was similar to the mutual respect and confidence that developed between Reagan and Gorbachev at the Reykjavik Summit in 1986 and for Baker and Soviet Foreign Minister Eduard Shevardnadze in September 1989 at their first meeting in Jackson Hole, Wyoming.

Prior to Malta, President Bush had dismissed President Gorbachev's spectacular speech at the United Nations in December 1988 as "nothing new." This was the speech that presaged Moscow's willingness to withdraw forces from Eastern Europe and its unwillingness to interfere with political reform in Eastern Europe. It was a seminal statement of policy to say the least.

In May 1989 White House spokesman Marlin Fitzwater referred to Gorbachev as a "drugstore cowboy." On the eve of the Malta Summit, Fitzwater predicted that Bush's approach to

Gorbachev would be one of "tough love." Baker was particularly concerned that the Bush administration's first strategic review of the Soviet Union was nothing but "mush," blaming Reagan administration holdovers for being "incapable of truly thinking things anew."[22]

The unusual setting for a summit, U.S. and Soviet battleships off the coast of Malta, was designed to permit President Bush to term the meeting "informal." Stormy weather in the Mediterranean, predictable in summer but not so in winter, nearly caused a disaster, however. The seas turned so violent during the first day of talks that the U.S. delegation nearly capsized in the presidential launch on the return to the USS *Belknap*. President Bush was scheduled to return to the Soviet cruiser *Maxim Gorky* the following day, but his secret service detail intervened and he remained on the U.S. ship for an additional day. During that time, there were more exchanges between Baker's and Shevardnadze's weather forecasters than between their political aides.

Despite the stormy weather and political turbulence, the Malta summit marked a new beginning for Soviet-American relations, even though no agreements were negotiated, let alone concluded. Malta produced the breakthrough that enabled completion of the Conventional Forces in Europe Treaty in 1990 and the Strategic Arms Reductions Treaty in 1991. Malta also produced the first joint press conference in the history of superpower summitry. Gorbachev told Bush, "We don't consider you an enemy any more," and Shevardnadze added that the two sides had "buried the Cold War at the bottom of the Mediterranean Sea."[23]

Despite the success of the Malta Summit, two major arms control treaties, and significant Soviet cooperation during the Gulf War of 1991, there continued to be a group in the Bush administration favoring increased defense spending and continued resistance to detente with the Soviet Union, then Russia.

The neoconservative group was led by Vice President Cheney with strong support from deputy national security adviser Gates and deputy defense secretary Wolfowitz. Cheney's promotion of the controversial Defense Policy Guidance seemed particularly ill-timed, with its emphasis on the absence of change in Soviet "fundamental objectives" in foreign policy, particularly the Third World. Cheney and Gates were especially stubborn regarding the notion of an unchanged Soviet threat. Baker's and Gates's successor as CIA director, William Webster, did not share the stubborn convictions of Cheney and Gates, but overall the Bush administration was slow to recognize the national security revolution of Gorbachev and Shevardnadze. Gorbachev and Shevardnadze were trying to end the Cold War, but the neoconservatives remained unimpressed.

Bush's "New World Order"

Before a joint session of Congress on September 11, 1989, the president declared the dawn of a "new world order . . . a world where the rule of law supplants the rule of the jungle . . . a world where the strong respect the rights of the weak."[24] Following a speaking engagement at the National War College in 2000, national security adviser Scowcroft was asked about the origin and meaning of the "new world order" that the president had declared. Bush's argument appeared to be that, with the collapse of the Soviet empire, the United States would reign supreme in a unipolar world and would dominate the world economy. Scowcroft's response indicated that the concept was far less ambitious and magisterial. The retired general, a man of few words, conceded that the "new world order" was a slogan, unaccompanied by any new ideas for changes in policy.[25]

In other words, the "new world order" was a phrase to hide the continuation of an anti-Soviet policy that would not use the dissolution of the Soviet Union and the end of the Cold War to stabilize the international arena and reduce reliance on military power. Bush never discussed changes to strategic policy or conceptual doctrine. He was not as cerebral as Jimmy Carter, not as programmatic as Richard Nixon, not as political as Lyndon Johnson, and certainly not as willing to pursue arms control as Ronald Reagan was in his second term. Bush and Scowcroft were simply unprepared for change after forty-five years of American policy dedicated to the breakup of the Soviet empire. For the first time in its history, the United States was a totally unrivaled global power with the ability to use military force with impunity and to dominate the diplomatic process in most regions of the world.

Bush and Scowcroft had the good fortune to be dealing with the last Soviet president, Gorbachev, and the first Russian president, Yeltsin, who were prepared to capitulate to reasonable demands from the United States. Gorbachev and Yeltsin as well as Shevardnadze deserve the major credit for the patience and determination to take the diplomatic initiative, to make unilateral initiatives and even concessions, and to bring a complete end to the Cold War. Their policies were designed to transcend detente, energize arms control, and create a new code of conduct between the superpowers. The forthcoming policies of the Kremlin made the initial obscurantism of Bush and Scowcroft particularly remarkable.

The Failure to Anchor

The collapse of the Soviet Union marked a virtual end to the long-standing military threat that Moscow represented as well as the ideological confrontation. Bush's greatest strategic failure was the failure to "anchor" the new Russia to the political and economic architecture of the Western alliance. George F. Kennan, in his containment doctrine of the 1940s, wisely argued that, once Russia demonstrated that it would behave in a moderate and conciliatory fashion in the world community, it would be essential for the Western states to "anchor" or tie Russia to the West.[26] In other words, the United States must not use such geopolitical and economic institutions as the International Monetary Fund, the World Bank, the World Trade Organization, GATT, and the Missile Technology Control Review merely to moderate Russian behavior, but must bring Russia into these institutions as a stakeholder to bolster international conciliation and to foster liberal trends in the Kremlin itself. The Bush administration needed to signal that it wanted to make Russia a vital part of the Western community, and that the United States had no interest in isolating or marginalizing Russia. It took two decades for Russia, in fact, to gain membership in the World Trade Organization.

Bush and Scowcroft, unwilling to test the waters of a new Russian approach, bought into the conventional wisdom of the former national security adviser to President Carter, Zbigniew Brzezinski, who argued that it would be premature to buy into the notion of a "strategic partnership" or any kind of partnership with a Russia that maintained its imperial impulses.[27] Brzezinski totally ignored the withdrawal of Russian forces from East Germany, Central Europe, and even the Baltics, and instead falsely accused Russia of encouraging an "ethnic explosion" in the Crimea. Thus a major opportunity was lost to build immediately on the arms control agreements of the past two decades or to exploit the opening for conflict resolution in the Third World. Yeltsin's Russia was in favor of reducing nuclear arsenals, reducing arsenals of weapons of mass destruction in developing nations, and becoming a stakeholder in managing the conflict zones in the global community. By the summer of 1994, Russia had withdrawn all of its forces from Central Europe and the Third World, leaving only small numbers of soldiers in those states where Moscow had basing agreements.[28] Soon after, Russia walked away from these agreements with Cuba and Vietnam.

Gorbachev and Shevardnadze had changed the basic assumptions driving Soviet-U.S relations, radically altered the nature of the dialogue, and effectively ended the Cold War, but President Bush and national security adviser Scowcraft lacked the imagination or perhaps the interest to capitalize on these new developments. They took steps to improve bilateral relations, but these were modest steps that failed to capitalize on the large strategic opportunity that the Gorbachev-Shevardnadze leadership and the Soviet decline had afforded. Gorbachev and Shevardnadze had fundamentally altered the direction of Soviet foreign policy in order to accommodate the United States and to reduce the Soviet presence throughout the Third World, which led to Gorbachev's being awarded the Nobel Peace Prize in 1991. Meanwhile, the Bush administration remained in the grasp of the Cold War thinking of the military-industrial complex, which prevented any significant changes in U.S. national security policy.

Gorbachev and Shevardnadze particularly deserve credit for putting Soviet relations with the United States as well as Soviet relations with Western Europe on the most solid footing since the end of the Second World War. They deserve credit for eventually breaking down the anti-Soviet attitudes of President Bush, which ultimately led to a degree of engagement and confidence. Soviet-American cooperation during the Iraq-Kuwait crisis in 1990 and the Gulf War in 1991 made it relatively easy for the United States to obtain the international sanctions that the Bush administration wanted against Iraq as well as a great deal of support for Desert Storm. More importantly, Soviet-American cooperation ended the Cold War by ending the military confrontation between East and West in Europe and cooperating in the reunification of Germany.

Bush and Panama

Too often, in their first year as commander-in-chief, presidents rely on the use of force to establish their bona fides. Bush was no exception, and deployed 26,000 soldiers to invade Panama. This took place as the Soviet Union was beginning to collapse, and moved one Soviet official to remark, "It seems we have turned the Brezhnev Doctrine [i.e., unlimited intervention in satellite nations] over to you."[29] Once again, a new president was demonstrating his machismo by using military force, as President Kennedy did so disastrously at the Bay of Pigs in 1961; Presidents Johnson and Nixon did in Vietnam; President Ford did in "rescuing" a U.S. merchant marine crew that had already been released by its captors; and President Reagan did in Grenada in 1983.

Panamanian dictator Manuel Noriega had been on the CIA payroll in the 1970s when George Bush was CIA director. He was dropped from the payroll in the late 1970s because President Carter was convinced that Noriega had negotiated one too many drug deals with Columbia's Medellin drug cartel and Cuba's Fidel Castro. By 1985, the Reagan administration had resumed the stipend to Noriega, which probably convinced the Panamanian dictator that he had a free hand to operate in Central America.

When two federal grand juries in Florida indicted Noriega on drug-trafficking charges, the Reagan administration began covert actions against Noriega, although it offered to drop prosecution if Noriega would leave Panama. Vice President Bush opposed this plan, believing (probably correctly) that it would backfire in the same way that Iran-Contra blew up. Vice President Bush believed that Noriega would have to be forcibly removed from power, although in 1989 he did not support a coup against the Panamanian leader. The coup leaders were asking the United States to block two critical routes so that Noriega couldn't call in reinforcements once the coup began.

A huge mistake was made in December 1989 when one of Noriega's thugs killed a U.S. soldier. This act gave President Bush the justification he needed to invade Panama on December 20, the first intervention of the post–Cold War era. By December 21 the Noriega government was gone. The Pentagon, true to form, was opposed to the use of force against Noriega, but the Bush administration believed that Noriega's forces had become a threat to the 40,000 servicemen and civilians in Panama. When the chairman of the Joint Chiefs of Staff, Admiral William J. Crowe, exhibited only tentative support for the operation, Secretary of Defense Cheney again let it be known that if you cross Bush, you pay, mentioning some who had found out the hard way. Crowe's successor, General Colin Powell, and the service chiefs were leery about getting involved in Panama, but they eventually realized that the time for diplomacy had passed. The commander of U.S. forces in Panama, General Maxwell Thurman, was initially opposed, but he too got on board. Secretary of Defense Cheney made sure there would be military support for Bush, and warned the Joint Chiefs again that the president "has got a long history of vindictive political actions."[30] As vice president a decade later, Cheney led the campaign for the war against Iraq in 2003, and favored an aerial strike against an alleged nuclear facility in Syria in 2007.

Nearly 25,000 U.S. troops launched combat operations just five days before Christmas in an operation labeled Just Cause, which many pundits offered as an explanation ("just cause") for U.S. action. Noriega was ousted from power within twenty-four hours but took refuge in the Vatican embassy, where he was bombarded with eardrum-shattering rock music for days. He eventually surrendered and was brought to the United States as a prisoner, although any reading of international law presumably would conclude that the U.S. invasion was unprovoked and therefore illegal. The 25,000 troops that Bush sent to Panama were minuscule compared to the 600,000 that he sent to Iraq in 1991 to fight the one-hundred-hour Gulf War under the name Desert Storm.

The U.S. Role in the Persian Gulf

Desert Shield and Desert Storm were the names given to the diplomatic and military campaigns, respectively, against Iraq's invasion of Kuwait in 1990. Both operations were startling and unusual in many respects. The Reagan and Bush administrations were slow to acknowledge the brutal nature of Saddam Hussein's regime, but Secretary of State Baker's diplomatic campaign was quick to isolate the Iraqi leader, to form a comprehensive international coalition against Saddam's invasion of Kuwait, and to obtain a United Nations resolution authorizing the use of force if he failed to leave Kuwait by early 1991.

Prior to the military campaign, the policy and intelligence communities had no idea that Saddam Hussein was preparing forces to occupy the entire country of Kuwait in 1990, although satellite photography showed the Iraqi army on the move. The collapse of the Soviet Union gave the United States freedom of action in the Middle East, unlike earlier confrontations when Washington had to worry about Soviet responses to use of force. Very few pundits expected a one-hundred-hour war, and some experts predicted a hard-fought campaign against Iraqi forces. The Pentagon ordered thousands of Purple Hearts and body bags before the campaign that resulted in fewer than 150 U.S. fatalities.

President Bush's use of force against the Iraqi invasion of Kuwait led to more intense U.S. involvement in the Middle East and Southwest Asia. "Desert Storm" was a short but devastating war that crippled the country's infrastructure but left Saddam Hussein in power and led to long-term engagements that involved three more administrations. In January 2011, former Secretary of State Baker told a reunion of Gulf War veterans that Desert Storm was "a textbook example of the way to go to war diplomatically, politically . . . militarily . . . and economically." Baker emphasized, "a lot of other countries contributed treasure to this effort."[31] The brevity of the campaign, however, led to the American military activism of the 1990s, misplaced confidence in the use of air power, and misplaced optimism involving use of force against Afghanistan and Iraq.

President Bush boldly proclaimed in the wake of Desert Storm that the United States had at long last kicked its Vietnam syndrome regarding the use of force. The president believed that the successful use of American military power would lead to less frequent uses of U.S. forces. "I think," Bush explained, that "when we say something objectively correct . . . people are going to listen."[32] If this was the new foundation for Bush's "new world order," then the paradigm was flawed from the start. The decade was marred by unprecedented U.S. military activism in the Balkans, the Horn of Africa, and the Persian Gulf.

Following the collapse of the Soviet Union, Russia and the United States cooperated in efforts to stabilize a range of regional conflicts, including those in El Salvador, Ethiopia, and Nicaragua, and sought to de-emphasize the superpower competition in Afghanistan, Angola, and Cambodia. The Soviets made serious efforts to avoid war in the Persian Gulf, but once the Bush administration used force, Moscow fully supported the U.S. role in Desert Storm. The Kremlin refused to let Desert Storm get in the way of a possible era of cooperation in the Third World as well as in arms control and disarmament. In addition to progress in bilateral strategic arms control and disarmament (including START and reciprocal unilateral reductions), there were multilateral arms control measures (including the Conventional Forces in Europe Treaty, the ban on chemical weapons, and efforts to stop the proliferation of nuclear weapons. Both Bush and Gorbachev spoke of a "new world order," although there were no efforts to institutionalize the Russian-American relationship.

Gorbachev's successor, Boris Yeltsin, went further in terms of policies that were pro-Western, pro-cooperative, and more consistent in developing "new thinking" in international affairs, but the Bush administration did not respond in its last year in the White House.

The increased U.S. military involvement in the Middle East and the Persian Gulf actually followed the United Kingdom's decision in 1970 to abandon its traditional interests in the region. President Carter issued the Carter Doctrine in 1977 to clarify U.S. interests in the region, but the presence of Soviet military power in the Mediterranean and the Indian Ocean restrained U.S. use of force. With the collapse of the Soviet empire in 1990 and the Soviet Union itself in 1991, there were no longer geopolitical constraints on the use of military power, and four consecutive American administrations have used the military instrument to protect perceived U.S. interests. The major winners in this policy trend have been Iran, which no longer worries about hostile regimes on its borders with Iraq and Afghanistan; Islamic interests, which have exploited the chaos in the region that protracted U.S. power has created; and the oil-producing states of the Persian Gulf that have profited enormously skyrocketing cost of oil since the introduction of U.S. force in Iraq in 2003.

In declaring the "new world order" before a joint session of Congress in January 1991, Bush had no way of knowing that he was inaugurating a post–Cold War era that would be marked by extensive use of military force that has seduced three successive American presidencies. All of these administrations have emphasized the importance of U.S.-style democracy in the region, but the operative goal of U.S. policy has been creating an "order" that was responsive to U.S. demands and dictates.

Desert Storm successfully liberated Kuwait and virtually destroyed the military machine of Saddam Hussein, but it could not secure Bush's reelection the following year. Wars typically elevate the power and prestige of U.S. presidents: Nixon and George W. Bush were reelected in the midst of losing wars in Vietnam and Iraq; America's most dovish post-war president, Jimmy Carter, was not. George H.W. Bush could not be re-elected despite his huge popularity in the wake of the success of Desert Storm; his son was reelected despite a controversial and unnecessary war. Bush's defeat in 1992 was reminiscent of Prime Minister Winston Churchill's defeat during WWII in 1945.

It must be asked, however, is this war necessary? Only days before the American-led ground offensive was getting under way on February 24, 1991, Saddam Hussein was desperately negotiating with President Gorbachev to arrange an Iraqi withdrawal from Kuwait. Iraqi forces had invaded and occupied Kuwait on August 2, 1990, and for months he had ignored the efforts of the United States, the United Nations, and the international community to arrange a withdrawal. It was not until the eleventh hour that Saddam Hussein offered to withdraw his forces. He told Gorbachev that it could be done within twenty-one days; after consulting with the Bush administration, Gorbachev said that it would have to be done within nine to ten days. U.S. aerial assaults had actually begun in mid-January and, as a result, Hussein's chief negotiator with the Soviets, Foreign Minister Tariq Aziz, could not even fly directly from Moscow to Baghdad. Instead, he flew from Moscow to Amman, Jordan, and traveled by road to the Iraqi capital, often reaching speeds of more than 130 miles an hour.[33]

An extraordinary Iraqi diplomatic archive, which was captured in the first weeks of the 2003 invasion, confirmed that sensitive diplomatic efforts were under way at the last moments to avert war. In the last hours before the start of the invasion, there were frantic calls between Gorbachev and Hussein as well as between Gorbachev and Bush. Saddam Hussein dispatched his foreign minister to Moscow on the eve of the U.S. invasion in an eleventh-hour bid to head off a ground war. Gorbachev convinced Hussein to offer to withdraw Iraqi troops from Kuwait within twenty-one days. In private, Hussein referred to the Soviet leader as a "scoundrel," who lacked the will or the influence to stop the United States. "He tricked us," Hussein said. "I knew he would betray us."[34]

On February 23, just minutes before the noon deadline, Gorbachev argued that joint Soviet-American action through the United Nations could establish a model for dealing with other crises. He believed that he could engineer a compromise to avert war that would protect the former Soviet client and establish the Soviet Union as an equal partner with the United States in international diplomacy and conflict resolution. At the same time, the archives make it clear that Hussein did not genuinely believe that the United States would resort to force, a strategic miscalculation that he repeated in 2003. He believed that the United States lacked the resolve to wage a grinding ground war and would not accept the casualties that would ensue.[35] "Let them come to Karbala City," Hussein said. "It will become their cemetery."

The previous day, however, Saddam had set the notorious Kuwaiti oil-well fires that President Bush described as a "scorched-earth policy" that justified the use of force.[36] Bush and Scowcroft had decided that it was essential to use military force. In their unusual joint memoir, they made it clear that they were going to act against Iraq "even had Congress not passed the resolutions" to use force.[37] Bush and Scowcroft had invested political energy and diplomatic imagination to create a multinational coalition that included 697,000 Americans. Bush and Scowcraft tried to mollify Gorbachev by emphasizing their concern for safeguarding the future of Soviet-American relations. At the same time, they realized that the economic and military decline of the Soviet Union gave the United States total freedom of action. Moreover, the international coalition included support from key Arab countries, even Syria. The president and his national security adviser had a clear field ahead of them for the use of force as well as an opportunity to put the memories of the Vietnam failure, the so-called "haunting legacy," behind us.

The United States argued publicly that it was going to war against Iraqi forces in Kuwait in order to leave behind a democracy in the occupied country. Ever since President Woodrow Wilson in WWI, U.S. presidents have justified the use of military force by stressing the importance of nation-building and democracy. Two decades later, Kuwait is no closer to being a democracy than it was when Iraqi forces entered the country and U.S. forces entered the war. The ruling al-Sabah family has maintained an authoritarian hold on power. The volcano of rage that exploded in the Middle East and the Persian Gulf in the Arab Spring of 2011 reached Kuwait, but with no democratic impact.

Nevertheless, Desert Storm and the U.S. role in ousting Saddam's forces from Kuwait, like the Vietnam debacle, left a haunting legacy for Washington. Following the war, President Bush endorsed a public and private campaign urging Iraqi Shiites to rebel against Saddam Hussein's government. When they did so, however, the United States stood by as Iraqi forces slaughtered the Shiites by the thousands. In 2011, in an extremely unusual gesture, U.S. Ambassador to Iraq James F. Jeffrey apologized to Iraqi politicians and tribal leaders for U.S. inaction during the popular uprising. President Bush had publicly encouraged the revolt and then allowed U.S. forces to stand by while Iraqi helicopter gunships and execution squads carried out a bloodbath that claimed tens of thousands of lives.

The Bush administration's response was to order the CIA to find ways to oust the Iraqi president with covert action, which led to one of the Agency's greatest operational failures. Most of the money was spent on useless propaganda, and the CIA operational officers who worked with the Kurdish resistance forces spoke neither Kurdish nor Arabic. Saddam's spies even penetrated the operation, but when a CIA officer warned of the penetration, he was ignored.[38] Twenty years later, the perception of U.S. betrayal still resonates deeply in the Iraqi psyche, and to this day Iraqi Shiites have never expressed thanks for the U.S. overthrow of the tyrannical reign of Saddam Hussein and his Baathist Party.

The Right Steps on Arms Control . . . Eventually

A remarkable change took place in President Reagan's second term when his administration shifted from a policy of opposition to the Soviet Union to one of engaging Moscow and its new president, Mikhail Gorbachev. As part of this new engagement and detente, there were just as many summits between the U.S. and Soviet presidents from 1985 to 1988 as there were in total during the administrations of Nixon, Ford, and Carter in the 1970s. There was significant progress on arms control and disarmament, including the first treaty that banned an entire class of weapons system—the medium-range missiles deployed in Europe that were banned in the Intermediate Nuclear Forces Treaty (INF). There was a definite slowdown in military spending in the second term as well and a recognition that arms control, peaceful coexistence, mutual deterrence, and even a code of conduct had to be pursued in the name of detente. President Reagan was prepared to go beyond detente, demonstrating a willingness to ban all nuclear weapons.

The incoming Bush administration, however, was not interested in pursuing the dramatic reduction of the nuclear arsenal that President Reagan had set in place. President Bush was not only unprepared to move in such a direction, but he and national security adviser Scowcroft emphasized in private that there would be a long timeout in the negotiation of disarmament treaties. Two of Scowcroft's key advisers, Bob Gates and Condi Rice, were anti-Soviet and skeptical that the turmoil in the Soviet Union and Eastern Europe, which included the collapse of the Berlin Wall, would lead to change. Fortunately, Secretary of State Baker had a different perception of Soviet-American relations and the need for continued summitry and arms control.

The Bush administration had a perfect opportunity to move boldly in the area of arms control and disarmament because of the worsening political and economic situation for Gorbachev. With the collapse of the Berlin Wall in 1989 and the Warsaw Pact in 1990, Gorbachev and Foreign Minister Eduard Shevardnadze clearly saw the writing on the wall and were persistent in their efforts to engage the Bush administration. The START I treaty was finally signed in July 1991, but Gorbachev was prepared to pursue deeper reductions in strategic weapons than Bush would accept. The Soviets made the key concession when they suggested a "range" for the reduction of strategic warheads rather than a one-number ceiling. This allowed the Soviets to reduce more missiles than the U.S. favored; Moscow wanted to have greater cuts in its strategic arsenal for economic reasons, and Washington favored a decrease for political reasons. The U.S. edge of a few-hundred-warhead advantage was strategically irrelevant, but it provided excellent cover for ratification in the U.S. Senate.

President Bush was initially adamant in resisting Soviet overtures regarding deep cuts in strategic forces, cessation of nuclear testing, elimination of tactical and naval nuclear weapons, reassurance on the ABM Treaty, and preventing an arms race in outer space. The only area of progress was in the field of naval nuclear weapons, with President Bush belatedly going ahead in September 1991. Actually, it never made any strategic sense for the United States to deploy nuclear weapons on its ships, because doing so had led the Soviet Union to do the same and thus compromise a clear U.S. advantage at sea.

The tough negotiating tactics of Reagan and Bush made it very difficult for Gorbachev and Shevardnadze to convince their more conservative Politburo colleagues that the United States was serious about detente and that the Soviet Union had something to gain from negotiations. Both administrations made certain that the Soviets made the key concessions in both the INF Treaty and the START Treaty. Instead of reciprocating, U.S. negotiators merely pocketed the Soviet concessions and moved on to the next demand. The terms of Soviet withdrawal from Afghanistan also catered to U.S. terms, with the United States reneging on a commitment from Secretary of State Shultz to assist Moscow to prevent disorder and the emergence of an unpredictable regime such as the Taliban, which established control in 1996 with the assistance of Pakistan. The United States continues to pay a staggering price in lives lost and resources squandered for its failure to secure the Najibullah regime left in place by Moscow.

President Bush did have some success in the area of arms control and disarmament, particularly the decision to remove tactical nuclear weapons from U.S. warships and the halt to B-52 alerts. Once again, the Pentagon, which consistently resisted negotiated reductions to the nuclear arsenal, tried to block these steps. Fortunately, President Bush took a page from the playbook of President Nixon, which was to conduct nuclear policy from the White House and not from the Pentagon, which President Clinton chose to do.

President Bush deserves major credit for his unilateral

decision in September 1991 to withdraw tactical nuclear weapons from Europe and from U.S. warships, a step that Soviet President Gorbachev matched and trumped several days later. These decisions produced rare disarmament measures that even the Pentagon favored. It never made sense to place tactical nuclear weapons on U.S. warships that already had a huge superiority in power projection and weapons lethality. It was wrong to encourage other nations to deploy nuclear weapons, which would compromise the U.S. advantage at sea and endanger U.S. forces. Similarly, ground-based tactical weapons made no sense because there was no way for Army commanders to fight on a nuclear battlefield, where soldiers engaged in close-range combat operations would be annihilated.

The other exception to the relatively hardline tactics of the Bush administration was in the case of the sudden collapse of all the communist regimes in Central and Eastern Europe. The Reagan administration made numerous calls for change in Eastern Europe and supported these calls with covert action, particularly in Poland. The Bush administration, however, held back from endorsing change in either the Soviet Union or Eastern Europe, and President Bush was heavily criticized for his condemnation of "infantile nationalism" in a speech in Kiev during uprisings in Ukraine. Conversely, Bush's initiatives pointed to a huge policy and intelligence failure with decision-makers and intelligence analysts totally unprepared for the wave of nationalism in Eastern Europe that pushed aside a series of community regimes in a few short months.

Gorbachev and Shevardnadze deserve plaudits for avoiding any involvement in the revolutionary activity in Eastern Europe, thus ending the Brezhnev doctrine, which proclaimed Moscow's right to intervene to defend communist regimes and to enforce Eastern European submission to Moscow. As a result, the Eastern European revolutions took place without military resistance.

This certainly was not the case with previous Soviet leaders, who resorted to the use or threat of force during counterrevolutions in Hungary (1956), Czechoslovakia (1968), and Poland (1981). Moscow's endorsement of non–use of force and nonintervention helped to unleash the dramatic changes that contributed to revolutionary developments in the former states of the Warsaw Pact in 1989, the reunification of Germany in 1990, and even the breakup of Yugoslavia in 1991. But Bush and Baker also deserve credit for not resorting to political or polemical support on behalf of the protestors and not gloating over their rapid political success.

Bush and Iran-contra. Bush was not a major player in the national security policy-making of the Reagan administration, but his denials of any role or understanding of the illegalities of Iran-contra were disingenuous. In his campaign for the presidency in 1987, Bush maintained that he didn't get to "see the picture as a whole" until December 1986, when he received a briefing from Senator David Durenberger (R-MN), the chairman of the Senate Intelligence Committee.[39] Bush created the impression that he had been deliberately excluded from key meetings on the Iran operation, that he had serious doubts about the operation, and that if he had known about the doubts of Secretary of State Shultz and Secretary of Defense Weinberger, he would have gone to the president and requested a meeting of the National Security Council on the subject. Bush was convinced that, if he had done so, he could have convinced President Reagan to see the "project in a different light, as a gamble doomed to fail."[40]

In fact, Bush was on hand for numerous high-level meetings to discuss Iran-Contra, including the principals meeting in January 1986, when Shultz and Weinberger forcefully presented their opposition to the operation. Bush was regularly briefed by national security adviser John Poindexter on the arms sales and the efforts to free the hostages, bringing the vice president up to date whenever Bush missed one of President Reagan's daily intelligence briefings. He was also briefed in Israel in July 1986 by Amiram Nir, President Shimon Peres's adviser on terrorism, at "considerable length and in intimate detail" about the background and status of the Israeli dealings with Iran and the arms-for-hostages deal.[41] Nir was a close confidant of the National Security Council's Oliver North; they collaborated closely on a series of counterterrorism operations, including the U.S. interception of the Egyptian plane carrying four Palestinian terrorists after the hijacking of the cruise ship *Achille Lauro* in 1985. Nir played the key Israeli role in creating a conduit to Iran for the delivery of surface-to-air missiles.

Bush knew that Israeli Defense Minister Yitzhak Rabin had been authorized to sell arms to Iran, including SAM missiles, and that the United States would replenish those weapons. Bush initially claimed that he lacked full understanding of the briefing from Nir regarding weapons for Iran, but eventually admitted in a television interview that he approved the project when he learned about the torture and death of a CIA station chief in the Middle East, William Buckley, who had been kidnapped in Beirut. Bush claimed that he "erred on the side of trying to get those hostages" out of Lebanon.[42]

Not only was Bush present at several key meetings that discussed Iran-Contra, his national security adviser was Donald Gregg, a CIA operational veteran. Gregg met regularly with Colonel Oliver North, Felix Rodriguez, and others who were closely involved with the weapons transfers and exchanges of intelligence that violated the Boland Amendment, which prohibited providing military support for the purpose of overthrowing the Nicaraguan government. It was reasonable to assume that Gregg regularly briefed the vice president, who was once director of the CIA, on these activities. Finally, Bush attended the so-called "bridging meeting" of the National Security Council on May 16, 1986, which arranged soliciting financial support from various Arab countries, particularly Saudi Arabia, to support the Contras.

Bush maintained that if he had sat there and heard Shultz and Weinberger express opposition strongly, maybe he "would have had a stronger view."[43] In fact, there were three meetings between the president, Secretary of State Shultz, and Secretary of Defense Weinberger in which the cabinet officers discussed their opposition to the sale of arms to Iran. Vice President Bush attended two of these meetings, including the first one in early August 1985, when national security deputy adviser Robert Mc-Farlane first proposed the sales and on January 7, 1986, when President Reagan authorized the continuation of sales directly from the United States. Therefore, Bush was dissembling when he said he was "out of the loop," and he never mentioned that he had been briefed regularly by national security adviser John Poindexter on the arms sales and the efforts to free the hostages.[44]

In addition to dissembling about his knowledge of and role in Iran-Contra, President Bush used the power of presidential pardon to prevent a public trial of key individuals involved in the scandal, including Secretary of Defense Weinberger and national security adviser McFarlane. The pardon for Weinberger was particularly damaging because his contemporaneous notes documented a "conspiracy among the highest-ranking Reagan administration officials to lie to Congress and the American public."[45] Notes from Weinberger and Shultz also revealed that they were stunned by Bush's claims not to have heard their opposition to Iran-Contra.

Lawrence E. Walsh, the independent counsel in the Iran-Contra investigation, believed that the concealment of the notes on Iran-Contra possibly forestalled timely impeachment proceedings against President Reagan and others. In addition to pardoning those officials who had lied to Congress and obstructed official investigations, Vice President Bush also concealed highly relevant notes that would have implicated himself and others. National security adviser Poindexter and his close aide, Oliver North, were actually convicted, but their sentences were vacated on appeal because of immunity agreements with the Senate concerning their testimony.

Bush and Defense Spending

The military buildup during the Reagan years, the greatest military spending in peacetime, was slowing down as Bush was coming into office. There had been a 40 percent increase in overall defense spending during the eight years of Reagan's stewardship of national security. Increased defense spending and major tax cuts in the 1980s created huge deficits; these policies were repeated during the stewardship of George W. Bush from 2001 to 2009, when decisions to go to war were accompanied by significant cuts in taxes.

The end of the Cold War provided an excellent opportunity to finally cut the high cost of the defense budget. President Bush took some tentative steps in that direction, but by 1990 the Iraqi invasion of Kuwait convinced him that there was no such thing as a "peace dividend," and he decided to raise taxes in order to maintain defense spending. Thus, President Bush broke his famous pledge "read my lips, no new taxes," which contributed to his election defeat in 1992. In an overall compromise, the president agreed to the Democratic demand for increased spending on social needs and to the Republican demand for increased defense spending, but angered the right wing of his own party by agreeing to increase taxes in order to get both guns and butter. The increases in defense spending in the administrations of Bush I and Clinton were minor. The administration of George W. Bush changed that pattern.

In his final State of the Union message, President Bush seemed to understand Eisenhower's message regarding the military-industrial complex, emphasizing that the demise of the Soviet Union meant that "we can look homeward even more and move to set right what needs to be set right."[46] Bush noted, "The American people have shouldered the burden and paid taxes that were higher than they would have been to support a defense that was bigger than it would have been if imperial communism had never existed." President Bush took credit for starting a round of defense cuts and argued that "with imperial communism gone, that process can be accelerated."

Bush and Cheney deserve credit for cutting back on some of the major weapons systems of the Cold War confrontation with the Soviet Union, particularly the B-2 bomber, which was originally planned to be a force of 135 aircraft, but was reduced to twenty. Bush and Cheney also tried to cut the intended production of C-17 Globemaster III transport aircraft nearly in half, from 210 to 120, although a case could have been made that the C-17 was not necessary. The existing transport aircraft, the C-5, could carry twice as many troops as the C-17, but the powerful Boeing Corporation and the equally powerful California congressional delegation lobbied the Bush and Clinton administrations for additional aircraft beyond the forty that had already been ordered.

In 1995, however, the General Accounting Office (GAO), which monitors government spending, determined that forty C-17s would "meet the Defense Department's airlift requirements . . . at a cost savings of upwards of $10 billion when compared to a fleet of 120 C-17s.[47] A lobbying team, led by Senators Barbara Boxer (D-CA), and Dianne Feinstein (D-CA), known for their antiwar views, saved the program at the level of 120 C-17 aircraft. Ten years later, Republican Governor Arnold Schwarzenegger led a similar lobbying effort on behalf of

Boeing to keep the program alive for another ten years. This marked a major victory for the military-industrial complex on behalf of Boeing's most profitable large aircraft program, which finds profit margins far exceeding profits on commercial aircraft. (According to the *Seattle Post-Intelligencer*, the profit margins on sales of the C-17 exceeded 13 percent while sales of the Boeing-747, then Boeing's most profitable commercial aircraft, were less than 5 percent.)

Bush and Cheney limited the number of Seawolf submarines, although Senator Joseph Lieberman (D-CT) fought for full funding. During the Clinton administration, Senator Lieberman, a powerful member of the Senate Armed Services Committee, intervened once again to make sure that the Seawolf would be fully funded until the next generation of strategic submarines, the Virginia class, could be procured.[48] The Seawolf is another example of a weapons system that was developed during the Cold War against a strategic Soviet submarine threat that was being eclipsed. The Bush and Clinton administrations allocated over $7 billion for several Seawolf submarines until the Virginia-class submarine could be deployed. The most recent Virginia-class submarine was christened in December 2011, marking a new generation of attack subs hailed as the world's most complex piece of machinery at a cost of $2.6 billion each.[49] Thus, the United States appropriated funds for two classes of strategic submarines against a largely mothballed Soviet Navy.

When Lieberman joined with presidential candidate Al Gore in 2000, the vice presidential candidate promised to "set aside more than twice as much" for a military buildup as their opponents, George Bush and Dick Cheney.

THREE

CLINTON'S PROBLEMS WITH THE PENTAGON

Prior to World War II, the U.S. military rarely influenced foreign and national security policy. It took the Cold War and the 1947 National Security Act (NSA) to give the military an integral role in formulating national security policy in peacetime and in war. The NSA created the position of chairman of the Joint Chiefs of Staff (JCS); successive amendments and reforms enhanced the power of the chairman and weakened the influence and leverage of the civilian secretaries of the Army, Navy, and Air Force. The Goldwater-Nichols Act of 1986 made the chairman the "principal military adviser to the president, the National Security Council, and the secretary of defense." The stature of JCS Chairman Colin Powell in the early 1990s added leverage to the position. The authority of force commanders in major regional areas (previously known as commanders-in-chief, or "Cincs," until Secretary of Defense Donald Rumsfeld abandoned the acronym, declaring that the country had only one commander-in-chief) was also strengthened, weakening the stature of assistant secretaries of state and key ambassadors in the field. These regional commanders became, in effect, proconsuls to the empire.

The unprecedented statutory authority of the regional commanders gave them greater influence in the budget process, foreign policy formulation, and national security decision-making, including the debate over the transformation of the military in the twenty-first century. These commanders, backed by the secretary of defense, have prepared regional engagement plans around the world without consulting the State Department, occasionally resulting in the overuse of U.S. forces. (In May 2003, several weeks after the end of the war in Iraq, the U.S. military conducted a raid on the Palestinian diplomatic mission in Baghdad without consulting any civilian official in Iraq. An official in the Bush administration explained that "Marines don't get paid to worry about any flags, other than the Stars and Stripes, and this unit carried out its disarmament mission with relish and *Semper Fi.*"[1])

In the post–Cold War era, no president has had as much difficulty dealing with the military as Bill Clinton. President Clinton entered office with no experience in national security or military affairs. Moreover, he demonstrated a suspicion of the military community, which was fully reciprocated. Coming to office with the reputation of having manipulated the draft laws in 1969 to avoid military service during the Vietnam War, his relations with the Pentagon were tenuous from the start. Although his opposition to the Vietnam War had been cautiously calibrated, the military pictured Clinton as an extreme activist. The fact that President Clinton wanted to reduce the defense budget in the wake of the collapse of the Soviet Union and the end of the Cold War didn't endear him to the military-industrial-congressional community. Finally, his campaign's endorsement of allowing homosexuals to serve openly in the military made him an object of scorn among many, if not most, military officers.

It is noteworthy that Republicans such as George W. Bush, Dick Cheney, and William Cohen dodged the draft but drew a pass from the Pentagon on this issue. But Democrats such as President Clinton and even a war hero such as Senator John Kerry did not, begging serious questions about the politics of the professional military, which has become increasingly conservative.

Clinton alienated the military shortly after his inauguration, suggesting in a press conference that he would allow homosexuals to serve openly in the military. This decision, virtually his first as commander-in-chief, set off a firestorm in the Pentagon. When his new secretary of defense, Les Aspin, tried to explain it to the Joint Chiefs of Staff, he was treated to an unprecedented ninety-minute tirade. Following the demands of the Joint Chiefs of Staff, Aspin arranged a meeting in the White House that was attended by the chairman of the Joint Chiefs, General Colin Powell. The Marine commandant, Carl Mundy, was the most vociferous opponent of allowing gays to serve in the military. He termed homosexuality a "moral depravity that could not be tolerated in the ranks."[2] Predictably, nearly twenty years later, when President Obama finally moved to end "don't ask, don't tell," the greatest opposition came from the Marine Corps.

Clinton was caught off-guard by the opposition of Senator Sam Nunn (D-GA), the chairman of the Senate Armed Forces Committee; forced to backtrack, he instructed Aspin to find a compromise. Senator Nunn, who was extremely influential on military matters and led the opposition to ending the gay ban, posed a series of fatuous questions for those activists who supported the president (e.g., "What would happen if a gay soldier brought a partner to a military ball?")[3] In a move that was beneath even Nunn, he scheduled a visit to a submarine to demonstrate the lack of privacy on board. Nunn made it clear that there would be no passage of President Clinton's first piece of domestic legislation, the Family and Medical Leave Act, until the White House abandoned its support for open military service for homosexuals.

The compromise, of course, was the cynical "don't ask, don't tell." In addition to the human damage this policy caused, the compromise signaled to the uniformed services that they could challenge the authority of the commander-in-chief with impunity. "I got the worst of both worlds," Clinton later wrote—losing the fight to allow gays in the military and earning taunts of betrayal from his gay supporters. Clinton did not understand that, by caving into pressure from the Pentagon, he also had demonstrated that he could be pushed around by the generals. His lack of credibility enabled the Joint Chiefs of Staff to drag their heels in the last several years of the Clinton administration, particularly when the president wanted the Pentagon to plan more aggressive steps in Afghanistan.

Soon after his inauguration, President Clinton tried to build a bridge to the Pentagon—but was rebuffed. During a March 1993 visit to the aircraft carrier USS *Theodore Roosevelt*, Clinton was treated rudely by the sailors, according to news reports; some even spoke in mocking tones about their commander-in-chief. An apocryphal story circulated that a sailor threw a beer at Clinton, but that there was no need to worry because it was "draft beer" and the president dodged it.[4] In April, Clinton was booed during a visit to the Vietnam War Memorial. I was on the faculty of the National War College during this period, and can personally testify to the ugliness of the remarks made about President Clinton, all in violation of law and military regulation.

Clinton repeatedly bowed to military pressure on important national security and foreign policy issues. His capitulations weakened or killed agreements dealing with the International Criminal Court, a ban on landmines, the Comprehensive Test Ban Treaty, and the Chemical Weapons Convention. And in walking away from confrontation overseas, he appeared to capitulate to foreign elements, which angered many members of the Joint Chiefs of Staff. The embarrassing withdrawal of U.S. forces from Somalia in September 1993, and the sudden withdrawal of the USS *Harlan County* from Port-au-Prince, Haiti, in October 1993 created a picture of U.S. impotence and irresolution that the Pentagon deplored, although the uniformed military initially opposed any active role in Haiti or Somalia. The fact that Senator Robert Byrd (D-WV) appeared to dictate the terms of the withdrawal from Somalia added to President Clinton's embarrassment.

The national security policies of the Clinton administration antagonized leading neoconservatives and influential members of the defense community, some of whom formed the Project for the New American Century in 1997. The Project was the natural heir of the Coalition for a Democratic Majority and the Committee on the Present Danger, which had been created in the 1970s to challenge the foreign policies of the Carter administration, particularly Carter's interest in arms control, disarmament, and conflict resolution in the Third World. The George H.W. Bush administration mildly frustrated the neoconservatives, but various policies of President Clinton and Vice President Gore drove them to distraction: support for international cooperation on climate change and the control of AIDS; humanitarian intervention and peacekeeping in the Balkans; nation-building; and the creation of the International Criminal Court. These were anathema to neoconservatives such as Dick Cheney, Richard Perle, and Paul Wolfowitz. Clinton's policies were dismissed as "globaloney" by the neoconservatives, who attacked his liberal agenda and his perceived failure to exploit the "new realities of power" as the United States moved into the post–Cold War world.

Although President Clinton committed more funds to defense spending than his predecessor, he was attacked by the neoconservatives for not committing sufficient funds to the Pentagon. Initially, the Clinton administration adopted the Pentagon's doctrine of funding wars on two fronts, designed to fill the vacuum created by the demise of the Soviet Union. Nevertheless, even the concept of a two-front war led to a modest decrease in defense spending, particularly for investment in military procurement. The last two years of the Bush administration and the first two years of the Clinton administration led to a decrease of 20 percent in the defense budget, resulting primarily from a 25 percent reduction in the force structure.

Nevertheless, the Pentagon was still spending more per soldier than it did in the 1980s. The overall budget was still somewhat higher than average spending during the Cold War, and Clinton failed to cut back on unnecessary weapons systems. A case in point was production of the controversial C-17 transport aircraft, which could lift only half the number of combat troops carried by the existing C-5 transport aircraft. The C-5s could have been rebuilt and modernized for about $250 million per aircraft. President Clinton inherited forty C-17s and maintained the Bush administration's plan to procure 120. The General Accounting Office concluded that a "fleet of 40 C-17s and 64 commercial aircraft could meet the Defense Department's airlift requirements . . . at a cost savings of upwards of $10 billion when compared to the fleet of 120 C-17s."[5]

While liberals criticized Clinton for excessive spending, they did little to help him cut back. Joining California's congressional Republicans, California's Democrats lobbied on behalf of the C-17 aircraft that was produced in Long Beach, California. The state's liberal, anti-war senators, Barbara Boxer and Dianne Feinstein, were not typically friends of new weapons systems—unless they were manufactured in California. There are few better examples of the insidious nature of the military-industrial-congressional complex.

Clinton's National Security Team
Although President Clinton had pledged to install a government that "looks like America," his national security team was a selection of establishment individuals, each of whom created

policy and management problems at his or her respective agencies. None of them was able to conceptualize a post–Cold War national security policy that would build on the success of George Kennan's containment policy. Clinton's choices for the four key positions for national security affairs brought no new thinking to U.S. national security policy. Warren Christopher as secretary of state, Representative Les Aspin as secretary of defense, Anthony Lake as national security adviser, and James Woolsey as director of Central Intelligence were not known for their thinking on grand strategy. None could play the role that Henry Kissinger played for President Richard Nixon or Zbigniew Brzezinski played for President Jimmy Carter. The inexperienced president needed a strategist who understood the opportunity to craft a grand strategy based on new principles for a post–Cold War world that would include arms control and disarmament, demilitarization, and conflict resolution in the Third World. He needed a sherpa for strategy, instead he ended up with four low-key mechanics much too lackluster to take the lead.

It was not surprising that no member of the national security team made it to President Clinton's second term. Secretary of Defense Aspin was the first to fall, leaving the Pentagon in December 1993 due to health problems that eventually required heart bypass surgery. Aspin's departure was also due to serious policy differences with high-ranking military officers over the issue of gays in the military, armored support for U.S. forces in Somalia, and the military budget. When asked about the causes of his resignation, Aspin conceded, "Oh, a bit of all three" in reference to his health, gays in the military, and Somalia. During his short tenure at the Pentagon, he also had to deal with controversies concerning the role of women on the front lines, cutting the reserve force, and base closures. His departure was a victory for the military-industrial complex.

Clinton was one of the least experienced commanders-in-chief in the twentieth century, and it was obvious from the start that Aspin was not going to fill the void for the president. Members of the Joint Chiefs of Staff considered Aspin aloof and abrasive, and his waffling over key substantive decisions regarding military support for the Contras in Nicaragua and the MX missile certainly didn't help his standing. He was an intellectual figure in a definitely anti-intellectual setting, slow to make decisions, unable to manage substantive disputes between the separate forces, and imprecise in debate. As one of his military critics opined, Aspin had the courage of his conclusions but not the courage of his convictions. By removing Aspin so abruptly, however, the Pentagon learned that it could challenge the president successfully.

Clinton went from the frying pan into the fire when he nominated Admiral Bobby Ray Inman to be Aspin's successor in a gesture to mollify the military-industrial complex. At the press conference announcing him as the nominee, Inman arrogantly stated he had reached a "level of comfort" with Clinton as a suitable commander-in-chief. No cabinet nominee has ever provided a better political epitaph than Inman, who soon after announced his withdrawal from consideration and told the press, "The country is better off with me in the private sector." In fact, it was the shady business practices of Inman that had called attention to his dubious qualifications. Clinton's embarrassment with this selection continues today, because nowhere in his 964-page memoir does Inman's name appear.

Clinton's eventual appointment of William Perry as secretary of defense was the best selection he made in the national security field and the only exception to the mediocre and largely unqualified appointees who populated his eight years as commander-in-chief. Perry had ideas about reforming the Pentagon, including significant reductions in military contracts, military suppliers, and even military weaponry. He was a great proponent of arms control and disarmament, and was able to stand up to the critics of arms control in the Pentagon. In an attempt to find a bipartisan solution for his second term, however, Clinton selected Senator William Cohen (R-MA), who created some of the same problems with the military that Aspin had created in the first term.

In 1994, the second key member of the national security team was forced to step aside, Director of Central Intelligence James Woolsey. He was confirmed unanimously in February 1993 but within months had antagonized key members of the Senate Intelligence Committee, including chairman Dennis DeConcini (D-AZ), as well as important players in the White House and the Office of Management and Budget, such as OMB chairman Leon Panetta. One of Panetta's senior staff officers commented on Woolsey's edgy demeanor and disposition in dealing with Panetta: "I've never seen a more graceless stonewall. . . ."[6]

Woolsey's mishandling of the espionage case involving CIA career operations officer Aldrich Ames, particularly the mild discipline he gave officers responsible for the worst security breach in U.S. history, led him to announce his resignation in December 1994. The seventh-floor suite of the director of Central Intelligence offers a wonderful view of the wooded hills of northern Virginia, but it was obvious that Woolsey could not see beyond the cloistered world of an agency that was overtaken by history, particularly the collapse of the Soviet Union and the end of the Cold War. Ames was responsible for the deaths of the twelve most important Soviet officials spying for the United States, but Woolsey could only bring himself to issue bureaucratic reprimands in the face of clear institutional dysfunction.

Ames was on the Soviet (and Russian) payroll for nearly a decade, but no one at CIA was fired, no one was demoted; there were only reprimands for the "old-boy" network that failed to respond aggressively to a traitor responsible for the deaths of every CIA asset in the Soviet Union and the loss of every espionage and counterintelligence operation against the Kremlin. When Clinton created a presidential commission to investigate the need for reform of the intelligence community, headed by former secretaries of defense Aspin and Harold Brown, Woolsey clashed repeatedly with Congress and even the White House over the work of the commission. He became increasingly combative and isolated, and, having lost the trust of the president and Congress, he had to go.

Clinton seemed to learn nothing from his disastrous nomination of Inman, choosing Air Force General Michael Carns to replace Woolsey, one more move to appease the military-industrial community. With the exception of the Pentagon, no government agency requires a stronger management hand than the CIA. It was obvious from the start that the Air Force general was not the right candidate. Carns ostensibly withdrew his nomination because of immigration and tax issues involving a member of his domestic work force, but from the outset it had been clear that Carns lacked the acumen and experience to deal with the nomination process, let alone the complexities of the U.S. intelligence community. As with Admiral Inman, there is no mention of General Carns in the Clinton autobiography. As in a Sherlock Holmes mystery, it is often the dog that doesn't bark that provides the loudest clue. Clinton's other directors of Central Intelligence, John Deutch and George Tenet, made their own contributions to the decline and fall of the CIA, and with the Intelligence Reorganization Act of 2004 the role of CIA director was significantly weakened.

If Aspin didn't let you know what he was thinking because he hadn't decided, Secretary of State Warren Christopher didn't let you know what he was thinking by design. Even before the dust had settled on the resignations of Aspin and Woolsey, there were rumors involving the possible resignation of Christopher.

Christopher remained in place until November 1996, but it was a bumpy and unsuccessful ride. His first major trip to Europe took place early in the first Clinton term, April 1993; his purpose was to persuade key Western European states to lift their arms embargo on Bosnian Muslims. European journalists and pundits immediately caricatured the secretary as a weak messenger for the Clinton administration. There were stories such as his bellying up to the bar to order a "virgin decaf Irish coffee" during a refueling stop in Ireland. The trip, needless to say, was a total failure; Christopher could not make a good strategic case for arming the Muslims, and no European nation was willing to follow the U.S. lead.

In the wake of this failure, the Clinton White House made things worse by secretly deciding to ignore European opposition and permit the Iranians to supply Bosnian Muslims with arms, informing the U.S. ambassador to Croatia, Peter Galbraith, of the decision but not the director of the CIA. Agency operatives in the Balkans learned of these arms transfers and reported incorrectly to the director of Central Intelligence that Ambassador Galbraith was secretly and illegally involved in negotiations to arms the Muslims.[7] The DCI took this information to the Senate Select Committee on Intelligence, which had not been briefed on this covert action, and an unnecessary political imbroglio took place on Capitol Hill. In addition to mishandling the Bosnia matter, Secretary of State Christopher and national security adviser Anthony Lake developed a reputation for multiple changes of direction on virtually all key decisions, particularly those involving Haiti and Somalia.

But the straw that broke the camel's back was Christopher's support of the 1994 reform plans for the State Department sponsored by reactionary Senators Jesse Helms (R-NC) and Mitch McConnell (R-KY). Helms and McConnell were opposed to arms control and disarmament and realized that changes in the bureaucratic process would lead to changes in the policy process. Their plan called for abolishing the Arms Control and Disarmament Agency and the U.S. Information Service, and moving their few remaining functions into the Department of State. This created an unwieldy and unmanageable department and deprived the executive branch of the independent expertise needed in areas of arms control and disarmament as well as the need to use information policy to combat anti-Americanism in the Middle East and Southwest Asia. The Agency for International Development remained, as an independent agency, but it was greatly weakened and suffered from morale problems that have never been cured. These bureaucratic maneuvers led to the decline in the stature and influence of the Department of State that the last four secretaries of state, including Colin Powell, have not been able to reverse. More importantly, it led to a weakening of the civilian role in decision-making in key national security areas as well as in the role of oversight.

Ultimately, it was Clinton who agreed with Helms's efforts to move ACDA and USIS into the State Department, defending the decision in his autobiography and never mentioning the unfortunate impact this reorganization had on the management of the State Department, let alone the loss of two important and independent agencies. Clinton contended that he had to agree to Helms's reorganization plan in order to get a vote on the Chemical Weapons Convention, which ultimately passed by a 74-26 margin after congressional conservatives weakened its ratification procedures.

It didn't help matters that on almost every key area of policy, particularly Haiti and North Korea, Christopher and his State Department were upstaged by the globe-trotting diplomacy of former president Jimmy Carter. Carter's successes in these areas made Christopher look irrelevant and led to a good deal of sniping and opposition within the department. As in the case of Aspin at the Pentagon, where he never took charge of the military culture, and Tony Lake at the National Security Council, where he never took command of the policy process, Christopher was never able to take command of the Foreign Service Corps.

Lake's management problems were used against him when he was nominated to be CIA director in 1995. In addition to being too liberal for the job of CIA director in the eyes of too many senators, Lake was criticized for his inability to manage a small staff, which did not prepare him for dealing with a huge organization such as the CIA. There is a certain irony here, because, alone among the key Clinton advisers, Lake was the only substantive expert who understood the need for developing operational strategies to deal with terrorism, the proliferation of weapons of mass destruction, and ethnic conflict. He was clearly someone who had his priorities in order and someone who could think outside the box. Lake could have been an outstanding director for getting the CIA into the world of strategic intelligence, which remains a major problem for the Agency.

Unfortunately, he could not translate his substantive expertise into command of the policy process, as witness his initiative to permit Iranian arms to reach the Muslims in Bosnia. It was Lake's idea not to inform the director of Central Intelligence, whom he didn't trust, or even the U.S. Congress, which became irate when it learned of this initiative. These missteps led to resignation rumors for Lake as early as October 1993. This is not the first time in Washington that a substantive and even strategic expert could not manage the politics and the process of decision-making.

In view of Lake's substantive expertise, he could have played a key role in the field of strategic intelligence at CIA, but not as the director of Central Intelligence. Strategic intelligence has suffered in recent years at the CIA, particularly since the politicization of intelligence by CIA director William Casey and his deputy, Robert Gates. Lake was out in front on the issue of international terrorism and the role of Osama bin Laden's al-Qaeda organization and might have prevented the huge intelligence failures surrounding the 9/11 attacks. A man of genuine character and integrity (unlike future directors such as George Tenet and Porter Goss), he would not have manipulated intelligence to support the policy process. Lake, who courageously resigned from the foreign service in 1971 to protest the secret bombing campaign against Cambodia, would never have caved in to policy demands to politicize intelligence as Tenet did in 2002.

Even though his conservative critics, especially Senators Richard Shelby (R-AL) and Pat Roberts (R-KS) from the Senate Intelligence Committee, cited Lake's management style to force the withdrawal of his nomination as CIA director, it was clearly part of an ideological campaign to defeat the nomination. Like Theodore Sorenson, President Carter's first choice for CIA director in 1977, Lake was simply too liberal for the Republican troglodytes on the Senate Intelligence Committee. In addition to resigning from the foreign service for reasons of principle, Lake was a supporter of arms control and human rights, and a critic of Casey's mishandling of the CIA in the 1980s. The bottom line was that he was just "too damned liberal" for the ideologues who opposed him. The confirmation struggles for Sorenson were more complicated, however, because the Carter nominee was a self-professed pacifist, an odd choice for a CIA director.

On balance, Clinton failed miserably in his choice of a national security team, which played a key role in the increased influence of the Pentagon in decision-making as well as the militarization of the national security arena and the intelligence process. Unlike his economic security team, which had such heavyweights as Robert Rubin and Larry Summers, the foreign policy players were weak and ineffective. Two of the four were gone within two years, one was clearly outmaneuvered by his deputy, and the fourth, Christopher, lasted nearly the entire first term but left behind a weak department that could not stand up to the growing influence and power of the Department of Defense. Christopher's successor, Madeleine Albright, did nothing to improve the standing of the State Department, and President Clinton soon tired of her constant moralizing on foreign policy issues, providing "advice that was devoid of politics."[8] The team failed to provide an outline of broad strategy for national security, the concepts for implementing strategy, or the leadership to guide the way against critics in Congress and the Pentagon. Clinton was virtually on his own in the field of national security, and this put a heavy responsibility on the chief executive, who was not up to the task and was having his own difficulties within the bureaucracy, particularly the Pentagon.

The Team Grapples with Somalia

U.S. involvement in Somalia, which started modestly in the last months of the Bush administration as a humanitarian mission to provide food to the starving poor, soon turned into a major embarrassment for the Clinton administration. Humanitarian missions are just the kinds of operation that the Pentagon doesn't favor and curiously labels "Operations Other Than War." Within months, the new Clinton administration was engaged in a classic "mission creep," taking the United States far beyond its humanitarian objectives to an investment of nearly $2 billion and, more important, the loss of eighteen Army Rangers and two helicopters in 1993. That engagement became well known as "Black Hawk Down," thanks to a gripping book and movie of that name. Clinton's inexperienced national security team, new to the tasks of use of force and new to each other, and extremely inexperienced on military affairs, gradually committed more force. President Clinton and even national security adviser Lake never really engaged the issue and played only minor roles in the crisis, which irritated the Pentagon. Senior military officers were not happy with the fact that the problem was subcontracted to an extremely inexperienced deputy national security adviser, Sandy Berger, whose international experience was limited to a practice as a trade lawyer. There was great tension over decision-making between Secretary of Defense Aspin and the Pentagon brass as well as Berger and the uniformed military.

There was plenty of blame to go around, although most of it was directed at the president. The chairman of the Joint Chiefs, Colin Powell, was a short-timer and focused on his upcoming retirement, only days away, as it turned out, before the failed operation. Secretary of Defense Aspin did not favor the mission, nor did the senior military officers for that matter. It simply collapsed like a house of cards.

Problems with the Pentagon

I served with the government for forty-two years, including twenty-four years at the Central Intelligence Agency and fourteen years on the faculty of the Department of Defense's National War College. During that time, dating back to the mid-1960s, there were deep controversies within the government over Vietnam and detente with the Soviet Union. There was only one period when I felt there existed a deep and abiding animosity at the Pentagon toward the president of the United States. The hostility the military had for Clinton, his first secretary of defense, and his national security team demonstrated the conservative, anti-liberal views of the professional military. Military officers are known for their jocular humor, but in this case they went over the line, setting the stage for the act of insubordination under President Obama that is discussed in Chapter V.

Clinton and Brutality: Haiti, the Balkans, and Rwanda

Unlike his predecessor, a veteran of World War II, President Clinton had no background in military affairs and was extremely uncomfortable with the use of military force. Like the senior Bush, Clinton believed that the use of force should always be the last resort after the failure of diplomacy and that wars of choice should have international support, if not participation. But military decisions were particularly difficult for Clinton, and in the case of Somalia and Haiti, they were extremely ill-defined as well. In all of these cases, the military dragged its heels, finding it difficult to justify humanitarian interventions. As mentioned, the Somali operation cost nearly $2 billion and led to the loss of eighteen Army Rangers in one battle. Haiti, which was labeled "Operation Uphold Democracy," required more than 20,000 U.S. troops and cost more than $1 billion. Neither operation brought the United States any advantage, and violence continues in both Somalia and Haiti.

Clinton's indecision with regard to the ethnic cleansing in Rwanda led to his worst decision of all, making no effort to stop the genocide in Rwanda in 1994, which has been termed the "fastest, most efficient killing spree of the twentieth century."[9] The president wanted to take some action to stop the genocide in Rwanda, but there were never any discussions in the White House about the possibility of intervention and the Pentagon provided no military options to the White House. After watching President Clinton pull the plug on operations in Somalia and Haiti, the Pentagon had no desire to get involved in Rwanda.

At the very least, the U.S. Air Force could have bombed the media facilities that were responsible for the hateful propaganda and the kill orders that the Hutus were giving against the Tutsis, but the Pentagon rejected this modest measure. In the wake of the twin disasters in Somali and Haiti, there would have been great resistance to using force or even allocating resources for opposing the genocide in Rwanda. Sadly, President Clinton didn't even try.

As for President Clinton, he has demonstrated more anguish over his failure to take action in Rwanda than he has over any other foreign policy issue. On a visit to Rwanda, he told an audience of Rwandans that he accepted responsibility for not intervening in the "slaughter in this blood-filled country," and accused the international community (including the United States) of parsing the definition of the word "genocide" instead of acting. Unfortunately, President Clinton disingenuously claimed that "all over the world there were people like me sitting in offices, day after day, who did not fully appreciate the depth and speed with which you were being engulfed in this unimaginable terror." The facts were quite different. The CIA's Presidential Daily Brief had provided the White House an accurate and up-to-date picture of the horrors that were taking place.

Clinton's memoir provides an important clue to his embarrassment over the mishandling of the situation in Haiti, making no mention of the role of the USS *Harlan County* in Haiti, where the dispatch and then panicky withdrawal of the ship from Port-au-Prince drew much criticism in senior military leadership circles. The combination of the withdrawal from Somalia and, only days later, the withdrawal of the *Harlan County* was an embarrassment to both the White House and the Pentagon. The televised images of these withdrawals from backwater situations on the Horn of Africa and in the Caribbean created the image of an administration that was totally out of its element.

Clinton very reluctantly agreed to use force in Haiti where operational initiatives could have cost the lives of the president's diplomatic negotiators, former JCS chairman Colin Powell, Jimmy Carter, and Senator Sam Nunn, an unusual grouping in view of the fact that the president didn't have good relations with any of them. Clinton didn't want to use military force and therefore picked three negotiators who were also opposed to armed intervention and hoped to make a political deal to avoid one. Clinton was particularly reluctant to select Carter for the mission in view of his headline-grabbing efforts in North Korea and elsewhere. But former president Carter was threatening to go to Haiti on his own, and President Clinton decided to practice damage limitation and include the former president. The two presidents from the South simply didn't like each other.

Clinton allowed the delegation very little time to succeed, and, when it was apparent that the Haitians were not taking the Carter group seriously and that Carter was far too optimistic about his chances of success, the president decided he had waited long enough and instructed Carter's group to leave the island immediately. Carter had been sent to Haiti with various conditions, including no discussion of Haiti's future political situation, but Carter ignored all of them. In any event, the U.S. invasion force was in the air as Clinton and Carter were holding a conversation about the possibility of an imminent deal, as Carter saw it. When the Haitian military rulers learned that the "U.S. was coming; the U.S. was coming," they agreed to leave the country. U.S. aircraft turned back to Pope air base in North Carolina on October 15, 1993, and the U.S. Army landed the next day as a peacekeeping force to restore Jean-Bertrand Aristide to power.

The Haitian operation could have been an embarrassment and failure for all concerned, but ultimately good fortune was on President Clinton's side. There were no U.S. military casualties; Aristide was returned to power; Haiti was given an opportunity to govern itself; Somalia and the Black Hawk Down incident were quickly forgotten. The short-term consequences were good; the long-term consequences were not so good, as Haiti, like Somalia, nearly two decades later is still overwhelmed with violence, corruption, and poverty.

The coercive use of military power in Haiti was a minor event compared to President Clinton's next challenge: Bosnia, where once again a humanitarian operation turned into a more conventional use of force, and the president had to deal with the opposition of the Pentagon, particularly General Powell, chairman of the Joint Chiefs. The senior military leadership was strongly opposed to involvement in Bosnia, but Clinton's autobiography merely talks about the "ambivalence" of Powell and his subordinates. Initially, the United States was going to commit troops to withdraw the failed UN mission, but—again, mission creep—this led to a U.S. confrontation against the Bosnia aggressors in order to bring the protagonists to the peace table. President Clinton was hesitant, but national security adviser Lake this time around was thorough and effective. The peace table, which led to the Dayton Accords, marked a success for the Clinton administration and the White House, and allowed Richard Holbrooke to seize the mediation from the Europeans and personally conduct the peace talks.

The end of the Cold War and the dissolution of the Soviet Union allowed the various ethnic groups that formed Yugoslavia to go their own way, which involved chaos and bloodshed. It was the worst fighting in Europe since the end of WWII, and it took a terrible slaughter in Srebrenica in July 1995, marking the failure of a UN peacekeeping mission, to get U.S. intervention in Bosnia. Despite the hesitation of the Pentagon, Clinton ordered 32,000 troops to the Balkans, with a total cost of more than $10 billion. Nevertheless, the United States displayed "unbearable timidity" in failing to use its peacekeeping forces to track down and arrest indicted Bosnian war criminals.[10]

The struggle with Serbia over Kosovo several years later was more complicated and involved far more U.S. involvement, with nearly 40,000 troops and a U.S.-led air campaign that marked the first use of NATO's air power in its history. The

White House was unprepared for this crisis because the Monica Lewinsky scandal was taking up a huge amount of time and resources. As in the case of Bosnia, UN Ambassador Madeleine Albright was a strong advocate for the use of force, and on this occasion she had strong support from an outstanding U.S. diplomat, the late Richard Holbrooke. The decision to use force became far easier for President Clinton in the wake of the Serbian massacre of civilians, which broke a ceasefire agreement. Unlike the decision-making for Bosnia, President Clinton was more assertive and confident.

Nevertheless, the modest U.S. and NATO intervention did not deter the forces of Serbian President Slobodan Milosevic, and before long U.S. and NATO planes were bombing Belgrade. This marked the first use of NATO's air power in its history. It also marked the failure of assumptions regarding an air campaign, particularly in light of the intelligence that led to the bombing of the Chinese embassy in Belgrade and the deaths of three Chinese. The intelligence community and Clinton's policymakers, particularly Ambassador Albright, believed that the bombing campaign would deter the Serbs from further attacks against the people of Kosovo.[11] Well, it didn't, and *Time* magazine's cover in the spring featured Albright on a tarmac in a flight jacket under the headline "Madeleine's War."

If you substitute Tripoli for Belgrade, Muammar Qadhafi for Slobodan Milosevic, and the Libyan rebels for the Kosovar Albanians, then you have history repeating itself. The uniformed military opposed the use of air power in both cases, citing the limits of air power; civilians are less familiar with these constraints. Over the past five decades, civilian officials have favored the use of military force over the opposition of their military counterparts. In doing so, the "best and the brightest" have blundered into long-term engagements in Vietnam, Iraq, and Afghanistan that didn't favor U.S. national security interests. In the case of the Balkans, the uniformed military was consistently opposed to the use of ground forces.

Chairman of the Joint Chiefs Powell was particularly unhappy with President Clinton's decision to use force in the Balkans. He was critical of the president for getting directly involved without a "clear political objective" and felt trapped between a president who was uncomfortable with the use of force and UN ambassador Albright, who favored intervention in Yugoslavia.[12] Powell recorded that he thought he "would have an aneurysm" when Albright, the future secretary of state, asked him "What's the point of having this superb military that you're always talking about if we can't use it?" Powell knew, of course, that Albright was paraphrasing the famous exchange between President Abraham Lincoln and General George B. McClellan ("If you don't want to use the Army, I should like to borrow it for a while"). Powell's immediate counter was that "American GIs were not toy soldiers to be moved around on some sort of global game board."

Paradoxically, the military is far less likely than their civilian counterparts to resort to the use of force. As with most senior U.S. generals, Powell was demonstrating great awareness of the limits and constraints on military power and a great reluctance to use it. However, once the confrontation begins, uniformed decision-makers are typically blind to the necessity of ending limited conflicts without clear victory. By taking his case to the public in an op-ed in the *New York Times*, however, Powell was demonstrating insubordination. On balance, civilians leaders should listen to the counsel of the uniformed military before taking a decision to use force, but be extremely careful of the Pentagon's advice once hostilities begin. President Eisenhower understood this fact.

Clinton vs. the Pentagon on Arms Control and Disarmament

The Pentagon has been a consistent opponent of arms control treaties, starting with its heavy-handed opposition to President Kennedy's negotiation in 1963 of a Partial Test Ban Treaty, which banned the testing of nuclear weapons on land, at sea, and in the atmosphere. Military brass, particularly Air Force chief of staff General Curtis LeMay, opposed Kennedy's diplomatic solution to the Cuban missile crisis and believed that the test ban represented an additional concession to Moscow. President Nixon had to override Pentagon opposition to the Strategic Arms Limitation Treaty (SALT) in 1972, which stabilized mutual deterrence on the basis of parity and equal security. He also took on military opposition to complete the Anti-Ballistic Missile Treaty (ABM) in the same year, which limited anti-ballistic missile sites in the United States and the Soviet Union to two sites, and eventually one. The ABM treaty prevented the deployment of a nationwide or comprehensive anti-ballistic missile system, until President George W. Bush abrogated the treaty in 2001.

President Clinton faced significant military opposition to much of his foreign policy agenda, including every aspect of his agenda on arms control and disarmament. Having rolled the president on the issue of "don't ask, don't tell," the Pentagon had no difficulty lobbying on the Hill against the wishes of the White House. President Clinton appeared totally unaware that his caving in to the demands of Senator Helms and other congressional conservatives, who lobbied for the destruction of the Arms Control and Disarmament Agency as well as the United States Information Service, had left the White House without key allies in the fight for arms control and disarmament. Foreign policy professionals recognize that these two important agencies must be reestablished, but, two decades later, there is no campaign to do so. As a result, a weakened Department of State continues to lumber along without any real influence on significant foreign policy decisions. The process of arms control and disarmament has particularly suffered.

Landmines Ban

The campaign to ban landmines is an excellent example of the Pentagon's power and influence as well as the U.S. failure to support its allies on key disarmament issues. By the 1990s, landmines in Afghanistan, Cambodia, Vietnam and dozens of other countries were killing or injuring 25,000 innocent children and civilians annually.[13] The campaign to ban landmines was international; it was headed by Jody Williams of the Vietnam Veterans of America Foundation and supported by more than one thousand Non-Government Organizations (NGOs) in eighty-five countries. Senator Patrick Leahy (D-VT) introduced legislation in the Senate to place a one-year moratorium on American exports of antipersonnel mines, and the bill was passed in 1992. Clinton called for the "eventual elimination" of landmines in his speech to the United Nations in 1994 and issued a policy statement in 1996 that called for negotiations of an international agreement to ban antipersonnel mines. The Ottawa Conference that year, attended by fifty governments, called for an immediate ban on all antipersonnel landmines. Then the United States and the Clinton administration began to waffle.

By 1997, it appeared that everything was in place to get U.S. approval for a landmines ban. President Clinton had announced his support, and over one hundred countries were positioned to support the ban. When the president bowed to pressure from the Pentagon and decided to oppose the ban, there was considerable shock in Washington, particularly on Capitol Hill. The Pentagon argued that, although landmines were killing and maiming innocent civilians and children, the offending landmines did not belong to the United States. The uniformed military claimed that U.S. mines were technologically superior, that they were "smart enough" to be set to self-destruct over a specific period of time, and that would not be a permanent risk to an innocent population. This, of course, was nonsense. The Pentagon opposed the international effort to ban landmines because it had deployed mines in the demilitarized zone between North and South Korea and it supported the use of mines in mixed antitank systems as well as the continued use of so-called "smart" mines that would self-destruct at a preset time.

Antipersonnel mines, unable to tell the difference between a combatant and a child, have created havoc in such disparate places as Cambodia, Angola, Afghanistan, El Salvador, Bosnia, and Mozambique. The Pentagon's regional commanders made landmines a readiness issue and would not budge. Not even the beginning of some signs of stability between the two Koreas and the beginning of high-level diplomacy between the United States and North Korea in 1994 led to new thinking at the Pentagon. Once again, Clinton bowed to the Pentagon's pressure, even though several retired generals supported the ban, including several former commanders in Korea and the former Superintendent of West Point. Clinton briefly mentioned his inability to sign the international treaty banning landmines in his memoir, but does not mention the Pentagon's opposition to the treaty.[14]

In announcing his sudden volte-face on landmines on September 17, 1997, President Clinton placed the United States in the dubious company of countries such as China, Iran, Iraq, Libya, Russia, and Somalia, which were opposed to an international ban on landmines. Fittingly, the Nobel Peace Prize that year was awarded to Jody Williams, the coordinator of the International Campaign to Ban Landmines.

Comprehensive Test Ban Treaty

The Clinton administration badly mishandled the Senate's vote on the Comprehensive Test Ban Treaty (CTBT), not preparing the Democratic Senators and particularly its Republican supporters for the vote. The defeat of the CTBT marked the first congressional rejection of a significant international agreement since Congress had rejected the Treaty of Versailles' establishment of the League of Nations eighty years earlier. The Pentagon has fought restraints on strategic and conventional arms, including testing, for the past four decades, starting with President Kennedy's partial test ban treaty in 1963 and President Nixon's Anti-Ballistic Missile Treaty (ABM) and Strategic Arms Limitation Treaty (SALT) in 1972. Kennedy and Nixon stood up to the Pentagon in supporting these treaties. President Clinton had been the first global leader to sign the CTBT, doing so at the United Nations in 1996, but he dropped the ball when he returned to Washington.

Clinton became the first president to fail to stand up to the Pentagon on a major arms control treaty, when he refused to challenge the Pentagon's opposition to the CTBT. In 1998, the Pentagon got unanticipated leverage in its opposition to the treaty when a relatively new intelligence agency, the National Imagery and Mapping Agency (NIMA, now the National Geospatial Intelligence Agency), failed to predict and monitor five nuclear tests in India. This failure led CIA director Tenet to tell Congress that the CIA could not monitor and verify the CTBT, marking the first time that a CIA director had told Congress that an arms control or disarmament agreement could not be verified. This contributed to the Senate's decision to reverse gears, with many Senators suddenly declaring that, if the United States could not monitor an international weapons treaty, then it should not be ratified. President Reagan had said of arms control and disarmament measures that the United States would "trust, but verify." With the emphasis on verification, Tenet's public remarks were fatal. The Senate accepted the Pentagon's position and defeated the treaty. Once again, Clinton's memoir failed to mention this controversial issue and the intelligence failure that led to the defeat of the CTBT in the Senate.

The intelligence failure regarding the Indian nuclear tests was due in part to assigning the important task of analyzing satellite imagery to the Pentagon, which gave a low collection priority to South Asia as a region and to arms control as an objective. This is precisely the reason that President Harry Truman had placed intelligence collection and analysis outside the realm of the policy community. The failure on the part of NIMA and CIA and the defeat of the CTBT are sufficient reasons to criticize the Clinton administration for shifting the analysis of satellite imagery from the CIA to the Pentagon, which is responsible for the staffing and funding of NIMA. With the creation of a director of national intelligence in 2004, there was the hope initially that the analysis of satellite imagery would be moved outside of the policy community or at least once again be made a joint Department of Defence–CIA responsibility. There has been no movement in that direction, however.

In mishandling the ratification process, the Clinton administration suffered its worst foreign policy defeat in the Congress. It was a decisive and humiliating defeat. The vote was a stark 48-51—not even a majority in the treaty's favor, and far below the two-thirds required for approval.[15] Briefing teams from the State Department and the National Security Council had been formed belatedly, but not even one Republican senator was interested in receiving a briefing in favor of the Comprehensive Test Ban Treaty. The fact that the defeat of the CTBT hurt U.S. standing in Europe, its role in the International Atomic Energy Agency, and its campaign for comprehensive verification measures was totally lost on the partisan resistance.

As National War College professor Terry Deibel noted in his useful case study on the defeat of the treaty, Clinton failed to mount a public campaign on behalf of the treaty, to appoint a high-level official within the administration to lobby for its passage, and to recruit a senior Republican senator such as Richard Lugar (R-IN) to work for the treaty in the Republican caucus. He also failed to block the behind-the-scenes efforts of the Pentagon to express its opposition to conservative senators such as Jon Kyl (R-AZ) and Byron Dorgan (D-ND). Senator Kyl still actively opposes cuts in defense spending and progress toward arms control and disarmament, even when the treaty at issue, such as START, is clearly in the interests of the United States.

Clinton's passivity on this issue convinced many Democrats that the White House was not genuinely committed to the comprehensive test ban. By the time that the NSC, the White House Legislative Office, and the State Department shifted into high gear to gain support for the treaty, it was too late. A majority of the Senate, realizing that the United States would suffer a significant diplomatic embarrassment with the defeat of the treaty, wanted to postpone a vote, but Senate Majority Leader Trent Lott (R-MS) demanded a letter from the president requesting the postponement and added the recommendation that the "CTBT not be considered for the duration of his presidency."[16]

It was obvious that the Republican leadership was more interested in embarrassing the Clinton presidency than in a genuine compromise with the White House. If they couldn't impeach the president in 1998, then at least they could defeat his national security agenda, including this bipartisan treaty that had been supported by six presidents over a thirty-five-year period, ever since the Kennedy administration stood up to the Pentagon and secured the Partial Test Ban Treaty in 1963. (The election of George Bush in 2000 effectively ended any further discussion of the International Criminal Court, the CTBT, and the landmine ban.)

International Convention on Cluster Bombs

The convention against cluster bombs offered one more example of the Clinton administration's unwillingness to endorse a treaty that faced opposition in the Pentagon and among the Pentagon's allies in Congress. Another victory for the military-industrial complex.

Cluster bombs have been banned by most of the world, but not by the United States, which used them in Yemen, Iraq, and Afghanistan. These bombs are essentially terror weapons, striking large areas with a dense succession of high-explosive munitions. The mortars or bombs typically have a range of up to four miles and can cover a land area comparable to a football field. When fired into populated areas, they place innocent civilians at grave risk. This was clearly demonstrated in Misurata, Libya, where Colonel Muammar Qadhafi fired these bombs into residential areas.

The cluster munitions often take the form of 120-millimeter mortar rounds that burst in the air and rain high-explosive bomblets down upon people and objects. In Libya, in April 2011, these mortar projectiles carried and distributed as many as twenty-one submunitions designed to kill people and penetrate light armor. Ironically, the cluster bombs used in Libya were made in Spain in 2007, one year before Spain signed the international convention against their use.

International Criminal Court

As with the ban on landmines, Clinton bowed to the interests of the Pentagon and walked away from the International Criminal Court (ICC). In walking away from the ICC, the United States joined hands with China, Iraq, Iran, Libya, Qatar, Sudan, and Yemen. In doing so, the United States rejected a court that was designed to bring the world's worst human-rights violators to justice. Every member state of the European Union favored the ICC. Initially Clinton did too, after the administration's successful involvement in war-crimes tribunals in Rwanda and the former Yugoslavia. But the Pentagon resisted exposing U.S. soldiers to international justice, claiming that the court would allow other countries with political motivations to prosecute U.S. military personnel. The Pentagon's interpretation of the ICC charter was misguided; nonetheless, its opposition drove U.S. policy, and the Clinton administration ended up dropping its support of the ICC.

In caving in to the Pentagon, the Clinton administration demonstrated no understanding of the growing international resentment of the U.S. government's unwillingness to subject itself to international law. Anger over U.S. highhandedness on human rights issues made U.S. allies less willing to compromise on matters of importance to the United States. There was significant international opposition to the State Department's efforts to pressure governments not to join the ICC, including the threat to renegotiate bilateral treaties that govern the stationing of U.S. forces overseas in order to protect them from the ICC. The latter policy had the enthusiastic support of Secretary of Defense Cohen. In any event, the ICC opened for business in 2002 and is surviving without U.S. participation, although the absence of the United States contributed to a slow start for the court and undermined Washington's opposition to terrorism and drug trafficking, which dominated the early agenda for the ICC.

In his memoir, Clinton mentioned his support for the ICC but made no mention of its defeat in the Senate, let alone the opposition of the Pentagon. He signed the Court's founding statute on the final day of his presidency, presumably as a cover for his failure to lead a campaign for U.S. ratification of the statute. An opportunity to ensure a serious effort to enforce accountability for international crimes was lost.

International Ban on Teenagers in Combat

Another low point for the Clinton administration took place in 1999, when the United States voted against UN efforts to ban using soldiers under the age of 18 in combat. Nearly two hundred nations voted in favor of the ban. Only Somalia, which for all practical purposes has no civil governance, joined the United States in casting an opposing vote. The Pentagon's opposition was particularly irrational in view of the fact that fewer than 3,000 Americans in uniform were under the age of 18 in 1999. In any event, Clinton reversed policy gears on the ban for teenagers in combat in July 1999 after six years of lobbying the Pentagon for support. Time after time, Clinton deferred to pressure from the Pentagon on key national security and arms control issues, unwilling to go to the mat for issues he strongly supported.

Clinton and Terrorism

It is noteworthy that President Clinton and both of his national security advisers, Tony Lake and Sandy Berger, were out in front of the Pentagon and the CIA on the terror threat from al-Qaeda. Unlike in 1993, when the White House, like most of the country outside of New York City, displayed no strong response to the bombing of the World Trade Center, the president's response to domestic and international terrorism was passionate in private but pusillanimous in public. Conversely, his response to the bombings of the U.S. embassies on the Horn of Africa in 1998 was a craven overreaction, with the United States bombing a pharmaceutical plant in Khartoum, Sudan, that was charged falsely with the production of lethal chemicals and connections to terrorism. The cruise missile attack on a ramshackle training facility in Afghanistan accomplished virtually nothing, but the fact was that there were really no strategic targets in Afghanistan, not even for al-Qaeda. Privately, President Clinton wanted the Pentagon to engage in more planning for a policy of counterterrorism, but senior military leaders were reluctant to engage either Afghanistan or the problem of terrorism. He did take steps to expand his authority to kill bin Laden in a covert action or a direct assault, and stationed two submarines in the area in order to conduct follow-up attacks with cruise missiles.

In 2000, the bombing of the USS *Cole* with the loss of seventeen U.S. sailors led to no U.S. action whatsoever, although it was clear from the start that al-Qaeda had planned and carried out the operation. President Clinton and national security adviser Berger testified that they wanted to retaliate, but that the CIA could not guarantee that al-Qaeda and bin Laden were behind the attack. Clinton and Berger, moreover, claimed that they gave the CIA clear and unambiguous orders to assassinate al-Qaeda leader bin Laden, but that is open to dispute as well. There were one or two incidents in which Attorney General Janet Reno blocked actions against bin Laden.

The attack on the USS *Cole* demonstrated the key role that the Pentagon played in the implementation of national security strategy. For two years prior to the attack, the State Department and the CIA had warned both the policy communities and the public at large of the dangers of using Yemen as a refueling stop for U.S. warships and of traveling to the Arab nation. The U.S. ambassador to Yemen, Barbara Bodine, had even vetoed several planned military ship visits to the country because of concern over terrorist attacks. But the powerful regional commander for U.S. forces in the Persian Gulf, General Anthony Zinni, insisted that the refueling of warships in Yemen would be part of his policy to improve relations with that country. On October 12, 2000, two men in a dinghy full of explosives rowed up to the *Cole* and blasted a 1,000-square foot hole in the hull of the ship, killing seventeen American sailors.

Clinton received heavy criticism for not retaliating more effectively against al-Qaeda's terrorist acts against the United

States, but there is no doubt that he provided ample warnings about terrorism to the new Bush team. The unfortunate fact for President Clinton is that one month before the election, he feared that any response to the USS *Cole* would be perceived as the White House taking action in order to buttress Vice President Gore's chances of winning the November election.

Clinton and the Expansion of NATO

Although Clinton became a more confident leader in his second term, he lacked a strategist who could define and describe foreign policy problems and solutions in broad terms. Perhaps the best example of a flawed strategic concept was the expansion of the North Atlantic Treaty Organization, which marked a return to military instruments for the conduct of foreign policy and ensured that there would be no progress in developing a strategic approach to the former Soviet Union. Clinton correctly observed that the liberated states of Eastern Europe had to be anchored to the West, but the appropriate vehicle for such an arrangement should have been the European Union, not NATO. Indeed, one of the greatest strategic failures of the Clinton administration was its effort to use NATO to marginalize Russia rather than seeking to anchor Russia to the West, as suggested by the late George Kennan in his strategy of containment.

The Russians had several reasons for opposing the expansion of NATO. First of all, former Soviet foreign minister Shevardnadze had received a verbal commitment from his U.S. counterpart, Secretary of State Baker, that the United States would not "leapfrog" over a unified Germany in order to put U.S. military forces in the former Eastern European states of the Warsaw Pact. It was difficult for Soviet President Gorbachev and Shevardnadze to accept the unification of Germany and German membership in NATO in view of longtime historical memories and huge World War II losses. Baker's assurances about no "leapfrogging" had a great deal to do with Moscow's fairly rapid acceptance of a unified Germany, which in turn led to a loss of influence and credibility for Gorbachev and Shevardnadze in the Politburo and in the Red Army. One of the few sources of Soviet pride in either domestic and foreign policy was the Soviet defeat of the German Wehrmacht, which was the key to the U.S. and British victory on the Western front. Without the huge Soviet sacrifices on the Eastern front, it is difficult to imagine the Western success at Normandy in 1944. After all, three-fourths of the German army fought on the Eastern front, and three-fourths of German losses took place on the Eastern front.

U.S. diplomats and academics, particularly those with expertise in European policy and the Soviet Union, made a valiant effort to convince the Clinton administration that NATO expansion was a bad idea for various national security reasons. Even members of the administration, including then deputy secretary for defense Bill Perry, tried to encourage President Clinton to slow down on expansion. Editorials in major U.S. newspapers and policy papers from elite U.S. think tanks made cogent arguments against expansion, and there were important congressional hearings that supplied ample arguments against bringing NATO to former members of the Warsaw Pact. The key testimony came from former ambassador George Kennan, who in congressional testimony three decades earlier warned against involvement in Vietnam. He testified that NATO expansion was a "strategic blunder of potentially epic proportions." He was right, of course, both times.

Clinton and the National Security Bureaucracy

The fiscal situation at the State Department was so weak in the late 1990s that a form of "Sovietization" was taking place in Foggy Bottom. The State Department lacked Foreign Service officers for more than three hundred overseas positions and, since the Pentagon and the CIA are traditionally overfunded and overstaffed, it began filling these overseas positions with officers from the military and the intelligence community. There were often more military attachés and CIA operations officers than foreign service political officers in U.S. embassies. When the former Soviet Union faced a similar problem in the late 1970s and 1980s, the KGB began to assign its personnel to fill foreign ministry slots overseas. Gorbachev moved smartly in 1985 to correct this situation, but the Clinton administration and the Office of Management and Budget did nothing to reverse the trend. Neither did the Congress, which has always taken better care of the Pentagon and the CIA than it has the Department of State.

The Clinton administration also permitted a lesser role for the CIA as a supplier of strategic and military intelligence and strategic intelligence. The Pentagon was permitted to dominate the analysis of satellite imagery, the single most important collection system in the intelligence community. The CIA, under the stewardship of Bob Gates in 1991 and 1992, and Jim Woolsey in 1993 and 1994, made another analytic turn to the right, becoming increasingly known for providing "worst-case views" on key national security intelligence issues. In 1999, for example, the agency produced an estimate on new strategic challenges to the United States that significantly increased the likelihood of a missile attack against the United States, a view favored by the Pentagon. The military was looking for a rationale for its national missile defense system, and the new estimate provided such a rationale, although it cited no new intelligence data since its previous estimate on the problem. (In a heartening show of independence, the State Department strongly dissented from CIA's position, arguing that the Agency's worst-case view gave "more credence than is warranted to developments that may prove implausible."[17])

Clinton and Defense Spending

The end of the Cold war in 1989 placed President Clinton in a unique position to address inflated defense spending. Unfortunately, this was a subject that the president was unprepared to address in an administration that had only one genuine expert on defense spending, Secretary of Defense William Perry.

There was some reduction in defense spending in the administrations of George H.W. Bush and Clinton, which permitted a decrease from the record highs of the Reagan administration, but these reductions were modest and were not in the context of a grand strategy that would explain the reductions, let alone the value of reduced spending on defense. By 1994, the Bush and Clinton administrations had reduced defense spending by nearly 20 percent from the record highs of the Reagan administration, but the new level was still 10 percent greater than the level that President Reagan inherited from President Jimmy Carter. The size of the U.S. military was reduced, but military spending remained higher than the Cold War average. In view of the dissolution of the Soviet Union and the significant reduction in the Russian army as well as the reduced defense spending around the world, the United States was in an unprecedented position to make far more significant cuts.

The Clinton administration inherited three new expensive fighter programs that were not strategically necessary and could have been canceled or significantly cut back. The F-22 Raptor, a troubled aircraft that was designed to replace the F-15 and counter a Soviet fighter that was planned but never built, was cut from 438 aircraft to 339 aircraft. The original plan called for 750 aircraft by 2010, but Secretary of Defense Cheney cut that number significantly with a savings of more than $30 billion. Each F-22 cost the Air Force more than $350 million, making it ten times as expensive as the plane that it replaced. The Navy was supposed to receive more than 1,000 modernized versions of its F-18 fighter aircraft, which the Clinton administration cut back to 548. But the most sophisticated and expensive program, the Joint Strike Fighter or F-35, was barely touched, with the Clinton administration agreeing to build 2,852 aircraft instead of 2,978.[18] Thus, President Clinton agreed to build more than 3,850 fighter aircraft at a cost of over $350 billion at a time when there was no significant rival in the skies.[19] The large number of fighter aircraft for the U.S. Navy was similarly striking in view of the absence of any other navy with a global presence or a power projection capability.

Another area that could have sustained significant reductions was the appropriations for nuclear weapons programs that made up one-quarter of the entire procurement budget during the Reagan administration. Reductions in defense spending also could have been applied to conventional weapons systems. Meanwhile, instead of limiting the deployment of U.S. forces, U.S. naval aircraft carriers were forced to extend their tours of duty by 50 percent, and the U.S. Air Force was on constant combat status because of operations in the Balkan experience as well as the declaration of "no fly zones" in Iraq in the 1990s.

The Clinton Legacy

President Clinton had no real background in foreign or national security policy and was not respected by the foreign policy community. The foreign policy community was not being cynical when they concluded that the president's expansion of NATO had nothing to do with U.S. foreign policy, but everything to do with domestic policy. The president was preparing for his reelection bid in 1996 and knew that the key Republican candidate, Senator Bob Dole (R-KS), had already shown his hand in favor of NATO expansion. Given the key electoral states with large Eastern European immigrant populations, such as Michigan,

Ohio, and Illinois, there should have been no surprise regarding President Clinton's decision to expand NATO.

President Clinton's problem, similar to President Obama's, was the lack of a strong nation security adviser to conceptualize and implement foreign policy. National security adviser Berger had the president's trust and confidence, but Berger was an international trade lawyer by background and lacked the credentials to impress foreign policy analysts or elite opinion makers. He understood the political realities of decision-making, but operated for the most part by the seat of his pants and not from a strategic worldview. "I really like him," said Henry Kissinger, "but you can't blame a trade lawyer for not being a global strategist."[20] One of Berger's unfortunate contributions to the U.S. playbook on strategy was the policy of "dual containment," which justified the non-recognition of both Iran and Iraq and complicated U.S. interests in the Persian Gulf.

This is not to say that the Clinton administration lacked successes in the area of arms control and disarmament. President Clinton secured a major success in 1994 when he negotiated the removal of so-called "loose nukes" from the Ukraine, which led to the removal of all strategic nuclear weapons in those former Soviet republics, other than the Russian Republic, that had deployed or stored such weapons. In this case, the White House had the support of an unusual bipartisan effort in the Senate, led by Senators Nunn and Lugar to take $500 million from the defense budget and apply that money to securing the nuclear inventories of the former Soviet republics. The Pentagon protested the cuts in defense spending to fund denuclearization in the former Soviet Union, but the Nunn-Lugar Cooperative Threat Reduction Act proved to be one of the best national security investments of the post–Cold War era.

President Clinton also engineered an indefinite expansion of the 1968 nuclear Non-Proliferation Treaty and ratified the second Strategic Arms Reduction Treaty. In 1994, Clinton negotiated a nuclear freeze with North Korea in return for promising Pyongyang two light-water reactors. Construction on a site for the reactors began in the 1990s, but the reactors were never delivered, which led North Korea to walk away from the agreement. The Bush administration was particularly critical of the "Agreed Framework" with North Korea, but in September 2005 it entered its own agreement with North Korea that called for an eventual light-water reactor for Pyongyang, thus replicating the very Clinton policy that the Bush team had trashed. The Bush administration also derided a 2000 communiqué that showed the Clinton administration pledging not to attack North Korea. Once again, the 2005 agreement had the same promise.

On balance, the Clinton presidency registered both positives and negatives, but overall it significantly contributed to the problems of the national security policy process by weakening the balance between the key instruments of foreign policy. There were bumpy roads in the use of limited force in Haiti, Bosnia, and Kosovo, but overall President Clinton brought a modest measure of stability to the Balkans. No one could create stability in Haiti or Somalia; unfortunately, no one is really trying.

Clinton made an attempt to reduce defense spending, but demonstrated no ability to go to the public in order to build a national consensus for reduced defense spending. President Clinton simply paid insufficient attention to foreign policy, which was his original intention in any event, and was too ready to read public opinion polls before acting. The unfortunate expansion of NATO was dictated by public opinion and an oncoming election, not geopolitical necessity.

As a result, President Clinton left no legacy in foreign policy or national security policy. He operated by the seat of his pants in the Middle East, moving belatedly to address the Israeli-

Palestinian problem where he had limited leverage. Clinton got off to a good start in dealing with the problem of North Korea, but once again he ran out of steam and moved belatedly to solve a problem that still begs for a diplomatic solution. There was no consistency in his agenda, and he lacked a strong strategic team to provide the necessary conceptual thinking for a strategic policy. President Clinton's worst crisis was at home—the Monica Lewinsky affair—and that one was self-inflicted.

The Clinton administration was in a position to achieve a great deal in the arms control and disarmament arena, but the president was simply unwilling to take on the Pentagon to fight for his agenda. The dissolution of the Arms Control and Disarmament Agency and the United States Information Service as well as the weakening of the Agency for International Development have compromised the work of the State Department. Two decades later, Secretary of State Hillary Clinton has not been able to reverse or correct this trend.

Meanwhile, the Pentagon emerged in the catbird seat on the making of national security and foreign policy; its leading role in the intelligence community was strengthened by the Intelligence Reorganization Act of 2004. By permitting an unacceptable level of military influence over national security policy, the Clinton administration paved the way for the Bush administration to pursue policies of unilateralism and preemptive attack, which lent an imperial dimension to U.S. policy that was unprecedented. To paraphrase Mark Twain, if the only tool in the toolbox is a hammer, then all problems will soon look like nails.

FOUR

BUSH'S SURRENDER TO THE PENTAGON

We face an enemy that has an ideology. They believe things. The best way to describe their ideology is to relate to you the fact that they think the opposite of the way we think. —President George W. Bush

Violence is the last refuge of the incompetent. —Isaac Asimov

How do you ask a man to be the last man to die for a mistake? —Senator John F. Kerry, 1971, congressional testimony on Vietnam

The last U.S. soldier to die for his country in Iraq was Army Specialist David Emanuel Hickman, who was killed in Baghdad on November 14, 2011, when a roadside bomb ripped through his armored truck. Hickman's death took place eight years, seven months, and twenty-five days after the U.S. invasion of Iraq; he was the 4,474th member of the U.S. military to die in the war. U.S. combat operations were officially over when Hickman's truck was hit; he was conducting a "presence patrol" in Baghdad to remind insurgents that the U.S. military was still there. A decade after the U.S. invasion, Iraqi security forces were still not up to the task of patrolling its own neighborhoods.

Specialist Hickman may have been the last man to die for his country in Iraq, but he will certainly not be the last man or woman to suffer from the stewardship of President George W.

Bush. No president since World War II has contributed more to the militarization of the United States than President Bush. Under his leadership from 2001 to 2009, the United States fought two unsuccessful wars; experienced a financial crisis; initiated irreversible tax cuts that burden the U.S. economy; and compromised the rule of law at home and abroad. President Bush's militarization of U.S. foreign and national security policy included the creation of an entrenched national security state.

The memoirs of President Bush, Vice President Dick Cheney, Secretary of Defense Donald Rumsfeld, and Secretary of State Condoleezza Rice should have helped explain why the United States embarked on the path of war against Iraq in 2003, a deadly one paved by lies and deceit.[1] Unfortunately, the memoirs provided no insight. All four principals are hopelessly unapologetic about their overall handling of the decisions to go to war, to conduct the war, and to handle the post-war situation. The memoirs are particularly egregious because we find no one taking responsibility for any decisions relevant to the use of force. Instead, the memoirs demonstrate the chicanery of public officials in taking uncertain and ambiguous intelligence, exaggerating it, and creating their own facts. It strains credulity that memoirs from the president, vice president, secretary of state, and secretary of defense fail to provide any sense of the strategic reasoning behind the urgency of preemptive war against Iraq, which they continue to claim has been "worth the costs."

The willingness of Cheney, Rumsfeld, and Rice to criticize their president, which is virtually unheard of in memoirs of high-ranking administration officials, is both noteworthy and revelatory. They blame the president for allowing "far too many hands on the steering wheel, which was . . . a formula for running the truck into a ditch."[2] According to Rumsfeld, there were too many National Security Council meetings, even with President Bush presiding, which ended without precise objectives for the way ahead. Cheney and Rice cite the president's inability to "clearly or firmly" resolve key differences within the NSC, which only the president could do.

The seeds for disarray within the administration began in the run-up to the war in 2002, when no plans were made for the post-war situation. In May 2003, the president belatedly named Paul Bremer to head the Office of Reconstruction and Humanitarian Assistance to manage the transition in Iraq to the post-war phase. Cheney, Rice, and especially Rumsfeld blame Bremer for botching the occupation and the president for ignoring the chain of command and enabling Bremer to "pick and choose" which senior Washington officials to consult. Bush often met alone with Bremer, linking Bremer to the White House instead of the Defense Department or the State Department and making decision-making opaque, even to cabinet secretaries. Bremer never had the experience or wisdom for such a post, and, to be fair to him, one must acknowledge that he had to create a post-war plan without proper staffing or expertise.

Rumsfeld consistently denies any responsibility for the mistakes. If there weren't enough troops in Iraq, that would be the fault of General Tommy Franks. If we were caught off guard by Turkey's sudden decision to refuse to allow troop movements through Turkey on the way to Iraq, that would be the fault of Secretary of State Colin Powell. As for the failure of the United States to find Iraqi weapons of mass destruction (WMD), Rumsfeld and his colleagues argue that "recent history is abundant with examples of flawed intelligence that have affected key national security decisions," ignoring the fact that intelligence was not merely flawed, it was politicized—skewed to bolster official positions irrespective of the facts. Bush, Cheney, and Rumsfeld, moreover, played key roles in assuring that the Department of Defense (DoD) and the Central Intelligence Agency lied about Iraq and WMD.

The memoirs document discussion about war with Iraq in the wake of 9/11, which served as the pretext for the Iraq War, not a cause. Even before 9/11, Rumsfeld had sent a memorandum to Cheney, Powell, and Rice, suggesting a principals committee meeting to develop a policy toward Iraq "well ahead of events that could overtake us." Rumsfeld's memoir did not discuss his order to military commanders on 9/11, only five hours after the attacks, which called on them to "judge whether [intelligence] good enough [to] hit S.H. [Saddam Hussein] @ same time—not only UBL [Osama bin Laden]."[3] A military aide conceded that it was "hard to get a good case," but that they would "sweep it all up. Things related and not."

None of the memoirs mention the fact that, the day after 9/11, the president told Richard A. Clarke, the NSC's leading specialist on counterterrorism, "See if Saddam did this. See if he's linked in any way."[4] Every agency and department of government agreed that there had been no cooperation between Saddam and al-Qaeda, and a memorandum to that effect was sent to the president. But the Pentagon's focus had already shifted from al-Qaeda to Iraq, reflecting the view of deputy defense secretary Paul Wolfowitz, who strongly believed that Iraq was the state sponsor for the attack on the World Trade Center in 1993 as well as 9/11.

Several days after 9/11, the decision-makers in the administration met at Camp David to discuss Afghanistan as the target of U.S. operations. Two weeks later, President Bush invited Rumsfeld to the Oval Office and asked the secretary of defense to take a look at the shape of military plans on Iraq, emphasizing the importance of not letting the review of war plans leak to the media. Rumsfeld claims to be nonplussed: "Two weeks after the worst terrorist attack in our nation's history, those of us in the DoD were fully occupied," but the president insisted on new military plans for Iraq. Nevertheless, Rumsfeld returned to the

Pentagon and "asked for briefings to cover several contingencies in various parts of the world," as a precaution, so that the request for Iraqi war plans did not stand out.

In their memoirs, Cheney and Rumsfeld eviscerated two key members of the decision-making team, Secretary of State Powell and national security adviser Rice.[5] Cheney is particularly critical of the Department of State (DoS) for failing to conduct post-war planning for Iraq, although Rumsfeld expressly forbade his colleagues from taking part in DoS meetings on the future of Iraq, which anticipated the systemic problems that the United States would inherit. Cheney is particularly immodest in taking credit for framing policy choices for President Bush (the self-proclaimed "Decider"), noting that he received the CIA briefing (the President's Daily Brief or PDB) at six-thirty in the morning and then joined the president for his briefing. Perhaps this is why high-level CIA officials referred to the vice president as "Edgar" (i.e., Edgar Bergen, the puppet master for Charlie McCarthy).

President Bush's memoirs hide his role in the advance planning for the Iraqi war. He uses his self-portrait to emphasize his hopes of avoiding war and points to Vice President Cheney as the impatient one. He cites Cheney asking him, "Are you going to take care of this guy, or not?" Several weeks before the start of the war, Bush told his daughters "I am working hard to keep the peace and avoid war. I pray that the man in Iraq will disarm in a peaceful way."[6] At the same time, he told his secretary of state, "I really think I'm going to have to take this guy out." One week after 9/11, moreover, the president told the first White House meeting of his war planners, "I believe Iraq was involved, but I'm not going to strike them now. I don't have the evidence at this point."[7]

The memoirs contend faulty intelligence was responsible for the decision to go to war, but the speeches of the principals, including the president and vice president, confirm that they were willing to go beyond evidence to justify a state of "permanent war" against terrorism. These major speeches included Bush's statement before the United National General Assembly in September 2002 and the State of the Union speech in January 2003; Cheney's speech in Tennessee to the Veterans of Foreign Wars in August, 2002; and Powell's speech to the UN Security Council in February, 2003.[8] These speeches were the best examples of the Bush administration taking phony intelligence to the Congress, the American people, and the international community. The speeches were given careful review inside the White House as well as in the intelligence community. Powell's speech to the Security Council, in fact, was written by CIA analysts and vetted by the Agency's director and deputy director, which was without precedent.

In their memoirs, Cheney and Rumsfeld depict a president presiding over a national security process marked by "incoherent decision-making and policy drift," and a dysfunctional national security process riven by tensions between the Pentagon and the State Department. Rice indicts the president for signaling to the Pentagon that he had no interest in a plan for maintaining law and order in Baghdad after the fall of Saddam. Bush dismissed the subject in front of senior generals, saying that such a plan was "something Condi wanted to talk about." Cheney and Rumsfeld ignored the fact that senior military officers disagreed with Rumsfeld's strategy, particularly the undermanned invading force; the officers requested additional troops. Actually, if Rumsfeld had had his druthers, the invading force would have been 75,000—even more inadequate than the eventual force of 155,000 the Joint Chiefs of Staff settled for. The Army chief of staff, Eric Shinseki, was rushed into retirement for suggesting 300,000 troops would be needed for the post-war phase. Cheney's memoir makes no mention of Shinseki; Bush merely chides Rumsfeld for skipping the general's retirement ceremony because it "helped feed the false impression that the general had been fired for policy disagreements over Iraq."[9]

Rumsfeld and Powell argued with each other throughout Bush's first term. Powell blamed Rumsfeld for using deputy defense secretary Wolfowitz to attack the State Department; Rumsfeld blamed Powell for using his deputy, Richard Armitage, to attack the Defense Department. Both Cheney and Rumsfeld blamed Powell for permitting the DoS to ignore the president's political direction and for making personal and anonymous attacks on the Pentagon in the media. Rumsfeld accused Powell of creating his own "media image" by describing himself as "battling the forces of unilateralism and conservatism," which "may have been beneficial to Powell in some circles, but it did not jibe with reality." Cheney cited Rice's failure to resolve differences within the policy community and to present the president with clear policy choices.

Rice used her memoir to defend herself from the charges by both Cheney and Rumsfeld that she had failed to control the decision-making process. All the memoirs made it clear, however, that the Pentagon called the major shots and that Rice, as national security adviser and then secretary of defense, played a subordinate role. Rice tacitly documented the increased power of the Pentagon and the declining power of the State Department over the past decade. More importantly, she acknowledged a "cycle of dysfunction" within the Bush administration; the backdoor dealings of Cheney; her own mishandling of intelligence on Iraqi WMD; and her own failure to make sure that the Pentagon had prepared a post-invasion plan for Iraq.[10]

Like her colleagues, she offered no explanation of how the decision to invade Iraq was made, no indication that the pros and cons of such an invasion were discussed, no indication of a policy process that allowed all views to be heard; she was particularly culpable for the last failure. The major duty of a national security adviser is to make sure that the president has sufficient evidence on all sides of an argument before making a decision, particularly one as momentous as the use of force. Her unwillingness to discuss her management of the policy process gives added credibility to those memoirs that cited her inability to conduct such management.

Rice is at her most disingenuous when she credits the war with having assured that Saddam was deprived of the ability to enter into a nuclear race with Iran's President Mahmoud Ahmadinejad—as the Iraqis possessed none of the key elements of a nuclear weapons program. She eventually conceded that even the president was "underwhelmed" by the CIA's intelligence on Iraqi WMD and Iraqi links to terrorism. No one described it better than UN weapons inspector Hans Blix, who asked "Could there be 100 percent certainty about the existence of weapons of mass destruction but zero percent knowledge of their location?"

The intelligence community, particularly the CIA, made numerous errors prior to the invasion and missed the strategic consequences of U.S. use of force. The CIA incorrectly concluded that the Iraqi military would remain intact and that whole units would defect to the United States; that the Iraqi police would stay on the job and contribute to stability in the wake of Saddam's ouster; and that the secular Baathists would cooperate strategically with jihadist religious extremists.[11] Some errors were due to politicization; others were legitimate intelligence mistakes. The failure to understand the weakness of the Iraqi economy and military, which would leave Iraq in a position of total chaos in the wake of the U.S. invasion, was probably the most egregious example of the latter. These errors were not made by the Department of State's study group on Iraq, which drew no support from either the Pentagon or the CIA.

None of the memoirs alluded to one of the most serious pre-war transgressions: the militarization and politicization of intelligence that was responsible for failing to report that Saddam had no WMD and that there had been no strategic weaponry in the country for the previous decade. White House and Pentagon pressure on the CIA was the source of some of these blunders, and the Bush memoirs make no mention of Vice President Cheney's numerous (and unprecedented) visits to the CIA to press for intelligence on WMD. When the CIA's director, George Tenet, made his infamous remark that it would be a "slam dunk" to provide intelligence to justify going to war, he was referring to the president's demands for intelligence to take to the American people and the international community regarding the need for war, not to support for the Bush administration's decisions regarding the use of force against Iraq.

The decision to invade was made long before the intelligence was in; Bush was merely seeking intelligence to rationalize the case for war. When he told CIA Director Tenet and deputy director John McLaughlin that their intelligence on Saddam's weapons programs was "not very convincing," he was talking about convincing public opinion—not convincing a skeptical president that there should be more discussion of the case for the use of force. The Cheney Doctrine ruled the day: Even a one percent chance of Iraqi WMD would be treated as a certainty, making firm evidence unnecessary.

The use of tailored intelligence to justify an immoral war was a direct result of the Bush administration's militarizing of the intelligence community. The Silberman-Robb Commission, which was created to review pre-war intelligence failures, confirmed that the militarization of intelligence collection prevented a focus on the serious strategic issues surrounding the Iraqi problem, particularly in the wake of Iraq's unanticipated invasion of Kuwait in August 1990. There was very little human intelligence, virtually no useful signals intelligence, and, most important, no effort to rectify this gap. Investigations of both the Silberman-Robb Commission and the Senate Intelligence Committee point to senior Defense Department officials, particularly undersecretaries of defense Paul Wolfowitz and Douglas Feith, who led the way in distorting and politicizing intelligence on Iraq.

The militarization of intelligence prior to the Iraq War resembled the militarization of intelligence that preceded the Vietnam War. Forty years after the Gulf of Tonkin Resolution legislated the use of force against North Vietnam, we learned that senior officials at the National Security Agency deliberately distorted critical intelligence to secure an overwhelmingly favorable vote in Congress. In 2001, the senior NSA historian, Robert J. Hanyok, found a pattern of uncorrected translation mistakes, altered intercept times, and selective citations of intelligence that pointed to the deliberate skewing of key evidence.[12] President Johnson had doubts that there had actually been a Vietnamese attack on U.S. ships, but the intercepted communications were key to the decisive vote on the resolution. Thus, doctored intelligence was used to justify the escalation of a war that led to the death of 58,226 Americans and more than 1 million Vietnamese people. NSA officials were moving in 2002 to declassify Hanyok's work, but the project was placed on the back burner because it would have been politically embarrassing to release the report at the time the Bush administration was moving toward a congressional resolution to use force against Iraq.

The Plan

It is not unusual for administrations to manipulate intelligence prior to embarking on war. This occurred before the Mexican-American War in order to support the policies of President James Polk, before the Spanish-American War in order to support the policies of President William McKinley, and in Lyndon B. Johnson's Vietnam War. The Bush administration was unique because of the institutionalization of the process. The president's chief of staff, Andrew Card, said it best, admitting that the White House had a "marketing plan," set to begin in September 2002 to justify the war.

The Bush administration's marketing plan included creation of a White House Iraq Group (WHIG) to convince public opinion of the need for war. Beginning in August 2002, the group met regularly in the White House Situation Room, coinciding with the twelve visits of Cheney and his senior aide, Lewis "Scooter" Libby, to CIA to meet with analysts. These unprecedented meetings were designed to gain intelligence justification for a war to conduct regime change in Iraq that would be credible to Congress, the American public, and the international community.

The WHIG produced phrases such as "the smoking gun should not be a mushroom cloud," which was a favorite for Cheney, Rice, and Rumsfeld.[13] Rice used the oft-repeated phrase on CNN on September 8, 2002, the same day that Vice President Cheney told *Meet the Press* that we know with "absolute certainty" that Saddam is "using his procurement system to acquire the equipment he needs in order to enrich uranium to build a nuclear weapon." Judith Miller and Michael Getler had a front-page story in the *New York Times* that day citing anonymous administration officials saying Saddam has repeatedly tried to acquire aluminum tubes "specially designed" to enrich uranium.[14] Four days later, President Bush took the aluminum tubes claim to the UN General Assembly. Deputy secretary of defense Wolfowitz conceded privately that the Bush administration had difficulty determining its rationale for going to war, but that the nuclear rhetoric regarding WMD was the "one reason everyone could agree on."[15]

Wolfowitz met regularly with British Ambassador to the United States Christopher Meyer to discuss ways and means to influence opinion in the British parliament and the U.S. Congress. British Foreign Secretary Jack Straw, like Secretary of State Powell, realized that regime change was no justification for the use of force and that the case therefore had to be built around WMD. The British were nervous about the public relations campaign and urged regular meetings between Prime Minister Tony Blair and Bush to get public acceptance of the Iraqi threat. A major victim in this legerdemain, besides the American and British people, was the intelligence community and its pursuit of objective and balanced intelligence. The biblical inscription "The truth will set you free" may be inscribed in the lobby of CIA headquarters, but no whistleblowers emerged in the intelligence community to set the record straight.

British Assessment of the Marketing Plan
The chief of the British MI6 intelligence service, Sir Richard Dearlove, was aware of the administration's plans for war and had no illusions about Andrew Card's marketing plan. High-level CIA officials made it known to their British counterparts that the Bush administration had already made a decision to go to war, that the option to petition the United Nations was merely a face-saving measure to appease Secretary of State Powell and the international community, and that the intelligence was being tailored to support the war. The memoirs of the key decision-makers made no mention of Dearlove and his incriminating memorandum.

In the Downing Street memorandum of July 23, 2002, Dearlove warned Prime Minister Blair of Washington's intentions. The memorandum, which was published in the *Sunday Times* of London on May 1, 2005, described the U.S. marketing plan and conceded that the British had agreed to the "establishment of an ad hoc group of officials under Cabinet Office Chairmanship to consider the development of an information campaign to be agreed with the United States."[16] Dearlove noted that there had been a "perceptible shift in attitude. Military action was now seen as inevitable. . . . The intelligence and facts were being fixed around the policy. . . . The most likely timing in U.S. minds for military action to begin was January." In fact, the timeline began months earlier with the U.S. Air Force attacking targets before the official start of the war in March 2003. As with most missed signals that could have challenged the administration's case for war, the Downing Street memorandum was ignored by the American press and dismissed by some pundits, such as Michael Kinsley of the *Los Angeles Times*, as the stuff of the "usual freelance chatterboxes."

Another British memorandum, in January 2003, described a meeting between Blair and Bush and made it clear that the United States intended to invade Iraq even if UN inspectors found no WMD. If it were necessary, Bush said, the United States would "fly U2 reconnaissance planes . . . over Iraq, painted in UN colors" to tempt Iraqi forces to fire on them, which would constitute a breach of UN resolutions. The justification for the war would be the "conjunction of terrorism and WMD," although there was never good evidence of Iraqi links to terrorist groups such as al-Qaeda or Iraqi holdings of WMD. Dearlove concluded that "there was little discussion in Washington of the aftermath of military action," which ultimately created a disastrous situation. In a separate memorandum, Foreign Secretary Straw conceded that Saddam was no threat to his neighbors.

The British requested the MI6-CIA meeting so that Blair could get an update on the thinking of the Bush administration on Iraq. The CIA and MI6 hold annual high-level meetings as well as regular exchanges of sensitive intelligence matters and are extremely candid with each other in their one-on-one meetings. The prime minister wanted a gut check on his exchanges with the president regarding Iraq and considered a candid exchange between U.S. and British intelligence chiefs essential. The day-long meeting at CIA headquarters included a private one-on-one meeting between Tenet and Dearlove. On the basis of those meetings, Dearlove reported that "military action was now seen as inevitable" and repeated that the "intelligence and facts were being fixed around the policy."

The Phony Case for War

Both the marketing case for going to war with Iraq and the use of force resolution were based on two false premises: that Iraq had huge stocks of WMD and that there were terrorist links between Saddam Hussein and Osama bin Laden. Much of the intelligence on key aspects of the WMD issue and the links between Iraq and al-Qaeda consisted of single-source reporting that lacked corroboration. This would not be an acceptable methodology in investigative journalism, but obviously it was good enough for the intelligence community.

Bush went beyond the credible evidence when he argued that Iraq was "reconstituting its nuclear weapons program" and that Saddam was seeking significant quantities of "nuclear materials from Africa" and "high-strength aluminum tubes suitable for nuclear weapons production." There was no reliable intelligence that supported these views; similarly, there was no intelligence to support Cheney's views that the "Iraqi regime has in fact been very busy enhancing its capabilities in the field of chemical and biological agents" and that "we now know that Saddam has resumed his efforts to acquire nuclear weapons." Powell, in his UN speech, argued without evidence that Saddam was "determined to get his hands on a nuclear bomb."

The intelligence community told the administration consistently that the Iraqis were several years away from developing a nuclear weapon, another worst-case view and a great exaggeration of the real situation. There was no reason to believe, as the administration contended, that Saddam was on the verge of developing such a weapon. The October 2002 National Intelligence Estimate concluded that, even if he had nuclear weapons, Saddam would not use such a weapon against the United States and would not share the technology with terrorist organizations unless the United States invaded Iraq and was on the verge of overthrowing his regime. This was one of the few sensible conclusions of the NIE, but the CIA produced an unclassified White Paper for the Congress and the U.S. public that omitted this assessment in order to help the administration's case for war.

Iraq's nuclear program, including weapons design facilities and production equipment, had been destroyed long before 9/11, let alone prior to the U.S. invasion of Iraq. The use of gamma detection equipment in Iraq produced no evidence of efforts to enrich uranium or produce plutonium. There was less certainty about the destruction of Iraq's chemical and biological weapons programs, because of the difficult verification and monitoring problems, but international disarmament specialists were not convinced that Iraq had active programs in this area. In fact, the disarmament specialists were convinced that Iraq lost its capability to fabricate new chemical and biological agents. Finally, in late 2004, in a formal acknowledgment, the CIA issued a classified report ("Iraq: No Large-Scale Chemical Warfare Efforts Since Early 1990s") revising its pre-war assessment and concluding that Baghdad had abandoned its chemical weapons programs in 1991.[17] In my twenty-four years at the CIA, there was no precedent for the CIA formally disavowing a previous judgment, and former deputy CIA director Richard Kerr testified that the Agency had never before issued a revisionist report on any subject.

The International Atomic Energy Agency (IAEA) issued its own report before the war, but unlike the intelligence community concluded there was "no indication of resumed nuclear activities . . . nor any indication of nuclear-related prohibited activities at any inspected sites."[18] The IAEA also reported that there had been "no indication that Iraq has attempted to import uranium since 1990" and termed the source of President Bush's assertion that Saddam was trying to purchase uranium in Africa a forgery. The obvious question in all this was why a UN inspection team with a limited budget was able to monitor and verify the decrepit state of Iraq's political, economic, and military situation when the $50 billion intelligence community, particularly the $5 billion CIA, was not.

The pre-war estimate of Iraq's nuclear program, as reflected in the politicized National Intelligence Estimate of October 2002, was that Baghdad was "reconstituting its nuclear weapons program" and "if left unchecked, [would] probably have a nuclear weapon during this decade," although not before 2007 to 2009."[19] The only "compelling evidence" of reconstitution, according to the Robb-Silberman report, was provided by a relatively junior CIA analyst (referred to as "Joe") who cited Iraq's "aggressive pursuit of high-strength aluminum tubes."[20] Iraq pursued these tubes on the open market, however, which argued against their use for nuclear weapons. Moreover, the Department of Energy and the State Department's Bureau of Intelligence and Research (INR) concluded that the tubes were for Iraqi artillery. The Energy Department dissented from the NIE on the issue of the aluminum tubes and, prior to the NIE release, sent a memorandum to the CIA that destroyed "Joe's" theory that the aluminum tubes were for nuclear centrifuges. This memorandum was given to national security adviser Rice, but she continued to maintain the tubes were clear evidence of an Iraqi nuclear program. It is incredible that a professional soldier, former JCS chairman General Powell, could get this one wrong. In any event, the tubes were not evidence, in the words of President Bush, of a "grave and gathering danger."

In addition to the phony case for Iraqi WMD, the White

House made a case for linkage between Saddam and bin Laden. President Bush said on September 25, 2002, that "You can't distinguish between al-Qaeda and Saddam when you talk abut the war on terror," and, at a press conference in December 2005, he made the same observation.[21] Secretary of Defense Rumsfeld claimed on September 27, 2002, that he had "bulletproof" evidence of ties between Saddam and al-Qaeda, and Secretary of State Powell described a "sinister nexus between Iraq and al-Qaeda, a nexus that combines classic terrorist organizations and modern methods of murder."[22] Secretary of Defense Panetta was still making this case in the summer of 2011, soon after his confirmation.

The information that Iraqis had trained al-Qaeda members to make bombs with deadly gases came from a top al-Qaeda operative, In al-Shaykh al-Libi, who had been tortured in Egypt. He had been in the custody of the CIA over the protests of FBI interrogators who favored standard law enforcement interrogation practices. Al-Libi was then rendered to Egypt, where he was tortured and invented the tale of al-Qaeda operatives receiving chemical weapons training from Iraq. He quickly recanted his claims upon his release in 2004. A CIA source told ABC on November 18, 2005, "This is the problem with using the waterboard. They get so desperate that they begin telling you what they think you want to hear."

The Phony Link Between Saddam Hussein and al-Qaeda

For several years, the Bush administration kept alive the charge of an Iraq–al-Qaeda link, using murky speculation, innuendo, and phony intelligence. As late as April 2004, when the 9/11 Commission was approaching its conclusion that there was no such link, nearly half the U.S. population had already been falsely persuaded to believe that the link existed and that Saddam was involved in the 9/11 attacks against the World Trade Center and the Pentagon. President Bush accused Iraq of sending "bomb-making and document forgery experts to work with al-Qaeda" and of providing al-Qaeda with "chemical and biological weapons training."[23] "The reason I keep insisting that there was a relationship between Iraq and Saddam and al-Qaeda," according to Bush, was "because there was a relationship between Iraq and al-Qaeda."[24]

In October 2002, President Bush asserted that "Iraq has trained al-Qaeda members in bomb-making and poisons and deadly gases." In responding to reports of chemical and biological assistance to al-Qaeda, the CIA concluded that "the level and extent of this assistance is not clear."[25] The Agency identified "many critical gaps" in the knowledge of Iraqi links to al-Qaeda because of "limited reporting" and the "questionable reliability of many of our sources."

Vice President Cheney referred to "overwhelming evidence" of these links, and Secretary of State Powell referred to links that existed "over the years" in a nexus that "combines classic terrorist organizations and modern methods of murder."[26] On the eve of Powell's UN speech, Secretary of Defense Rumsfeld said that the link existed "over a span of some eight to ten years" and, when Iraq denied any linkage, Rumsfeld flippantly replied, "And Abraham Lincoln is short."[27] Even after the invasion of Iraq, national security adviser Rice repeated the myth of Iraqi training in chemical and biological weapons for members of al-Qaeda and stated that the United States needed to prevent the day that Saddam would hand "just a little vial of something" to the terrorists.[28]

Among senior intelligence officials, only Tenet argued that there was evidence of connections between Iraq and al-Qaeda. Ignoring his own analysts, Tenet wrote a letter to the Senate intelligence committee claiming evidence of ties between the two. When the CIA was crafting a UN speech for Secretary of State

Powell, Tenet again referred to the "sinister nexus" between Iraq and al-Qaeda, which is the formulation that Powell used in his speech to the Security Council on February 5, 2003. The CIA never suggested there was a connection between Iraq and the 9/11 attacks, but when NSC official Richard Clarke reported to the White House that there was no such connection, he was told "Wrong answer. . . . Do it again."[29]

Several days before the president's remarks in Cincinnati in October 2002, the NIE on Iraqi WMD programs reported that the sources on training and support for al-Qaeda are "second-hand or from sources of varying reliability.[30] It also noted that the intelligence community "cannot determine . . . how many of the reported plans for CBW (chemical and biological warfare) were actually realized." As late as January 2003, the CIA noted the "lack of evidence of completed training" and admitted that the reporting never made "clear whether training" was "actually implemented."[31] The Agency report noted that much of the reporting was based on "hearsay" and that some of the reporting was "simple declarative accusations of Iraqi–al Qa'ida complicity with no substantiating detail or other information that might help us corroborate them." The Agency confirmed that the only source for Iraqi–al-Qaeda links had been tortured by the Egyptian security service and had recanted all of his accusations.

Cheney to this day argues that, despite the absence of good evidence, there were substantive contacts between Iraq and al-Qaeda prior to 9/11. There was no good evidence of either Iraqi training to al-Qaeda in WMD technologies or a meeting between Mohammed Atta and an Iraqi intelligence official before the 9/11 attacks, although Cheney told Tim Russert of *Meet the Press* that he had been given a "pretty well confirmed" report of such a meeting in Prague.[32] The Defense Intelligence Agency (DIA) destroyed the credibility of reports and the reliability of sources on these issues.

Only Cheney aggressively argued that one of the hijackers, Atta, met with a senior official of the Iraqi intelligence service in Czechoslovakia in April 2001.[33] The Czech intelligence service denied such a meeting had ever taken place, but in September 2002, Cheney asserted that Atta had traveled to Prague "on a number of occasions. On at least one occasion, there was unsubstantiated reporting that placed him in Prague with a senior Iraqi intelligence official a few months before the attack on the World Trade Center." In January 2003, the CIA reported that the "most reliable reporting casts doubt" on the possibility of any such meeting.[34] In fact, the CIA had sensitive telephone intercepts that placed Atta in the United States at the time of the so-called meeting with Iraqi intelligence officials. Nevertheless, as late as January 2004, Cheney was arguing that Atta traveled to Prague and met with Iraqi intelligence officers.

Nonexistent Mobile Labs

Among the unproven claims regarding Iraqi WMD, one of the most bizarre involved an Iraqi source who was debriefed by German intelligence. The Iraqi defector, code-named "Curveball," who was described by his German handlers as "not psychologically stable," an alcoholic and a convicted sex offender, provided information on so-called mobile laboratories that were producing biological and chemical weapons.[35] The Germans repeated their concerns to the CIA over and over again, and British intelligence also informed the CIA prior to the 9/11 attacks that "elements of Curveball's behavior strike us as typical of . . . fabricators." CIA operatives asked to debrief Curveball, but the Germans never permitted this customary step. Curveball, who was granted political asylum in Germany in September 2001, still lives in southern Germany under an assumed name, in a furnished apartment, receiving a generous stipend.

The Germans had warned U.S. intelligence authorities,

including the CIA and DIA, that Curveball had exaggerated his claims during the run-up to war, and, as a result, they were shocked when President Bush and Secretary of State Powell used this intelligence in their speeches prior to the war.[36] Senior members of the German Federal Intelligence Service warned the United States that Curveball never claimed to produce germ weapons and never saw anyone else do so. "We were shocked," the official said. "Mein Gott!! We had always told them it was not proven . . . it was not hard intelligence."[37] Even Iraqi colleagues of Curveball dismissed his accounts as "water cooler gossip" and "corridor conversation."

The fact that Curveball was trading information, in this case disinformation, for possible German citizenship seemed obvious to many members of the German intelligence service and even to several clandestine officers from the CIA, including the chief of the directorate of operation's European Division, Tyler Drumheller. Even before publication of the intelligence estimate on Iraqi WMD in 2002, which emphasized the importance of the mobile biological labs, German intelligence officers had told Drumheller that Curveball was "crazy, probably a fabricator," and that it would be a waste of time for the CIA to debrief him.[38]

Drumheller kept pressing German intelligence for access to Curveball, but to no avail. Drumheller and one of his senior agents passed this information along to CIA deputy director McLaughlin, who ignored all of the caveats on the Curveball information. As a result, the October 2002 estimate embraced Curveball's information, and Secretary of State Powell's speech to the UN Security Council in February 2003 shamelessly exaggerated it. Powell was reportedly furious when he learned in the summer of 2003 that there were CIA officers who had doubts about the information, but that these doubts had not reached him before the speech.

Curveball's ability to pass information to the Pentagon agent and Iraqi exile Ahmed Chalabi gave his disinformation instant play at the Department of Defense and the White House. Chalabi himself was the source of other disinformation, such as a report that an Iraqi general had witnessed Iraqi training of Arabs to hijack airplanes. Chalabi's disinformation was given to the Office of Special Plans (OSP), which delivered the information to the White House and to Stephen Hayes at the *Weekly Standard*.

President Bush mischaracterized Curveball's information when he warned that Iraq had at least seven mobile laboratories brewing biological weapons; Secretary of State Powell did the same before the United Nations in February 2003. Yet, Vice President Cheney in November 2005 lashed out at administration critics who accused the Bush administration of manipulating key intelligence information to make the case for war. DIA analysts referred to Curveball's intelligence as "garbage," but this didn't stop the information from reaching the White House.

The president, the vice president, the national security adviser, and the secretary of defense made it clear what they wanted in the way of "intelligence" and kept sending reports back to be redone until they got the "right" answers. Cheney and Libby were also involved with Secretary of Defense Rumsfeld in the creation of the OSP, which was more than willing to prepare the intelligence assessments on Iraq that the CIA blocked or challenged. On at least two occasions, Cheney was even guilty of shooting the messenger, demanding the replacement of at least two senior briefers for the President's Daily Briefing whose intelligence assessments did not correspond to the views of the White House. It is particularly noteworthy that neither Bush, Cheney, nor Rumsfeld bothered to mention the OSP in their memoirs, presumably because the Pentagon's inspector general confirmed in 2006 that OSP had a role in "fixing" intelligence to justify the Iraq War.

When David Kay, the chief of the Iraq Survey Group, told CIA director Tenet that Curveball was a liar and that Iraq had no mobile labs or other illicit weapons, he was assigned to a windowless office without a working telephone. When President Bush used the State of the Union message on January 20, 2004, to praise Kay and his Iraq Survey Group, Kay resigned and went public with his concerns.[39]

The Niger Fabrication

Sixteen words in President Bush's State of the Union message in January 2003 ("The British government has learned that Saddam Hussein recently sought significant quantities of uranium from Africa") had much to do with moving the country and the Congress toward war with Iraq. Among the various deceitful measures employed to support the war, the use of these sixteen words based on an obviously fabricated document was the most egregious. First and foremost, virtually every key member of the Bush administration had been told that the allegation linking Iraq and Niger was based on a forgery. CIA director Tenet tried to convince the White House in 2001 and 2002 that there was no reason to believe Iraq was seeking uranium in Africa. In December 2001, Department of State and CIA analysts believed that the issue "was done, shot down," but the White House wanted the Niger story in the president's speech in October 2002 and the State of the Union in January 2003.[40]

In 2002, Tenet personally kept a reference to an Iraq purchase of uranium out of the president's speech in Cincinnati, convincing deputy national security adviser Hadley to remove the offensive language. Tenet delivered the same message to Hadley before the State of the Union speech in January 2003, but Hadley claimed to have forgotten both the October and January conversations. Two months after the start of the Iraq war, Hadley conceded that he had received Tenet's warnings but had forgotten them in the run-up to the war. CIA officials told Cheney on numerous occasions of the forgery.

Rice remembered no warning from the CIA but former deputy director of intelligence Jamie Miscik said she had warned Rice before the State of the Union message. The director of Bureau of Intelligence and Research, Carl Ford, told Secretary of State Powell about the forgery, and Powell deleted the information from his address to the UN Security Council in February 2003.[41] Alan Foley, the director of the CIA's Weapons Intelligence, Nonproliferation, and Arms Control Center (WINPAC), told Robert Joseph, the senior NSC official responsible for counter-proliferation, that the intelligence was based on a fabrication. Foley repeated his warning to Joseph several months later. In late December 2002, however, Joseph asked Foley if he would accept language on the uranium issue that was linked to British intelligence instead of U.S. intelligence, and Foley gave in, satisfied that at least the link to the CIA had been removed.

Cheney and Rumsfeld were particularly aggressive in pushing the intelligence community to accept the disputed Niger documents. Prior to the president's speech, they told the press that Iraq was trying to purchase uranium from Niger. Secretary of State Powell told the vice president personally that the Niger documents were phony, and received considerable pressure from Libby and Hadley to cite the allegations in his UN speech. The Rumsfeld memoirs make no mention of the bureaucratic imbroglio over the allegations regarding uranium for Iraq.

The pressure from the vice president and the secretary of defense became so great in 2002 that the State Department, the CIA and the Joint Chiefs of Staff decided to send high-level representatives to Niger to look into the allegations and to check into the security of Niger's uranium. The JCS representative, Marine General Carlton Fulford Jr., was convinced that the uranium supply was secure and reported this finding to the chairman of the JCS, General Richard Myers. Myers never shared Fulford's findings with the vice president. The State Department sent Ambassador Barbro Owens-Kirkpatrick to Niger, and, as in the case of Fulford, she reported emphatically that there was no substance to the reports that Iraq was trying to buy uranium yellowcake from Niger.

The greatest controversy over the so-called Niger documents concerned the CIA and its emissary to Niger, Ambassador Joseph Wilson, who traveled to Africa and, in the summer of 2003, wrote an op-ed for the *New York Times* that concluded Iraq and Niger had no dealings over uranium and that no dealings could be completed without the knowledge of the international consortium responsible for the uranium industry in Niger. The CIA had picked Wilson for the Niger trip because of his knowledge of the uranium industry and of African politics, hoping that his bona fides would disabuse Cheney of his zeal in using the Niger documents to link Saddam to reconstituting Iraq's nuclear capabilities. Wilson's op-ed infuriated Cheney, who orchestrated a program to vilify Wilson and thus intimidate and prevent other government officials from revealing the misuse of intelligence in the run-up to the Iraq War.

Cheney's campaign led to the outing of Wilson's wife, Valerie Plame, a clandestine operative at the CIA who worked in the Counter-proliferation Division (CPD), which had selected Wilson for the Niger trip. Plame's role in CPD led to administration accusations that Plame had recommended her husband for the trip. According to *Long Island Newsday* reporters Tim Phelps and Knut Royce, and CNN correspondent David Ensor, the proposal to send Wilson to Niger came from Plame's colleagues and not Plame.[42] It is rarely mentioned that, during the same period that Wilson traveled to Niger and reported back to the CIA, State Department and Defense Department emissaries had corroborated Wilson's conclusions. Although the findings of the Senate Intelligence Committee tried to impugn Wilson's motives in criticizing the Bush administration's case for war, it conceded that it agreed with the findings of Ambassador Owens-Kirkpatrick, the four-star marine general, and Joe Wilson.

Ambassador Wilson made his points in a trip report to the CIA. As a result, on October 5, 2002, the day of the release of the NIE, the CIA's associate deputy director for intelligence reported "concerns about the sourcing and some of the facts of the Niger reporting, specifically that the international control of the Niger mines would have made it very difficult to get yellowcake to Iraq."[43] The CIA also provided this information in a memorandum to Hadley, suggesting that the reference to an Iraqi purchase from Niger be removed from the president's speech in Cincinnati. And on October 6 the CIA sent a second memorandum to the White House with additional reasons for dropping the reference to Niger, including the fact that the clandestine reporting referred to a uranium oxide mine that was actually flooded and a second mine that was controlled by the French.[44] Senior CIA officials knew that the British reporting on Niger was from 1999, that it had never been substantiated or corroborated, and that there had been subsequent evidence challenging the possibility of an exchange of uranium involving Iraq.

Nevertheless, Cheney authorized Libby to leak the specific language of the 2002 intelligence estimate, linking Iraq to uranium purchases from Niger, to Judith Miller of the *New York Times*. Libby and Karl Rove, the president's senior aide, were also instructed to provide the name of Wilson's wife, and to reveal her affiliation with the CIA as a clandestine operative. This information was given to syndicated correspondent Robert Novak and five other journalists, but only Novak published the information. Novak did so even though it is a felony to disclose an undercover agent's name, violating the Intelligence Identities Act of 1983. Cheney's role in undermining Wilson and outing his wife serve as prima facie evidence of the vice president's passionate commitment to war and to protecting the phony reasons for doing so. Libby was sentenced for lying to the FBI and a grand jury about his role in the affair, although no charges were brought against Rove, who spoke to reporters from *Time* magazine.[45] President Bush commuted Libby's sentence, but refused to issue the pardon that Cheney wanted.

In the same week that the estimate on Iraqi WMD gave credibility to the possibility that Iraq was pursuing uranium in Niger, CIA deputy director McLaughlin, in response to a question from Senator Jon Kyl (R-AZ), disagreed with a British White Paper that charged Iraq with "seeking uranium from various African locations." The National Intelligence Officer for Strategic and Nuclear Programs testified that "there's a question about those attempts [to buy uranium in Africa] because of the control of the material in those countries," an obvious reference to the international consortium that controls Niger's uranium industry. Later in the year, the Agency became involved with additional efforts to deny the fabricated reporting on Niger. The State Department inserted the claim into a fact sheet in December 2002, but the CIA's intervention caused State to remove it. The Pentagon asked for an authoritative judgment from the National Intelligence Council and was told unequivocally, "The Niger story was baseless and should be laid to rest."

The CIA tried to have it both ways, however, initially trying to stop the White House from citing the Niger report in public statements, but reporting the allegations in their own intelligence products. The national intelligence estimate (NIE) in October 2002 and the draft of Powell's address to the United Nations in February 2003 incorporated references to Iraq and Niger. The estimate concluded that Iraq was "shifting from domestic mining and milling of uranium to foreign acquisition." Thus, the highest ranking members of the intelligence community's analytic staffs gave credibility to the phony charge, although the consensus within the intelligence community was that the clandestine reporting on a Niger deal was a fabrication produced by members of the Italian military intelligence service. Apparently, once leading intelligence officials realized there was no way to challenge a Bush administration preparing for war, they would protect their access to the White House by telling the decision-makers what they wanted to hear. There is no better example of the politicization of intelligence.

Rice briefly took responsibility for the president's use of discredited intelligence about the Niger yellowcake. "No one is to blame for this but me," she wrote at one point.[46] Eventually, however, she shifted the blame to CIA director Tenet for his failure to read the advance text of the State of the Union speech. Even more egregious, she allowed her deputy, Stephen Hadley, to take the blame for the entire affair.

The fact that we still do not know everything about who created the phony intelligence and why it was created points to inept counterintelligence capabilities at the FBI and CIA, or perhaps a cover-up of an investigation that would implicate U.S. intelligence officers. If the Niger forgery was, in fact, an example of CIA "black propaganda," it would not be the first time that CIA disinformation designed for a foreign audience ended up in the United States, even in the White House, as unintended blowback.

There has never been a serious attempt by the Senate intelligence committee to learn why the administration used the fabrication or other controversial intelligence that it received. Senate intelligence chairman Pat Roberts (R-KS) promised an investigation, the so-called "Phase Two" investigation, but never conducted one. The exaggeration of intelligence by the president, the vice president, the secretary of defense, and the national security adviser, particularly with reference to Iraqi nuclear programs ("the smoking gun cannot be a mushroom cloud"), and Iraqi links with al-Qaeda, was obvious, but there has been no attempt to build an official record of their distortions.

The President's Defense

Fifty days after the fall of Baghdad, on May 29, 2003, President Bush emphatically proclaimed that the United States "has found the WMD," which turned out to be the so-called mobile biological laboratories.[47] This purported vindication for the invasion of Iraq was repeated by every prominent member of the Bush administration over the next nine months. The CIA and the DIA even jointly published a White Paper in May 2003 that described the labs as the "strongest evidence to date that Iraq was hiding a biological warfare program." It emphatically refuted an explanation by Iraqi officials, reported in the *New York Times*, that referred to the trailers as mobile units for producing hydrogen.[48]

Two days before the president's remarks, however, the Pentagon had received a three-page field report from a team of U.S. and British experts that it had sent to Iraq to examine the trailers, which one of the experts referred to as "the biggest sand toilets in the world."[49] Thus, at the highest levels of the Pentagon and the CIA, it was known authoritatively that there no mobile biological laboratories prior to the president, the vice president, the secretary of state, and the secretary of defense heralding the find as justification for the invasion of Iraq. David Kay's Iraq Survey Group, which had been dispatched by the CIA, informed CIA director Tenet in October 2003 that the trailers were not only "impractical" for biological weapons production but were in fact "almost certainly intended" for manufacturing hydrogen for weather balloons, just as Iraqi officials had claimed six months earlier.

President Bush selected his Veterans' Day address on November 11, 2005, to deny that his administration skewed intelligence to make the case for war and to charge that he received the same intelligence on Iraq that the Congress and his immediate predecessor, President Clinton, had received. Bush maliciously charged that those Democrats accusing the White House of militarizing intelligence were providing aid and comfort to the insurgents and hurting the morale of American servicemen. This was a major reversal of his previous defense, which was to blame the CIA for providing faulty intelligence on Iraqi WMD. On balance, the deterrence policies of the Clinton administration had worked, with the destruction of all WMD programs achieved by 1998, the same year that the UN inspectors left Iraq. Bush's preemptive war, based on lies and deceit, had been a costly failure.

President Bush argued that no political pressure was put on the intelligence community to provide analysis to make the case for war. This aspect of Bush's defense is particularly frustrating because Senate Intelligence Committee chairman Roberts blocked an investigation of how the administration manipulated intelligence from the community. The minority chairman of the committee, Senator Jay Rockefeller (D-WV) called for such an investigation before the war began in March 2003, but Roberts blocked such efforts for the next two and a half years, yielding only in October 2005, after the Senate Democrats demanded an unusual secret session of the Senate to work out a compromise on investigating the White House's handling of sensitive intelligence matters.

President Bush was disingenuous in stating that the Congress had the same intelligence that was available to the president. Actually, the White House blocked sensitive intelligence from going to the committee, and Vice President Cheney played a particularly aggressive role in this campaign. Cheney asked for the removal of at least two CIA briefers who failed to deliver the kind of tough message that the vice president was seeking. In any event, the committee had no access to the President's Daily Brief, which contained the most sensitive intelligence available to the community.

A senior CIA analyst, Paul Pillar, wrote an authoritative account of the Bush administration's misuse of intelligence to "justify decisions already made," but maintained that the Agency did not compromise its own assessments in the process.[50] The CIA had nothing to do with the decision to go to war, which was decided upon early on in the first year of the Bush presidency, but the CIA knowingly corrupted intelligence, and Pillar was part of the process, managing and directing the unclassified White Paper on Iraqi WMD. Pillar finally conceded in a PBS *Frontline* documentary that he was directly responsible for militarizing intelligence for the Bush administration. In the documentary, broadcast in June 2006, Pillar said that the White Paper was "clearly requested and published for policy advocacy purposes . . . to strengthen the case for going to war with the American public."[51] It is unconscionable for an intelligence analyst to distort intelligence information in order to help a president make a case for going to war. Pillar merely conceded that it wasn't "proper for the intelligence community to publish papers for that purpose."

The CIA intelligence ombudsman, Barry L. Stevenson, told the Senate Intelligence Committee that the administration's "hammering" on Iraq intelligence was harder than anything he had seen in his thirty-two years at the CIA, and a former deputy director of central intelligence, Richard Kerr, remarked in 2003 that there was "significant pressure on the intelligence community to find evidence that supported a connection" between Iraq and al-Qaeda.[52] Kerr headed a group of former senior intelligence officers who prepared three reports on the intelligence community's performance in the run-up to the Iraq War: These carefully concluded that there had been "intense policymaker demands in the run-up to the war, which some in the community believed "constituted inappropriate pressure on intelligence analysts."[53]

In any event, the Bush administration paid little attention to overall intelligence assessments on Iraq and, more importantly, requested no specific intelligence on Iraq other than specious summaries regarding WMD and ties between Iraq and al-Qaeda. Pillar told a Senate committee in June 2006 that he received no requests from any administration policymaker on any aspect of Iraq until more than a year after the war began.[54] This is in stark contrast to the era of the Vietnam War, when there was a healthy debate within the community on Southeast Asia and the White House and National Security Council were well aware of every aspect of the debate, including the controversy between the CIA and the Pentagon over the numbers of Viet Cong fighting in South Vietnam.

The Case for Militarization

The Kerr Group conceded that the analytical community took a "purposely aggressive approach" in conducting exhaustive and repetitive searches for such links. The CIA produced a classified post-mortem on the intelligence failure regarding Iraq's non-existent weapons of mass destruction in 2006, which was declassified six years later in a highly redacted form. The study made no attempt to discuss the politicization of intelligence; instead, it lamely argued that CIA analysts failed to account for "Iraq's extensive history of deception" on its weapons programs.[55] In any event, the CIA produced no study on lessons learned to explore the difficulties of understanding closed societies such as Iraq, which could be applied to similar problems regarding weapons programs in Iran and North Korea.

The CIA and Defense Intelligence Agency thoroughly politicized the intelligence on Iraq prior to the war, but the Bush administration did not decide to go to war on the basis of intelligence. Whenever the United States has pursued a war that was not in self-defense, the decision has been a political one and not one based on intelligence. Even if the CIA had gotten the intelligence picture right; if Robert Walpole had not managed the specious October 2002 National Intelligence Estimate; if Paul Pillar had not drafted the specious unclassified White Paper; if CIA director Tenet and deputy director McLaughlin had not orchestrated the phony speech for Secretary of State Powell to deliver to the UN in February 2003; the Bush administration would have gone to war.[56] Secretary of State Rice provided the most cynical explanation for the war: "The fact is we invaded Iraq because we believed we had run out of other options."[57]

Whenever the intelligence community had it right, it was ignored by the White House. The CIA and Bureau of Intelligence Research told the administration that undersecretary of defense Wolfowitz's dream of a democratic Iraq was a pipe dream and that it would take a "Marshall Plan" to restore the Iraqi economy. The intelligence community dismissed Wolfowitz's view that Iraqi oil revenues, and not the United States, would pay for the restoration of the Iraqi economy. Nor did anyone take seriously the views of the chief of the Agency for International Development, who told faculty members of the National War College that the war would cost less than $2 billion. When the economic adviser in the White House, Larry Lynn, candidly predicted in September 2002—just as the White House was beginning its marketing campaign—that the actual cost of the rehabilitation effort would be over $200 billion, he was forced to resign. The actual price tag exceeded $1 trillion by 2012.

CIA analysts anticipated the serious sectarian fighting that took place in post-war Iraq, a line of analysis that supported the thinking of Army Chief of Staff Eric Shinseki, who predicted that it would take more troops in the post-war situation than during the battle against Saddam. Like Lynn, Shinseki was marginalized and humiliated for his prescience.[58] When Shinseki had his retirement ceremony in 2003, Secretary of Defense Rumsfeld refused to attend, which caused more anger among the Pentagon's general officers than his callous disregard for the inadequate and unprepared force that was sent into Iraq. Rumsfeld's memoir merely includes a parenthetical reference in a footnote to the retirement.

The CIA does not deserve credit for anticipating sectarian strife in Iraq, because anyone familiar with the British experience in Iraq in the 1920s knew that occupation of an Arab country would produce anarchy, not democracy. After WWI, Lawrence of Arabia warned that the British have been led "into a trap from which it will be hard to escape with dignity and honor. . . . Things have been far worse than we have been told, our administration more bloody and inefficient than the public knows. . . . We are today not far from a disaster." The CIA's Middle East analysts anticipated that the war and occupation would further politicize the Islamic community against the United States, would increase support for terrorists within the Islamic community, and would bring Arab extremists into Iraq to fight the infidels. In January 2003, a paper from the National Intelligence Council warned the president that war in Iraq could lead to an anti-U.S. insurgency and "increased popular sympathy for terrorist objectives."

Just as the White House ignored good intelligence on Iraq, the CIA omitted definitive intelligence that was not compatible with the administration's positions on the war. The White House simply created its own intelligence or politicized the community's intelligence to make its case for war. As the Downing Street memorandum concluded in July 2002, "intelligence was being fixed to policy." The CIA ignored some of the best intelligence gathered from Saddam's son-in-law, General

Hussein Kamal, who knew about the destruction of WMD in the 1990s; Foreign Minister Naji Sabri, who corroborated information on the WMD destruction; and a group of Iraqi-Americans who traveled to Iraq prior to the war to collect intelligence and confirmed the end of the Iraqi nuclear program in the late 1990s. The thirty American relatives of Iraqis who were sent to Baghdad in 2002 to elicit information on the nuclear industry returned to the United States and reported that Saddam had abandoned all his WMD programs, but this intelligence never got outside of the CIA building and was never briefed to the White House. The Bush administration even stopped the CIA from recruiting Sabri as a clandestine source.[59]

Despite the documented evidence of the militarization of intelligence from the 9/11 Commission, the Senate and House Intelligence Committees, and the CIA ombudsman, CIA director Tenet continued to defend the intelligence analysis of the CIA, resorting to an unprecedented public campaign to proclaim that the "integrity of our process was maintained throughout and any suggestion to the contrary is simply wrong."[60] Tenet's remarks coincided with President Bush's claim that two trailers found in Iraq were evidence of the mobile biological weapons labs that the CIA introduced to the draft of Secretary of State Powell's UN speech in February 2003. The CIA and the DIA even rushed a joint paper into print, declaring the trucks part of Iraq's biological weapons program, an unprecedented rush to judgment. The DIA eventually disavowed the information; British and Australian intelligence officers resigned over their governments' use of this material. The CIA reluctantly became the last intelligence agency to disavow the legitimacy of its reports; there were no resignations.

The Kerr Group conceded that the analytical community took a "purposely aggressive approach" in conducting exhaustive and repetitive searches for such links. Nevertheless, the

CIA and the newly established director of national intelligence displayed no interest in understanding the analytical failures that took place. No post-mortem and no lessons learned were produced to explore the difficulties of understanding closed societies such as Iraq, which could have been applied to similar problems regarding Iran and North Korea.

The problem of intelligence collection targeting closed societies was hardly a new one. The CIA had limited understanding of the processes and pathologies typical of authoritarian societies in the Soviet Union and China, and there is no indication that the Agency will do better in dealing with perceptions and behaviors of non-state terrorist organizations in the next crisis. This is particularly troublesome because twenty-first-century violence is dominated by the work of thugs dealing in drugs (e.g., Colombia, Afghanistan) or organized crime syndicates (e.g., Congo and the nations of the Caucasus and Central Asia) or fanatics (e.g., Somalia, Nigeria, and the Philippines).

The CIA made numerous errors in analyzing terrorism in the 1980s because it bowed to political pressure to paint the Soviet Union as the chief organizer of all terrorist activities. The CIA made additional mistakes in the 1990s, again because it underestimated the impact of non-state organizations. The lack of analytical growth in this regard had profound consequences for the nexus of intelligence and policy, convincing policymakers that the CIA could not be trusted for premonitory intelligence and creating a rationale for worst-case analysis. Michael Eisenstadt has concluded, "If U.S. intelligence analysts and policymakers fail to understand the assumptions and choices of enemies in past wars, they will almost surely be surprised again by enemies in future wars."[61]

Intelligence Costs of Militarization

The bottom line on the militarization of intelligence was that the Bush administration cherry-picked the intelligence it wanted, whether it was bogus intelligence on Niger's uranium industry or unsubstantiated intelligence on Saddam's links to bin Laden. The infamous National Intelligence Estimate of October 2002 on Iraqi WMD was not requested by the Bush administration, which was aware of the differences within the intelligence community on key aspects of the Iraqi problem, but by the Senate Intelligence Committee. Bush and Cheney had their assumptions about Iraq, and sensitive intelligence information would not change their thinking. In any event, the intelligence community largely steered away from the intelligence that the White House wanted to avoid.

The militarization of the intelligence community created serious problems for U.S. interests in the Middle East and continues to compromise U.S. credibility on wide-ranging issues.

- International cooperation is needed for dealing with WMD, but the distortion of evidence on Iraqi WMD makes it harder to gain cooperation in the war against terror and the campaign to prevent the spread of WMD. Information from foreign intelligence services has been essential in the capture of al-Qaeda terrorists; any success in stopping the strategic weapons programs of Iran and North Korea, both more advanced than those of pre-war Iraq, will require international help.
- Misuse of intelligence by the White House, such as the forged documents on Niger, or politicization of intelligence by the CIA such as the NIE of October 2002, undermines the credibility of intelligence as well as U.S. efforts to forge international cooperation

to prevent further terrorism. The misuse of intelligence during the Vietnam War prolonged a brutal and costly war. The manipulation of intelligence during Iran-Contra in the 1980s led to political embarrassment for the Reagan administration. The misuse of intelligence on the Soviet Union led to unprecedented peacetime increases in defense spending despite the decline and decay of the Soviet Union. Any administration's use of intelligence for political ends is unacceptable, particularly to make a specious case for war.

- Former White House spokesman Ari Fleischer noted during the Iraq war that WMD "is what this war was about and is about. And we have high confidence that it will be found." If so, then the United States lost an opportunity to verify any remnants of WMD in Iraq in the spring of 2003 when the U.S. military occupation made no attempt to investigate possible WMD sites, not even Tuwaitha, where Iraqis previously had stored enriched materials. If the Pentagon believed its own intelligence reporting on Iraqi WMD, then it was pure negligence not to order U.S. forces to make securing WMD an extremely high priority. The disposition of forces in Iraq suggested that the U.S. military commanders did not believe a word of the Pentagon's propaganda on WMD.

- The United States initially faced resistance in getting international support for tough sanctions against Iran's nuclear program because too many governments distrusted information that the U.S. government was providing. The memory of phony U.S. intelligence on Iraq's so-called nuclear program has not been forgotten.

In order for the United States and CIA to regain their credibility, the intelligence ethics of collection and analysis must be revived and revamped. The German intelligence service never had confidence in Curveball's reporting and was stunned by continued American use of his allegations. The al-Qaeda source for the false reporting on Iraqi chemical and biological weapons laboratories was a fabricator, and the Pentagon's DIA gave the intelligence community sufficient warning. Finally, the sole documentary source for Saddam's efforts to purchase "yellowcake" uranium from Niger was known to be a fabrication by the Italian military intelligence service from the beginning. Only British and American officials used the forgery, which suggests they were fooled or, more likely, decided to take advantage of the allegation. The pattern of illicit tradecraft points to a larger problem within the intelligence community that will require more than bureaucratic reorganization or new layers of authority.

President Bush's National Security State

In addition to leaving President Obama with two costly and unwinnable wars, President Bush left his successor with the excesses of a national security state that violate civil rights at home and human rights abroad, a situation that Congress prefers to ignore. Over the past decade, in addition to the outing of Valerie Plame, a violation of the Intelligence Identities Act, there has been solitary confinement for Pvt. Bradley Manning in the WikiLeaks case and the legal harassment of Thomas Drake, a National Security Agency whistleblower. The government's handling of these cases was designed to intimidate and prevent others from coming forward with embarrassing details about government malpractice.

President Bush's creation of the national security state included the most profound bureaucratic expansion of government since the New Deal in the 1930s, including creation of the outrageously named Department of Homeland Security, which failed the nation during Hurricane Katrina in 2005; the Office of the Director of National Intelligence, which added a layer of bureaucracy to an already sclerotic intelligence community; and the National Counter-Terrorism Center, which was responsible in part for the intelligence failure regarding the Nigerian "underwear bomber" in 2009.

At home, the Bush administration expanded domestic intelligence gathering that permitted U.S. law enforcement and intelligence agencies, as well as the Pentagon, to collect, store, and analyze vast quantities of digital data on law-abiding American citizens. The clandestine collection involved no congressional oversight, rare judicial review, and almost no public scrutiny. Since much, if not all, domestic surveillance is conducted secretly, there has been no public debate on the consequences of this activity. Lawsuits that challenge improper eavesdropping are blocked by the Department of Justice's use of "state secrecy" to prevent disclosure of so-called classified information. The Obama administration has resorted to the state secrecy defense even more often than the Bush administration and has made greater use of the Espionage Act than all presidents since its inception in 1917.

The increase in domestic surveillance, often illegal and—in the case of warrantless eavesdropping—unconstitutional, appears irreversible. The FBI has wiretapped conversations between lawyers and defendants, challenging the legal principle that attorney-client communication is inviolate. The NSA is permitted by law to eavesdrop on foreign targets but was once required to get a court-approved warrant to monitor a U.S. citizen's communications over wires traversed in the United States. Warrants for monitoring U.S. citizens are longer required as long as the ultimate target of the surveillance is a foreigner.

Advocates of civil liberty finally achieved a rare victory in

January 2012, when the Supreme Court voted unanimously that police violate the Constitution when they place Global Positioning System (GPS) tracking devices on a suspect's car without a warrant. This decision has been called a "signal event in Fourth Amendment history," and it could bring into question various searches in the digital age that permit law enforcement officials to gather information without entering an individual's home or vehicle.[62] Since 9/11, there has been an explosion of technological surveillance, including video surveillance in public places, automatic toll collection systems on highways, and location data from cell phone towers.

After 9/11, the FBI received the authority to issue National Security Letters without the review or approval of a judge or prosecutor. Indiana University professor Fred H. Cate, who has written extensively on privacy and security, has argued that "we are caught in the middle of a perfect storm in which every thought we communicate, every step we take, every transaction we enter into is captured in digital data and is subject to government collection."[63] In May 2011, Senate Intelligence Committee members Ron Wyden (D-OR) and Mark Udall (D-CO) said that Americans would be disturbed if they knew the facts of the situation, but that they (Wyden and Udall) were prevented by law from discussing them.

National Security Letters are a form of administrative subpoena used to obtain records from third parties, such as hotels, banks, phone companies, Internet providers, and even libraries in order to collect data on unsuspecting citizens. The U.S. government issued nearly 200,000 of these letters between 2003 and 2006, and nearly 25,000 in 2010. Presumably the decline in numbers was due to the complaints of civil rights groups such as the American Civil Liberties Union, Human Rights Watch, and the Center for Constitutional Rights. Once upon a time, when the "government wanted to find out what you read, and what you wrote, it would have to get a warrant and search your home," said Daniel J. Solove, a law professor at George Washington University.[64]

The Justice Department's former inspector general, Glenn Fine, determined in 2007 that the FBI had engaged in "serious misuse" of its authority to issue National Security Letters, claiming urgency in cases where none existed. Meanwhile, FBI agents have acknowledged that this form of data mining has developed useless and often irrelevant information that has interfered with the real work of the FBI. Senator Obama condemned the practice of warrantless eavesdropping and National Security Letters in his presidential campaign in 2008, but President Obama supported legislation that granted retroactive legal immunity to telecommunications companies that had secretly helped the government conduct eavesdropping. The law retroactively legalized other forms of surveillance, including bulk monitoring that allows the government to intercept all email traffic between U.S. citizens and suspect email addresses in countries such as Pakistan. Obama, moreover, has refused to use the Convention Against Torture to investigate those individuals who commit torture or to seek disciplinary action for those Justice Department lawyers (John Yoo and Jay Bybee) who justified the use of torture and abuse at the direction of the White House.

The Cost of American Militarism
Members of the Bush administration often referred to their war plans for Iraq with the term "shock and awe." The same term could be used to describe the Bush administration's defense budgets from 2001 to 2009, when total military spending exceeded the peak spending of the Cold War era, including the Korean War, the Vietnam War, and President Reagan's unprecedented peacetime defense buildup from 1981 to 1986. Defense spending during the Clinton administration had reached a post-

WWII low of 15 percent of the federal spending by 1999. By President Bush's last year in office, defense spending was more than 20 percent of the federal budget and the largest part of the budget's discretionary spending. The combination of a doubling of the defense budget and the major tax decreases had much to do with climbing U.S. debts and deficits, which doubled during the Bush era. For the first time since WWII, U.S. debt is rivaling U.S. gross domestic production.

Increased defense spending, particularly unnecessary over the past three decades, contributed to increased deficits. During the stewardship of President Jimmy Carter, the federal budget deficit remained under $55 billion annually. President Reagan pursued tax deductions while doubling federal spending, creating huge increases in the federal deficit. Increases in defense spending, during a period of Soviet decline, were a major part of the budgetary expansion. President Reagan emphasized that "defense is not a budget item," thus justifying these huge increases. President George W. Bush went one step further than President Reagan; he reduced taxes and fought two (unsuccessful) wars that already have cost the United States more than $1.5 trillion.

Key members of the Bush administration were committed to increasing the defense budget long before the 9/11 attacks, although they had different rationales. Even before 9/11, the Bush administration was seeking a rationale for expanding defense spending. Bush and Rumsfeld began to argue on Capitol Hill that shipbuilding was underfunded, that military aircraft were aging, and that pay was not competitive. The charges concerning U.S. naval ships and fighter aircraft were particularly ludicrous in view of the strategic edge of the United States over air and naval power the world over.

President Bush wanted greater defense spending, knowing that it would require reduced domestic spending; Vice President Cheney wanted a more powerful military (and even war), knowing that it would create a more powerful presidency; and Secretary of Defense Rumsfeld wanted to militarize a new arena, outer space. When Cheney served as secretary of defense in Bush I's cabinet, he was responsible for the largest weapons system cancellation in the Pentagon's history, the A-12 carrier-based stealth bomber. After serving as CEO of Halliburton in the 1990s, he returned to Washington as vice president in 2001 in no mood to argue against Cold War weapons platforms. Only Secretary of State Powell was skeptical of Bush's goals; however, it was more important to him to be part of the Bush administration than it was to fight for important issues.

Just as the North Korean invasion of the South in 1950 enabled the Truman administration to expand the defense budget, the 9/11 attacks opened the door to greater defense spending and militarization of the government. The Bush administration endorsed such big-ticket items as national missile defense (NMD) and the F-22 fighter aircraft, reversing the Clinton administration's efforts to limit these weapons systems. Republicans were totally supportive of President Bush's war aims and defense spending, and Democrats were too intimidated by the impact of 9/11 to offer any effective resistance. Several days after 9/11, the Democrats dropped their opposition to funding for NMD as well their efforts to stop missile testing that would violate the Anti-Ballistic Missile Treaty.[65] President Bush added to the budgetary problems by pushing a major tax reduction through Congress while making sure that war appropriations would be handled as emergency supplemental appropriations that were separate from the overall defense budget.

President Bush became the first U.S. president to expand defense spending, go to war, and provide tax relief for all Americans. The Bush administration started with a defense budget increase of $30 billion, which represented a 10 percent increase in defense spending, the greatest annual increase in defense spending since the Reagan administration. Although President Bush proclaimed that his "administration was going to have to winnow [military spending priorities] down" because "we cannot afford every weapons system," he introduced major spending initiatives and found that the Congress was willing to increase, and not challenge, the appropriations on defense items as well as provide earmarks for nearly $4 billion in additional defense spending.

The pressures of defense spending contributed to the re-ordering of the national security community and the entire foreign policy process. When Secretary of State Powell initially demurred over the use of force against Iraq, he was marginalized, then co-opted by Cheney to make a totally spurious speech on the case for war to the Security Council of the United Nations in order to influence international opinion. When the CIA moved too slowly in providing intelligence to take to the American people, Bush and Cheney increased the pressure on the intelligence community until CIA director Tenet agreed that it would be a "slam dunk" to provide information to influence domestic opinion. When the CIA was too slow in following up, Cheney and Rumsfeld conspired to create an illegal intelligence organization in the Pentagon to deliver so-called intelligence to the White House and the U.S. media.

Agencies that appeared to get in the way of the march to war, such as the Department of State, were marginalized and ultimately ignored. Agencies that appeared to move too slowly, such as the CIA, were privately vilified and publicly humiliated. White House browbeating was instrumental in getting the Agency to sign off on spurious information in President Bush's State of the Union message in January 2003; to produce a totally politicized national intelligence estimate in October 2002; and to produce an illegal White Paper on Iraqi WMD, which was the unclassified version of the NIE. All of the CIA officials involved in this dubious activity received promotions and career advancements, with CIA director Tenet garnering the government's highest award for a civilian, the Presidential Medal of Freedom. Nevertheless, the CIA ultimately lost a great deal of bureaucratic clout with the creation of the post of Director of National Intelligence, which took over the duties of the CIA director as the leader of the intelligence community.

President Bush's Defense Budget

The policies of President Bush, particularly the wars in Iraq and Afghanistan, put the lie to Bush's campaign promises in 2000 to pursue a more moderate and less arrogant foreign policy that would not involve the use of force or nation-building. The Bush administration used the immoral war against Iraq to justify unnecessary increases in the military budget, with military spending by the end of the Bush era (nearly $700 billion annually) exceeding the peak spending of the Cold War era.[66] By the end of Bush's second term in office, military spending was growing at a rate of 7 percent a year. The 9/11 attacks were probably responsible for some of the developments discussed above, but not for the huge investment in nation-building. Condi Rice exposed the lie on the invasion of Iraq: "We did not go to Iraq to bring democracy any more than Roosevelt went to war against Hitler to democratize Germany, though that became American policy once the Nazis were defeated."[67]

The strategy of preemptive or preventive attack was used to justify the military buildup as well as the doubling of the intelligence budget. The reliance on unilateral use of force also created the need for greater defense and intelligence budgets, and the president's warning against the "axis of evil" in 2002 promised more aggressive policy toward Iran, Iraq, and North Korea, eventually leading to war against Iraq and a political impasse with Iran and North Korea.

President Bush walked away from the constraints of international diplomacy and coalition strategy, which would have provided opportunities to bring defense spending under control. He demonstrated no interest in joining the International Criminal Court, the ban on landmines, or the Comprehensive Test Ban Treaty. Under the stewardship of President Bush, verification was no longer a part of arms control and disarmament. He abrogated the ABM Treaty of 1972, the cornerstone to deterrence and arms control. The Pentagon was encouraged to revise strategy in order to allow the use of nuclear weapons against non-nuclear states, thus reversing a bipartisan tenet of U.S. foreign policy. His administration sent thousands of U.S. soldiers to their death to wage a war without evidence of a threat, but managed to oppose genuine scientific evidence and, as a result, ridiculed the Kyoto accord on climate change.

The Opportunity to Reform

Ironically, Secretary of Defense Rumsfeld, who will go down in history as one of our most unpopular secretaries, had more ideas about reforming the Pentagon than most of his predecessors. He understood that he would have to challenge the "iron triangle"—the network of entrenched relationships between the military and civilian bureaucracies in the Defense Department, Congress, and the defense industry. These institutions were permanent members of the establishment, but secretaries were mere political appointees who would come and go. In his first term as defense secretary in the 1970s, Rumsfeld achieved a higher level of standardization of military equipment among the NATO allies and improved logistical efficiency; there were substantial cost savings in these steps. He won a major battle with the iron triangle in 1976, when he favored Chrysler's M-1 Abrams tank over the Army's favorite candidate, which was designed by General Motors. The M-1 was used in combat for the first time fifteen years later, when it performed on a high level in Iraq and Kuwait.

In his next term as defense secretary twenty-five years later, Rumsfeld favored a much smaller military, including the possible cuts of two Army divisions and two naval aircraft carrier battle groups. He identified one major weapons system in each service for cancellation, including the Army's Crusader mobile artillery system; the Marines' V-22 Osprey tilt-rotor aircraft; the Air Force's F-22 Raptor fighter aircraft; and the Navy's new DD-21 destroyer. The Crusader was, in fact, two different vehicles; one was a tracked, automatic-loading 155mm howitzer and the other a tracked ammunition carrier that trailed behind. Together, they weighed more than seventy tons, which made them too heavy to be transported on the C-130 and virtually useless in developing nations where U.S. forces have been fighting in the past decade. Moreover, the idea of going into battle with a "Crusader" tank in such Islamic areas as Iraq and Pakistan would have created a propaganda opportunity for Islamists everywhere. Nevertheless, Rumsfeld's ideas for a smaller military force created a storm of criticism within the Pentagon and on Capitol Hill, and there were calls for his resignation long before the failure of force in Iraq.

Rumsfeld's job was saved temporarily by 9/11 and the Iraq and Afghan Wars, but his strategic decisions on the two wars created more problems for the secretary of defense. In Iraq, he was prepared to invade with a small force merely to prove his point about the new mobile, highly sophisticated Army and Marine Corps. His Joint Chiefs of Staff talked him out of that idea, but even the force of 150,000 was inadequate to contain the breakdown of law and order following the U.S. invasion. In Afghanistan, the real credit for the success of the initial operation in 2001 belonged to the CIA, which had operational plans for confronting the Taliban government and al-Qaeda as well as logistical ties to the Northern Alliance, the Tajik organization that opposed the Taliban.

The CIA's success surprised and embarrassed Rumsfeld, who offered no conceptual or operational approaches for dealing with Afghanistan. Even when CIA and Army special forces had bin Laden trapped in the Tora Bora mountains, Secretary Rumsfeld was against sending reinforcements that could have captured or killed the al-Qaeda leader a decade before his eventual assassination. What at the time seemed to be initial tactical successes in Iraq and Afghanistan quickly deteriorated into strategic nightmares, however, leaving U.S. forces in a geopolitical cul-de-sac in the Middle East and Southwest Asia, the new arc of crisis. By the time Rumsfeld was forced to resign, he was even more unpopular than he had been before 9/11.

Eventually, President Bush realized he had been ill served by his vice president and his secretary of defense on important matters of national security. He replaced Rumsfeld with a loyal servant to the Bush family, Robert M. Gates, who quickly abandoned his support for troop withdrawal as a member of the Iraq Study Group in order to support the surge of forces in Iraq as a new member of the Bush administration. Bush couldn't replace Cheney, which would have been politically embarrassing, but he stopped taking his advice on matters involving use of force against Iran, Syria, and North Korea. But the damage had been done to U.S. foreign policy and to the national security bureaucracy. In the hands of Condi Rice, the State Department sank to a new low in prestige and influence. The Defense Department in the hands of Bob Gates became more self-aggrandizing in its accumulation of power and influence. When Obama, unwilling to roil the waters, took the unusual and unprecedented step of retaining his predecessor's secretary of defense, it appeared that the country would not soon disentangle itself from a decade of irresponsible governance.

As a result, an arc of instability now dominates U.S. national security policy: a difficult post-war situation in Iraq and an unwinnable war in Afghanistan; the use of force in Pakistan, Somalia, and Yemen; and special operations throughout North Africa, the Middle East, and Southwest Asia. The management of the arc was central to the conduct of the Bush administration for eight years; disengagement from the arc will be the central task of President Obama and his immediate successors.

FIVE

PRESIDENT OBAMA'S DEFERENCE
TO THE MILITARY

God help this country when someone sits in this chair who doesn't know the military as well as I do. —President Dwight D. Eisenhower

No one starts a war, or rather, no one in his senses ought to do so, without first being clear in his mind what he intends to achieve by that war and how he intends to conduct it. —Prussian military strategist Carl von Clausewitz

At the Democratic convention in the summer of 2008, former president Clinton exhorted the people of the United States to rely more on the power of influence than on the influence of power. In his inauguration address, President Obama also called for an end to reliance on military power. After campaigning on the basis of change and the audacity of hope, however, both Clinton and Obama seemed unwilling to challenge the Pentagon's influence.

President Obama would not be the first president to contribute or accede to the militarization of U.S. national security. Over the past three decades, all of our presidents have done so to some degree. President Reagan was responsible for unprecedented peacetime increases in defense spending even though the Soviet Union was in decline. He endorsed the Goldwater-

Nichols Act in 1986 that enhanced the political role of the regional commanders-in-chief and marginalized the State Department and the civilian leadership of the Department of Defense. President George H.W. Bush's deployment of 26,000 troops (Operation Just Cause) to Panama only one month after the collapse of the Berlin Wall demonstrated his commitment to the use of force. President Clinton further weakened the State Department by abolishing the Arms Control and Disarmament Agency and the United States Information Service and substantially reducing funding for the Agency for International Development. He became the first president in three decades to submit to the Pentagon on arms control, failing to challenge the military's opposition to the Comprehensive Test Ban Treaty.

President George W. Bush initially turned over the leadership of national security policy to Vice President Cheney and the Pentagon. The war on terror became permanent war, leading to a decade of civil rights abuses, just as President Eisenhower warned. We have seen warrantless eavesdropping, the abrogation of habeas corpus, torture and abuse, and an atmosphere of fear and anxiety, which all combine to make us less secure. With a justice system that defers to the national security state; a compliant, all but dysfunctional, Congress; and corporate media that have long abandoned their watchdog role, there has been little opposition to the illegal excesses of the national security state. In the wake of 9/11, U.S. presidents have brandished their belief in the necessity of U.S. global hegemony and have proved unwilling to challenge the power of the Pentagon. The United States goes to war without congressional approval and, lacking a draft, with less than 1 percent of Americans over the age of 18 who serve in the active-duty military. As a result, the United States has become increasingly alienated from its own constituency as well as the international community.

President Obama's National Security Team

Like President Clinton, President Obama failed to appoint a strong or cohesive national security team that shared a belief in the president's original message. His team was extremely weak; its members were virtually unknown to each other and, with the exception of Secretary of State Hillary Clinton, unknown to the president. President Obama's hopeful inaugural speech in 2009 suggested an understanding of the need to revamp U.S. national security policy. He rejected the "false choice between our safety and our ideals," which was a denunciation of the Bush administration's subversion of the Constitution in the wake of 9/11. His emphasis on earlier generations who "understood that our power alone cannot protect us, nor does it entitle us to do as we please," appeared to be a rejection of Bush's "long war" against terror, which has created more enemies than friends. In stressing that "the world has changed, and we must change with it," Obama sounded the clarion call for new policies.

Obama's national security team had little experience in foreign policy decision-making and strategic thinking, and hardly shared the president's message on national security. His leading policy adviser (General James Jones) and his leading intelligence advisers (Admiral Dennis Blair and Leon Panetta) were not known for national security expertise; his secretary of state (Hillary Clinton) was chosen for domestic political reasons (to keep Bill and Hillary inside the Obama tent) and had little familiarity with difficult foreign policy matters; and his secretary of defense (Robert Gates) was also chosen for domestic political reasons (to appease the Pentagon as well as conservatives in both parties).

The turbulence that engulfed the team was not surprising. National security adviser Jones and intelligence tsar Blair were the first to go, but Jones was replaced by a domestic political specialist (Tom Donilon), and Blair was replaced by another general officer (Lt. Gen. James Clapper), who had a strong technical background but little experience with strategic intelligence. CIA director Panetta replaced Gates at the Pentagon in the summer of 2011, an appointment that promised business as usual. General David Petraeus replaced Panetta at the CIA, indicating further militarization of the intelligence community. Within the national security team, only Secretary of State Clinton will have served the complete first term, and she will be leaving as soon as a new secretary of state is confirmed.

President Obama's most curious choice was his retention of Bob Gates as secretary of defense, making him the first defense secretary to serve both Democratic and Republican presidents. Gates, a veteran of the Cold War, had served conservative masters of policy such as CIA director William Casey and General Brent Scowcroft. His initial speeches made it clear that he did not share the president's conciliatory instincts.

Replacing Donald Rumsfeld in 2006, Gates had easy shoes to fill. His predecessor had become unpopular in the Pentagon, on Capitol Hill, and even in the White House. Rumsfeld was particularly uncivil in dealings with subordinates. As a result, the confirmation process for Gates was not a grilling; rather, it was a love fest. He was not questioned about his politicization of intelligence at the CIA in the 1980s; his knowledge of Iran-Contra, which had been documented in the independent counsel's investigation and forced him to withdraw his nomination as CIA director in 1987; or his lack of experience on vital matters such as weapons acquisition and the need for military reform. Members of the Senate Armed Forces Committee treated Gates as the "morning-after" pill that would abort Rumsfeld. They had forgotten that Gates was also a Cold War ideologue who had suppressed intelligence in order to advocate his own hardline agenda.

Gates brought his hardline views into the Obama presidency. He gave a provocative speech at the National Defense

University in 2009 that revealed his Cold War thinking. With language reminiscent of the worst days of the Cold War, Gates argued that the "demilitarization of Europe—where large swaths of the general public and political class are averse to military force and the risks that go with it—has gone from a blessing in the twentieth century to an impediment to achieving real security and lasting peace in the twenty-first century." He concluded that a perception of European weakness could provide a "temptation to miscalculation and aggression" by hostile powers. Gates didn't name these so-called hostile powers; by this time, there were none.

Gates's speech was a harbinger of a three-year campaign to turn NATO into an instrument for power projection abroad and to malign the European members of NATO for their failure to support U.S. national security goals in Iraq and Afghanistan. On his farewell tour in 2011, he used his last NATO meeting in Brussels to strongly criticize NATO members for "shortages" in military spending and for what he termed a "dim if not dismal future" unless member states increased their military participation in NATO activities.[1] Gates's bitter language was a self-fulfilling prophecy, contributing to discontinuity within NATO, which no longer has a common perception of threat to maintain its cohesion. Gates failed to take into consideration the serious domestic tensions in many European capitals over the deployment of force in Afghanistan; on the eve of his speech, the coalition government in the Netherlands collapsed over the issue of keeping Dutch troops there.

What Gates (and Obama) failed to acknowledge is the reality that Europeans increasingly do not share the domestic or foreign policy goals of the United States. On domestic issues, Europeans cannot understand why the United States continues to expand its economic support for corporations while continuing to shrink or dismantle its services and support for its citizens; does not adopt comprehensive national health insurance; refuses to acknowledge and act on global climate change; fails to regulate the purchase of lethal weapons; accepts the deterioration of its cities; and appears intimidated by religious fundamentalists who limit political choice, civil liberties, and public education. Most European politicians could not be elected if they took the positions that many Americans take on gun control, capital punishment, and global climate change. On foreign policy issues, most Europeans oppose U.S. support for NATO expansion; the installation of missile launch sites; unconditional support for Israel; use of force in areas where no national, let alone vital, interests are at stake; the urgency of Afghanistan, and humongous budgets for the military and national security. U.S. policies involving torture and abuse, extraordinary renditions, and secret prisons were particularly reprehensible to the European public, although some of their governments participated in U.S. rendition policy. The U.S. agreement with Poland for permanent basing rights for U.S. fighter aircraft also was shocking to most Europeans, who disapprove of the gratuitous U.S. challenge to Russia.

In a closed-door session with European defense ministers in June 2011, Gates broke with diplomatic protocol and criticized Germany and Poland for failing to join the Libyan campaign as well as the Netherlands, Spain, and Turkey for refusing to take part in the aerial assault against Libya. He even attacked Britain, Washington's closest ally in Europe, for its defense cuts. The criticisms demonstrated the ignorance of U.S. policymakers, particularly Gates, with respect to the political and economic realities of Europe that have led to smaller allocations for defense. According to the *Financial Times*, only Spain responded directly to Gates's criticism, noting that, as a democracy, it was flying all the missions it could under its current parliamentary mandate.[2]

White House officials tried to distance themselves from Gates's speech, claiming that he had not received White House clearance for his disparaging remarks. But the damage had been done. Secretary of State Clinton never publicly objected to Gates's rhetoric even though it complicated her own diplomatic efforts in Europe. Even the conservative military analyst Max Boot, a senior fellow at the Council on Foreign Relations, stated that he wasn't sure "what point is served by jawboning the Europeans on defense spending" at this time.[3]

Secretary Gates's decision to retire and return to his home in the State of Washington forced President Obama to make changes in his national security team that he probably preferred to avoid. Obama was no longer following Gates's advice on Afghanistan, the raid against Osama bin Laden, and the handling of the insubordination of General Stanley McChrystal, and objected to Gates's heel-dragging on ending "don't ask, don't tell," but the cautious president, feeling politically hamstrung, did not want a confirmation struggle in the Senate. Therefore, he made three appointments that were certain to get unanimous approval: Panetta as secretary of defense; Petraeus as director of the CIA; and Ryan Crocker as ambassador to Afghanistan. All were approved in June and July 2011 with no negative votes. Unlike the others, Crocker had excellent credentials for his position and was privately pessimistic of success in Afghanistan. He has never believed that U.S. forces can build a civilian government in Afghanistan and mediate between the government and the Afghan people, objectives that are central to the Petraeus-McChrystal counterinsurgency strategy.

Petraeus was a particularly perplexing choice for CIA director. As commander of U.S. and NATO forces, General Petraeus had strong policy views on Iraq and Afghanistan and no strategic intelligence experience. Giving this sensitive position to Petraeus (and further militarizing the intelligence community) should have elicited more criticism. He should have received serious scrutiny from the Senate Intelligence Committee (and the news media) during confirmation hearings in June 2011, but the sessions were a love-fest with no attention paid to his lack of a background in intelligence; his strong policy views; and his potential problems dealing with dissent, a challenge for any general officer. Petraeus faces the same issues he faced as a four-star general (e.g., wars in Iraq and Afghanistan; terrorist challenges from within Pakistan, Yemen, and Somalia; the Arab Spring; and the Taliban insurgency), and he almost certainly shares the worst-case approach that military careerists typically favor. This could well compromise the intelligence picture. One of the reasons for creating the CIA was to neutralize the worst-case thinking of the military.

At the CIA, Petraeus faces a less deferential culture than he dealt with in the military. CIA officers have been traditionally skeptical toward the views of the military and the conclusions of military intelligence, and have challenged the views of their directors, such as Richard Helms (Vietnam) and William Casey (the Soviet threat and terrorism). These challenges have not always succeeded, but they forced directors to expend limited political equity or appoint surrogates to mount the battle. Intelligence careerists such as George Carver, Bob Gates, and John McLaughlin were most willing to help politicize intelligence on behalf of CIA directors Helms, Casey, and Tenet, respectively. Former general and CIA director Michael V. Hayden, discussing the Petraeus appointment, said that there are some CIA officers who "don't do the hierarchy thing very well at all. That'll be a bit of an adjustment."[4]

Nevertheless, the appointment of Petraeus was one more step in the blurring of the line that previously existed between the military and the intelligence community, including the merging of military special operations and CIA covert operations.

General Petraeus is responsible for a secret "Execute Order" in September 2009 that authorized American Special Operations troops to carry out reconnaissance missions and create intelligence networks throughout the Middle East and Central Asia in order to "penetrate, disrupt, defeat and destroy" militant groups and "prepare the environment" for future U.S. military actions. The order greatly expanded the role of the military in clandestine activities; these missions have received no scrutiny from congressional intelligence committees responsible for oversight of covert operations.

In moving to the Pentagon, Panetta had a tough act to follow. He had to step into the shoes of the most influential member of the Obama administration, Bob Gates, who has been canonized for his performance over the past five years. Gates, moreover, spent the last two months of his stewardship as secretary of defense on a farewell tour of U.S. think tanks, universities, and military academics, advocating policies that make Panetta's job extremely difficult. He took hardline positions against a full withdrawal from Iraq; against beginning the withdrawal from Afghanistan; against significantly reducing the defense budget; and against reforming the Pentagon's weapons acquisition process. In his last weeks, he traveled to Baghdad and Kabul, where he contradicted President Obama's positions on Iraq and Afghanistan.

Panetta has inherited procurement policies and military missions that the United States can no longer afford, but, even before he settled into his spacious office in the Pentagon, he had labeled further cuts in the defense budget "disastrous" and "unacceptable." As the former director of the Office of Management and Budget, Panetta presumably understands that the United States, with less than 25 percent of the world's economic output and more than 50 percent of the world's military expenditures, will have to curtail certain weapons and missions. The defense budget has grown over 50 percent in the past ten years and now exceeds the pace of spending during the Cold War era as well as the peacetime buildup of President Reagan. So much for those pundits who believed that Panetta's experience at the Office of Management and Budget would enable him to take on the Pentagon's sacred cows.[5]

Panetta's first task was to find a new deputy defense secretary. Only one week after Panetta took over the Pentagon, William J. Lynn III resigned, leaving behind the difficult task of finding at least $485 billion in defense cuts over the next twelve years. Lynn's departure meant that, in Obama's mid-term, he had to deal with three new faces in the Department of Defense: the secretary of defense, the deputy defense secretary, and the chairman of the Joint Chiefs, Army General Martin Dempsey. Lynn's departure was particularly noteworthy because his specialty was the defense budget, where he had a wealth of experience. Informed observers of the Pentagon noted, however, that Lynn never had a real relationship with Secretary of Defense Gates, who had left sensitive defense initiatives to his chief of staff, Robert Rangel. According to Loren B. Thompson, the chief operating officer of the Lexington Institute, a Washington-based think tank, "Lynn got cut out of a lot of the action."[6]

Lynn should not have been surprised, since Gates had never been surrounded by strong subordinates. His deputy at CIA, Dick Kerr, had been a journeyman naval analyst. When President Obama tried to make Richard Danzig, an experienced military analyst with definite ideas about reform, the deputy defense secretary, Gates vetoed the choice. Gates didn't want a senior expert who had closer relations with the president than Gates himself.

It is likely that Gates favored Panetta as his successor, hoping to maintain the firewall against military reform. Panetta will have to address the weapons acquisition process that Gates ignored for the past five years, however, and he will have to determine the fate of increasingly expensive (and some dubious) weapons systems such as the F-35 Joint Strike Fighter, a new class of ballistic missile submarine, and a new fleet of aerial refueling tankers for the Air Force. One of Panetta's first decisions did not augur well, continuing production of the expensive Marine variant of the F-35, which had been on a virtual probation status because of cost and risk.

The acquisition process has been beset with military mismanagement, huge cost overruns, and little congressional scrutiny. Gates, who falsely labeled himself a cost-cutter, left the Pentagon with more defense acquisition programs at a greater cost than those existing at the time he became Obama's secretary of defense. He called these systems "absolutely critical" to the nation's defense, although these are weapons that no longer reflect a balance between cost effectiveness and national security.

Gates also left Panetta with the task of shaping deployment plans. A reexamination of current troop deployments must include the tens of thousands of U.S. troops stationed in Europe and Asia more than six decades after the end of World War II; hundreds of bases and facilities the world over; and excessive capabilities for projecting power in Iraq, Afghanistan, and Libya. The United States needs to abandon the chimera of national missile defense systems at home and in Eastern Europe. There should also be a serious examination of the campaign to build up forces in Asia against China, now including amphibious training for U.S. Marines in Australia.

Panetta has the background, but not necessarily the inclination, to take on the Pentagon, Congress, and the defense-industrial complex with which he has close ties. He served in the House of Representatives, where he led the House Budget Committee; the Office of Management and Budget; and in President Clinton's administration as its first budget director.

He was praised for bringing order to the unruly Clinton White House and, as CIA director, kept the Agency out of the news, which any president would appreciate. Panetta has bipartisan credentials. He entered the House originally as a Republican, but switched parties after President Nixon removed him from the White House's Office of Civil Rights because he was enforcing discrimination laws too enthusiastically. Panetta is the oldest man to be named secretary of defense in U.S. history, however, and may lack the stamina for this demanding position. He flies home to the family walnut farm in California on most weekends, and he is perceived as an avuncular figure who brought his dog to CIA headquarters on a daily basis and does the same at the Pentagon. Panetta was referred to privately as "Uncle Leon" at the CIA; the uniformed military presumably will find its own dismissive nickname.

Unlike Gates, Panetta is approachable and jocular, which may help him on the Hill but will not necessarily do the same in the Pentagon. Those who know him best, such as American University professor Gordon Adams, credit him with knowing "how to hang tough . . . when to concede . . . and when to close a deal." All of these attributes will be important in dealing with the $485 billion in defense cuts demanded by President Obama by 2023. Since senior military officers are known for resorting to back channels to take their case to Congress, Panetta's experience on the Hill should put him in a position to anticipate and block such efforts.

By the end of his first term, Obama's closest advisers, the ones who sat in on the sensitive briefing sessions at the start of the day, still had limited experience in conceptualizing and implementing foreign policy. Vice President Biden, former chairman of the Senate Foreign Relations Committee, and national security adviser Donilon, a congressional staffer for domestic affairs, had never distinguished themselves in the field of foreign policy. Deputy national security adviser Brennan was an intelligence professional who lacked policy experience.

President Obama's Briar Patch

Alexander the Great couldn't do it; Queen Victoria couldn't do it; four successive Soviet general-secretaries from 1979 to 1985 couldn't do it. But President Obama initially believed he could stabilize Afghanistan. Unfortunately, he is likely to join his illustrious predecessors in failing to build a nation commonly referred to as the "graveyard of empires." He also has taken on the Sisyphean challenges of strengthening Pakistan's frail democracy, forging economic and military cooperation between Afghanistan and Pakistan, and stabilizing relations between India and Pakistan. Afghanistan has become Obama's war; Southwest Asia could become his briar patch.

President Obama should have followed the lead of Soviet President Gorbachev, who recognized immediately that fighting a war in Afghanistan was a fool's errand. In March 1985, President Gorbachev acceded to power; within several weeks he had repudiated his predecessors, giving a secret speech to the Politburo that referred to Afghanistan as Moscow's "bleeding wound." In 1987, Foreign Minister Shevardnadze privately told Secretary of State Shultz of Soviet plans to withdraw. In 1988, Gorbachev announced the timetable for withdrawal, and in 1989 all Soviet forces were gone. Gorbachev wanted U.S. support for a coalition government in Kabul, but the United States refused to cooperate, setting the stage for the Taliban triumph in 1996.

Rather than emulate Gorbachev, Obama approved a compromise plan that combined the advice of Vice President Biden, General David Petraeus, and Ambassador Richard Holbrooke. Petraeus, who has been given too much credit for the questionable success of his counterinsurgency doctrine and the surge in

Iraq, favored a long-term commitment in Afghanistan to protect the population and wage a campaign to win hearts and minds. Holbrooke, who cut his teeth on a failed Vietnam policy in the 1960s as a junior Foreign Service Officer, wanted to widen assistance programs to governments in Afghanistan and Pakistan, despite their corruption and incompetence. Only Biden understood that our primary objective in Afghanistan was to insure that al-Qaeda did not regain its sanctuary in Afghanistan, and this objective did not require a large military presence.

President Obama made two major, albeit contradictory, course changes in Afghanistan, adding 33,000 U.S. troops in December 2009 and announcing that the United States would begin to withdraw these forces in 2011. Ten thousand U.S. troops were withdrawn by the end of 2011, and the remaining 23,000 troops were scheduled for withdrawal in 2012. By 2014, the president implied that there would no longer be any need for U.S. combat forces, and said that the "Afghan people will be responsible for their own security." He dramatically returned to the language and substance of his Inaugural Address in January 2009, when he said that it was "time to focus on nation-building here at home" and that "what sets America apart is not solely our power—it is the principles upon which our union was founded." Upon learning of the U.S. decision to deploy and then begin the withdrawal of its forces, Afghan President Hamid Karzai querulously muttered, "Good riddance," which—as Jim Hightower reported—put the "dumb in dumbfounding."[7]

In making the decision to withdraw, President Obama finally demonstrated a willingness to stand up to his military leaders, rejecting advice from Secretary of Defense Gates, commander of U.S. and NATO forces General David Petraeus, chairman of the Joint Chiefs Admiral Mike Mullen, and the new commander of U.S. and NATO forces in Afghanistan, Marine General John Allen. These senior officials continued to oppose any significant withdrawal of U.S. forces before 2014. All recommended a gradual withdrawal from Afghanistan and believed that the president's plan was more aggressive than they considered prudent. General Allen indicated that winding down the war would require great progress on a wide front, including more help from allies, and that there would be a residual force of 10,000 to 30,000 troops even after 2014. U.S. Ambassador Ryan Crocker also asserted in January 2012 that the year 2014 is not a hard deadline for U.S. withdrawal.

Gates and his senior military commanders failed to appreciate Afghanistan as the lethal trap that it has always been, nor did they comprehend the difficulty of the geography and tribal culture of Afghanistan. Nevertheless, there have been general officers who have argued against the surge and who favor the withdrawal on the president's timetable. This group included vice chairman of the Joint Chiefs General James Cartwright; a former ambassador to Afghanistan, retired general Karl Eikenberry; and the current tsar for Afghanistan, General Douglas Lute. When President Obama tried to name Cartwright as the successor to Admiral Mullen as chairman of the Joint Chiefs in 2011, Secretary of Defense Gates and senior military officers resisted the selection because of Cartwright's support for withdrawal from Afghanistan.

Although the Obama administration professed to favor a policy debate on the proper level of U.S. forces in Afghanistan, the White House never requested a National Intelligence Estimate to inform such a debate. An estimate would have exposed the arguments against successful military involvement, and provided President Obama with the kind of intelligence cover he needed in order to deal with the Pentagon, the press, and the public. The administration may have feared those examples of intelligence estimates in the 1960s and 1970s that failed to support officials in the White House and the Pentagon who wanted to increase the U.S. military presence in Vietnam. The Pentagon Papers on Vietnam, which were finally declassified in 2011—forty years after their compilation—were replete with intelligence estimates that exposed Vietnam as unwinnable. The White House would have benefited from an intelligence estimate on Afghanistan in 2010–2011 that did the same.

President Obama's decision in 2009 to escalate the use of military force was based on a series of myths and false assumptions, not the web of lies spun to justify the Iraq War in 2003. These myths have dominated the debate on U.S. policy. Obama tried both counterterrorism and counterinsurgency in Afghanistan, beginning with counterterrorism in his first few months in office, then promoting counterinsurgency with a surge of troops, contractors, clandestine operators, infrastructure construction, and so-called coalition members to defeat the fundamentalists that U.S. policy toward Afghanistan had helped create in the 1980s. The acceptance of six major myths led to the so-called surge. Vice President Biden challenged these myths, but it appears that President Obama initially believed them.

Myth #1: The Pentagon endorsed a counterinsurgency strategy that viewed the Taliban as a collection of armed groups with different political and economic objectives. The Pentagon believed an additional 40,000 U.S. troops would make it easier to divide the Taliban and wean a significant number of fighters away from the insurgency. In fact, it was the international coalition that lacked clear direction and it was the Taliban that had the strategic initiative. The Taliban had demonstrated an increasingly coordinated and centralized approach in their tactics and operations over the past several years, and there is ample evidence that the Afghan population recognizes this fact and has provided significant support to the insurgency. The U.S. offensive in Helmand in the summer of 2011, which involved nearly 20,000 troops, failed to weaken the Taliban on the southern front; the British offensive there in 2008 also failed. The belief that a significant number of Taliban forces can be brought to our side has proved dead wrong. But this type of wishful thinking was central to the counterinsurgency strategy. The Taliban may not be monolithic, but they have maintained control of their forces.

In any event, the Taliban has had a sanctuary in Pakistan, and no counterinsurgency has ever been successful against an insurgency with safe haven. Without the ability to cut the insurgents' supply lines, their recruitment efforts, and their fundraising, which the United States has never achieved, there was little likelihood of success.

Myth #2: A Taliban presence would lead to a renewed sanctuary for al-Qaeda, and once again the United States would be vulnerable to a terrorist attack. There are very few al-Qaeda elements in Afghanistan, and both the Bush and Obama administrations have been successful in using Predator strikes against al-Qaeda leadership in Pakistan, Somalia, and Yemen. In the past year, U.S. and Pakistani intelligence agencies have enabled the Predator to eliminate al-Qaeda leaders and restrict al-Qaeda's ability to operate; they also have eliminated some of its financial support. More importantly, al-Qaeda's leadership does not need a sanctuary or safe haven in Afghanistan to plan its operations. The training and preparations for the 9/11 attacks took place in U.S flight schools and in European apartments. Paul Pillar, the former deputy chief of the CIA's counterterrorist center, has argued that bin Laden's role was "less one of commander than of ideological lodestar, and for that role a haven is almost meaningless." In May 2011, with the killing of bin Laden in Pakistan, al-Qaeda lost its lodestar.

Myth #3: Military defeat in Afghanistan would have a domino effect in the region that would affect Pakistan, India, and Iran, with the United States and NATO suffering a significant loss of credibility. The domino effect and the credibility argument represent old saws from the Vietnam era that were discredited thirty-five years ago and should be dismissed today. Internal political machinations in Afghanistan, even the restoration of a Taliban government in Kabul, would not have significant implications outside the country, and there is no indication that the Taliban has aspirations beyond Afghan borders. The international community has a good understanding of U.S. military capabilities; a reduced U.S. military footprint would not lessen the international perception of U.S. power.

Myth #4: As part of its counterinsurgency strategy, the United States must invest billions of dollars to create more capable, accountable, and effective governments in Afghanistan and Pakistan. U.S. nation-building will enhance civilian control and stabilize constitutional government in both countries. Afghanistan and Pakistan are two of the most corrupt nations on earth. U.S. aid to both countries has been siphoned off to individuals and institutions that do not contribute to U.S. national security. U.S. assistance has been particularly ineffective in Afghanistan, which is 70 percent rural, and there is no indication that the weak Pakistani government can make the reforms needed to use U.S. assistance effectively. We have been supplying military and economic assistance to Pakistan since the 1950s, when we based U-2 spy planes there, and successive Islamabad governments have misused and diverted this aid to the military front against India. The Taliban and al-Qaeda regrouped in Pakistan between 2002 and 2008, but the $6.6 billion in U.S. aid to Pakistan did not fund Islamabad's military efforts against the Afghan Taliban.

Myth #5: The Pakistani army would give up its fight against the Pakistan Taliban if the United States reduced its own military efforts in Afghanistan. No matter what strategy the United States adopts, Pakistan cannot give up its efforts to defeat or co-opt the Pakistan Taliban. The Pakistan Taliban represents a domestic problem for Islamabad because of the short distance between the Pakistani capital and the Taliban zone of operations. The Pakistani army will defend its nuclear weapons against the Pakistan Taliban, and it will resist Taliban military and terrorist attacks. If the ineffective and corrupt government of President Asif Ali Zardari is not up to these tasks, then a military government could replace Zardari. Until now, no civilian government in Pakistan has completed its term in office in the country's history.

Myth #6: The defeat of the Taliban would ensure success in Afghanistan. A civil war has waged in Afghanistan for the past forty years, and there is no guarantee that the defeat of the Taliban would end the war between the Pashtuns and the Tajiks. The Soviet invasion in 1979 was designed in part to end this battle; the Soviets failed. The United States is on a similar mission; it, too, is failing. Unlike Iraq, where the fighting was concentrated in several key urban areas, the Afghan fighting is widely dispersed and there are many adversaries other than the Taliban. Many of the current Afghan fighters are "simply rural Afghans who have taken up arms out of a sense of honor or nationalism, or because of economic incentives, or because they have relatives who have been killed or injured."[8]

Other myths influenced U.S. politicians to waste lives and money by extending the U.S. presence in Afghanistan, particularly the belief that the "surge" in Iraq in 2007 was a strategic victory. The surge may have been a short-term tactical success, but it created no strategic advantage because of Iraq's inability to capitalize on the increased U.S. presence to stabilize and strengthen its government. Similarly, a "surge" in Afghanistan has had no impact on the corruption and abuses of the government of President Hamid Karzai. Most agree that the Afghan election in August 2011 exposed the fraudulence and corruption of the Karzai government. It also exposed the inability of U.S. and international forces to provide sufficient security for the Pashtuns, Uzbeks, and Tajiks to cast their ballots.

These myths have led to blunders on every level—strategic, operational, and tactical—ignoring lessons from Vietnam in the 1960s and 1970s as well as the Soviet experience in Afghanistan in the 1980s. On the strategic level, the United States totally ignored the Taliban at the beginning of the military mission in 2001. On the tactical level, the United States was slow to recognize the absence of an Afghan infrastructure due to a continuous civil war that began in 1973 and a Soviet occupation that lasted ten years. As a result, there have been a series of logistical problems in supplying a 100,000-solidier U.S. force, and Pakistan has been given great political leverage as the holder of the keys to the Khyber Pass, the major supply route into Afghanistan. Like the Soviet Union, the United States attacked the Afghan problem as one that called for a centralized approach, whereas a decentralized approach was needed, one that would emphasize the creation of security forces on village and district levels.

Members of Obama's administration claim success for the surge, but the facts do not support the proclamation. The level of violence in Afghanistan was 15 percent higher in 2011 than it was in 2010; the insurgents were as resilient as ever and were targeting high-level members of the national and provincial governments even in key cities such as Kabul and Kandahar. When the president announced the beginning of the end of the U.S. war in Afghanistan, he said, "These long wars will come to a responsible end." It is difficult to decipher what that phrase means, but neither the occupation of Iraq nor the occupation of Afghanistan point to "success."

The U.S. needs to end the high cost of keeping tens of thousands of troops in Afghanistan; it costs $1 million a year for each soldier and Marine in the country. A good part of this cost is involved in the logistical problems of resupply in a country that lacks any infrastructure, including roads and storage for oil and even water. All U.S. facilities have been built from scratch, which means that we will be leaving the Taliban an excellent infrastructure somewhere down the road. As Dexter Filkins of the *New York Times* reported, the president's "prediction for Afghanistan . . . seems more like a prayer."[9]

Now, in the second decade of war in Afghanistan, the United States still lacks a policy, let alone a strategy, for funding an Afghan government that will require U.S. assistance through 2025, according to President Karzai. It is believed that the cost of governance and security in Afghanistan over this decade will amount to more than half of Afghanistan's gross domestic product, particularly to cover the costs of an Afghan army that numbers more than 300,000.

There has been little progress thus far in building the Afghan military and police forces even though the United States spends $8 billion to $10 billion annually to train and maintain these forces. The United States, in other words, is building an army that Afghanistan will never be able to fund. As one U.S. official noted, "We're going to have to pay for it for years and years to come."[10] Few believe that the Afghan army, which is not capable of planning and conducting operations on its own, will be able to maintain control of the country as the United States and its NATO allies withdraw.

Secretary of Defense Gates was an enthusiastic promoter of nation-building in Afghanistan, telling the Association of the U.S. Army that "reviving public services, rebuilding infrastructure and promoting good governance" had become soldiers' business. According to Gates, "All these so-called non-traditional capabilities have moved into the mainstream of military thinking, planning, and strategy—*where they must stay*." He believed that military power was the all-purpose answer to geopolitical challenges. In other words, the military would serve as the pointy end of the nation-building spear. The United States has claimed throughout that it has been helping the Afghan people rebuild their society, which has been battered by war and civil war for the past four decades.

The killing of bin Laden in May 2011 essentially ended the major reason for any large-scale U.S. presence in Afghanistan. The fact that bin Laden had been in Pakistan—and not Afghanistan—raised serious questions, moreover, about al-Qaeda's relations with Pakistan. The capture of a huge trove of al-Qaeda documents in bin Laden's Pakistani compound also raised questions about the ability of al-Qaeda to conduct large-scale terrorist operations and the ability of bin Laden's successor to lead the organization.

Historians will ask why President Obama kept the United States in a position to lose so many American lives (more than two thousand as of September 2012) and so much in taxpayer dollars in a place that has been fighting an ethnic and tribal civil war for the past four decades, has never had a centralized government, has never conquered its poverty and illiteracy, is considered the second-most-corrupt country in the world, and has never represented a threat to U.S interests, let alone the United States itself. No amount of U.S. forces or U.S. aid dollars will stabilize Afghanistan, let alone create a democratic government.

President Obama was skeptical about U.S. success even when he agreed to the surge of forces in 2009. The first surge, which took place in mid-2009, was designed to make sure that Afghanistan conducted free and fair elections, which of course it didn't. The second surge was designed to slow down the Taliban's advance in the eastern and southern portions of the country, which it didn't. High-level U.S. officials, including former national security adviser Jones, former CIA director Panetta, and current CIA director (and former commander of forces in Afghanistan) Petraeus have conceded that the United States has achieved its only genuine mission in Afghanistan (i.e., making sure that al-Qaeda is never again in position to attack the United States from Afghanistan). All of them have testified that there are fewer than one hundred al-Qaeda members in Afghanistan. Each year from 2008, however, Taliban activities and U.S. losses have increased, and the U.S. military presence in Southwest Asia has contributed to the destabilization of Pakistan. The stability of Pakistan is far more important to regional and global security than any outcome in Afghanistan.

President Obama can be credited, at least, with ignoring the polemics of Senators John McCain (R-AZ), Lindsay Graham (R-SC), and Joe Lieberman (I-CT), who have urged a continued military buildup in Afghanistan without explaining where the force structure for a major expansion of forces would come from and how to deal with the logistical nightmare that has complicated our military presence. The Mujahideen forces in the 1980s shut down the Salang Tunnel on a regular basis, compromising the Soviet military campaign. The opposition in western Pakistan has successfully hampered our supply route through the Khyber Pass. Too many U.S. officials advocate the use of force in Afghanistan without recognizing the importance of logistics and the overwhelming limitations on a U.S. military presence at any level.

The president eventually understood that he had been boxed in by Gates and Petraeus on the escalation of force in Afghanistan; this appeared to be the start of a learning curve for him in dealing with the Pentagon. According to *Newsweek* columnist Jonathan Alter, President Obama asked Petraeus in 2009 "If you can't do the things you say you can in eighteen months, then no one is going to suggest that we stay, right"? Petraeus replied, "Yes sir, in agreement."[11] Although Petraeus told the President in their meeting on November 29, 2009, that he would not ask for more troops and more time even if the counterinsurgency strategy was not going well, the general began singing another tune less than a year later. When asked on *Meet the Press* on August 15, 2010, whether he might tell the president that the draw-down of forces should be delayed beyond the summer of 2011, Petraeus said, "Certainly, yes."

The president has denied that he was "jammed" by the military in the fall of 2009, when one of the toughest decisions of his presidency had to be made. It is clear, however, that the military was trying to manipulate the president for the next round of decision-making. Obama gave Petraeus too much influence over Afghan policy when he reappointed the general to command forces in Afghanistan; he compounded his error by permitting the general to box in the White House on strategy.

In fact, one high-ranking general after another, as well as the secretary of defense, walked away from discussions of a major review of Afghan policy and made on-the-record comments in support of an extended stay. The Pentagon's campaign began in the fall of 2010, when General Petraeus stated that he had not returned to Afghanistan to preside over a "graceful exit." Petraeus indicated that his support for any decision to begin the withdrawal of forces in 2011 would depend on how the war was proceeding, and said he could repeat the so-called success of the surge in Iraq, which he had campaigned for in 2007. Petraeus told ABC News that there could no clear "hand-off" of primary responsibility for security to the Afghan Army in the summer of 2011 and that the United States might "do a bit less and the Afghans do a little bit more."

In the wake of General Petraeus's remarks, the top military leadership has ignored the president's pledge to withdraw and has made the case for keeping U.S. forces in Afghanistan beyond 2014. Former chairman of the Joint Chiefs Mike Mullen was the most aggressive military leader making the case for a long-term commitment to Afghanistan. General James Conway, the commandant of the Marine Corps, said that President Obama's July 2011 deadline to begin U.S. troop withdrawal was "giving our enemy sustenance." General Conway was particularly dismissive of any discussion of withdrawal, noting that President Obama was "talking to several audiences at the same time when he made his comments regarding July 2011." The senior commander in Afghanistan, General John R. Allen, indicated in January 2012 that he favored a long-term presence.[12] The U.S. commander in charge of training Afghan security forces, General William Caldwell IV, told Pentagon reporters on August 23 that he would not complete his mission of training an Afghan force until after the deadline.

Even Secretary of Defense Panetta testified to Congress that the United States would continue to support Afghan development as an important partner for the long haul. "We will not repeat the mistakes of 1989," he said, "when we abandoned the country only to see it descend into chaos and into Taliban hands." Panetta's remarks were particularly troublesome because he must understand that, if we are going to continue funding both military and civil spending in Afghanistan beyond 2014, there needs to be a planning process. There is no indication that such a process is under way.

Meanwhile, the Pentagon's public campaign was different from the private comments made by the military leadership to President Obama in 2009, when he conducted his high-level review of Afghan policy. In the Oval Office in October 2009, Secretary of Defense Gates and Admiral Mullen pledged their support to President Obama, and committed themselves to making sure that the battlefield commanders, Generals McChrystal and Petraeus, would stop their public discussion of the policy debate. The vice chairman of the Joint Chiefs, General James Cartwright, also pledged fealty. In late November 2009, only days before the West Point speech, President Obama asked General Petraeus if he was sufficiently certain that progress over the next eighteen months would allow the withdrawal to begin in 2011. Gates, Mullen, and Petraeus agreed that it could be done and that the Afghan army could take over the mission at that time.

The pace of U.S. military construction in Afghanistan does not suggest an expectation of an imminent withdrawal. Major expansion continued at three U.S. air bases in southern and northern Afghanistan in 2012, and one air base was completed in January 2012 at a cost of more than $20 million. Military spokesmen disingenuously indicated that the base was needed for the logistics of withdrawal. In other words, long after President Obama had pledged to begin the withdrawal of U.S. forces, the Pentagon was allocating tens of millions of dollars for the expansion of U.S. air bases in key regions. The House of Representatives has approved more than $1 billion for additional base construction in addition to the more than $5 billion allocated to build facilities for the Afghan army and the national police. Neither Afghan institution has demonstrated that it can maintain security in the country, let alone take on the growing Taliban forces.

Of course, high-ranking military commanders typically sing a different song after they leave the military. Retired General Stanley McChrystal, who commanded the U.S. and NATO force from 2009 to 2010, had the gall to tell the Council on Foreign Relations in October 2011 that the United States began its war in Afghanistan with a "frighteningly simplistic" view of Afghan history over "the last fifty years," citing the lack of knowledge of Afghan culture and language.[13] "We didn't know enough," he said, and "we still don't know enough." President Eisenhower presumably would have cited that lack of knowledge as one of the best reasons for avoiding the use of force in Afghanistan.

Dealing with Insubordination

The public comments of Generals Petraeus and Conway and others may not amount to insubordination in challenging policy favored by the White House, but there was no question that when General McChrystal, the commander of U.S. and NATO forces at the time, privately denigrated senior members of the Obama administration, he was being insubordinate. In remarks that found their way into *Rolling Stone* magazine, General McChrystal, who was legendary for running eight miles a day, eating one meal a day, and sleeping four hours a night, went out of his way to denigrate senior leaders associated with decision-making on Afghanistan, particularly Vice President Biden, Ambassador Eikenberry, and then tsar for Afghanistan, the late Richard Holbrooke. It was clear that McChrystal and his handpicked staff had no respect for the president or for the civilian decision-making process on Afghanistan. Secretary of Defense Gates favored a reprimand, but President Obama realized he had no choice but to fire the general. Anything less would have labeled the president a political weakling in the eyes of senior military officers.

The contemptuous remarks of McChrystal and his aides ring true to those who have spent time around senior military officers, particularly special operations officers, who are even more bellicose and conservative than their colleagues. Upon arrival at the National War College in 1986 to join the faculty after a twenty-year career at the Central Intelligence Agency, I assumed that the major threats to U.S. security emanated from the Soviet Union, China, and various Third World trouble spots. I soon learned that many senior U.S. military officers believed the major threats to U.S. security came from the media, Congress, and liberal Democrats. Since the end of the draft, the officer corps has become increasingly conservative and libertarian, and it is the rare officer who votes Democratic. In the 1970s, more than half of all senior officers considered themselves independents; currently, the overwhelming majority of senior officers consider themselves Republicans. Ironically, McChrystal, whose Army nickname was "The Pope," is a registered Democrat and a social liberal, and was an Obama supporter in the 2008 election.

President Obama recognized the McChrystal affair as a challenge to civilian control and leadership, although the reappointment of Petraeus enhanced the political power of the military, marking another obstacle to the president's exercise of civilian control. Too many influential people viewed Petraeus as the answer to our Afghan problems; he wasn't. In fact, the forced resignation of McChrystal and reappointment of Petraeus as commander of forces merely meant a change of waiters in Afghanistan without changing the Afghan menu. Meanwhile, retired General McChrystal is earning $60,000 for his speaking experiences; he was permitted to retire with four-star rank even though he hadn't held the rank for three years, which is a military requirement; and he's been named to several advisory boards. In April 2011 President Obama appointed him to an advisory board to provide support for military families, in order to end any appearance of a civilian-military breach following his forced retirement.

The mainstream media, meanwhile, downplayed the critical issue that dominates this sad affair—the fundamental importance of civilian supremacy in military policy. The *New York Times'* David Brooks minimized General McChrystal's remarks as mere "kvetching." For the *Times'* Maureen Dowd,

McChrystal and his "smart-aleck aides" were merely engaging in "towel-snapping" jocularity. The *Washington Post* editorial board, noting that President Karzai called McChrystal the "best commander of the war," concluded that the general should be retained as the Afghan commander.

The Return to Arms Control and Disarmament

There is good news in that President Obama ended the Bush administration's campaign against disarmament and returned to traditional approaches toward arms control. The bad news is that the president's modest steps do not match his rhetorical support of nuclear disarmament and that he remains unwilling to take the necessary steps to advance his previous strategic agenda—support for the Comprehensive Test Ban Treaty and opposition to national missile defense.

President Obama turned back to arms control and disarmament in April 2011, when he took command of the global dialogue on nuclear arms control. He authorized the release of the Nuclear Posture Review; signed a strategic arms agreement with Russia; and hosted a Nuclear Security Summit that moved arms control back to the U.S. national security agenda for the first time in a decade.

Unfortunately, on the eve of the summit, Secretary of State Hillary Clinton proclaimed that the United States was "stronger than anyone, as we've always been, with more nuclear weapons than are needed many times over." With this provocative utterance, reminiscent of Secretary of State Albright's reference to the United States as the "indispensable nation," Secretary of State Clinton gave the international community good reason to be skeptical of Washington's goals and objectives. President Obama sent a similar signal during the State of the Union address in January 2012, when he vowed that the United States would remain the one "indispensable" nation.[14]

The Nuclear Posture Review of April 5 returned U.S. nuclear policy to the bipartisan approach established more than fifty years ago, when the Eisenhower administration ruled out nuclear war against non-nuclear states. President Eisenhower emphasized that the primary role of nuclear weapons would be deterrence of nuclear war, a posture designed to address the foolish notions of then Harvard professor Henry A. Kissinger that the United States could wage and win a "limited" nuclear conflict. President Obama has taken on neoconservative critics such as John Bolton, who argue that U.S. advances in nuclear weaponry could make nuclear war winnable. Unlike President Reagan, however, Obama has not proclaimed that "nuclear war cannot be won—and must not be fought."

Moreover, President Obama did not challenge the Pentagon's unwillingness to consider a pledge of no first use of nuclear weapons, which would offer the best incentive for non-nuclear states to disavow development of nuclear weapons. For the past two decades, the former Soviet Union/Russia has been trying to engage the United States in a serious dialogue to pledge no first use of nuclear weapons; no militarization of outer space; and the creation of nuclear-free zones. The Soviets broached the subject of no first use as early as the 1960s, hoping to place such a pledge in either the Nuclear Non-Proliferation Treaty or the Strategic Arms Limitation Treaty. Moscow made its first unilateral pledge not to be the first to use nuclear weapons in 1982; China and India have also renounced the first use of nuclear weapons. The Pentagon has opposed taking such a step, and President Obama, like his immediate predecessors, has not taken on the Defense Department on essential issues germane to genuine nuclear disarmament.

The new Strategic Arms Reduction Treaty (START), signed in Prague on April 9, 2011, brought an expected reduction of strategic launchers to 800 vehicles and strategic warheads to 1,550, but did nothing about the 200 tactical nuclear warheads that the United States maintains in Western Europe (over the opposition of many Western European governments); the several thousand tactical nuclear warheads in American and Russian inventories; or the thousands of reserve nuclear warheads. The United States continues to pursue a national missile defense that is highly objectionable to the international community and wants to place conventional warheads on strategic launchers, which would create a serious early warning problem regarding detection.

A major opportunity was missed in 2011 to introduce the concept of minimal deterrence, which could lead to reducing strategic warheads to several hundred instead of the goal of several thousand that won't be reached until 2017. Russia is willing to reduce its warheads to 1,000 and such U.S. hardliners as former CIA director John Deutch agree with the 1,000 level. A recent article in an authoritative strategic journal by several writers associated with the U.S. Air Force argued for a minimal deterrence of 311 warheads, which would protect the strategic triad of missiles, bombers, and submarines. As long as we pursue flexible deterrence and not minimal deterrence, we allow the Pentagon to pursue war-fighting strategies with nuclear weapons, which former secretary of defense Robert McNamara warned against fifty years ago.

The Nuclear Security Summit in April 2011 brought needed attention to the issue of non-proliferation and highlighted announcements from Ukraine and Chile that they would turn over their stocks of highly enriched uranium to Russian and the United States, respectively. The United States and Russia agreed to reduce their huge stocks of excess plutonium, the key ingredient in thousands of nuclear weapons, but this will not be completed until the 2030s. Mexico pledged to convert its research reactor to low enriched uranium.

Like the Kellogg-Briand Pact of 1928, a worthless pledge to outlaw war, the nuclear summit relied on long-term pledges and not written commitments. Participating nations did not introduce mandatory standards for securing nuclear facilities or universal commitments to stop producing weapons-grade materials. The nuclear states of India and Pakistan, which have never joined the NPT, are the main obstacles to a ban on producing fissile materials. Israel is another nuclear state that refuses to sign the NPT, and its hardline president, Benjamin Netanyahu, stubbornly refused to even attend the Washington summit. President Obama's major mistake in this instance was the failure to invite Iran and North Korea, two of the key anomalous states on nuclear issues, thus missing an opportunity to conduct genuine international diplomacy. The United States missed a similar opportunity in 1998, when it failed to join the Comprehensive Test Ban Treaty (CTBT), which was the price India and Pakistan had set for joining the NPT.

In abjuring an opportunity to declare no first use of nuclear weapons; to renounce tactical and reserve nuclear warheads; to diplomatically engage Iran and North Korea; and to endorse the notion of minimal deterrence, President Obama missed opportunities to make the "peace and security of a world without nuclear weapons" our new strategic objective, as he proclaimed in Prague in 2009. We may never get rid of nuclear weapons entirely, but we could do more to significantly reduce nuclear stockpiles and to restrict technologies that make nuclear weapons easier to use. Significant nuclear reductions by the United States and Russia would make it easier to demand stringent inspections of the non-nuclear states and the acceptance of the NPT by India and Pakistan, if not Israel.

President Obama needs to press the Congress to ratify the CTBT, which Presidents Clinton and Bush failed to do; press China for more transparency and confidence-building measures on strategic weapons; and press nuclear states to take steps to prevent collisions between nuclear missile submarines, such as last year's British-French collision of submarines armed with more than one hundred nuclear warheads. Finally, Obama needs to take advantage of the bipartisan group of elder statesmen, including William Perry, Sam Nunn, George Shultz, and Henry Kissinger, who support a comprehensive disarmament agenda, which would provide cover for conservatives who dismiss disarmament as appeasement.

Military Lessons from Libya

Prior to Libya, the United States had supported three successful no-fly zones: Operation Northern Watch over northern Iraq from 1991 to 2003, to prevent Iraqi repression of the Kurdish population; Operation Southern Watch over southern Iraq from 1991 to 2003, to protect the Shia population; and Operation Deny Flight over Bosnia and Herzegovina from 1993 to 1995, to protect the Muslim population from Bosnian Serb repression. Operation Deny Flight was the most successful because it supported the UN Security Council's resolution insuring the delivery of humanitarian assistance and strengthened the case for ending hostilities in Bosnia and Herzegovina. It protected Muslims from the terror of Serbian President Slobodan Milosevic. The no-fly zones in Iraq were not linked to any specific strategic mission in determining the political situation in that country, but they contributed to the safety of vulnerable civilian populations from the terrorism of Iraqi President Saddam Hussein.

Like Operation Deny Flight in the Balkans, Operation Odyssey Dawn in northern Africa was based on a clear-cut Security Council resolution, this one passed on March 17, 2011, which authorized member states to "take all necessary measures . . . to protect civilians and civilian populated areas under threat of attack in the Libyan Arab Jamahiriya, including Benghazi, while excluding a foreign occupation force of any form on any part of Libyan territory."[15] Prior to the resolution, several key congressmen, including Senator John McCain (R-AZ), Representative Ron Paul (R-TX), and the chairman of the Senate Foreign Relations Committee, John Kerry (D-MA), introduced resolutions endorsing a no-fly zone, although Rep. Paul noted the importance of obtaining congressional approval before any "use of U.S. forces in response to civil unrest in Libya." Unfortunately, the "no-fly" zone to protect civilians actually became the thin edge of a wedge to destroy Qadhafi. Once again, there was an exaggerated belief in the surgical precision of air power.

President Obama's endorsement of a no-fly zone over Libya in March 2011 was one of his biggest gambles. It rivaled President Carter's hostage rescue attempt in Iran in 1980, which contributed to his election defeat later that year. A mistake of President Obama's regarding Libya was one of the most avoidable ones he has ever made. In March 2011, on a state visit to Brazil, the president announced that authorization for "limited military action" in Libya, making a commitment that it would last "days, not weeks."[16] Actually, NATO military action lasted for eight months, and there is no telling when Libya will be stabilized. The coordinated attack on the U.S. consulate in Benghazi in September 2012, which killed several Americans, including the U.S. ambassador, points to continued difficulty for U.S. interests not only in Libya, but throughout the Arab world.

The Obama administration was clearly making policy by the seat of its pants in conducting the no-fly zone. While in Chile on a state visit, the president told a group of reporters five days after the imposition of the no-fly zone that the United States would be achieving "clarity and a meeting of the minds" in the next few days.[17] While on a visit to Russia, Secretary of Defense Gates told a group of Russian military officers in St. Petersburg that never before in history had the United States created a "command and control [system] on the fly."[18] Prior to the start of the operation, Air Force Chief of Staff General Norton A. Schwartz warned that it would take "upwards of a week to establish a no-fly zone and would require U.S. forces to first neutralize Libyan ground-to-air anti-aircraft sites," which in any event "would not be sufficient" to reverse Libyan government gains against the anti-Qadhafi forces.[19]

These comments added to the confusion that was created by the failure of the major proponents of the no-fly zone (the United States, Britain, and France) to reach an understanding on command and control prior to the start of the operation. For nearly a week, there were high-level exchanges between the major NATO states regarding who would take the lead for commanding the no-fly zone over Libya. French President Sarkozy was the most insistent head of state in calling for the no-fly zone, which probably saved the people of Benghazi in eastern Libya from Qadhafi's murderous threats. But Sarkozy's efforts to remain the leader and coordinator of the intervention strained relations with key members of the coalition and created problems for Obama. The U.S. president and his administration were divided over policy from the outset and, as a result, France and Britain took the lead in obtaining the Security Council resolution. Sarkozy's unwillingness to turn over the operation to NATO, moreover, irritated key NATO members such as Italy, Norway, and Turkey.

Unfortunately, one of President Obama's advisers told a reporter that President Obama chose to be cautious in Libya and was "leading from behind."[20] In fact, the president was leading from behind the scenes, which made a great deal of sense in view of the country's preoccupation with Iraq and Afghanistan and the need to get the European powers more involved in crisis management in North Africa, where the European capitals have more at stake than the United States does. Secretary of

Defense Gates and members of the Joint Chiefs of Staff were opposed to any U.S. intervention in view of the over-extension of U.S. forces. Similar to the decisions on General McChrystal's insubordination and the withdrawal of forces from Afghanistan, President Obama chose to ignore his secretary's recommendations and follow his own lead. The president also ignored Senators McCain, Lieberman, and Graham, who wanted boots on the ground.

President Obama was right to get involved and to take a cautious approach in doing so. There was the risk that Muammar Qadhafi would take advantage of the chaos in Libya to slaughter innocent civilians, which is why the international community was generally supportive of NATO's involvement. The Arab League supported the use of force, and several Islamic countries (United Arab Emirates, Jordan, and Qatar) got involved operationally. The Security Council's vote on the NATO operation drew five abstentions (including Russia and China), but no negative votes. There was an international consensus that, in view of the events of the Arab Spring, this would be the wrong time to permit a tyrant such as Qadhafi to reverse one of the most events in Middle Eastern history in the recent past.

Nevertheless, Obama erred in approving military operations in Libya without consulting Congress. First, he ignored the War Powers Resolution of 1973, which called for congressional approval for hostile actions beyond a sixty-day period. Second, in choosing not to invoke the WPR—and no president has invoked it in four decades—Obama should have at least consulted the congressional leadership of both parties to get some acquiescence to U.S. actions. As a result of these errors, in June 2011, the House of Representatives introduced two measures: a successful one calling for the president to provide justification for U.S. actions in Libya; and an unsuccessful one calling for U.S. withdrawal from Libya within fifteen days. The congressional response represented four decades of frustration over successive presidents ignoring the War Powers Resolution as well frustration over U.S. use of force in the Middle East, Southwest Asia, and now North Africa.

The administration also missed an opportunity to call attention to an obscure principle that the United Nations adopted in 2005, with the support of more than 150 nations, and has been refining since. The doctrine of "Responsibility to Protect" (R2P) declares that when a sovereign state fails to prevent hostilities against innocents, foreign governments may intervene to stop them. R2P was obviously designed to give some international weight to the doctrine of "never again," which has been observed in the breach, most recently in Rwanda twenty years ago. Human rights advocates believe that R2P saves lives, although the doctrine can be misused. In 2008, Russia invoked the doctrine to justify its harsh attack on Georgia. To defend his policy, President Obama should have invoked the example of Srebrenica, where UN forces failed to act to avert a massacre of Bosnians in July 1995; the Sudanese government's campaign of genocide in Darfur; the Khmer Rouge massacres in Cambodia in the 1970s; Iraq's use of chemical weapons in 1988; and ethnic cleansing in Bosnia and Kosovo in the 1990s.

The overwhelming congressional vote in June 2011 against U.S. participation in Libya would not have taken place if the Obama administration had taken the simple step of authorizing the operation several months earlier. Even Pentagon lawyers and advisers from the Justice Department's Office of Legal Counsel considered the Libyan operation to be "hostilities" and counseled the White House to seek authorization or to honor the sixty-day deadline of the War Powers Resolution on U.S. involvement in hostilities. White House lawyers and State Department lawyer Harold H. Koh disagreed, however, presumably not believing it would take two months of aerial bombardment to defeat Qadhafi. Koh's opinions allowed the administration to bypass the WPR, which requires that U.S. forces be withdrawn from hostilities within a certain period unless Congress approves continued military action.

Koh's views are particularly noteworthy because the Yale University law professor has written widely about the importance of acknowledging the balance of power in the making of foreign policy, particularly the use of force. But where you sit (in this case, the Department of State) typically determines where you stand, so Koh the theoretician and academician argued against the validity of the WPR, thus supporting the kind of national security arrogance he once had criticized. In his major work on the national security system, Koh had praised the passage of the WPR as a useful counter to the arrogance of the Nixon administration during the Vietnam War and an instrument for preventing "undeclared creeping wars that start and build before Congress or the public are fully aware."[21] He was even critical of the resolution for failing to include covert wars, in which intelligence operatives acting under civilian supervision conduct paramilitary activities against foreign governments. Koh also believed the resolution should address short-term military strikes that could be completed well within the resolution's sixty-day time limit; this certainly would have applied to the Libyan operation if U.S. involvement had lasted "days, not weeks," as the president indicated.

The WPR has typically been "observed in the breach." The Reagan administration deployed force in Lebanon in 1983, leading to the deaths of more than two hundred Marines, without any reference to the WPR; President Clinton deployed force in Somalia in 1993 that led to the worst firefight for American forces since Vietnam without reference to the WPR. And now the United States is using unmanned drone aircraft overtly and covertly in at least six countries without any reference to the WPR or consultation with the Congress.

One of the lessons that needed to be learned from U.S. policy toward Libya is the folly of providing military assistance to allies that are capable of torturing and killing their own citizens. As recently as 2009, the United States concluded a multimillion-dollar arms deal with Qadhafi, despite the State Department's human rights report of that year documenting the brutal torture techniques of Libya's security forces. Just months before the Libyan uprising began, the Obama administration was moving ahead on another arms deal with the Qadhafi regime.

Reinhold Niebuhr and President Obama: Not a Match

President Obama often calls Reinhold Niebuhr, the most influential American theologian of the twentieth century, his "favorite philosopher." Many editorial writers viewed the president's acceptance speech at the Nobel Prize ceremony in Oslo in 2009 to be a "faithful reflection" of Niebuhr's political philosophy. George Packer, in the *New Yorker* magazine, said that Niebuhr's spirit "presided over the Nobel address."

In fact, one of President Obama's greatest failures in dealing with national security issues has been his failure to address the moral issues he inherited from the Bush administration, particularly the CIA's use of torture and abuse and the destruction of the so-called torture tapes that documented the abuses; the Pentagon's increased role in covert actions that avoided congressional oversight; drone warfare, assassinations and extra-judicial killings; and the unwillingness to appoint strong inspectors general at the Pentagon and the CIA who would be responsible for internal oversight. His unwillingness to explore the conduct of torture and abuse is arguably the president's greatest failure, because it ignored the criminality of the recent past as well as domestic and international law, and perhaps insured that a future president would resort to such practices. In September 2012, Attorney General Eric Holder announced that no one would be prosecuted for the brutal deaths of two prisoners held in CIA custody. This decision is the latest example of the Obama administration's efforts to avoid any legal scrutiny of the Bush administration's abuses.

Thus, President Obama has placed himself and the United States in the hypocritical position of encouraging the pursuit of investigation and prosecution of torture and abuse that takes place abroad, but being unwilling to conduct such a pursuit at home. In doing so, he has put his own military and intelligence forces at risk in Developing World situations where they could be captured or detained by insurgents groups or other hostile forces. It was politically convenient for President Obama to ignore the issue of torture and abuse, but it was morally and ethically wrong.

Niebuhr warned against the "dangerous dreams of managing history." There is probably no better example of managing history than Afghanistan, where Alexander the Great, Queen Victoria, Brezhnev, and now Obama have tried to manage the ethnic and tribal communities of this region. Ironically, the United States and the CIA helped to "manage history" in one respect, providing aid to the anti-Soviet Mujahideen, who now comprise the ultra-repressive Taliban who are fighting NATO forces to a draw in Afghanistan. In his memoir, *From the Shadows*, Gates called the support of the Mujahideen the greatest covert action in the history of the CIA. The consequences of U.S. support, however, have proved this to have been a major strategic failure.

A half century ago, Niebuhr warned that the "trustful acceptance of false solutions for our perplexing problems adds a touch of pathos to the tragedy of our age." Indeed, with the United States facing severe domestic problems as well as international challenges from an unstable nuclear state (Pakistan) and an unstable near-nuclear state (Iran), President Obama has committed the future expenditure of hundreds of billions of dollars to Afghanistan, a corrupt and undeveloped land considered the "graveyard of empires."

President Obama has succumbed to what Niebuhr termed the "false security to which all men are tempted"—the security of power. The president used the Oslo Nobel ceremony to declare Afghanistan a just war, without defining the Afghan threat to U.S. security. His numerous references to a coalition of foreign forces are, in fact, a good example of the kind of pseudo-internationalism that Niebuhr warned against. The small contingents sent by such countries as Macedonia, Georgia, and Montenegro merely add to the problems for U.S. forces, which have had to provide force protection for undermanned and poorly trained foreign forces.

Obama and the Military Culture

One of President Obama's greatest weaknesses in his role as steward for national security policy was his lack of military experience, particularly his lack of understanding of the military culture. As far back as 1997, senior Defense Department officials, including then secretary of defense William Cohen, warned about a "chasm developing between the military and civilian worlds, where . . . the military doesn't understand . . . why criticism [of the military] is so quick and unrelenting."[22] Others have noted a "gap" in values between the armed forces and civilian society, which could threaten civil-military cooperation as well as the military's loyalty to civilian authority.

My own experience at the National War College, where I was on the faculty for eighteen years, is that the all-volunteer military has drifted too far away from the norms of American society, is inordinately right-wing politically, and is much more religious (and fundamentalist) than America as a whole. The "Republicanization" of the officer corps is well known. Too many career military officers believe that their moral code is superior to civilian norms, and there has been constant criticism within senior ranks about the moral health of civilian society. At the same time, these senior officers ignore their own opposition to change over the years, particularly opposition to the service of African Americans, women, and homosexuals in their ranks. Secretary of Defense Gates and the Pentagon's military leadership worked energetically to undermine the president's call for an end to the cynical policy of "don't ask, don't tell," which compromised the place of gays in the military. When the Obama administration was discussing Afghan policy at the highest levels last year, senior general officers campaigned for a significant expansion of U.S. forces long before any decision was actually made and failed to provide requested plans for troop withdrawal.

Unfortunately, the service academies and the war colleges spend very little time in their curriculum dealing with developing a coherent understanding of U.S. society and culture as well as the tradition of civil-military relations in the United States. A commandant at the National War College in the late 1980s, in the wake of the Iran-Contra revelations, which found military officers ignoring their own code of conduct, reduced the few hours devoted to U.S. policy and politics—just when these hours should have been expanded. Faculty members arguing against the cuts told the commandant that the curriculum should try to make sure that service members understood the U.S. political culture, particularly the rule of law.

Indeed, there is no more important task in political governance than making sure that civilian control of the military is not compromised and that the military remains subordinate to political authority. Unfortunately, President Obama has demonstrated too much deference to the military, retaining the Bush administration's secretary of defense as his own; appointing too many retired and active-duty general officers to key civilian positions such as national security adviser and intelligence tsar; and making the Pentagon's budget sacrosanct in an age of restraint.

The imbalance in civilian-military influence is more threatening to the interests of the United States over the long term than developments in Afghanistan. President Nixon's ending of the draft has created a professional military, which has fostered the cultural behavior that General McChrystal demonstrated in his outspoken contempt for civilian leadership. The Goldwater-Nichols Act in 1986 created regional commanders-in-chief (CINCs) who expanded the martial reach of the United States in the post–Cold War world; these CINCs have become more influential than U.S. ambassadors and assistant secretaries of state in sensitive Third World areas. The Act created a powerful chairman of the Joint Chiefs of Staff, and, during Desert Storm in 1991, the chairman often ignored the secretary of defense and personally briefed the president on war plans. It is noteworthy that the Act passed the Senate without one vote of opposition.

No Grand Strategy, But Perhaps a Vision

The uneven performance of the Obama administration has led to the pillorying of the president for a lack of a grand strategy. This criticism has come from all quarters: journalists such as the *Washington Post*'s Jackson Diehl; academicians such as the University of Chicago's John Mearsheimer; and historians such as Niall Ferguson. According to these critics, the "root cause of America's troubles . . . is the lack of any kind of a coherent grand strategy."[23] With the exception of Presidents Theodore Roosevelt, Woodrow Wilson, Franklin D. Roosevelt, and perhaps Richard Nixon, there have been no presidents in the past century with a strategy for national security, let alone a grand strategy. President George W. Bush is falsely credited with having a grand strategy of preventive war and the promotion of democracy, but the emphasis on democracy was designed to conceal the fact that the so-called preventive war against Iraq was based on a pastiche of lies and phony intelligence.

But if President Obama lacks a grand strategy, it does not mean that he lacks a vision for American foreign and national security policy, a vision that has the potential to reverse the militarization of the past two decades since the end of the Cold War. In the president's short speech to the nation on June 22, 2011, announcing his plans for withdrawal from Afghanistan, there was a recognition of the need to limit the role of the United States in counterinsurgency campaigns.[24] The capture and killing of bin Laden in May 2011 gave the president the opportunity to begin to exercise control over the Afghan operation, and he may have done just that. Bin Laden and al-Qaeda were the original reasons for entering Afghanistan in October 2001, and the key to controlling the political narrative of Afghanistan is using bin Laden's death to capture the initiative. By setting the first two rounds of withdrawal in the context of the successful operation against bin Laden, President Obama could point to progress in weakening al-Qaeda. The United States is now in a position to leave Afghan security to the Afghan forces themselves, and the president has set a date of 2014 for the Afghan military to take over the fighting from allied forces.

The announcement in January 2012 that there would be $485 billion in defense cuts over a ten-year period certainly pointed to a new era of austerity for the Pentagon, although there was no change in the large-scale investment in hugely expensive weapons platforms, such as F-35 fighter aircraft. The Obama administration's emphasis on a threat from China, which has been greatly exaggerated, does not suggest that the White House is genuinely interested in a fundamental restructuring of U.S. forces. There was no sign of cuts in the nuclear force and no indication that President Obama will look to further reductions in defense spending in order to come to grips with the need for stabilizing federal finances, which require at least $4 trillion in spending cuts and revenue increases over the next decade.

It is also disheartening to find the United States providing continued military assistance to so-called allies such as Bahrain, Saudi Arabia, and Yemen, where there has been well-documented government repression of nonviolent pro-democracy activists. The human rights abuses perpetrated under Israel's occupation of Palestinian territories also calls for limits on military aid and arms sales. Many of the tear gas canisters that assailed protestors during the Arab Spring in 2011 had a "Made in the USA" label, a reminder of the decades of support the United States has provided to repressive governments in Egypt and Tunisia.

President Obama, a constitutional lawyer, has also wasted an opportunity to challenge the abuses of the Bush administration, particularly failing to address torture and abuse, secret prisons, and extraordinary renditions that were conducted in violation of international and domestic law. He has contributed to the "lost decade" of the Bush era because of his unwillingness to challenge the power and influence of the Pentagon; to significantly reduce defense spending; and to use diplomacy to improve relations with Cuba, Iran, or North Korea. Until he abandons his excessive caution, the United States will remain mired in its current international cul-de-sac and its domestic stalemate. Time is not on Obama's side: congressional majorities have been lost in the House and are threatened in the Senate, the "youth vote" has been weakened, independents are abandoning the Democratic Party, and a discredited conservative movement has reinvented itself in a more virulent form.

The greatest disappointment may have been identified by longtime educator Marshall Ganz, who observed in an editorial in the *Los Angeles Times*, after the shocking results of the 2010 mid-term elections, that President Obama had "entered office wrapped in a mantle of moral leadership" that included a "call for change rooted in values that had long been eclipsed in our public life: a sense of mutual responsibility, commitment to equality and belief in inclusive diversity."[25] Ganz believed that these values "inspired a new generation of voters, restored faith to the cynical and created a national movement." One of the greatest disappointments with the Obama administration has been the unwillingness to impose meaningful accountability for the torture and abuse committed against prisoners during the Bush administration, particularly the brutal deaths of two prisoners held in the custody of the CIA. Attorney General Eric Holder stated that the decision not to bring prosecutions should not be seen as a moral exoneration, but there has never been an explanation of why charges could not be brought. Without legal accountability, there is no guarantee that these lawless practices would not happen again. Obama may be brighter than his critics in either party, but he has been too cautious and often unable to demonstrate a propensity for leadership.

SIX

THE PENTAGON'S GRIP
ON THE INTELLIGENCE COMMUNITY

The President of the United States and the Secretary of Defense would not assert as plainly and bluntly as they have that Iraq has weapons of mass destruction if it was not true, and if they did not have a solid basis for saying it. —Ari Fleischer, White House Press Spokesman, December 4, 2002

Don't worry, it's a slam dunk. —CIA Director George Tenet's response to President Bush's demand for intelligence on Iraq's weapons of mass destruction to provide to the American people.

But for those who say that we haven't found the banned manufacturing devices or banned weapons, they're wrong, we found them. —President George W. Bush, May 30, 2003

The first casualty when war comes is truth. —Senator Hiram Johnson, January, 17, 1941

The Central Intelligence Agency (CIA) was created as an independent, non-departmental agency because President Harry S. Truman saw the need for an intelligence service that was not part of the policy community and would therefore be less susceptible to manipulation in support of policy goals. Throughout CIA's sixty-year history, there have been many efforts to slant analytical conclusions, skew estimates, and repress evidence that challenged a particular policy or point of view. As a result, the litmus test for the Agency's credibility and integrity is its ability to recognize and resist such pressure, and to institutionalize barriers to politicization. Unfortunately, the CIA has often failed to meet the challenge.

The surprise attack of Pearl Harbor in 1941 and the start of the Cold War in 1947 were the immediate causes for the creation of the CIA. President Truman wanted an institutional challenge to the Pentagon's worst-case analysis, which tilted toward exaggerations of perceived threats. The CIA had many successes during the worst days of the Cold War from the 1950s to the 1970s. CIA imagery analysis determined there was no bomber gap between the Soviet Union and the United States in the 1950s and no missile gap in the 1960s. President Eisenhower accepted CIA analysis and avoided an unnecessary round of increased defense spending. In the 1960s, however, Presidents Kennedy and Johnson ignored CIA analysis for political and policy reasons, and initiated an unnecessary round in the strategic arms race.

The CIA's greatest analytical successes occurred in the 1960s and early 1970s, when it presented an intelligence case against involvement in Vietnam and prepared assessments on Soviet military capabilities that justified ratification of the Strategic Arms Limitations Treaty (SALT) and the Anti-Ballistic Missile (ABM) Treaty. In both cases, the CIA successfully challenged intelligence provided by the Pentagon, and if the Kennedy and Johnson administrations had paid attention to CIA estimates on Vietnam, the United States would have been spared the tragic and costly conflict that dragged on for twelve years. On Vietnam, the CIA provided evidence that the Pentagon had intentionally under-counted Viet Cong forces in South Vietnam; it also predicted the failure of strategic bombing and the overall U.S. military effort in Southeast Asia.

As early as 1963, the CIA and the State Department's Bureau of Intelligence and Research (INR) believed that the Vietnam War was slipping away. In that year, an INR analyst on Vietnam, Louis G. Sarris, wrote a memorandum for Secretary of State Dean Rusk providing analysis critical of the U.S. military effort in Vietnam. Rusk forwarded the memorandum to McNamara.[1] The chairman of the Joint Chiefs, General Maxwell Taylor, "hit the ceiling" over the report, and McNamara warned Rusk not to issue "military appraisals without seeking the views of the Defense Department." Rusk agreed that the State Department would never again issue an "independent assessment of the overall military situation in Vietnam." My friend and colleague Lou Sarris was given a new assignment in INR. Several years later, another colleague, CIA analyst Sam Adams, was reassigned after correctly detailing the number of Viet Cong operating in South Vietnam, which the Pentagon had deliberately under-counted.

The Sarris memorandum was corroborated by intelligence assessments from the CIA that demonstrated there was an "unfavorable shift in the military balance" and a decline in Viet Cong casualties and weapons losses as well as an increase in South Vietnamese defections and Viet Cong military attacks. Nevertheless, in 1967, General William Westmoreland, the commander in Vietnam, told a joint session of Congress that there was great progress in the war; several months later, the Tet offensive, which was predicted by Sarris at State and Robert Layton at the CIA, took place. Sadly, it took the United States another seven years and the killing of 58,226 U.S. soldiers and more than one million Vietnamese people for it to withdraw.

The Tonkin Gulf Resolution, which gave the Johnson administration a blank check to pursue victory in South Vietnam, was based on an intentional misreading of intelligence. Forty years after the Resolution legislated the use of force against North Vietnam, a National Security Agency (NSA) study confirmed that the NSA had distorted critical intelligence used by the White House to secure an overwhelmingly popular vote in the Congress to endorse the use of force. In 2001, the senior NSA historian, Robert J. Hanyok, found a pattern of uncorrected translation mistakes and altered intercept times that indicated a deliberate skewing of key evidence.[2] President Lyndon B. Johnson doubted the intelligence supporting the Tonkin Gulf Resolution and never believed there had actually been a second attack on U.S. ships. Nevertheless, he escalated a war on the basis of intelligence that had been doctored and partially covered up.

CIA analysts also argued that expanding the war to Cambodia would be counterproductive. In 1970, when the Nixon administration was planning the "incursion" into Cambodia, the CIA's Board of National Estimates concluded that an "American invasion of Cambodia would fail to deter North Vietnamese continuation of the war."[3] Despite his willingness to bring unwanted intelligence to the White House on arms control issues, CIA director Helms refused to deliver the estimate on Vietnam and Cambodia to the White House, knowing the decision had already been made to invade Cambodia. He was one messenger who did not want to be shot. He also suppressed accurate CIA analysis on the numbers of Communist guerrillas and self-defense forces in South Vietnam, preferring to forward the politicized figures of the Pentagon that deliberately under-counted the enemy presence in Vietnam. Like so many CIA directors, Helms was not willing to take on the Pentagon.

It is not unusual for decision-makers to blame intelligence when their policies fail. In 1995, former Secretary of Defense McNamara wrote a memoir, *In Retrospect: The Tragedy and Lessons of Vietnam*, bemoaning the lack of reliable information on Vietnam for the crucial decisions made in the early 1960s. In fact, the CIA and INR had produced outstanding intelligence on Vietnam that accurately anticipated the failure of military force in

Vietnam. Military leaders refused to listen, however; even when one of their own, Lieutenant Colonel John Paul Vann, returned to Washington in 1963 with his account of the corrupt South Vietnamese government, he was not permitted to brief the Joint Chiefs of Staff. Similarly, in their memoirs, President Bush, Vice President Cheney, Secretary of Defense Rumsfeld, and Secretary of State Rice blame the decision to go to war against Iraq in 2003 on the incorrect intelligence of the CIA, never acknowledging their role in lobbying for false intelligence and actively misinforming the Congress and the American public.

In the late 1960s, CIA analysts battled policy agencies on sensitive issues related to arms control and disarmament, particularly SALT and the ABM Treaty. In doing so, the CIA convinced Congress that arms control agreements could be successfully monitored and verified, and that U.S. strategic advantages made the SALT and ABM treaties worthwhile. If the Nixon administration had ignored CIA estimates on Soviet military capabilities, it is possible that we would not have negotiated the SALT and ABM Treaties in 1972.

The key to achieving the first strategic arms agreements with the Soviets in 1972, the SALT Treaty, was dealing with the problems of Soviet capabilities regarding multiple independently targeted reentry vehicles (MIRVs) and ABMs. The opponents of the SALT agreement argued that the SS-9 had a MIRV capability that made a SALT treaty a risky proposition. National security adviser Henry A. Kissinger and Secretary of Defense Mel Laird initially shared this incorrect assumption, but the CIA confirmed the analysis of the INR and the Arms Control and Disarmament Agency (ACDA), arguing that the SS-9 was not MIRV capable.

The SS-9 issue was particularly important because, if the Soviet ICBM was a MIRVed weapon with three warheads and these warheads could be fired independently at separate and distinct targets, then the Pentagon could argue that the USSR had a first-strike capability. Kissinger and Laird argued that the fourth version of the SS-9 was a MIRVed weapon; the CIA disagreed. The intelligence community eventually agreed that the SS-9 was a maneuverable reentry vehicle (MRV) weapon with warheads, which could place a cluster of explosions in a single area, and not a MIRV, which could reach multiple targets. The CIA's analytic community, led by Sayre Stevens, who became the chief of the directorate of intelligence for his efforts, stuck to its guns, however. Kissinger was eventually persuaded, enabling conclusion of the SALT Treaty in 1972.

On several occasions, CIA director Helms ran into intense resistance from military representatives on the United States Intelligence Board (USIB) on estimates dealing with Soviet strategic forces. Since USIB coordination was required for National Intelligence Estimates, Helms would send these documents back for revision but typically supported the Agency's decision not to alter the substance of the estimate. CIA analysts were under a great deal of pressure from Kissinger, who initially wanted the CIA to argue the Soviet Union already had a MIRV capability. Helms defended his analysts, and CIA assessments correctly argued that the SS-9 had not been MIRVed.

When the CIA demonstrated that Soviet surface-to-air missiles could not be upgraded to an anti-ballistic missile defense, it opened the door to negotiations on the ABM treaty of 1972. The opponents of arms control, particularly the Pentagon, argued that there was no verifiable difference between a national missile defense and a nationwide air defense system, and therefore no way to verify an anti-ballistic missile system. The Intelligence Community, led by the CIA and INR, argued correctly that it had monitored both the installation of the Soviet air defense system and the technological upgrades of these components. The CIA asserted that the components of the air defense system were too slow to use against intercontinental ballistic missiles (ICBMs) and therefore posed no threat to U.S. strategic forces. Analysts from the Pentagon's Defense Intelligence Agency (DIA) eventually conceded that the air defense system could not be upgraded to a national defense missile system, which removed the last negotiating barrier to the ABM Treaty.

Many CIA directors, including Helms, James Schlesinger, Bill Casey, Bob Gates, and George Tenet, have been guilty of politicizing intelligence. President Nixon was so disgusted with the CIA's analysis on the Soviet Union and the Vietnam War that he wanted a "study made immediately as to how many people in CIA could be removed by Presidential action."[4] He wanted the CIA to stop recruiting "from any of the Ivy League schools or any other universities where either the university president or the university faculties have taken action condemning our efforts to bring the war in Vietnam to an end."[5] Presumably realizing that these steps would take too long, he simply fired Helms and appointed Schlesinger to "get rid of the clowns . . . [the CIA'S] info is worthless."[6]

Schlesinger put nothing in writing, but he assembled the Agency's Soviet experts and warned them, "This agency is going to stop fucking Richard Nixon." I was one of those Soviet analysts. Schlesinger's objective was to rein in the CIA, which had produced analysis that challenged Nixon's policy on Vietnam. He immediately abolished the Board of National Estimates, which had guided the production of the accurate and troubling estimates. Schlesinger's announcement to the Board was classic: "I understand that this is like a gentleman's club. Well, I want you to know that I am no gentleman."[7]

No director, however, was more direct and vocal on politicizing intelligence and less understanding of the role of intelligence in the policy process than Porter Goss. In the 1980s and 1990s, Casey, Gates, and Goss made sure that Agency briefings did not counter or compromise administration positions on sensitive issues. Gates issued constant warnings to his analysts to avoid "sticking your fingers into the eyes of policymakers." Two weeks after President Bush's reelection in 2004, Goss sent an internal memorandum to all Agency employees telling them their job was to "support the administration and its policies in our work. As agency employees, we do not identify with, support, or champion opposition to the administration or its policies."[8]

A declassified study on Soviet intentions during the Cold War identified significant failures in U.S. intelligence analysis on Soviet military intentions and demonstrated the Pentagon's constant exaggeration of the Soviet threat. The study, released in 2011 by the National Security Archive, was prepared in 1995 by a Pentagon contractor who had access to former senior Soviet defense officials, military officers, and industrial specialists. It demonstrated U.S. exaggeration of Soviet "aggressiveness" and its failure to recognize Soviet fears of a U.S. first strike. The Pentagon study concluded that the Soviet military high command "understood the devastating consequences of nuclear war" and believed that the use of nuclear weapons had to be avoided at "all costs."

Cooking the Books

Two major examples of the militarization of intelligence demonstrate the resulting corruption. The first occurred in 1975, when the Ford administration, with the prodding of presidential chief of staff Dick Cheney and Secretary of Defense Donald Rumsfeld, placed a group of neoconservatives in the CIA. The purpose was to challenge the professionally produced National Intelligence Estimates (NIEs) on Soviet military power and to ensure more dire estimates of Soviet power and more skepticism of arms control. In order to accomplish this, Cheney and Rumsfeld persuaded President Gerald Ford to remove a professional, William Colby, as CIA director and to replace him with the Agency's first political appointee, George H.W. Bush. Colby would not allow a clearly polemical group, led by Harvard professor Richard Pipes and referred to as Team B, to hijack the production of intelligence estimates. Bush had no qualms about doing so. Ford removed Colby, and Pipes—with the help of Cheney and Rumsfeld—named a team of right-wing academics and former government officials to draft their own intelligence estimates on Soviet military power. It is noteworthy that neither Cheney nor Rumsfeld mention the Team B chicanery in their recently published memoirs.

Team B predicted a series of Soviet weapons developments that never occurred. These included directed energy weapons, mobile ABM systems, and anti-satellite capabilities. Pipes's team concluded (falsely) that the Soviet Union rejected nuclear parity, was bent on fighting and winning a nuclear war, and was radically increasing its military spending. CIA deputy director Gates used this worst-case analysis in a series of speeches in the 1980s to ingratiate himself with the Reagan administration. Ironically, the Pipes politicization process was taking place during the period (1977–1983) when several Soviet leaders (Brezhnev, Andropov, and Chernenko) were trying to bring Soviet defense spending under control.

Pipes's Team B represented the hard right on U.S. foreign policy; this group consistently labeled the Soviets an aggressive imperialistic power bent on world domination. Team B estimates were drafted in order to reify this worldview, which Cheney and Rumsfeld supported three decades before they combined to militarize intelligence and take the country into war against Iraq. Members of Team B, particularly Paul Wolfowitz, deputy secretary of defense in the administration of George W. Bush, argued that Moscow would use its nuclear advantage to wage conventional war against developing nations.

Having seen the writing on the wall, the CIA team known as Team A exaggerated its own assessments of Soviet military spending and Soviet military technology. It took a decade for the CIA to correct the record and lower these inflated estimates. But the damage had been done. The Reagan administration used these inflated estimates of Soviet military power to garner a trillion and a half dollars in defense spending in the 1980s. These vast expenditures were directed against a Soviet military threat that was greatly exaggerated and a Soviet Union that was in decline.

The Pentagon welcomed the hardline intelligence and its threat of Soviet militarism to oppose all arms control and disarmament measures during the Cold War. The military-industrial complex, particularly the weapons laboratories, were vehemently opposed to any restrictions on strategic testing and weapons modernization. In the wake of the Cuban missile crisis of 1962, President Kennedy courageously promoted a partial test ban treaty with the Soviet Union. Fortunately, in this case the CIA and INR vouched for the U.S. capability to monitor any partial test ban treaty, and the treaty was ratified with bipartisan support.

The Team B experience was the first instance of institutionalized militarization of intelligence imposed on the CIA from the White House. The first instance of the CIA's internal militarization of intelligence took place in the 1980s, when President Reagan appointed a right-wing ideologue, Bill Casey, to be CIA director, and Casey appointed a right-wing ideologue, Bob Gates, to be his deputy. Casey and Gates combined to "cook the books" on a variety of issues, including the Soviet Union, Central America, and Southwest Asia, tailoring intelligence estimates to support the military policies of the Reagan administration. After he left the CIA in 1993, Gates admitted that he had become accustomed to Casey "fixing" intelligence to support policy on many issues. He did not describe his own role in support of Casey.

Casey's first National Intelligence Estimate as CIA director became an exercise in politicization. The estimate dealt with the Soviet Union and international terrorism. Casey and Gates speciously argued that a Soviet conspiracy was behind global terrorism. They pushed this line in order to justify more U.S. covert action in developing nations and to defend increased defense spending. In 1985, they ordered an intelligence assessment of a supposed Soviet plot against the Pope, hoping to produce a document that would undermine Secretary of State George P. Shultz's efforts to improve relations with Moscow. The CIA also produced an NIE in 1985 that became the intelligence rationale for arms sales to Iran. Former clandestine operative and national intelligence officer Graham Fuller collaborated with the National Security Council to prepare an estimate that supported the Reagan administration's (illegal) arms sales to Iran and (illegal) diversion of the profits to Contra forces in Nicaragua.

Casey and Gates supported an aggressive policy in Central America that included covert action in Nicaragua and CIA involvement in the civil war in El Salvador, where the CIA and the Pentagon backed the brutal Salvadoran government. The U.S. ambassador in El Salvador, Robert E. White, challenged the CIA's role and charged the CIA station chief in San Salvador with filing politicized reports in order to justify continued military support for the government. He charged that Casey had "put intelligence at the service of policy and provided justifications for ever-deeper involvement."[9] White also took issue with a State Department White Paper, drafted by CIA analysts, that falsely described a "flood of arms" to the Salvadoran insurgents from such Soviet allies as Vietnam, Ethiopia, and Bulgaria.

Casey and Gates pressured CIA analysts to ensure assessments matched the reports of the CIA station chief in El Salvador. Secretary of State Alexander Haig eventually fired White, and several analysts were forced out of the CIA's Central America branch because of their opposition to this politicization.

During their tenure, Casey and Gates undermined the culture of the directorate of intelligence, introducing a successful corporate-style takeover of the CIA's finished intelligence. If you are unfamiliar with the organizational culture of the CIA in the 1980s, then think of Thomas Wolfe's *Wall Street*, with Casey serving as the corporate raider, Gordon Gecko, and Gates serving as his protégé, Bud Fox.[10]

The militarization of intelligence was a major reason for the CIA's failure to track the decline and demise of the Soviet Union. In the 1970s and early 1980s, SOVA analysts had "reported Soviet military spending growing at the enormous rate of 4 to 5 percent a year."[11] But, in 1983, these analysts realized they had significantly exaggerated the growth rate and that a rate of 1 percent was closer to the mark. Gates would not permit the publication of a paper with the revised growth rates, and he warned Secretary of Defense Weinberger about the reassessment. Weinberger "went nuts," according to two former CIA analysts. Two years later, in 1985, Gates finally permitted that paper to be circulated. He refused, however, to publish another paper arguing that the "Soviets had made a deliberate decision to curtail their spending on strategic forces in the mid-seventies, when they attained strategic parity with the U.S."[12] Even in 1987, when analysts were arguing that Gorbachev's failure to modernize Soviet industry would lead to lower defense spending, Gates ordered his analysts to prepare an assessment for Weinberger that projected increased Soviet military and economic power.[13]

The CIA vs. the Pentagon

There is chronic tension between the worst-case assessments of military intelligence and the typically less polemical views of the CIA. At the same time, there were episodes in which the CIA pulled its punches in order to produce intelligence that favored the Pentagon's worldview. If the Agency had not tailored its intelligence on the Soviet military in the 1980s, it might have been more difficult for President Reagan to get his unprecedented peacetime increases in the U.S. defense budget from 1981 to 1986. Accurate assessments of the troubled Soviet economy and the backward aspects of the Soviet military might have produced congressional challenges to increased defense spending. The late Senator Daniel P. Moynihan (D-NY), for example, asked in 1990, "Would we have spent as much on our military during the 1980s if we had believed that the Soviet defense burden simply was not sustainable? I think not, and if I am correct, then the issue has been a momentous one for the state of the American economy."[14]

Some of the mistakes were honest errors in judgment. Until satellite photography became available in the 1960s, the intelligence community had no direct evidence of the size of Soviet ICBM production. In view of the surprise launch of Sputnik in October 1957, there was a strong tendency to exaggerate the size of the Soviet force and to accept the boasting of Soviet leader Nikita Khrushchev. As a result, the NIE in 1960 stated that the "ICBM provides the USSR, for the first time, with an efficient means of delivering a heavyweight attack on the United States, and the Soviets have strong incentives to build up a substantial force."[15] This view was a key element in the notorious "missile gap" argument during the presidential campaign in 1960. Overhead photography revealed in 1961 that actual ICBM deployment was far lower than projected.

The CIA track record on Soviet military capabilities was not perfect, but it was typically more accurate than any other agency's record despite the examples of politicization. The CIA overestimated the projected number of warheads deployed on submarine-launched ballistic missiles, but challenged military intelligence that grossly exaggerated the numbers of MIRVed launchers. The high and low CIA projections in the 1970s on

MIRVs successfully bracketed the actual number of nuclear weapons in the Soviet force, with correct estimates of the numbers of MIRVs on ICBMs and the rate at which these missiles would be deployed. Overall, the CIA significantly overestimated the rate of strategic force modernization, with an NIE in 1985 projecting that virtually the entire ICBM force would be replaced within ten years. Less than 10 percent of the force had been replaced by 1989, more than a third of the projection period. In the overestimates of force modernization, the CIA exaggerated the rate of deployment and the date of initial operational capability of each weapons system. It is noteworthy that some of the CIA errors were due to an analytic bias, an unwillingness to accept that the Soviets would actually slow some weapons programs in order to conform to arms control limits.

Uses and Misuses of Satellite Imagery

Since the Soviet Union, Eastern Europe, and China were denied areas that prevented firsthand observation of the military environment, the United States had to develop sophisticated systems that could provide hard data on Soviet and Chinese intentions and capabilities. Traditional espionage methods were inadequate in monitoring the Soviet Bloc and China, and U.S. satellite imaging systems became essential. The CIA played a central role in developing the first remote sensors, both the U-2 spy plane and the Corona reconnaissance satellite. New collections methods had to be accompanied by sophisticated analytical methodologies for eliciting useful information from the collection, and the CIA's Office of Scientific Intelligence, later the Directorate of Science and Technology, led the way in both collection and analysis. Currently, the CIA lacks the scientific capability to develop sophisticated technological systems.

There are particular risks in allowing the military to dominate the satellite imagery used to critique the defense budget, gauge the likelihood of military conflict against developing nations, and verify and monitor arms control agreements. During the worst years of tension between the United States and the Soviet Union, there were major battles between the Pentagon and Defense Intelligence Agency against the CIA and INR. I participated in the preparation of numerous National Intelligence Estimates from 1966 to 1986, when the Pentagon's military analysts consistently exaggerated the quantitative and qualitative aspects of Soviet strategic forces.

With the development of satellite technology, the CIA successfully monitored the technical difficulties that the Soviets were experiencing in their strategic programs, particularly their anti-ballistic missile program's difficulties in detecting, identifying, and intercepting ballistic missiles. CIA estimates often were issued over the objections of the Pentagon, when military intelligence could not accept evidence of Soviet setbacks. In the 1980s, however, CIA assessments were ignored by CIA director Casey and deputy director Gates, who conducted their own public campaign to exaggerate Soviet capabilities and justify greater U.S. spending on President Reagan's "Star Wars" program.

Following President Reagan's announcement of the Strategic Defense Initiative to the National Association of Evangelicals, a ministers' organization, in Orlando, Florida, in March 1983, Gates made a series of speeches promoting Star Wars and politicizing CIA intelligence on Soviet strategic defense. Prior to the president's Star Wars speech, CIA director Casey hired a right-wing polemicist, Constantine Menges, to peddle the idea of Star Wars. The public policy advocacy of Gates and Menges on strategic defense was a violation of the CIA charter, which prohibits the use of intelligence information in the public arena.

CIA analysis of satellite imagery was the primary tool used to address key U.S. policy questions regarding the capabilities of Soviet strategic weapons systems and how they could be used against U.S. interests. In the 1980s, however, the CIA suppressed sensitive satellite intelligence on key issues such as Pakistan's nuclear program. The Symington Amendment in 1961 demanded that Washington terminate military assistance to any nation developing a nuclear weapons capability. This legislation forced the Carter administration to stop military assistance to Pakistan in early 1979, when the U.S. intelligence community discovered Pakistan was operating a clandestine uranium enrichment facilty at Kahuta. During the campaign against Carter in 1980, Reagan asserted that "nuclear nonproliferation is none of our business," which foreshadowed the shift to a closer military relationship with Pakistan and an abandonment of our policy of nonproliferation. The Reagan administration turned a blind eye to the program because the Pressler Amendment in 1985 had stipulated an end to U.S. military assistance to Pakistan if there were evidence of Pakistani possession of a nuclear explosive device. Since Pakistan was the conduit for record amounts of covert assistance to the Afghan rebels, the Reagan administration put a higher priority on building bilateral relations with Islamabad than on preventing nuclear proliferation.

In 1984, there were reports that Pakistan was trying to circumvent U.S. export controls to purchases krytron switches to trigger a nuclear device, and a leading Pakistani nuclear scientist, A.Q. Khan, began bragging about Pakistan's achievement of a nuclear weapons capability. In the previous year, U.S. intelligence had discovered that China was providing the Pakistanis with a design for solid-core nuclear weapons and that Pakistan was having success in uranium enrichment. Khan confirmed this in 1984, when he announced that Pakistan had crossed the nuclear threshold.

In 1986, however, CIA deputy director Gates issued an ultimatum that there would be no reporting on Pakistani nuclear activities in the *National Intelligence Daily*, the CIA product that was sent to the Senate and House intelligence committees. CIA leaders made sure that no finished intelligence on Pakistani nuclear activities got beyond the six or seven readers of the President's Daily Briefing. The annual certification of Pakistan became a farce. In 1993, the former deputy director of the CIA, Richard Kerr, told Seymour Hersh that "there is no question that we had the intelligence basis in 1987 to deny military aid to Pakistan."[16]

The military's willingness to suppress sensitive intelligence is a threat to the conduct of U.S. national security policy. One example of the dangers of entrusting satellite collection and sensitive imagery analysis to the Pentagon is an incident that took place during the Persian Gulf War in 1991. Colin L. Powell's memoir, *An American Journey*, revealed that during Operation Desert Storm, General Norman Schwarzkopf claimed a smart bomb had destroyed four Iraqi SCUD missile launchers. Intelligence imagery showed that it had actually destroyed four Jordanian fuel tanks. General Schwarzkopf's intelligence officers would not tell him he was wrong. Nor would General Powell, who concluded that preserving General Schwarzkopf's "equanimity" was more important than revealing the truth. This type of military bias and respect for the chain of command were primary reasons for creating an independent CIA in 1947 outside of the policy process, removed from the Pentagon's emphasis on worst-case analysis and exaggeration of the threat.

The Pentagon's control of satellite imagery caused a major intelligence failure in 1998, when the National Geospatial Intelligence Agency failed to monitor five Indian nuclear tests. This failure led CIA Director Tenet to tell Congress that the CIA could not monitor the Comprehensive Test Ban Treaty; as a result, the Senate failed to ratify the treaty. In piecing together the reasons for the intelligence failure, it was learned that the Pentagon had placed a low priority on satellite collection against India because the military was not concerned with threats from

South Asia and was not interested in issues that would support an arms control agreement.

The following year, the CIA and military intelligence combined to provide the outdated maps that led to the bombing of the Chinese embassy in Belgrade. The bombers hit the intended target, but outdated CIA maps did not show that the building was no longer a Serbian military office. This failure led to a political crisis in Sino-American relations, with Premier Jiang Zemin refusing to take calls from President Clinton in the immediate aftermath of this blunder.

The Pentagon's New Clandestine Role

President Bush's "Global War on Terror" brought the Pentagon into clandestine areas of activity that had been the province of the CIA. Until 9/11, the CIA had statutory privileges in both clandestine and finished intelligence areas. Title 50 of the U.S. Code gave the CIA the exclusive role to conduct "deniable" activities in foreign countries where the United States had not declared war. The Pentagon's war-fighting authority under Title 10 does not include a role in countries where war has not been declared. When Navy Seals conducted their successful operation against bin Laden in Pakistan, a country with which the United States was not at war, CIA director Leon Panetta was ostensibly the commander for the mission and the CIA ostensibly supervised the mission. Special forces have conducted similar activities in Pakistan, Somalia, Sudan, and Yemen against terrorist targets. Congressional intelligence committees should examine these operations and determine whether such operations are legal. In the wake of 9/11, however, many highly questionable activities have been conducted and even illegal activities have been ignored.

According to John McLaughlin, CIA deputy director from 2000 to 2004, Secretary of Defense Rumsfeld was "frustrated that he sat on this enormous capability that he could not fully utilize."[17] Rumsfeld's response, described by McLaughlin as an "awkward, stumbling, improvisational, crash-bang kind of thing," was designed to get the Pentagon fully engaged in the global war on terror. Rumsfeld, a creative manipulator of the national security bureaucracy, developed a three-part program to give the Pentagon an even bigger voice in the intelligence community, enable it to conduct operations abroad, and establish a special department to prepare and distribute intelligence assessments to rival CIA assessments.

Rumsfeld's first step, the appointment of Stephen Cambone to the new post of undersecretary of intelligence in 2003, should have been challenged by the intelligence community and the Senate Intelligence Committee. Cambone was in place a year before the creation of the post of Director of National Intelligence, the so-called intelligence tsar. He made sure that the tsar would have no control over the budgetary and personnel policies of the community, particularly combat-support institutions such as the National Security Agency (NSA) and the National Reconnaissance Office (NRO), which are managed by the Pentagon.

Secretary Rumsfeld's next step was the authorization of forward-deployed Special Forces units overseas, often without the knowledge of the appropriate U.S. embassy or CIA station chief. These units became known as "Military Liaison Elements" (MLEs). They often worked with indigenous special forces units, including "operational preparation of the environment" in countries that were not considered war zones, such as Iran.[18] The CIA's resistance ultimately forced Rumsfeld to create rules for coordinating activities with CIA station chiefs and ambassadors. The role of the military in these situations was extralegal because the Pentagon lacked authority to conduct "covert" activities, particularly in countries where there has been no declaration of war.

The Pentagon's role in clandestine collection and covert operations was unaccompanied by the constraints of oversight that govern the undercover activities of the intelligence community. Rumsfeld dispatched intelligence teams overseas, often without the knowledge of U.S. ambassadors and CIA station chiefs, to gather intelligence for military and counterterrorist operations. Special operations forces are active in Iran without oversight from Congress.

Finally, in addition to dominating the intelligence community and conducting clandestine operations, Secretary of Defense Rumsfeld, with the encouragement of Vice President Cheney, created his own intelligence analysis division in the Pentagon, the Office for Special Plans. OSP manipulated and in some instances, created the intelligence case for war against Iraq. The creation of the OSP marked the merger of intelligence and the Pentagon in order to militarize intelligence and make the case for war. This is presumably what President Bush meant when he proclaimed the "marriage" between intelligence and the Pentagon. The OSP was managed by undersecretary of defense Douglas Feith and Abram Shulsky. They supplied bogus intelligence to the White House on Iraqi WMD and links to terrorist groups. The OSP absorbed the staff of the Pentagon's Iraq Desk, grew to eighteen members, and reworked intelligence that the CIA and other members of the intelligence community found lacking in credibility.

The OSP coordinated activities with Ahmed Chalabi's Iraq exile opposition and organized military training in Hungary for his Free Iraqi Forces. Chalabi had his own special liaison officer in 2003 and 2004 who connected him to Centcom and top Pentagon officials.[19] The CIA had warned the policy and intelligence communities in the 1990s that Chalabi, the head of the Iraqi National Congress, was a fabricator and not to be trusted. Chalabi was also a favorite source for the *New York Times*' Judith

Miller, who headlined his views on Iraq's purported holdings of weapons of mass destruction. Vice President Cheney and his chief of staff, Lewis "Scooter" Libby, were also key sources for Miller's disinformation.

The OSP took Chalabi's disinformation and delivered it regularly to key members of the Bush administration, who, in turn, passed it to Congress and the U.S. public in order to make the case for war. The OSP also conducted meetings with such unreliable sources as Manucher Ghorbanifar, who was part of the Iranian arms-for-hostages talks in the 1980s. Both Cambone and Feith played major roles in relaying the views of Chalabi and Ghorbanifar to congressional and media sources.

Feith claimed that his office "didn't do intelligence assessments," but one of his briefings to the White House and the NSC was titled, "Assessing the Relationship between Iraq and al-Qaeda," which maligned the work of the CIA and DIA, and was designed to prove the so-called link between Iraq and al-Qaeda.[20] Another OSP document was titled "Iraq and al-Qaeda: Making the Case." It argued that a "massive, symbiotic relationship" existed between the two; it was released on July 25, 2002, soon after the British intelligence chief charged in a private memorandum that intelligence in Washington was being "fixed" to support the administration's policy. Feith personally delivered a briefing at the White House that contained a slide presentation termed "Fundamental Problems with How Intelligence Community Is Assessing Information." The directors of the CIA and DIA were never given the "Fundamental Problems" briefing.

The OSP's most important consumer was Vice President Cheney, who played a major role in cooking the intelligence books. The OSP also had close links with the Defense Policy Board, whose members—particularly Richard Perle, former CIA director Jim Woolsey, and former Republican speaker of the House Newt Gingrich—peddled the OSP's disinformation to audiences at home and abroad.

The Senate Intelligence Committee looked into the problem of the OSP, which had an exclusive pipeline to the White House without coordination within the intelligence community, but gave OSP a free pass, concluding that no regulations had been broken. Ironically, the Pentagon's own Inspector General concluded in 2006 that the OSP had "fixed" intelligence to produce "alternative intelligence assessments," which had been "inappropriate," a gentle way of describing illegal activity to make the case for war.[21] The so-called intelligence included "reporting of dubious quality or reliability" that supported the views of the White House and lacked the imprimatur of the intelligence community. The IG referred to Feith's activities as an "alternative intelligence assessment process" that was created to make the phony case for war.

Feith also passed classified intelligence to Stephen Hayes of the *Weekly Standard*, which regularly published the OSP's disinformation. Vice President Cheney often referred to the *Weekly Standard* as the "best source" of information on the relationship between Saddam Hussein and al-Qaeda. Cheney used the Feith-Hayes pipeline to trumpet the canard that 9/11 hijacker Mohammed Atta had met with Iraqi intelligence officers in Prague.

When media coverage became intense in the summer of 2003, Secretary of Defense Rumsfeld quietly folded the OSP into the Northern Gulf Affairs office under the Pentagon's Near East and South Asia policy office. Under this arrangement, the Gulf Affairs office had more adult supervision than the OSP, but it still danced to the tune of Cheney's office in the White House, specifically to the tune of Scooter Libby. Cheney and Libby had staffed the OSP with reliable neoconservatives and ideologues such as David Wurmser and Michael Maloof, who were loyal to the goal of regime change in Iraq and bent on using Chalabi's reporting to make the case for war. Cheney and Rumsfeld resorted to the same technique they had used in 1976, when they had worked for President Ford. In the 1970s, they had created Team B at the CIA in order to politicize intelligence on Soviet military power. In 2002, they politicized intelligence in order to take the country to war against Iraq.

In addition to the OSP, the Pentagon created the Counterintelligence Field Activity (CIFA) to conduct surveillance against American citizens near U.S. military facilities or at antiwar meetings. In the summer of 2004, CIFA monitored a small protest in Houston, Texas, against Halliburton, the giant military contractor once headed by Vice President Cheney. Undersecretary of defense Wolfowitz created a fact-gathering operation called TALON (Threat and Local Observation Notice) to collect "raw information" about "suspicious incidents."[22] The unauthorized spying of CIFA and the computer collection against innocent people and organizations for TALON were illegal, the type of threat to civil liberties that President Eisenhower had anticipated in an environment of continuous war.

The CIA's Contribution to the Militarization of Intelligence

The CIA played a major role in the militarization of intelligence on Iraq during the run-up to the war. CIA analysts in the early 2000s totally misread the crippled and demoralized dictatorship of Saddam Hussein and the picture of WMD, although they refuted the so-called evidence of links between Saddam Hussein and al-Qaeda. It was CIA director Tenet who misused intelligence to make a specious case for links between Hussein and al-Qaeda, and Cheney's memoirs emphasize the briefings he received from Tenet.

Tenet also misinformed the White House about the nature of the Taliban relationship with bin Laden's al-Qaeda. In his briefings in 2002, the CIA director stressed that the "Taliban and al-Qaeda [are] one and the same," which ignored the distance that the Taliban, a nationalist movement, wanted to keep from al-Qaeda, a global jihadist movement.[23] Tenet never understood the political and operational differences between the two different radical strains in Afghanistan—one that was local and contingent, the other global and unyielding. Al-Qaeda, moreover, consisted of largely intellectual Arab interlopers who were a generation older than their largely rural Afghan hosts.

Overall, the CIA missed nearly every call that needed to be made about Saddam Hussein's Iraq. As in the case of the CIA's corporate failure regarding the decline and fall of the Soviet Union in the 1980s, CIA analysts were fundamentally wrong about most issues involving Saddam Hussein's Iraq. One of the rare exceptions to this disturbing record was the warning that U.S. troops would face significant resistance from Iraqi irregular forces employing guerrilla tactics. Policymakers were told that the irregulars would fight more fanatically than regular army forces.

The egregious examples of politicization undermined the credibility of the CIA as well as the United States itself. The CIA cherry-picked the evidence to support the case for war and thoroughly corrupted the intelligence process to convince the Congress and the American people of the need for war. The Bush administration would have gone to war even if the CIA had gotten the intelligence right, had not drafted a specious NIE and unclassified White Paper, and had not prepared a phony speech for Secretary of State Powell. It is possible, however, that honest leadership from CIA could have created more opposition from the Congress, the media, and the public.

Three years after the invasion of Iraq, a senior CIA analyst, Paul Pillar, documented the efforts of the Bush administration to politicize the intelligence of the CIA on Iraqi WMD and so-called links between Iraq and al-Qaeda.[24] Pillar accused the Bush administration of using policy to drive intelligence production, which was the same argument offered by the chief of British intelligence in the Downing Street memorandum prior to the war, and aggressively using intelligence to win public support for war. Pillar does not explain why no senior CIA official protested, let alone resigned, in the wake of the president's misuse of intelligence, and understated his own role in the politicization process. Pillar falsely claimed "the intelligence community's own substantive judgments do not appear to have been compromised," when it was clear that the CIA erred on most key judgments and had to politicize the intelligence to be so egregiously wrong.[25]

Bush, Obama, and the Militarization of the National Security State

The Bush administration managed to militarize virtually every part of the national security arena, particularly intelligence. In addition to the politicization of intelligence to make the case for war, the CIA entered the "dark side," a world of "secret prisons," extraordinary renditions, and torture and abuse. The similarities between the Inquisition's interrogation regime and the role of the CIA in the twenty-first century are chilling.

Several months after the 9/11 attacks, President Bush ordered the NSA to eavesdrop on the conversations of Americans inside the United States without court-approved warrants as part of the war against terrorism, thus threatening the privacy of all Americans.[26] His secret executive order ignored criminal prohibitions against such surveillance in the FISA Act of 1978. The wiretapping program was conducted without congressional or judicial approval, and it was far more comprehensive than we were led to believe. It was eventually challenged by Attorney General John Ashcroft and Senator Jay Rockefeller (D-WV), the ranking minority member of the Senate Intelligence Committee. In the meantime, the NSA's spying inundated the FBI with thousands of "leads" that turned out to go nowhere.[27]

The Bush administration used 9/11 and the Iraq War to expand the powers of the Pentagon's DIA, which received authorization to allow its personnel to hide the fact that they work for the government when they seek domestic intelligence sources. The Pentagon unsuccessfully sought an exemption from the Privacy Act in order to gain access to FBI intelligence on Americans who had nothing to do with terrorism. Bert Tussig, director of Homeland Defense and Security Issues at the U.S. Army War College and a former Marine, says, "There is very little that could justify the collection of domestic intelligence by the U.S. military. If we start going down this slippery slope it would be too easy to go back to a place we never want to see again."[28]

Even the State Department got into the politicization game, with undersecretary of state for Arms Control and Disarmament John Bolton running his own intelligence program that he coordinated with Feith's efforts. Bolton provided the White House with "white papers" on WMD that lacked support within the intelligence community. He used these papers in testifying to congressional committees, exaggerating the WMD programs in Iraq, Syria, and Cuba. In 2002, he presented misinformation to the Congress on a Cuban biological weapons program. When the CIA challenged the accuracy of Bolton's information in 2003, he was finally forced to cancel a briefing on Syrian WMD for a House International Relations subcommittee. CIA director Tenet and the congressional intelligence committees should have been more aggressive in countering the activities of Feith and Bolton and their neoconservative cohorts.

In the political panic that followed the 9/11 attacks, the Bush administration permitted the creation of two large bureaucratic entities—the Department of Homeland Security and the Office of National Intelligence—that have contributed to intelligence and policy failures. These large bureaucratic entities made it easier for the White House and the Pentagon to control the context and timing of terrorist alerts, which Karl Rove influenced at the Office of Homeland Security, as well as the direction of intelligence activities, which Steve Cambone influenced from the Pentagon. These departments failed in their response to Hurricane Katrina in 2005 and the attempted suicide bombing of a commercial airliner in 2009, respectively. Unfortunately, the Obama administration convinced the mainstream media that James Clapper's predecessor, retired Admiral Dennis Blair, was force to resign because of the pathetic performance of the intelligence community in December 2009, when a young Nigerian boarded a commercial airliner with explosives and a key CIA facility in Afghanistan was hit by a suicide bomber.

These failures were systemic, and Blair should not have been blamed for them. The CIA, the National Counter-Terrorism Center (NCTC), and the NSA were blameworthy in the attempted suicide bombing of a commercial airliner. The U.S. embassy and the CIA station ignored warnings from the Nigerian's father; the NSA didn't exploit collection opportunities that would have provided significant information; and the NCTC failed to pursue information that would have placed the Nigerian on a no-fly list.

The NCTC should have had operational control of counterterrorism operations, but the 2004 statute that created Blair's position specifically states that the NCTC director "may not direct the execution of counterterrorism operations." Even the State Department's Bureau of Intelligence Research (INR) ignored the Nigerian's multiple-entry visa for the United States. President Obama's principal adviser on counterterrorism, John Brennan, should have taken the problem of operational responsibility to the Congress where it needs to be corrected; he still hasn't done so.

Similarly, the CIA, not Admiral Blair, demonstrated profound incompetence in the events leading up to the successful bombing of its most important operational base in Afghanistan. The base itself was in the hands of an inexperienced and unprepared CIA officer; too many CIA officers were exposed to the suicide bomber; the bomber himself had never been properly vetted; and, in any event, the bomber should never have been permitted to enter such a sensitive facility. None of the numerous human errors that were made in both failures could be placed at Blair's door. The blame resided at the highest levels of the National Clandestine Service, but CIA director Panetta praised the work of the clandestine service and no one was held accountable or even responsible.

Blair did have a major weakness as the intelligence tsar, a weakness he shares with many general and flag officers who lack experience in Washington. He simply lacked the geopolitical background for providing briefings to the president on strategic issues. President Obama placed too many general officers in sensitive political positions for which they are not prepared. General James Jones as national security adviser is a case in point. Blair and Jones started unnecessary—and losing—battles within the intelligence and policy communities. Blair tried to control the appointment of CIA station chiefs, who have traditionally been CIA operations officers. It made no sense to raise the possibility of replacing them with NSA officers or DIA officers who have no experience in intelligence liaison. Blair also tried to halt certain clandestine operations that would have weakened the CIA's counterterrorism mission in countries penetrated by foreign intelligence. Jones tried to get Ambassador Karl Eikenberry removed as ambassador to Afghanistan, which made the Marine general no friends in the White House or the State Department. Neither Blair nor Jones established a personal rapport with President Obama, despite their considerable contacts with him.

The last three intelligence tsars have been general officers, which means the absence of an independent civilian voice to counter the power of military intelligence and its worst-case analysis. In addition to the fact that active-duty general officers traditionally head the major intelligence collection agencies, many of the top positions at the National Counter-Terrorism Center are occupied by flag officers who lack any background in strategic intelligence. This compromises civilian oversight of the decision to use military power and makes it more likely that intelligence will be tailored to suit the purposes of the Pentagon. The current intelligence tsar, General Clapper, is certainly familiar with these problems, having served as undersecretary for intelligence for both secretaries of defense Gates and Rumsfeld. At that time, moreover, he was responsible for managing the Counterintelligence Field Activities Office, which managed the illegal database that included information about antiwar protests. These issues were not raised at his Senate confirmation hearings.

The Pentagon tried to interfere with the intelligence process in 2011, when it moved to delay an intelligence estimate on Afghanistan that supported President Obama's arguments in favor of the withdrawal of forces. On this occasion, no less a figure than General Petraeus did his best to throw a monkey wrench into the process and at least delay the publication of the estimate. This time, however, the intelligence community stood firm, key intelligence principals backed up the working analysts, and General Petraeus clearly suffered a bureaucratic defeat. Now that General Petraeus is CIA director, it seems likely that the CIA intelligence directorate and the National Intelligence Council will be subject to pressure on key intelligence issues, particularly where Petraeus has well-defined positions.

Presidents George W. Bush and Barack Obama created strong ties between the Pentagon and the Intelligence Community, which has contributed to the militarization of intelligence. Bush boasted of a "marriage" between the Pentagon and the CIA, which acknowledged an intelligence community subordinate to military priorities. After reappointing Clinton's CIA director, Tenet, and naming Congressman Porter Goss to succeed Tenet, a thoroughly unsuccessful appointment, Bush named Air Force General Michael Hayden as director of the CIA.

The notion of a "marriage" between these two major international security institutions stands in sharp contrast to Truman's idea of an intelligence community independent of the policy community, particularly the Pentagon. The Department of Defense, which was created by the same National Security Act that created the CIA in 1947, has become the chief manager of the $80 billion intelligence industry. The Pentagon controls more than 80 percent of the intelligence budget and more than 85 percent of all intelligence personnel. Most collection requirements for intelligence flow directly from the Pentagon and support the needs of the "war fighter." Deference within the congressional and policy communities for the war fighter, moreover, has elevated tactical military considerations over strategic political considerations. Two (losing) wars against Iraq and Afghanistan over the past decade have also skewed the interests and priorities of the intelligence community in the direction of the Pentagon.

President Obama has strengthened Bush's "marriage" between the military and intelligence communities with the appointment of Petraeus, the country's most popular military figure, to run the CIA. Petraeus's stature in the administration and in the halls of Congress will make it more difficult for the current intelligence tsar to introduce strategic change to the intelligence community. Petraeus has no background in intelligence and is strongly attached to sensitive policies on counterterrorism and counterinsurgency as well as bilateral policies involving Iraq and Afghanistan. This has already led to the CIA director's efforts to influence intelligence judgments because of his personal policy preferences. CIA analysts hold more pessimistic views of the war in Afghanistan than Petraeus does, which could lead to confrontations.

In addition to Petraeus at CIA and James Jones at NSC, President Obama gave key ambassadorial appointments to retired generals in Afghanistan and Saudi Arabia, and Secretary of State Clinton named a retired general who was responsible for special operations in Afghanistan as the State Department's coordinator for counterterrorism. The numerous military appointments in the national security field were unprecedented.

In undermining the kind of intelligence community that President Truman wanted to create, one that was outside the policy process, particularly the military policy process, President Obama has threatened civilian control over the decision to use military power. The militarization of intelligence risks increased tailoring of intelligence to suit the interests of the military community and its legion of supporters on Capitol Hill. The military domination of the intelligence cycle will also make it more difficult to rebuild the important role of strategic intelligence, which has been largely absent from the development of national security policy.

Obama's appointment of General Petraeus completed the militarization of the intelligence community with only the State Department's INR outside the orbit of the Pentagon's influence. The general is accustomed to a chain-of-command, top-down process at the Pentagon and would have been shocked by the original contrarian nature of the intelligence culture as well as the bottom-up culture of the CIA. He is used to "Sirs" and salutes, which were once antithetical to the intelligence culture. The military culture considers contrarians, the source of many intelligence successes, to be dissenters. Conventional wisdom reigns at the Pentagon, where contrarians are pushed aside.

As General Hayden said on his way out of the CIA in 2009, the CIA doesn't do "hierarchy at all. Some called me 'general,' some 'sir,' but many called me 'Mike.'"[29] Conversely, a former senior CIA officer seemed closer to the mark when he asked, "Are they going to have a civilian intelligence service, or is it going to be a giant counterterrorism center?"[30] The CIA must decide if it is going to be a civilian intelligence service or a paramilitary center in support of the war fighter.

President Obama's appointments of Panetta to the Department of Defense and Petraeus to CIA suggest that he did not want to make changes or waves at either organization and, in the interests of a speedy confirmation process, made very safe choices. The president got more than he hoped for when both men were confirmed without a negative vote and with hardly a negative question. In an election year, the president is unwilling to look beyond his own team and to countenance change. He went from a so-called team of rivals at the outset of his administration to a team of like-minded group thinkers going into the 2012 election.

The CIA has become the most militarized civilian intelligence organization in Washington, which wasn't the case in its first fifty years. The first directors of the CIA were general officers, including Office of Strategic Services veteran General Walter Bedell Smith, who ran the CIA from 1950 to 1953, but they had good relations with the president and never traded on their military culture. No less an authority than General Hayden contradicted his earlier remarks when he noted that Petraeus will find "all the values you find in the services," presumably a reference to the paramilitary nature of the organization as well as the obedience of a "chain-of-command" bureaucracy.[31] Hayden advised Petraeus to do all the things that made him successful as a company commander, such as "Eat with the troops, walk around and talk to them, and, by all means, protect them." Hayden and his successor, Panetta, certainly provided protection even when CIA employees destroyed the torture and abuse tapes, an illegal destruction of evidence in the criminal investigation that took place from 2009 to 2011.

General Petraeus, at least, did not repeat the mistake that Admiral Stansfield Turner made in 1977, when he arrived at the CIA with a small retinue of naval officers, including his young son. Like Turner, who ran into early difficulties at the CIA, Petraeus has very limited experience in Washington or in dealing with Washington. As one senior intelligence officer observed, it would be a mistake for Petraeus to arrive with an entourage, creating the impression that he was coming to Langley "to fix us and show us how to do things." If so, the "antibodies will start rejecting the transplant."[32]

Over the past fifteen years, the CIA has lost its standing as the leading civilian intelligence organization in the government. The Agency once stood apart from such combat-support agencies as the National Security Agency, the National Reconnaissance Office, and the National Geospatial-Intelligence Agency. Once upon a time, the CIA understood that it was a civilian organization with major responsibilities to the president and, after the creation of the congressional oversight committees in 1976, to the Congress.

Demilitarizing National Security at Home and Abroad

The opportunity to fundamentally reorient U.S. defense, intelligence, and national security policy, which was afforded with the collapse of the Berlin Wall, the Warsaw Pact, and the Soviet Union between 1989 and 1991, has been squandered. If President Obama were truly interested in intelligence reform he would have abolished the office of national intelligence and the position of intelligence tsar or at least placed the Director of National Intelligence in civilian hands to counter the Pentagon's control of intelligence personnel and intelligence spending. Active-duty and retired general officers now command nearly all of the major institutions of the intelligence community, although my eighteen years on the faculty of the National War College confirmed my impression that military officers are not distinguished in the fields of strategic intelligence or geopolitical problem solving.

The militarization of intelligence has become a factor on every level, not simply the role of worst-case thinking in making intelligence assessments and estimates. The military has too much budgetary and management authority over the collection agencies such as NSA, NRO, and NGA, which gives the Pentagon great influence over intelligence collection. Military control of intelligence collection leads to serious neglect of nonmilitary priorities such as arms control and disarmament and ethnic politics and violence.

The Pentagon has too much clout in the production of intelligence analysis as well; only the State Department's INR appears to demonstrate the required integrity and independence needed to tell truth to power. The military drove the exaggeration of the Soviet threat in a series of estimates on Soviet strategic power; presumably the military is having the same impact on estimates on China. Since the intelligence community lacks sufficient knowledge of U.S. military capabilities, let alone U.S. military operations and war plans, there is a tendency to exaggerate threats in making net assessments. In an era when the major intelligence concern is the problem of terrorism, the military simply lacks the skill-set for understanding the cultural and political roots of terrorist organizations, let alone their intentions and capabilities.

Bad intelligence will hurt the possibility of good national security policy, but good intelligence is no guarantee that there will be sound national security policy. If the Kennedy and Johnson administrations had been reading CIA estimates and assumptions on Vietnam in the 1960s, they would have found good reasons for not resorting to force in Southeast Asia. But Kennedy was convinced of the need to check what he believed to be the actions of a Soviet proxy, and Johnson, who was never personally committed to the use of force in Vietnam, was insufficiently confident to push his intuition against the policy arguments of the key players of the John F. Kennedy administration, particularly the Rostow brothers (Walt and Eugene) and the Bundy brothers (McGeorge and Bill) as well as Secretary of State Rusk and Secretary of Defense McNamara. If the Reagan administration had been reading CIA intelligence on the Middle East, presumably he would have thought twice about sending U.S. Marines into Beirut in 1983 to pull Israeli chestnuts out of a fire that was smoldering in Lebanon.

The Reagan administration exaggerated the Soviet threat and was prepared to increase the defense budget in the 1980s regardless of the intelligence presented to the White House. Even if the CIA had correctly and honestly presented the White House a picture of Moscow's interest in arms control and detente as well as the constraints on the Soviet defense budget, there would have been record peacetime increases for the military. Reagan had no interest in arms control and favored a 600-ship navy and a Strategic Defense Initiative that has resulted in an additional $100 billion in defense spending over the past twenty-five years without getting the United States any closer to a strategic defense against ballistic missiles. Sadly, the policy process will always overrule or ignore the intelligence process, no matter how prescient and credible that intelligence is.

The budgetary and collection authority for the major technical collection agencies (the NSA, which intercepts signals and communications and is essential to strategic warning; the NRO, which designs and launches spy satellites; and the NGA, which interprets satellite imagery) must be taken from the Pentagon and transferred to the DNI. The NRO, one of the largest enterprises in the intelligence community with a budget of more than $8 billion, began as a joint venture with the CIA; the NGA's responsibility for analysis was once a joint CIA-military operation that allowed civilian intelligence analysts to provide a check on the work of military analysts. The Pentagon opposes any transfer of responsibility for the agencies to the DNI, and congressional intelligence committees have been negligent in proposing reforms for the community or preventing the Pentagon from establishing corporate control over the process.

The Senate Select Committee on Intelligence and the Senate Armed Forces Committee must abolish the position of undersecretary of defense for intelligence, which was created by Rumsfeld to solidify the Pentagon's control over the intelligence community. The Senate Armed Forces Committee routinely approved the position without any vetting from the SSCI. Unfortunately, the DNI has had no support from the Congress in trying to obtain control over the Pentagon's resources on these key intelligence issues.

The failure of the U.S. intelligence community to pick up signals of the death of North Korean leader Kim Jong-il in December 2011, similar to the CIA's failure to provide warning of Soviet leader Yuri Andropov's death in 1984, pointed to problems in the field of strategic intelligence. North Korea is a closed society, which makes it a difficult intelligence target. The country is armed with nuclear weapons that are controlled by unpredictable leaders, which makes it an intelligence priority. The situation is similar to that of Iran, where there is a nuclear weapons program and great political turbulence, but little premonitory intelligence of strategic value.

The United States presumably has military options for any North Korean or Iranian efforts to use military force, but lacks political thinking and intelligence requirements for dealing with the possible unraveling of the opaque regimes in Tehran and

Pyongyang. In the middle of the Iraq War, North Korea managed to assist Syria in building an undetected nuclear reactor based on its own reactor in Yongbyon, with North Korean officials traveling regularly to the Syrian site. The U.S. intelligence community also failed to detect a new facility for uranium enrichment in Yongbyon, which was discovered in 2010 by a scientist from Stanford University. The militarization of intelligence has led to a lower priority for collecting intelligence on nuclear proliferation, a situation that needs to be corrected.

In the final analysis, the only protections against politicization are the integrity and honesty of the intelligence analysts themselves and the institution of competitive analysis to serve as a safeguard against unchallenged acceptance of conventional wisdom. The CIA's fundamental flaws, which contributed to the 9/11 failure, have gone largely uncorrected. The Bush and Obama administrations have compromised the CIA's Office of the Inspector General, which provided excellent investigations over the years, particularly in the wake of the 9/11 intelligence failure.

There is far too much attention given to current and tactical intelligence support for the war fighter and insufficient attention to the big-picture needs of strategic intelligence for decision-makers. There is too much investment in day-to-day intelligence involving weapons systems for the war fighter, but insufficient attention to the geopolitical developments and social tensions that are needed by the policymaker. As a result, the United States has too much information on the various military forces in the Middle East, yet its intelligence efforts failed to give any strategic warning of the Arab Spring. Serious attention must be given to improving the production of National Intelligence Estimates, which remain the best source of strategic intelligence.

Finally, the CIA must acknowledge its politicization of intelligence on the Soviet Union in the 1980s and its militarization of intelligence on Iraq in 2002–2003, which revealed an element of moral bankruptcy. These failures have made it more difficult to convince an international audience of U.S. intelligence on sensitive issues such as Iran's nuclear program. The CIA's unconscionable activities, particularly extrajudicial assassination, the preventable killing of civilians, torture, abuse, and secret prisons, have complicated the task of maintaining credible relations with our allies in the battle against terrorism. More attention must be given to the biblical inscription at the entrance to the CIA building in Langley, Virginia, that only "the truth will set you free."

SEVEN

THE PENTAGON'S PHANTOM MISSILE DEFENSE

*The release of atomic energy has not created a new problem. It has
merely made more urgent the necessity of solving an existing one.*
—Albert Einstein

*You can't say civilizations don't advance . . . in every war they
kill you in a new way.* —Will Rogers

There is probably no bigger bust or boondoggle in the history
of U.S. defense spending than the investment in national missile
defense (NMD), with annual appropriations of $10 billion, still
the most expensive and least effective weapons system in the U.S.
arsenal. According to John Arquilla of the Naval Postgraduate
School in California, this boondoggle has been unworkable and
unnecessary, with costs that are typically uncontrollable.[1] There
are boondoggles that have cost more, such as the F-35 Light-
ning II, which is already responsible for more than $325 billion
in spending since 2000. There have been boondoggles that have
made less sense, such as the Global Information Grid, which is
responsible for interconnecting all military networks, thus making it easier for international hackers to break into U.S. defense
information systems. But no boondoggle has been around longer and will end up wasting more U.S. taxpayer money than national missile defense.

Not even the initial skepticism of the uniformed military

has stopped the military-industrial complex from throwing money at strategic defense. As with other weapons systems, a constituency of defense contractors, conservative think tanks, and congressional forces has formed, making it difficult to stop its development or even deployment, no matter how little NMD contributes to national security.

Just as President Eisenhower had warned in 1961, defense contractors, conservative politicians, and scientists kept the idea of NMD alive. They formed political lobbying groups in 1978 consisting of politicians, retired generals, and industrial leaders.[2] These groups were led by the Committee on the Present Danger, formed by conservative Democrats, and High Frontier, formed by Republicans. High Frontier became a kind of kitchen cabinet to Ronald Reagan and eventually moved under the institutional umbrella of the Heritage Foundation, an ultra-conservative think tank with close ties to President Reagan. High Frontier was established by Karl R. Bendetsen, the retired CEO of the Champion International Corporation, and retired Lieutenant General Daniel O. Graham, who formerly headed the Defense Intelligence Agency. Initially, the Pentagon had no interest in NMD, preferring to develop offensive and not defensive weapons, but it played a key role in establishing links between these groups and their military supporters on Capitol Hill. The contractors, of course, have profited obscenely from the hundreds of billions of dollars thrown at NMD.

Influential members of the military-industrial complex took advantage of the American faith in technology to solve problems. This has worked in many areas of national security, but not for NMD. The United States has been chasing the gossamer of NMD for nearly sixty years. President Eisenhower's secretary of state, John Foster Dulles, began the pursuit, seeking large increases in spending to build such a defense. But even Dulles eventually concluded that the system would at best "degrade gracefully;" in other words, it would be over-whelmed by an increasingly large number of incoming missiles as well as the limited time needed for interception. Neverthe-less, U.S. strategists exaggerated the threat of ballistic missiles and, with the help of the military-industrial complex, continued the pursuit.

Both Democrats and Republicans have been willing to pursue the illusion of national missile defense, the "Star Wars" illusion. The funding for NMD began in the Eisenhower ad-ministration more than sixty years ago. Republican administra-tions have been more supportive than Democratic ones, and presidents from both parties ignored the initial opposition of the Pentagon. The position of the uniformed military was that arms should be developed and deployed for their lethality and not for defensive purposes and that, in any event, disarmament negotiations in any context were not a worthwhile enterprise vis-à-vis the Soviet Union. In the early 1970s, the secretary of defense and the joint chiefs of staff were opposed to the limits on offensive weapons in SALT and on ballistic missile defense in the ABM treaty.

After a decade of research, moreover, both the United States and the Soviet Union concluded in the 1970s that they could not develop a successful missile defense. For three decades, from the signing of the Anti-Ballistic Missile (ABM) Treaty in 1972 until President George W. Bush's abrogation of the treaty in 2001, the United States and the Soviet Union and Russia agreed that NMD would not work and that it would be impossible to limit offensive strategic weapons if one or both sides would deploy even a vulnerable national missile defense. Both sides accepted the logic of mutual assured destruction—MAD for short—re-quiring both to renounce an effective missile shield, since its owner might be tempted to attack the other in the belief that it would be safe from a counter-strike. This "balance of terror" gave the United States and Russia the confidence to cut their nuclear arsenals in the 1970s through the 1990s.

Pentagon planners were concerned that the massive amount of dollars spent on a missile defense system would drain away money from offensive systems that the military favors to guarantee U.S. security and protect U.S. forces. With the fiction of anti-missile defense inescapable, President Nixon and Soviet leader Brezhnev agreed to an ABM Treaty to limit the deployment of defensive systems and to ban testing that might make a comprehensive system possible. Leading members of Congress also were concerned that, even though an ABM system would not work, the Soviets would develop additional offensive capability to counter the United States. The Soviets were convinced from their research that they could not develop a successful system, but did not rule out the possibility that the United States could do so.

The ABM Treaty was a major arms control achievement that ultimately banned ballistic missile defense. The treaty initially limited ABM systems to a strategically insignificant deployment, which served to constrain the need for a continued race in offensive systems as well as defensive systems. The treaty initially allowed two ABM sites, with one site for each nation's capital and the second at an ICBM field. Two years after the treaty was signed, there was a further restriction to one site, which the Soviets had been willing to accept in the original treaty. After Congress refused to fund a site around the nation's capital, however, the issue of a second site became moot. As a result, the Soviets retained its defense system around Moscow, and the United States built its system (Safeguard) at Grand Forks, South Dakota, to protect the deployment of intercontinental ballistic missiles (ICBMs). In 1974, after an expenditure of $6 billion, Safeguard was dismantled as useless, which the critics of ABM knew it was all along. At that point, the United States and the Soviet Union agreed to ban all ABM systems. The Pentagon, which initially had not supported deployment of ABMs, reversed itself and opposed the total ban because it wanted to keep ABM technology alive, as did the defense industrial community.

Background of Missile Defense
The initial rationale for an ABM system during the Johnson and Nixon administrations was the need to protect civilian populations against attack. The protection for strategic missile sites was a secondary objective. In order to justify the cost of an ABM system to Congress, the stated mission became defending against a Soviet attack; this marked a fundamental altering of the character and objectives of our ABM program. There was no basis to justify such a mission, and the State Department and the Arms Control and Disarmament Agency realized this, but Nixon's national security adviser, Henry A. Kissinger, was determined to get funding for an ABM system regardless of the illogic of the administration's case. Kissinger wanted a bargaining chip against the Soviets no matter how expensive and regardless of its utility.

When the director of ACDA, Gerald Smith, who led the U.S. delegation to the Strategic Arms Limitation Talks (SALT), made it clear that he was "lukewarm at best" in support of ABMs, Nixon ordered Kissinger to tell Smith to get on board or resign.[3] Smith, in fact, continued to oppose the ABM and recommended that the SALT delegation pursue a total ban on ABMs with the Soviets. Smith had support from such stalwart conservatives as John McCloy, who was then the chairman of the President's General Advisory Committee on Arms Control and Disarmament. When Smith successfully negotiated the SALT and ABM treaties in 1972, he was pushed aside by Nixon and Kissinger. In order to get congressional ratification of the treaties, Kissinger had to cut an ugly deal with influential Senator Henry "Scoop" Jackson, guaranteeing that none of the U.S.

principals at the talks would be permitted to negotiate another arms control treaty with the Soviets. The substantive leader of the U.S. SALT delegation, Raymond L. Garthoff, was made ambassador to Bulgaria.

With the two key nuclear powers agreeing to forgo NMD, the strongest argument in favor of developing such a defense was the need to counter the proliferation of ballistic missiles in Third World states as well as the spread of technology to tip such missiles with nuclear, chemical, or biological weapons— the so-called weapons of mass destruction. Because countries such as North Korea or Pakistan have been willing in the past to provide WMD technology to anybody willing to pay for it, the conservative community has been preoccupied with the pace of proliferation by so-called rogue actors. Although no developing nation has demonstrated a capability to develop long-range systems that could reach the United States, the potential threat has framed the political campaign for NMD. The fact that such an act from a developing nation would be suicidal never seems to enter the geopolitical equation.

The obstacles to ballistic missile defense have not changed over the fifty-year period of testing and research and development. Pentagon planners have never developed a system capable of distinguishing between genuine warheads and the hundreds (or even thousands) of decoy missiles designed to thwart any missile defense. These planners have acknowledged the Soviet argument that any missile defense system can be overwhelmed by offensive missiles, and there was generally low confidence in the ability of any system to work perfectly or even effectively in a genuine testing scenario, let alone its first and perhaps only use against an actual missile attack. The problem of designing a battle management system of command, control, and communications that would function in a nuclear war has never been solved.

Reagan and National Missile Defense

At the 1980 Republican convention, the Republican platform called for the United States to conduct "vigorous research and development of an effective ABM system, such as already at hand in the Soviet Union, as well as more modern ABM technologies." The threat of an effective Soviet system was an outright deception, because the only Soviet system was the totally ineffective one around Moscow. The Pentagon and CIA had agreed on the ineffectiveness of the system, which the United States branded "galosh," a disparaging reference to the Soviet ABM system meaning "old man."

President Reagan was prepared to go far beyond the Republican plank. He made sure that more than $60 billion was spent to develop Star Wars, although no aspect of the system ever passed an operational test during his administration. He was introduced to the technology during a 1979 visit to the North American Aerospace Defense Command (NORAD), built inside a mountain in Colorado. The uniformed military had been skeptical of missile defense, but civilian defense intellectuals warned that America's land-based missiles in silos were vulnerable to attack, and therefore a defensive system was needed to prevent nuclear war. This theory was wrong for many reasons—not least of which was the invulnerability of the U.S. strategic submarine force, which could destroy the Soviet Union as a functioning society regardless of a Soviet first strike. Neoconservatives favored NMD because they anticipated that it would be a game changer regarding disarmament negotiations and arms control treaties with the Soviet Union, which was a major objective to such groups as the Heritage Foundation.

A basic element of Reagan's strategic vision was a belief that American technology could develop and deploy NMD, thus putting an "end to the threat of nuclear war."[4] According to his first biographer, Lou Cannon, Reagan believed in the "science-fiction solution" he had proposed without consultation with his secretary of state or his secretary of defense. He was convinced that "American ingenuity could find a way to protect the American people from the nightmare of Armageddon." For Reagan, the Strategic Defense Initiative was a "dream come true."[5]

The impetus for Reagan's decision to launch Star Wars came from a small group of military-industrial scientists; the renowned scientist Edward Teller was the most prominent member of this group. Probably no single individual was more influential with Reagan than Teller, who urged Reagan to launch a major Strategic Defense Initiative (SDI) based on the scientist's idea of a futuristic laser weapon. Although Teller's commitment to Star Wars was presumably based on science, President Reagan's commitment was solely based on faith and the vision to make nuclear weapons "impotent and obsolete."[6]

Various defense intellectuals, meanwhile, convinced President Reagan that the Soviets were developing powerful directed-energy weapons that would permit them to dominate both space and the Earth, and thus alter the geopolitical balance of power.[7] In addition to Teller and his colleagues, they had support from Senator Malcolm Wallop (R-WY), Harvard professor Richard Pipes, and Lieutenant General Danny Graham, who once headed the DIA. Wallop may not have been the most persistent advocate of SDI, but he was the first to reach the president with his policy of abandoning the strategy of "mutual assured destruction" and moving to a strategy of "assured survival." Graham was also responsible for briefing Reagan on the findings of Team B, the group of neocons responsible for politicizing national intelligence estimates, before the presidential candidate faced off in a debate with his key challenger, George H.W. Bush. All of the supporters of Star Wars were helped by CIA director Casey and his deputy, Bob Gates, who gave credence to the idea of directed-energy weapons, although CIA analysts had no evidence of a Soviet program.

Teller initiated a series of false claims in making the case for NMD, arguing for example that a single laser module might destroy more than a thousand speeding missiles by generating as many as 100,000 independently aimed beams. Teller and others falsely cited Soviet advances in beam weaponry for missile defense, and demanded that the United States close the "beam gap." After the false claims for the bomber gap in the 1950s, the missile gap in the 1960s, and the intentions gap in the 1970s, it was unsurprising that a new gap would be found. Whereas the CIA denied the claims of earlier gaps, this time around the beam gap had the support of Casey and Gates. At Gates's controversial confirmation hearing in 1991 for the position of director of central intelligence, several senior members of the Senate Intelligence Committee noted that CIA analysts didn't support his claims on various Soviet weapons systems, particularly those associated with missile defense. Gates had no response.

Reagan is falsely credited with bringing down the Soviet Union and ending the Cold War, but in truth the Reagan administration, with the support of disinformation from Casey and Gates, inflated the Soviet threat and then claimed false credit for its demise.[8] Supporters of Reagan cite his Star Wars speech on March 23, 1983, as the trumpet blast that brought down the Berlin Wall and the walls of the Soviet Union. President Reagan was not responsible for the collapse of these walls, but he was responsible for the largest peacetime buildup of the defense budget, a buildup that was conducted without a strategic plan.

Despite the scientific and intelligence information that challenged the utility of NMD, President Reagan's "Star Wars" speech stressed the need to eliminate the threat of nuclear weaponry. The idea was ridiculed by scientists and defense experts, and, on the same day the speech was given, Air Force officials were testifying that space-based laser weapons were insufficiently promising to justify additional funding. The services wanted defense appropriations to go toward the procurement of large offensive weapons systems, but Reagan's aides were convinced that an emphasis on strategic defense was needed to counter the public perception that President Reagan was pushing the country toward confrontation with the Soviet Union. As a result, President Reagan's senior advisers recommended that the Star Wars speech focus on defensive weapons to end the possibility of war between the superpowers and to form an image of the president as a man of peace and not a warmonger. When the Soviet Union collapsed eight years later, these advisers absurdly claimed that the idea of NMD had convinced the Soviets to give up the competition with the United States.

President Reagan's SDI could have had some utility as a bluff or a bargaining chip, but the president was so enamored with his "vision" that he lost an opportunity for a major arms control agreement at the Reykjavik Summit in 1986 as well as comprehensive strategic reductions during his second term. Secretary of State George P. Shultz was opposed to the initiative, and national security adviser Robert McFarlane saw its real potential only as that bluff or bargaining chip. Even Secretary of Defense Weinberger opposed committing resources to a very questionable capability.

But President Reagan persisted, and NMD became the sticking point at the Reykjavik summit, bringing an abrupt halt to the nascent Soviet-American disarmament dialogue that could have and should have produced a groundbreaking strategic arms agreement. The following year at the Washington summit, President Gorbachev called his bluff. Counseled by a newly freed dissident, Andrei Sakharov, who had helped to design the Soviet hydrogen bomb, Gorbachev was convinced that SDI was not workable and that its primary mission to destroy incoming missiles could not be achieved. He told Reagan, "I think you're wasting money. I don't think it will work. But if that's what you want to do, go ahead." The U.S. president warned that the United States was "going forward with the research and development necessary to see if this is a workable concept, and if it is, we are going to deploy it." "Who am I to tell you what to do," Gorbachev responded. "You do what you think you have to do."

The neoconservative justification for SDI was that it would increase Soviet defense spending, but Moscow was committed to reducing such spending. Far from spending vast amounts of money to counter SDI, the Soviets ignored it. U.S. intelligence estimates, moreover, eventually concluded that Soviet spending throughout the 1980s was flat.[9] Nevertheless, the arguments of the neocons were helped by military intelligence that was leaked to the military-industrial complex with its consistent exaggerations of the capabilities of Soviet strategic defense. In the 1960s and 1970s, for example, military intelligence predicted that the Soviet would deploy six thousand launchers on Moscow's ABM system. There were never more than one hundred launchers on a system that was considered totally inadequate.

The uniformed military and senior State Department officials, led by Secretary of State Shultz, shared the Soviet skepticism. They believed that the idea of SDI was lunacy, but very quickly enthusiasm and wishful thinking overwhelmed common sense. A former undersecretary of state, George Ball, who tried to convince President Lyndon Johnson not to expand the war in Vietnam, described the state of mind in Washington. "Although the project clearly had many closet opponents," he wrote, "there was now a mass conversion reminiscent of that decreed by King Ethelbert of Kent in the sixth century."[10]

Star Wars became a touchstone for conservatives; liberals and doubters were dismissed as unpatriotic. Senators such as Malcolm Wallop (R-WY), Dan Quayle (R-IN), and Pete Wilson (R-CA); congressmen such as Jack Kemp (R-NY) and Jim Courter (R-NJ); and scientists such as Edward Teller wrote

President Reagan in the mid-1980s to urge revocation of the ABM Treaty and development of strategic defense in the near term. Moderate senators such as Sam Nunn (D-GA), William Cohen (R-ME), William Proxmire (D-WI), and J. Bennett Johnston (D-LA) tried to slow down the movement toward expanded funding for NMD, but they were outgunned.

In addition to the big guns in the military-industrial-congressional complex, the moderates were up against a popular president who dealt in homilies and aphorisms and was motivated by superstition and simplistic visions. According to Michael Deaver, one of President Reagan's closest allies, the president regularly "consulted his horoscopes in the newspapers and habitually carried around a pocketful of lucky charms that people had sent him."[11] The president's dog was named Lucky, and the president believed in all sorts of oddities, such as UFOs and ghosts in the Lincoln bedroom of the White House. His wife Nancy followed her horoscopes and regularly consulted a mystic whose beliefs helped to determine the exact timing for the signing of the Intermediate-range Nuclear Forces Treaty in 1987.

The Pentagon didn't brandish the president's lucky charms or sign off on the first lady's horoscopes, but the senior military leadership decided to make the best of the situation and publicly jump on board with a program it had questioned in private. In early 1984, it created the Strategic Defense Initiative Organization (SDIO) to create a programmatic organization for dealing with the defense industry in procurement and deployment of NMD. Secretary of Defense Weinberger, who had criticized the notion of appropriating funds for NMD only two years earlier, indicated that it was unpatriotic to doubt that SDI could render ballistic missiles obsolete. Lieutenant General James Abrahamson Jr., who previously had been critical of NMD, was selected to head the office and began to award huge contracts to those firms who had lobbied for the program, including Boeing,

Hughes Aircraft, Lockheed, Rockwell International, and TRW Inc. Frances Fitzgerald, the preeminent historian of SDI, noted that "history has shown, big military programs are rarely canceled once Congress and the contractors are on board."

Lasers and X-ray lasers were a major part of President Reagan's SDI in the early 1980s. In an op-ed in the *New York Times*, Edward Teller took credit for introducing the president to such weapons. Many of Reagan's advisers, particularly national security adviser McFarlane, believed that SDI would be a great bargaining chip in negotiations with the Soviets, calling it the "greatest sting operation in history."[12] They were shocked upon realizing that Reagan had fallen in love with SDI and even accepted failure at the Reykjavik summit meeting with President Gorbachev in order to protect the administration's ability to deploy a strategic NMD that would incorporate laser weaponry.

In the 1980s, there were serious misrepresentations of the tests supporting the X-ray laser program. In 1987, a physicist at the program in Livermore Laboratory, W. Lowell Morgan, informed Representative George E. Brown (D-CA) that the tests and experiments were yielding "minuscule returns of poor quality" in the wake of an "obscene investment of money." He called the program a "laughingstock" of the technical staff at the Laboratory and stated that the interpretation and presentation of the "few scientific results that we had was fraudulent."[13] Even the Defense Department's Science Board concluded unanimously that it was "too soon to attempt to accelerate space-based laser development . . . for any mission, particularly ballistic missile defense." The Board rejected the arguments of such defense firms as TRW, Boeing, Rockwell International, Lockheed, United Technologies, Textron, and Hughes, which favored heavy investment in laser technology. Meanwhile, the Committee on the Present Danger, led by the charismatic Teller, the father of the H-bomb, continued to lobby the Congress for laser technology.

Tax money that could have been constructively served the nation was instead gushing into a fraudulent cause.

Bush I and National Missile Defense

Leaving Washington on Air Force One after the inauguration of George H.W. Bush, Reagan proclaimed, "The Cold War is over." Several days later, Bush and his national security adviser, General Scowcroft, went out of their way to proclaim that "the Cold War is not over." The Bush administration essentially shut down communications with Moscow and made it clear that arms control would be on the back burner and NMD would move to the front, marking a fundamental shift in Bush's position.

Shortly before the elections of 1988, the Defense Acquisition Board approved a plan for developing Phase I of the Strategic Defense System. Phase I called for a partial defense system consisting of kinetic weapons based in satellites and terminal defense on the ground. The projected cost of the project, which was supported by presidential candidate Bush, was over $70 billion. Bush said he was committed to "rapid and certain deployment of SDI" as the "most significant investment we can make in our nation's future security."[14] During the 1988 presidential debates, Bush proclaimed that he would "research it fully, go forward as fast as we can. . . . And when it's deployable, I will deploy it."[15] So Bush, who had not been enthusiastic about SDI as vice president, used the 1988 presidential campaign to support full deployment and for reinterpretation of the ABM Treaty in order to do so.

Immediately following his election, however, Bush abandoned his grandiose plans to protect the nation against a massive Soviet first strike. He supported a more modest, reconstructed system because of SDI's severe technological problems and exorbitant cost. Estimates were exceeding $250 billion for a full system.

Instead of a full system to "reduce Soviet confidence in the military utility of its ballistic missile force" and to "complicate Soviet attack plans," Bush proposed a limited system that would be compliant with the ABM Treaty. The new system, renamed GPALS (Global Protection Against Accidental Launch System), was designed to protect against very limited or accidental attacks. Bush appeared to concede that GPALS would be most effective against tactical nuclear weapons, and Secretary of Defense Cheney told the Senate Armed Services Committee in February 1991 that the "effectiveness" of tactical missile defense was established during the Gulf War with Iraq.

Actually, there was a major dispute over the actual success of the missile defense established in Israel during Desert Storm, when 158 Patriot missiles were fired against Iraqi SCUD missiles, a notoriously inaccurate missile. The military-industrial-congressional complex tried to exploit the so-called success of the effort, but a study by the General Accounting Office put these boasts to rest. The Patriot missiles hit no more than four of the forty-five incoming SCUDs that were targeted.[16] This provided sufficient evidence that the Patriots did more harm than good, because they merely added to the number of missiles that fell on Israel. Even Israeli officials concluded that the Patriot anti-ballistic missile system merely hit one or none of the SCUD warheads that it attempted to intercept.

Clinton and National Missile Defense

Bill Clinton's inauguration coincided with reduced interest in Star Wars and SDI. The Cold War was over; the Gulf War was already a distant memory; domestic issues were foremost, with some congressional interest in reducing defense spending. And just as he left office, President Bush signed the START II Treaty to eliminate MIRV land-based missiles and to affirm the traditional interpretation of the ABM Treaty. In May 1993, Secretary of Defense Aspin declared that the era of Star Wars and SDI was over and that the deployment of space-based weapons would be downgraded.

As the Clinton administration moved closer toward reelection in 1996, however, the president, who had tried to control defense spending in its first two years, reluctantly moved to legislate increases in defense spending, over $100 billion over the next six years. In the latter years of his second term, President Clinton approved even higher defense spending, in part to strengthen Vice President Al Gore's candidacy against the expected Republican candidate, George W. Bush. Bush had already come out in favor of greater defense spending, in part to finance NMD.

Initially, President Clinton preferred not to amend the 1972 ABM Treaty to allow limited land-based defenses against a limited missile attack, such as North Korea's. When Congress passed legislation in 1995 mandating deployment of a limited NMD by 2003, he vetoed the legislation, arguing that there was no threat justifying NMD deployment. In the face of congressional pressure, however, the Clinton administration announced a "3+3" program in 1996 to develop an NMD system in two phases of three years each. If, after the first three years, no threat justified deployment, then development would continue without deployment so that the system would be three years from deployment and up to date technologically. The "3+3" program assumed that there would be at least three years' warning of ICBM deployment by an emerging missile state, and for several years the program helped deflect continued Republican pressure to commit to a national defense.

President Clinton eventually agreed to approach the Soviets in order to amend the 1972 ABM Treaty and thus to allow land-based defenses against a limited missile attack, such as North Korea's. Once again, this was a political step to protect

Gore's candidacy for the presidency in 2000, since the obvious Republican challenger—George W. Bush—made it clear that he would renounce the ABM Treaty and deploy a widespread missile defense as soon as possible. The Clinton system was far less grandiose than President Reagan's SDI, which envisioned a space-based shield against a massive Soviet nuclear attack, and George H.W. Bush's system, a sophisticated, multilayered system of interceptors based at sea and in space as well as on land. Clinton's proposed system used ground-based interceptors to destroy incoming warheads by colliding with them, and it used existing rather than speculative technology. The Clinton administration argued that, unlike SDI, which would have accelerated the U.S.-Soviet arms race, the limited ground-based system would have fewer economic and political costs.

U.S. officials assumed that the end of the Cold War and the declining economy of Russia would lead to fewer problems with Russia, but Moscow's reaction to the unexpected revival of NMD and the expansion of the North Atlantic Treaty Organization was extremely negative. Russian spokesmen believed that the end of the Cold War obviated any need for a sophisticated NMD and that the United States was simply exploiting Russia's economic, political, and military weakness. The Pentagon estimated that the limited Clinton system would cost around $30 billion for a single interceptor site in addition to costs for the radar technology. The Congressional Budget Office estimated that the full system could cost upwards of $50 billion with additional costs for additional satellites.

On balance, the Clinton administration tried to slow down the development of NMD by basing deployment decisions on four criteria: the missile threat, the cost of the system, the strategic and arms control implications of deployment, and the readiness of the technology. Initially, these criteria led to the decision to move the deployment date from 2003 to 2005, but the

Republicans continued to press for deployment, and as a result President Clinton signed the National Missile Defense Act of 1999 that stated it was U.S. policy to deploy a limited NMD "as soon as technologically feasible."

As late as the elections of 1996, the Clinton administration had stymied the conservative forces that wanted to deploy NMD. As long as the ABM Treaty was valid, banning deployment of a nationwide missile defense, there was no legal way to begin construction. Abrogation of the ABM Treaty required six months' notice of intent to withdraw, which the Clinton administration was unwilling to do. The Bush administration had no such qualms, however. Developments in1998 ultimately eroded President Clinton's position, and the opposition to NMD collapsed.

Neoconservatives and National Missile Defense
A series of serendipitous political and military developments in 1998 made it difficult for President Clinton to continue his unwillingness to pursue NMD. These developments included a National Intelligence Estimate with an overstated assessment of the global missile threat, and the intelligence community's inability to provide warning of a series of Indian missile tests. The neoconservatives moved quickly to exploit both developments, which permitted President George W. Bush in his first year in office to abrogate the ABM Treaty and to start the legislative clock for funding NMD.

There is no question that 1998 was a watershed year for NMD, profoundly shaping the perception that nuclear threats to the United States had intensified and that Americans were living in a dangerous world of proliferation of weapons of mass destruction and terrorist acts against Western interests. In May 1998, India and Pakistan tested nuclear weapons, with the intelligence community failing to anticipate the Indian tests despite the political signals out of New Delhi and sophisticated U.S. surveillance technology.

In July 1998, the high-level bipartisan Commission to Assess the Ballistic Missile Threat to the United States, known as the Rumsfeld Commission after its chair, former secretary of defense Rumsfeld, released a report concluding that North Korea or Iran could develop an ICBM within five years (wrong!) and with little warning (wrong!). The report created great interest because, in that same month, Iran tested its Shahab-3 medium-range ballistic missile.

Rumsfeld was intensely interested in the militarization of space as well as NMD. When Congress moved in 1998 to establish a commission to "assess the nature and magnitude of existing and emerging ballistic missile threats to the United States," Rumsfeld was named to head the group. Rumsfeld was hardly an unbiased observer in these policy issues. He was a major contributor to the Center for Security Policy, which was the most prominent lobbying group pushing for NMD. The Rumsfeld Commission predictably exaggerated the missile threat to the United States, concluding that "rogue states" such as Iran, Iraq, and North Korea were on the verge of developing operational intercontinental ballistic missiles (ICBM) with "little or no warning." The commission's estimate that such missiles would be capable of targeting the United States within five years was significantly shorter than that of the intelligence community. As of 2012, the international community has still not encountered the testing, let alone deployment, of such missiles by Iran, Iraq, or North Korea.

In August 1998, however, North Korea launched a three-stage Taepo-Dong I missile over Japan in an attempt to put a satellite into orbit. The test launch of the Taepo-Dong was only 1,320 kilometers, but its international impact was enormous. Secretary of Defense Cohen proclaimed that the test was "another strong indicator that the United States will, in fact, face a rogue nation missile threat to our homeland against which we will have to defend the American people."

Also in August, the Cox Commission, chaired by Representative Chris Cox (R-CA), submitted its report to the White House on U.S. nuclear weapons and Chinese espionage programs, which documented China's alleged theft of nuclear secrets from U.S. weapons laboratories. The Commission's report alleged, which China stole ICBM designs that enabled Beijing to accelerate its own development and deployment of missile systems. As a result of the report, two major defense contractors (Hughes Electronics Corporation and Loral Space) were fined a total of $46 million for violating U.S. export laws.

Since the United States had begun focusing on the alleged construction of a secret nuclear facility in North Korea only several months earlier, Pyongyang's August test significantly enhanced the perception of a threat from emerging missile states and undercut the Clinton administration's key argument against an immediate decision to deploy an NMD system—namely, that the United States would have adequate warning before deployment. The first criterion for deployment of NMD had been met: There was a threat to warrant deployment, and technological readiness would become the primary independent variable for a decision to proceed.

Just as with NSC-68, a hardline document that might have been ignored were it not for the North Korean invasion of South Korea in 1950, the Rumsfeld Commission's report in 1998 received greater attention because of events that contributed to the perception that missile and nuclear threats to the United States had intensified and that Americans were living in an increasingly dangerous world.

The possible merger of WMD and international terrorism became more real in August 1998, when al-Qaeda terrorists attacked U.S. embassies in East Africa. Two weeks later, U.S.

Tomahawk missiles struck and destroyed one of the world's most prominent terrorist training camps in Afghanistan and a pharmaceutical plant in Khartoum, Sudan, that had nothing to do with terrorism. President Clinton's national security adviser, Sandy Berger, contended that the attack on the pharmaceutical plant was based on the "best intelligence we've ever collected on terrorism," but it is more likely that CIA director Tenet tailored the intelligence, possibly due to pressure from the White House.[17] The White House clearly picked targets believed to be linked to bin Laden, who had publicly announced the day before the strikes that more Americans would be murdered. The pharmaceutical plant, however, produced Sudan's aspirin supply, and not lethal chemicals. It is not certain if a staff member of the NSC, Richard Clarke, was lying when he told a National War College audience that the plant was producing a chemical used to manufacture nerve gas or if he had been given false intelligence from CIA director Tenet. When pressed, Clarke refused to take questions on the subject at the college although he was speaking off the record and not for attribution.

Finally, in December 1998, President Clinton ordered U.S. armed forces to strike military and security targets in Iraq in order to "attack Iraq's nuclear, chemical, and biological programs, and its military capacity to threaten its neighbors." This decision produced one of the more bizarre scenes in the Clinton presidency, as his national security team was providing updates on the situation in Iraq at the same time his domestic political aides were briefing the president on the imminent impeachment vote in the House of Representatives.

Militarized Intelligence on Missile Threats from the CIA
The report of the Rumsfeld Commission placed a great deal of political pressure on CIA, which was preparing its own National Intelligence Estimate (NIE) on the ballistic missile threat. The

CIA pulled many punches in the estimate, creating the impression that states such as Iran and North Korea were closer to developing intercontinental ballistic missiles than they actually were.[18]

The intelligence community added more hysteria to the general atmosphere when, in 1999, it issued an unclassified version of the NIE on missile threats to the United States, altering previously established intelligence criteria for judging nuclear threats. There was no new intelligence in the estimate or changes in the capabilities of the nations that were examined compared to previous iterations on this subject, but there were changes in three evaluative criteria. Instead of trying to estimate when Iran, Iraq, or North Korea "would" deploy a long-range missile, the new estimate emphasized whether these nations "could" test a long-range missile over the next five to ten years. (Twelve years later, we were still waiting for the first evidence of the development and testing of such a long-range missile, let alone the actual procurement and deployment.) The State Department's Bureau of Intelligence Research inserted an unusual dissenting opinion into the estimate, arguing that the use of "could" provides more credence than is warranted to developments that may prove implausible. In his briefing on the estimate, Secretary of Defense Cohen made the assessment even more threatening when he stated unambiguously, "The threat is here today. If it's not here right now it will be here tomorrow."

The 1999 estimate also increased the threat level to the United States by measuring the range of missiles on the basis of hitting Alaska and Hawaii rather than solely the continental United States, which had been the standard on previous estimates. This shift in potential targets actually brought the United States significantly closer to a potential launch site in North Korea in view of the distance from Seattle to the westernmost tip of Alaska's Aleutian Island chain. Although there is reason to be concerned about the potential of striking Hawaii or Alaska, it would seem unlikely that North Korea or any other nuclear weapons state would target sparsely inhabited areas instead of the continental United States in view of the certain annihilation it would face. In any event, the Taepo-Dong test in August was not particularly successful, failing to orbit a small satellite. Thus, the missile did not have the range to strike any part of the United States, including Hawaii and Alaska, with a large payload such as a nuclear warhead, although it might be able to strike parts of Hawaii and Alaska with a small payload.

The shift in standards in the newest version of the estimate, which pointed to politicization of the intelligence product, was the new emphasis on when a country would *test* a long-range missile rather than *deploy* a long-range missile, which moved back the target date by at least five years. "With shorter flight test programs—perhaps only one test—and potentially simple deployment schemes," according to the estimate, "the time between the initial flight test and the availability of a missile for military use is likely to be shortened."[19] The estimate did not state the obvious, which is that fewer flight tests for ballistic missiles would carry the risk of less reliability in the deployed weapons, particularly for the unpredictable North Korean program.

These changes accounted for the major differences between the 1999 NIE and earlier estimates. The new estimate, rather than representing a dramatic change in the ballistic missile threat, represented a lower standard for judging the threat. The 1999 estimate led some observers to conclude that there had been a significant technological leap forward in the Third World missile systems; in fact, there had been only modest and incremental developments in programs well known to intelligence analysts for years.

The 1999 estimate was enthusiastically received in the military-industrial-congressional complex as a justification for greater defense spending, particularly on NMD. It contributed to an exaggerated sense of the missile threat by focusing its assessment only on weapons programs in a few developing nations, whose political evolution will be a determining factor in whether they remain threats to the United States. Focusing on these few countries gave the distorted view that the global ballistic missile threat was growing. In fact, it was shrinking. The threats the United States faces remain serious, but they are orders of magnitude removed from threats confronted during the Cold War.

A more balanced net assessment of global ballistic missile arsenals over the past fifteen years would reveal that the threat is confined, limited, and changing slowly. The threat to the United States should be neither ignored nor exaggerated in order to justify the rush to deploy NMD. Of course, the Republican leadership in the Senate and the House did exactly that, using the Rumsfeld Commission's report to pass bills in March 1999 calling for antimissile defense "as soon as it is technologically possible."

The experience of India, which has a strong technological base and a sophisticated defense industry, is illustrative of the problems involved in creating a ballistic missile arsenal, and should have been addressed in the NIE. The Indian program demonstrated long lead times for flight tests, let alone procurement and deployment. The Agni missile program began in the mid-1980s; an Agni-1 missile was flight-tested in February 1994, and the Agni-2, a medium-range 2,000-kilometer version, was tested in April 1999. Despite substantial financial and scientific resources devoted to the Agni program, the Agni-1 did not have successful flight tests until 2010, and there were test failures for the Agni-2 in 2010 as well.

George W. Bush and the Compromise of Deterrence
George W. Bush ran his campaign in the year 2000 based in part on the determination to scrub the ABM treaty and to pursue NMD. He signaled his intent to deliver the death knell for

multilateralism and the issue of nuclear deterrence at the National War College in May 2001. In his first presidential address on global issues, President Bush announced that the United States "must move beyond the constraints of the thirty-year-old ABM Treaty" to deploy an extensive shield against nuclear missiles. Several months earlier, Secretary of Defense Rumsfeld had "derided the ABM Treaty of 1972 . . . as 'ancient history,'" thus presaging Bush's address.[20] Rumsfeld, a fervent supporter of NMD, wanted the militarization of space to be the centerpiece of his stewardship of the Pentagon. In his memoir, he took the bizarre position that the ABM Treaty was of "dubious legality" because the Soviet Union no longer existed.[21]

Despite becoming the most expensive weapons system in the Pentagon's procurement budget with an annual allocation of $9 billion to $10 billion, NMD was a defensive system that provided no defense against ballistic missiles. President Bush explained that, in the post–Cold War world, NMD would not be aimed at nuclear weapons states such as Russia or China, but rather against the "world's least-responsible states." The president did not name these states, but Iran, Iraq, and North Korea—the eventual "axis of evil"—were high on the list. Iraq's putative program became the phony cause for war in 2003. Iran's program became the justification for both the Bush and Obama administrations to extend the missile defense system to Eastern Europe. For states such as Iran, President Bush declared, "Cold War deterrence is no longer enough."

Without providing the notice required by the treaty, Bush simply abrogated the ABM Treaty in December 2001 and endorsed an NMD system based in Alaska and California. His appointment of Rumsfeld as secretary of defense, no friend of the president's father, probably had much to do with the fact that Rumsfeld was a strong advocate for NMD, one of Bush's major campaign positions. Secretary of Defense Rumsfeld made it clear that his two priorities at the Pentagon were the development of a national defense against ballistic missiles and the overall militarization of space. The post-9/11 environment and the unwillingness to challenge any new weapons system in the age of terrorism meant an absence of any real opposition to abrogation of the ABM Treaty, either from the arms-control lobby or from the Democratic Party. Rumsfeld's arrogance and truculence, however, soon antagonized uniformed members of the military, who have a direct and influential pipeline to senior Republicans on the Hill. As a result, there was a steady decline in Rumsfeld's influence and stature on Capitol Hill.

President Obama's Volte-face on NMD
Despite Senator Obama's skepticism regarding NMD and European regional defense during the campaign, President Obama changed his views for political reasons in order to appease the Pentagon. Unlike Bush's plan, Obama's plan for regional missile defense relied on a new generation of anti-missile technology, which he pronounced "proven and effective." His ostensible confidence was presumably based on a new rocket-powered interceptor known as the Standard Missile 3, or SM-3, which he had criticized as a senator and a presidential candidate. President Obama relied on a dubious Pentagon assessment from September 2010, which claimed that the SM-3 had intercepted 84 percent of incoming targets in various tests. MIT professor Theodore A. Postol and Cornell University professor George N. Lewis sampled this testing and found that only 10 to 20 percent of the tests could be considered successful. They concluded that most of the approaching warheads would have been knocked off course, but not destroyed. This might be considered a success against a conventionally armed warhead, but hardly a success against a nuclear warhead that would still detonate and cause mass destruction.

In September 2011, in its first flight test, the advanced

SM-3 interceptor missile failed to hit its target over the Pacific Ocean. The SM-3, part of the Aegis ballistic missile defense system, was launched from the Navy cruiser USS *Lake Erie* against a short-range ballistic missile launched from Hawaii. Both missiles had sensors to make the intercept more likely, which is typical in tests run by the Pentagon's Missile Defense Agency. Failed tests typically lead to long delays in the program, and the SM-3 program has been no exception.

Missile defense in Europe is destined to fail for the same reason that NMD continues to fail in the United States. Both systems use interceptors with infrared vision to attack warheads and decoys. There is no way that NATO's missile defense in Europe or the national system in the United States can distinguish between a warhead and a decoy. The *New York Times* cited NATO's "real progress" toward an "effective" missile defense at the Lisbon Summit in November 2010, ignoring the fact that the system relies on technology that is fundamentally flawed and will never work reliably in genuine combat.[22]

Why National Missile Defense Doesn't Work

NMD is a classic case of the military-industrial complex at work draining away oceans of taxpayers' money. There has never been a reliable series of tests that suggests NMD would work; there is no reason to believe that the United States would be safer with the deployment of such a system. There are doubts about the likelihood of a genuine threat from rogue states such as North Korea and Iran, and, in an age of serious budgetary constraint, the economic costs of the system are as unacceptable as the diplomatic costs. Any NMD system would contribute to greater proliferation of technology and worsen U.S. relations with both China and Russia.

When President Reagan made his stunning charge in 1983 regarding SDI, he trumpeted a "call to the scientific community in this country, who gave us nuclear weapons, to turn their great talents to the cause of mankind and world peace; to give us the means of rendering these weapons impotent and obsolete." Secretary of State Shultz did his best to tone the statement down, but failed. The president's science adviser, George Keyworth, referred to Shultz and other critics as "lunatics." When Shultz learned that President Reagan could not be stopped from making his "Star Wars" speech, he told his aides, "We don't have the technology to say this." None of the descendants of Star Wars works—from President Clinton's limited version to President Bush's comprehensive system, including the idea for an annex to the system in Eastern Europe and the Middle East to protect U.S. allies. It is only a matter of time before the military-industrial complex promotes deployment in East Asia against any threat from North Korea (read China).

The bottom line on the performance of any NMD is simple: The infrared sensors and radars that have been developed thus far cannot distinguish between real warheads and decoys. There is no indication that after fifty years of research and development as well as hundreds of billions of dollars of investment, the United States or any other country is about to break the code. The problem is about technology and physics. Decoys and warheads can always be made to emit almost identical signals in the visible, infrared, and radar bands; in other words, their signatures are virtually the same.

The impossibility of the task has not prevented the United States from investing billions of dollars in NMD over the past six decades. This money has been used to develop defense to cover the three phases of missile trajectory: powered flight, during which the rocket fuel is burned; free ballistic flight, which is known as "mid-course" flight covering the time the warhead spends in space; and the missile's aerodynamic re-entry. Mid-course trajectory accounts for 80 percent of the flight time.

Defenses can be designed to attack the missile or the warhead during any of these phases: the boost phase for the missile or the mid-course or re-entry phase for the warhead. Each approach, however, has its own unique virtues and difficulties. Many of the NMD systems thus far are designed to attack ICBM warheads in mid-course flight (i.e., in space before warheads re-enter the atmosphere), thus relying on a maneuverable "kill vehicle" designed to strike the warhead dead-on, thereby destroying it by force of impact. This is commonly referred to as "hitting a bullet with a bullet." This is achievable, but not with certainty, let alone with a high success rate.

Serious problems are posed by a missile that carries multiple warheads. In other words, the payload may carry lightweight chaff (essentially small pieces of wire or aluminum) and decoys that would confuse the interceptor's sensors. The decoys can be lightweight—a metal-coated mylar balloon, not dissimilar from mylar balloons sold in supermarkets. Once the payload of the mid-course part of the rocket's trajectory is in the vacuum of space, all its elements (e.g., warheads, decoys, and chaff) travel at the same velocity without any slowing due to atmosphere. In the case of chemical or biological payloads, the warhead can be subdivided into many small bomblets known as submunitions. The proposed defenses would be useless against a missile carrying submunitions, since they cannot target separate objects.

Decoys, moreover, cannot be distinguished from warheads. Warheads can be enclosed in a metal-coated balloon or similar device—a concept called "anti-simulation"—to make it appear to the interceptor's sensors to be a decoy. As long as there is no unique signature that can be used to determine which object in the threat cloud is the warhead, no amount of development of the defense sensors will allow discrimination of the warhead from a decoy.

Although it was technically feasible to "hit a bullet with a bullet" on the test range, U.S. adversaries would be in a position to create decoy missiles that would make it difficult to separate a decoy from the real thing. If a country could develop ICBMs, it could also deploy decoys and chaff; presumably the production of strategic offensive missiles would be accompanied by a test program to defy strategic defensive missiles. The U.S. Air Force's National Air Intelligence Center reported that China's testing of its road-mobile Dongfeng-31 (DF-31), for example, has included penetration aids, including decoys and chaff, since 1999. The CIA estimate of 1999 on ballistic missile threats and the Air Force report also concluded that Russia and China have developed numerous countermeasures and "probably will sell some related technologies." The development and deployment of countermeasures is technically far simpler than building and deploying ICBMs with nuclear warheads, and it is well within the capability of developing nations that could deploy the missiles. As long as the United States devotes resources to NMD, it is likely that decoys, chaff, and anti-simulation will be part of any potential adversary's program to develop long-range ballistic missiles.

These highly effective countermeasures, moreover, are extremely inexpensive. An effective tactic would be cooling the warhead with a shroud of liquid nitrogen, making it more difficult for the interceptor to succeed. Defending against these devices would be extremely expensive and, as the military experts like to say, "not cost effective at the margins." In fact, countermeasures are estimated to cost one-hundredth of the cost of the defensive missile needed to knock it out. In addition to not being cost effective, NMD would be highly vulnerable because its interceptors and radars are ground-based, and would be prime targets for destruction before launching an attack.

If the NMD system opts for attacking and destroying the warhead after it enters the atmosphere, the time available for the intercept would be dramatically shortened, and thus not reliable. The Soviets deployed such a system around Moscow during the Cold War, but it was never taken seriously by U.S. planners, who termed it the "galosh," and gave it no weight in their targeting strategy. When I was an intelligence adviser to the SALT delegation in 1972, my Soviet counterparts told me that their missile experts were highly insulted by this terminology.

The Moscow system was highly vulnerable to countermeasures such as a small number of Minuteman missiles equipped with highly effective chaff and decoys. U.S. experts contend that, if the Soviets had deployed more advanced defenses, the United States would have developed new maneuvering re-entry vehicles to evade interceptor missiles. Military men, whether Russian or American, would prefer to spend their investment rubles or dollars on lethal offensive weapons and not on technologically sophisticated defensive systems. So, in the case of NMD, the arms race is driven not by the military, but by the military-industrial-congressional complex. The bottom line: NMD is a fool's errand and is a complete waste of taxpayers' money, except for those congressmembers who have NMD projects in their states or districts.

In addition to trumpeting anti-missile defense, one element in the so-called Revolution in Military Affairs, the military-industrial complex has stressed the military impact of cyberwar, space weapons, lasers, pulses, and other directed-energy beams. In fact, it already appears that the Pentagon's investment in cyber-security and space-based capabilities is designed in part to make sure that defense contractors such as Northrup Grumman and Lockheed Martin have programs online to replace those weapons systems that face reductions. Typically, Russia and China are being blamed for stealing sensitive economic and commercial data that will require technological safeguards, which resembles Cold War justifications for major military platforms and the charges of espionage and reverse engineering. A recent report from the National Counterintelligence Executive, an advisory panel of senior U.S. intelligence officials, said that the pace of cyber-espionage is accelerating and threatening an estimated $400 billion in spending on research and development over the next ten years.[23] Increased reliance on satellites and drone aircraft, however, will raise legitimate security issues that will require sophisticated technology.

As a result, the military-industrial complex has begun feeding "inside information" on these new systems to journalists, such as David Ignatius of the *Washington Post*, who offer editorials on the "Future of Warfare."[24] Special attention was given to the Navy and Air Force development of exotic weapons systems. The Air Force was cited for its "Directed Energy Directorate," which has invested in gamma rays, lasers, and microwaves.

Ignatius's editorials bring to mind Will Rogers's warning that, "You can't say civilizations don't advance . . . in every war they kill you in a new way." After years of apologizing for the actions of the CIA, Ignatius has turned his public relations efforts in the direction of the Pentagon. He has argued there is less need for the so-called "legacy systems" of past wars, such as manned bombers and fighters, aircraft carriers, cruisers, and submarines that are "wrapped in red, white, and blue."[25] Ignatius now supports the new demands of the military-industrial complex that favors futuristic weapons such as lasers, directed-energy weapons, unmanned aerial vehicles, and even "unmanned ships, subs, and tanks, too." These systems are the new darlings of the think-tank community that relies on funding from the Pentagon and beams its research into congressional offices that support the Pentagon's arsenal.

More Defense Against a Lesser Threat

Ironically, the United States favors increasing its investment in strategic nuclear defense at a time when there is a reduced strategic threat and an opportunity to reduce strategic offensive arsenals. Let's start with the biggest missiles of them all: intercontinental ballistic missiles (ICBMs). The number of ICBMs with ranges over 5,500 kilometers has decreased dramatically since the height of the Cold War. These are the only missiles that can reach the continental United States from any likely attacker. During the 1980s, the Soviet Union deployed more than 9,540 nuclear warheads on 2,318 such long-range missiles. Currently, Russia has fewer than 5,200 missile warheads deployed on 1,100 missiles. This is a greater than 50 percent decrease in the number of missiles capable of striking the United States, and nearly a 50 percent decrease in the number of nuclear warheads. China has maintained a force of approximately 120 ICBMs for the past two decades. China will probably keep its force at this level for the near future, although U.S. deployment of NMD, let alone a regional system in East Asia, could prompt significant increases in the Chinese inventory. Even a limited missile defense could be perceived as a threat to a modest nuclear deterrent such as China's. The United States, Russia, and China are the only nations that have developed missiles with an intercontinental range.

The number of deployed intermediate-range ballistic missiles (with ranges of 3,000 to 5,000 kilometers) has decreased even more dramatically. President Reagan negotiated an arms control treaty in 1987 (the INF Treaty) that eliminated the entire class of intermediate-range missiles from the U.S. and Soviet arsenals. The Pentagon opposed the treaty, and Secretary of Defense Weinberger and his deputy for arms control and disarmament, Richard Perle, resigned in protest, although they gave the standard reasons (i.e., health and family time) for their departure. Previous presidents have encountered military opposition from the Pentagon for entering arms control and disarmament treaties, including President Kennedy (for the Partial Test Ban Treaty in 1963) and President Nixon (for the SALT and ABM Treaties in 1972). The Pentagon opposed the INF Treaty even though the Soviet Union destroyed more than twice as many missiles as the United States—1,846 missiles in the Soviet inventory; 846 missiles in the U.S.—and made the European theater safer for U.S. forces stationed there.

Throughout the 1990s, the Pentagon's worst-case assessments emphasized that at least twenty countries possessed either short or medium-range ballistic missiles and that another twenty-four countries could develop a missile capability. But none of these countries has developed a missile capability that threatens the United States—and, among so-called rogue states, only North Korea appears to have the incentive, if not the technology, to develop intercontinental ballistic missiles.

Six additional countries have medium-range missiles with a 1,000- to 3,000-kilometer range, which do not threaten the territory of the United States. These countries are India, Iran, Israel, North Korea, Pakistan, and Saudi Arabia. The technology of the North Korean Nodong missile is the basis for Pakistan's Ghauri and Ghauri II missiles as well as Iran's Shahab-3, which have been flight-tested. India, Iran, North Korea, and Pakistan have programs for extending the range of these systems to over 3,000 kilometers over the next three years.

In addition to the quantitative reduction in ballistic missile arsenals, the number of countries trying or threatening to develop long-range missiles has decreased significantly. The nations now attempting to do so are smaller, poorer, and less technologically advanced than the nations with missile programs fifteen years ago; this list includes North Korea and Pakistan. The intelligence projections, particularly from military intelligence, were significantly wrong in predicting the dramatic increase in missile technology around the world. Fifteen years ago, there was the perception of a threat from India, Iraq, Brazil, Argentina, Egypt, South Africa, and Libya, but only India has systematically and steadily continued its program. Israel, India, and Pakistan remain worrisome because they refuse to sign the Non-Proliferation Pact; fortunately, neither India nor Israel is a likely exporter of nuclear technology.

There are twenty-seven nations with short-range missiles;[26] most of these nations have only aging SCUDs, which are declining in military utility over time and have a range of no more than 300 kilometers. Thus, there is a decreasing number of long-range missiles that can threaten the United States; a slowly growing, but still limited, capability to launch medium-range missiles; and no threat from short-range missiles such as SCUDs. In any event, there is no compelling reason to deploy NMD or a regional mission defense in Eastern Europe to protect against the unlikely threat from Iran's weaponry to the European theater. Presumably, the military-industrial complex's next target for a regional missile defense would be North Korea, which would be particularly worrisome to China.

The Worst of All Possible Worlds

In sum, President George W. Bush created the worst of all possible strategic worlds. He abrogated the ABM Treaty, the cornerstone of deterrence and one of the pearls of Soviet-American arms control policy. He inflicted the diplomatic wound of abrogating a treaty without cause and incurred the expense of moving into the murky world of NMD without any guarantee that even rogue missiles could be stopped. There is probably no better example of the creation of national insecurity than the actions taken by the Bush administration in the foolish belief that we could create an impenetrable nuclear umbrella.

The deployment of NMD and the plans for regional missile defense in Eastern Europe (and perhaps in Asia against North Korea) have antagonized Russia (and China) and contributed to the problem of global instability. Both Russia and China have plausible concerns that missile defense would threaten their nuclear arsenals and allow the United States to use its own missiles with impunity. U.S. diplomats have worked overtime without success to convince their Russian and Chinese counterparts that NMD and the European missile defense system are not threats against their nuclear deterrents. As strategic missile inventories are reduced by arms control and disarmament treaties, any ballistic missile defense would take on greater importance.

The U.S. deployment of NMD was a setback to the goal of NATO unity. European members of NATO were opposed to such a deployment because they considered it an unnecessarily provocative step and believed it marked a departure from the concept of "shared risk" that had held the alliance together for five decades. The Europeans want to know what happened to good old deterrence—the trigger-blocking threat to respond to any attack on the United States or its close allies with massive retaliation. They now worry that, in a crisis, the United States might hunker down under its shield, decoupling its security from that of its allies. Our response has been that national or regional missile defense would complement deterrence, not substitute for it. The biggest problem, however, is that the United States is placing too much reliance on technological breakthroughs and has paid much less attention to good old-fashioned diplomacy, arms control and disarmament, export controls, and international sanctions to prevent or contain regional threats.

Despite the political and economic problems associated with the deployment of any national missile defense, there are still groups that favor an expanded system in the United States. After two years of study, a panel co-chaired by the retired president of

Lockheed Martin Missiles and Space concluded that the United States is vulnerable to "some kinds of long-range strikes."[27] The panel favors an expansion of the system favored by President George W. Bush, requiring new sensors and interceptor rockets as well as a base in Maine or upstate New York. The report ignores the problem of simple countermeasures that could foil any national missile defense and, having no realistic threat in mind, refers to the "likely development" of Iranian missiles designed to rain warheads down on the United States. Since the 1980s, when President Reagan began spending enormous sums of taxpayers' money for missile defense, the United States has clearly gone from the sublime to the ridiculous.

In fact, there is a considerable downside to the continued deployment of any national missile defense, particularly the creation of an incentive for others to deploy additional intercontinental missiles (Russia and China); to modernize strategic inventories (Britain and France); or to rely on more weapons of mass destruction (Third World nations). A greater level of NMD will lead to greater defense budgets. There is no good reason to deploy a technological system that does not work. The United States appears to be doing so because it can do so; there could not be a worse reason. Once again, only the interests of the military-industrial complex are being served.

EIGHT

DEFENSE SPENDING:
EISENHOWER'S "CROSS OF IRON"

A smaller military will be able to go fewer places and do fewer things. I can't imagine being part of a nation, part of a government . . . that's being forced to dramatically scale back our engagement with the rest of the world. —Secretary of Defense Robert Gates

Endless money forms the sinews of war. —Cicero

Over the past decade, the United States has engaged in the most significant increase in defense spending since the Korean War sixty years ago. Trillions of dollars have been allocated for the Pentagon with insufficient congressional monitoring and internal oversight. Defense planning in the 1990s had little relevance to the weapons that were needed for future wars, particularly in Iraq and Afghanistan, let alone the problems of counterinsurgency and counterterrorism. When Secretary of Defense Donald Rumsfeld said in 2003 that we would go to war "with the army we have and not the army we would like to have," he conceded the lack of preparedness.

At the end of the Cold War, Pentagon planners demanded a continuation of the high levels of spending that existed during the Cold War, much of which had been based on an exaggerated Soviet threat. The threat of international terrorism and "Islamoterrorism" as well as the exaggerated threat from China now feeds the military machine. If we don't rethink our national security commitments and objectives, there will be no end to this inflated spending. Even Secretary of Defense Gates, paraphrasing General Douglas MacArthur, said that a future president "would have to be out of his mind" to consider future land wars such as those in Iraq and Afghanistan.

Since 1998, defense spending has doubled, with the defense budget in 2011 exceeding $600 billion, equaling the combined defense spending of the rest of the world. The defense budget grew at a rate of 7 percent per year during this period, with military spending moving from its post-WWII low of 16 percent of the federal budget in 1999 to 21 percent by 2010.[1] The defense spending of the United States and its allies in Europe, Asia, and the Middle East accounts for more than 70 percent of global defense spending. In real terms, the U.S. defense budget is higher than at any time since the end of WWII, including the peak years of the Korean and Vietnam Wars as well as the peacetime buildup of President Reagan in the 1980s.

U.S. spending on the military, intelligence, and homeland security adds significantly to U.S. debt and deficits without necessarily strengthening security. Each U.S. taxpayer spends twice as much for national defense as each British citizen; five times as much as each German; and six times as much as each Japanese. Nevertheless, there is no sign that American security has been enhanced or that the international community has become more stable as a result of U.S. deployments.

In the wake of 9/11, the United States adopted ambitious security goals that extended the reach of American forces as the United States responded to perceived security challenges. A great part of the spending dealt with wars in Iraq (Operation Iraqi Freedom) and Afghanistan (Operation Enduring Freedom) that began with little congressional debate and virtually no public concern, let alone opposition. These wars have cost more than $1.2 trillion to date, according to the National Priorities Project, with costs of $120 billion for the war in Afghanistan, and another $50 billion for Iraq in 2011. U.S. participation in the coalition effort against Libya in 2011 (Operation Odyssey Dawn) cost additional hundreds of millions of dollars. The emphasis on nation-building added a new dimension at a Pentagon ill-equipped for such a task.

The factors that drive costs are obvious. The military is too large; its mission too great; and its demand for resources too intense. Costs for modernization are skyrocketing. The amount spent on procurement of military weapons as well as research and development totals more than $40 billion—more than the total defense budgets of all but a few nations. The United States has nearly 1,000 overseas bases and facilities, many of them in regions that no longer require a U.S. presence, such as Europe, or are opposed to a large U.S. presence, such as the Middle East and the Persian Gulf.

The final bill for the Iraq and Afghanistan wars, if President Obama sticks to his plans for withdrawal, will run to at least $3.7 trillion and could reach as much as $4.4 trillion. These numbers will continue to soar with long-term costs such as obligations to wounded veterans; interest payments of up to $1 trillion; and billions of dollars for the logistical costs of withdrawal.[2] Meanwhile, supporters of the wars in the military-industrial-congressional complex justify this spending by noting that *half of a percentage point* (emphasis added) has been added to growth in the gross domestic product, a rather paltry increase.

Columbia University professor Richard Betts observed in 2007 that "Washington opened the sluice gates of military spending after the 9/11 attacks not because it was the appropriate thing to do strategically but because it was something the country could do when something had to be done."[3] Even senior military officers have difficulty explaining the need for some of these U.S. expenditures. Newly named chairman of the Joint Chiefs, General Martin Dempsey told his confirmation hearings that he needed a "better understanding of the economy, which seemed likely to define" his tenure in the way that counter-terrorism and counterinsurgency had preoccupied his predecessors over the past decade.[4]

President Eisenhower warned that military demands on U.S. spending would become a "cross of iron" that would limit spending on domestic needs. Now, at a time when there are no serious challenges to U.S. security or military supremacy, more than 60 percent of U.S. discretionary spending goes to support defense, including the budgets of the Pentagon, Veteran's Affairs, Intelligence, and Homeland Security, and the costs of various nuclear weapons. No other agency in the U.S. government gets as much as 10 percent of U.S. discretionary spending: Health and Human Services gets less than 7 percent; Education less than 6 percent; and Housing and Urban Development less than 3 percent.

Eisenhower's "cross of iron" also needs to take into account the impact of defense spending and military operations on the global economy and the environment. In less than one hour, an F-16 consumes almost twice as much gas as the average American motorist during one year. A battle tank's fuel consumption is so high that it can be measured in gallons per mile. Approximately one-quarter (50 million tons per year) of the world's jet fuel is used by military forces, and the worldwide military use of aluminum, nickel, and platinum is greater than the entire demand for these materials among developing nations.

Military activity has a huge impact on the physical environment with pollution of the air, land, and water in peacetime; agricultural degradation from landmines in African and Asian countries particularly; and the unexploded remnants of war such as cluster bombs in places such as Kosovo and Afghanistan. The use of chemical agents and the burning of oil wells did terrible damage in the Gulf War in 1991. In addition to using vast amounts of energy, the military uses more than its proportional share of rare and expensive raw materials.

Land used for war games is prone to suffer severe degradation. Maneuvers demolish natural vegetation, disturb wildlife habitat, erode soil, silt up streams, and cause flooding. Bombing ranges transform the land into a moon-like wasteland, pockmarked with craters. Shooting ranges for tanks and artillery contaminate soil and groundwater with lead and other toxic residues. The Department of Defense is a major user of halon 1211 and CVC-113, which account for 15 percent of overall ozone depletion. Overall, the Pentagon generates five times more toxins than the five major U.S. chemical companies combined.

There is no better example of the insidious nature of the military-industrial complex than the Pentagon's willingness to recruit retired four-star generals who have become executives at defense companies to take part in exercises involving weapons systems that their companies are vying to build for the military. In 2009, the Air Force altered a war game to allow retired General Charles Robertson to take part as a "senior mentor." The war game itself involved an aerial tanker that Robertson's firm, Boeing, was hoping to build for the military in a $50 billion contract.[5] In 2011, the Pentagon awarded Boeing a $3.5 billion contract to develop the KC-46A tanker that will eventually become a $51 billion contract for 179 tankers. An investigation determined that the overwhelming majority of Pentagon "mentors" had ties to the defense industry.

Nevertheless, a two-year Inspector General study found no conflict of interest involving classified Pentagon briefings for retired generals who worked as military analysts for television and radio networks. These officers, referred to by the Pentagon as "message force multipliers," were originally recruited by Secretary of Defense Rumsfeld to sustain public support for wars in Iraq and Afghanistan. When these officers, including four-star generals Barry McCaffrey and Wesley Clark, began to challenge U.S. policy, they were no longer considered "team players" and were denied the briefings.[6] The fact that many of the retired generals were affiliated with defense contractors makes the conflict of interest even more apparent.

For the first time since 1998, the United States has moved to restrain the growth in defense spending. In view of the U.S. financial and employment crisis as well as the absence of a major geopolitical threat, there has never been greater incentive for cutting the budget. The United States has a huge technological and geopolitical advantage; no nation or group of nations challenges the U.S. ability to project power. The major industrial states of Europe (Britain, France, and Germany) and Asia (India and Japan) are reducing defense spending to stabilize domestic economies. Russia is emphasizing domestic economic growth, and China allocates one-tenth of U.S. defense spending to its own military budget. Eastern European countries that were so anxious to join NATO and even agreed to devote 2 percent of their gross domestic product (GDP) to defense budgets are spending 1 percent or less. The United States spends 5 to 6 percent of its GDP on defense; among NATO states, only Britain spends as much as 2 percent of its GDP. Russia allocates a little more than 3 percent to defense despite its ailing economy, China less than 4 percent.

In an attempt to cut defense spending by $485 billion over the next decade, which was mandated by the 2010 Budget Control Act, the United States will reduce the Army from 547,000 troops to 490,000 and the Marines from 202,000 to 182,00, still leaving the ground forces larger than the level before 9/11. The Air Force and Navy, which have dominance of the sea and sky, will undergo modest cuts: the Navy will keep its eleven aircraft carriers and merely delay construction of missile submarines and coastal combat ships; the Air Force will maintain the three variants of its F-35 fighter aircraft, but stretch out the purchases of 179 of these aircraft over the next five years and eliminate one hundred older F-15s and F-16s fighter aircraft. Although President Obama has often referred to the need to reduce nuclear forces, there will be no changes in the three legs of the nuclear triad—bombers, submarine-launched missiles, and land-based missiles. From 2013 to 2018, there will only be a slight cut of 1.6 percent in defense spending, which critics of inflated defense spending have referred to as a "rounding error."[7]

The savings will be limited because the United States will continue to invest in unmanned aerial vehicles; offensive and defensive cyber strategies; special operations in Third World countries; and new submarines with cruise-missile capabilities. The Air Force will be getting a next-generation long-range bomber to replace the B-2, and aircraft and warships will be modernized. As a result, the budget for 2013 will still be nearly 50 percent larger than the 1998 budget.

The Over-Financed Military

Since the end of the Second World War, there has been no decade comparable to the current one for a sustained rise of defense spending. In the wake of the demise of the Soviet Union, defense spending reached a post–Cold War low in 1998, dropping to $360 billion. Over the past ten years, however, defense spending nearly doubled, reaching a level of $660 billion in 2011. President Obama's campaign in 2008 referred to reduced defense spending, but the defense budget went up in his first four years. The United States spent a mere $450 billion a year during the worst days of the Cold War, when we faced a serious opponent with a nuclear weapons triad aimed at the United States. Now we are spending 50 percent more money and face no existential threat whatsoever. The United States could easily cut its defense budget by more than $1 trillion over the next ten years without sacrificing any element of national defense.

Spending on weapons procurement has doubled over the past ten years along with the costs of fighting wars in Iraq and Afghanistan. The U.S. military has been able to modernize and improve its weaponry across the board during a period that finds the Russian military still in disarray two decades after the collapse of the Soviet Union. China's air force and navy are two or three decades behind U.S. forces, but Pentagon spokesmen and their Capitol Hill supporters claim that the Chinese military poses a threat to us in order to justify larger and larger defense budgets. There is little likelihood of a Sino-American military confrontation anywhere around the world in the near term.

Pentagon announcements of defense savings are never what they appear. Half of these so-called savings consists of sums that have been diverted to other weapons systems. Other "savings" have been appropriations for weapons systems that were never finalized; they are thus hypothetical savings for systems that were never built. When former Secretary of Defense Gates announced in February 2010 that the Pentagon had saved $330 billion, he should have said that his budget proposal reflected the cutting, curtailing, or ending of programs that either were performing poorly or were in excess of contemporary needs.[8] If these programs had been pursued to completion, they would have cost $330 billion, but Gates kept using the $330 billion figure in his congressional testimony and the media kept repeating the number as if genuine savings had been realized.

Defense spending and procurement should be linked to actual threats to the United States. If this were done, Pentagon planners would take into account the fact that the United States is the only country in the world with a global naval presence. The Russian navy has been radically reduced and is an operational backwater. The only other serious rival, China, possesses a regional navy, not a global one. No country can compare to the United States in terms of naval aviation and global power projection. There is no air force that rivals the U.S. Air Force. No country has huge military bases the world over or access to countless ports and anchorages. And no other country has used lethal military power so often and so far from its borders in pursuit of dubious security interests.

Reducing the Defense Budget

Every aspect of the Pentagon's budget, including research and development, procurement, operations and maintenance, and infrastructure, needs to be scrutinized for additional savings.[9] The starting place should be the size of the active-duty military, which numbers 1.48 million service members.[10] Of this total, 40 percent are Army; 23 percent are Navy; 14 percent are Marines; and 23 percent are Air Force. With the wars winding down, the personnel costs of the military should wind down. In addition to the reductions in the Army and the Marines, which could lead to a savings of $147 billion over ten years, the Navy and Air Force as well as the civilian work force should also be cut. Cutting the civilian work force by 20 percent to a level of 630,000 would lead to a savings of $73 billion over ten years.

There are nearly 300,000 U.S. military personnel on duty overseas. This equals the number overseas during the last decade of the Cold War. Nearly one-third of the overseas force is engaged in combat; nearly 40,000 have been killed or wounded in action since 9/11. U.S. forces in combat are supported by 400,000 service members in infrastructure positions, including 85,000 in the health profession, 60,000 in personnel administration, and 45,000 in departmental management.[11] The military has more members in its marching bands than the State Department has foreign service officers.

Decades after the end of WWII and the Korean War, there are still 65,000 troops in Europe and another 65,000 in East Asia and the Pacific. More than 50,000 personnel are needed to support these overseas deployments. Reducing military personnel in Europe and Asia from 150,000 to 100,00 would bring additional savings of $70 billion over ten years.

Outside of Iraq and Afghanistan, the largest U.S. deployments are in Europe, particularly Germany (55,000), Italy (10,000), and the United Kingdom (10,000); in Asia, the leaders are Japan (35,000) and South Korea (29,000). These forces are in place more than six decades after the end of WWII. The U.S. presence in Germany declined significantly after the fall of the Berlin Wall and the dissolution of the Soviet Union, but even today there are twenty-one U.S. military bases in Germany, with associated forces fulfilling NATO commitments. There are twenty-three U.S. bases in Japan, which continues to favor military cooperation with the United States because of concerns about both China and North Korea, but there is significant opposition to the U.S. base in Okinawa. There are fifteen U.S. military bases in South Korea sixty years after the Korean War.

Military pay is currently more than $5,000 a year higher than comparable civilian employment; it is more than $10,000 a year higher when the military's special allowances and benefits are taken into account. Simply freezing non-combat pay for three years would save $3 billion a year. A lieutenant colonel with a family and twenty years of service took home $84,000 tax-free in 2001, compared with $120,000 in 2012—a 16 percent increase. Capping increases in military pay would mean savings of $17 billion; freezing DoD civilian salaries for three years would save $15 billion. Military benefits total nearly 100 percent of pay, compared with 55 percent for federal civilians. Over the past 15 years, service members have seen their out-of-pocket costs for housing eliminated and their pensions enriched. They also have gained the right to transfer their subsidized college tuition to a child or a spouse.

In addition to cutting the ranks of all the services, there is particular need to place restrictions on the overseas deployment of our military personnel, which is a moral issue as well as a cost issue. In 2011, a noncommissioned officer was killed in Afghanistan while on his fourteenth tour of Iraq and Afghanistan. This is unconscionable. Larry Korb, a former assistant secretary of defense in the Reagan administration, has proposed that no unit or individual be assigned to a combat zone for more than one year, and that they not be sent back involuntarily without spending at least two years at home.[12] The Guard and Reserve should be returned to their status as a strategic reserve. No unit or individual in the reserves should be activated for more than one year out of every six.

Two of the main drivers of increased defense spending are the cost of operations and maintenance (O&M), which nearly doubled between 2004 and 2008, and the cost of weapons procurement, which has been out of control over the past several years. Funds for O&M have gone from $42 billion to $80 billion between 2004 and 2008. Thus, when the number of deployed personnel increased by 25 percent, O&M costs tripled.[13] These costs include operations in Afghanistan as well as the huge logistic costs of transporting military equipment into a country with no logistics infrastructure. The O&M costs also were driven by the huge growth in requirements for force protection gear as well as much of the health care program, which will increase by $26 billion over the next few years.

The Congressional Budget Office (CBO) concluded that the "costs of developing and buying weapons have historically been, on average, 20–30 percent higher" than Pentagon estimates.[14] Spending for procurement in 2004 was only $7.2 billion, but it reached $61.5 billion in 2008, marking an eightfold increase and representing half of the total increase in the costs of the Iraq and Afghan wars in that year. These costs were accelerated by the purchase of Mine Resistant Ambush Protected (MRAP) vehicles and heavy trucks with a V-shaped hull designed to increase survivability against roadside bombs or Improvised Explosive Devices (IEDs).

Tens of billions are spent annually on Cold War systems ill-suited to the needs of the twenty-first century; cost overruns on these systems contribute heavily to the U.S. deficit. In 2010, the General Accounting Office (GAO) reported that cost overruns on the Pentagon's ninety-five largest weapons acquisitions systems totaled about $300 billion even as the Pentagon cut procurement orders and reduced performance expectations. Serious reductions are needed in the numbers of aircraft carriers, nuclear attack submarines, stealth destroyers, and manned fighter aircraft.

Since 9/11, the Pentagon has doubled its spending on modernized weapons systems, with more than $700 billion allocated for procurement and research and development. Accordingly, there has been huge waste on sophisticated technological systems that have been overpriced, underutilized, and often canceled. Secretary of Defense Gates conceded that these weapons systems "resulted in relatively modest gains in actual military capability," an outcome he called both "vexing and disturbing."[15]

Procurement boondoggles have robbed the U.S. treasury of hundreds of billions of dollars. In addition to the $100 billion that has been wasted on national missile defense over the past fifty years, several hundred billion dollars have gone to the Army's Future Combat System, which consists of interconnected vehicles, robots, and sensing devices. Althought it was originally priced at $100 billion, the development costs are closer to $400 billion, with Boeing and Science Applications International Corporation (SAIC) garnering huge profits over the past ten years.

In a bipartisan effort, Senators Carl Levin (D-MI) and John McCain (R-AZ) introduced legislation in 2009 that created a new Pentagon position, a director of independent cost assessments to review cost estimates independently of the military service requesting the program. Unlike previous efforts, these reviews would take place at key points in the acquisition process before a weapons program can proceed. At a hearing on the bill in March 2009, Senator McCain predicted that a "train wreck is coming" if the Pentagon didn't pull the plug on unneeded weapons with huge cost overruns.[16] There is a belief that the new office has been effective in reducing inefficiencies, but the money that is saved has thus far merely been moved back into other weapons programs. Major General James E. Cartwright, former deputy chairman of the Joint Chiefs of Staff, praised the effort because of the ability to apply savings to "more deserving projects."[17]

Complaints are already being heard that the new office merely duplicates existing regulations, adds a fresh layer of bureaucracy, and introduces new reporting mandates that make an already sluggish system even more sclerotic and inflationary. The Levin-McCain bill actually weakened the earlier Nunn-McCurdy Bill, which required the secretary of defense to seek special approval from Congress to continue funding a program that was 15 to 25 percent over budget. In any event, the Pentagon is skirting the intent of the new bill by cutting quantities of weapons systems, which actually increases unit cost.

If the Congress had been doing its job of constitutionally mandated oversight, it would not have been necessary to create this new position. In view of the Pentagon's waste of hundreds of billions of dollars in cost overruns, it is reasonable to expect Congress to try to control this Leviathan. Unfortunately, Congress has failed the test of oversight and is either unwilling or unable to scrutinize hugely expensive national security programs. The Congress did the same with intelligence reform in 2005, when it added a new layer of leadership (e.g., director of national intelligence) without significant changes, let alone improvements, in the process.

In announcing the budget for 2013, Secretary of Defense Panetta stated that the president would request another round of base closings in the United States, but it is unlikely that Congress would accept base closings at home until there is a commission to examine the closing of overseas facilities. Senator Carl Levin remarked immediately after the Pentagon's announcement regarding defense savings that he would not be "able to support" closing bases at home until the United States "shut down some of its bases in Europe."[18]

In an unusual bipartisan effort, Senators Jon Tester (D-MT) and Kay Bailey Hutchinson (R-TX) submitted legislation in 2011 to create a commission to review the situation overseas. U.S. bases in Europe cost more to operate than U.S. bases at home, and few U.S. European bases can be justified on the grounds of U.S. or European security. Too many U.S. forces deployed in non-combat zones abroad are in stable areas that do not require a military presence.[19] Closing bases in the United States and overseas, and curbing construction costs, including suspending plans to locate families with troops deployed in South Korea, could save an additional $5 billion to $7 billion over the next decade.

In 2006, the Department of Defense, as part of its Quadrennial Defense Review (QDR), envisioned the need to reduce our overseas footprint and created a comprehensive strategy to "shift the large, permanent overseas garrisons toward expeditionary operations utilizing more austere bases abroad." In response to the QDR, the Congress appropriated $14 billion for military construction at key U.S. installations to enhance U.S. readiness and create greater capability for rapid worldwide deployment in the eventuality of fewer overseas facilities. However, the Pentagon's QDR in 2010 shifted from reducing the size of large overseas bases to building greater capacity for supporting allied military forces, which if anything will lead to higher levels of investment.

Military construction costs more than tripled between 2005 ($0.5 billion) and 2008 ($1.7 billion), reaching a high point of $2 billion in 2010. Another $1.3 billion was requested for 2011 even though the United States is supposed to complete its withdrawal from Iraq in that year and begin withdrawal from Afghanistan. Recent defense appropriation and authorization acts prohibit the United States from establishing permanent bases in either Iraq or Afghanistan, but this has not stopped the Pentagon from building huge, permanent-looking facilities.[20] All infrastructure costs were heightened by the fraud and waste in providing contractor services to U.S. forces.[21]

The most sensitive area for reduced expenditures, an area referred to as a serious budget buster, has been health care. The United States has a sacred obligation to servicemen and women in combat zones, but former defense secretary Gates glibly remarked that health costs were "eating the Defense Department alive." These costs were $19 billion ten years ago, have reached $50 billion today, and are projected to grow to $92 billion by 2030. Spending on drugs in the defense program grew by an average of 2.2 percent a year from 2006 to 2010, while the national average growth was only 1.2 percent.

The current premium for Tricare, the military's health insurance program, is only $460 a year for military families. Raising the Tricare premium for employed working-age military retirees to $1,000 a month would save $28 billion over ten years. Raising the co-pay for Tricare drugs from $3 to $15 would save $26 billion over ten years. Military families have not faced an increase in health care premiums in more than fifteen years;

meanwhile, civilian federal workers pay more than $5,000 for a comparable health plan. Congress presumably will not allow the Pentagon to seek savings in health care at a time when two long wars have created terrible medical and psychological problems for servicemen and women and their families.

If we are going to ask our senior citizens to work longer and take social security payments later, then we should question a military retirement system that allows U.S. troops to retire as early as 38 years of age with inflation-adjusted payments for the rest of their lives. Reducing pensions for men and women serving only twenty years from 50 percent of salary to 40 percent of salary would save $86 billion. Nevertheless, Secretary of Defense Panetta favors increasing retirement spending even further by offering retirement pay to individuals who serve as few as twelve years.

Reducing the Air Force

The excessive spending on the Air Force is the most wasteful of all military expenditures. The Air Force is obsessed with fighter superiority in an era without a threat. The United States has not been threatened by air power in nearly seventy years, and the U.S. Air Force holds an advantage over any combination of air powers. Pentagon briefings on Capitol Hill have always exaggerated the capabilities of air defense forces, particularly the systems deployed by Russia and China, the only two countries with serious air defenses. Senior air force officers even had the effrontery to argue against the establishment of no-fly zones in Libya (2011) and Syria (2012) because of the so-called sophistication of their air defense systems.

The ability of U.S. fighter aircraft to deliver highly accurate guided weapons significantly reduces the number of aircraft needed as well as the number of combat sorties flown each day. The Air Force spent billions of dollars on advanced aircraft, such as the B-1 bomber and the F-22 fighter, that were never deployed in Iraq or Afghanistan or any other combat zone.

The tortured history of the F-22 fighter program illustrated the unnecessary expansion of U.S. procurement and deployment of fighter aircraft. The F-22 was designed in the mid-1980s to confront Soviet fighter planes that were never built. The first flight of a F-22 prototype took place in 1990, only one year before the collapse of the Soviet Union and thirteen years before the plane achieved initial operating capability. The original idea of a production run of 750 F-22s was incrementally reduced to the production of 187 aircraft when it was recognized that there was little utility for an air-to-air combat plane that lacked an obvious adversary. When the final F-22 rolled off of Lockheed Martin's assembly line in December 2011, its cost to the nation was $153 million—compared to the estimated cost in 1988 of $35 million per plane. When development costs were included, each F-22 was estimated to have cost more than $300 million.

The overall cost of the F-22 program was $65 billion; this included $30 billion in research and development costs and nearly $35 billion in procurement costs.[22] The Air Force has also allocated more than $12 billion to upgrade the F-22, which will bring the total cost of 187 of these aircraft to nearly $80 billion.

The F-22 program was killed in 2011 to make way for the F-35, an even more costly and contentious program. Nevertheless, the F-22 was the world's most effective and lethal air-to-air combat aircraft; it had a significant stealth capability, high maneuverability, and the ability to cruise at supersonic speeds without using engine afterburners. The plane became the nation's primary and most expensive fighter with unmatched capability for air supremacy and homeland defense. The combination of speed, stealth, maneuverability, and integrated avionics ensured air dominance for the United States. Like so many U.S. weapons programs (e.g., the Joint Strike Fighter, ballistic missile defense,

Navy shipbuilding), however, the F-22 has no relevance to the Global War on Terror.

The Air Force and its supporters defended the F-22 as a hedge against a revived Russian threat, a familiar rationalization. Pentagon planners also have cited unpredictable Third World dangers in the years ahead and the need to maintain U.S. industrial capabilities for the development and production of advanced aircraft. The Pentagon and its contractors advance the argument "It's a plane that sends a message to the world, 'Don't even think about competing with the U.S.'"[23] Perhaps, but it should be remembered that in fighting two wars over the past decade, the F-22 was never used in a combat mission anywhere. It is still considered to be a superior air-to-air combat fighter to the F-35, but its major assignment at present consists of intelligence gathering, for which the F-22 is an extremely expensive platform.

The Congress did not want to let go of the F-22 because Lockheed Martin relied on forty-seven states for spare parts and construction. Congressmembers viewed the F-22 as a jobs program for their constituents, not a defense necessity. The F-22 involved as many as thirty major subcontractors and 4,500 suppliers, and generated 28,000 jobs at peak production, with indirect employment adding up to 112,000 jobs.[24] In response to Gates's effort to end production of the F-22, Lockheed Martin sponsored an expensive ad campaign that claimed the potential loss of 95,000 jobs should production end. Fortunately, the Pentagon and Congress agreed to end the program, if only because one of the most expensive platforms, the F-35, was soaking up hundreds of billions of dollars.

The F-35: A Case of Sticker Shock
There is no better example of President Eisenhower's warning regarding the military-industrial complex than the procurement history of the F-35 Joint Strike Fighter. In view of U.S.

air superiority and the fact that only one U.S. aircraft has been shot down by an enemy over the past forty years, it is still not clear why the F-35 is necessary. There would be a savings of $15 billion to $20 billion annually by reducing the F-35 fighter fleet to 1,000, which is far more than needed in any event. Like the Marines' V-22 Osprey aircraft, the F-35 has been a troubled program, with cost overruns, military mismanagement, and no political scrutiny. Nevertheless, the Air Force is still planning to spend vast sums of taxpayer money to buy 2,440 F-35s, making it by far the Pentagon's largest program.

An unfortunate example of bipartisanship is Democratic and Republican convergence to spend astronomical sums on unnecessary weapons. Lockheed Martin, the manufacturer of the F-35, is the greatest beneficiary of the Pentagon's largesse, and the F-35 is Lockheed's most important and profitable weapons project. Lockheed Martin is also the top donor to the chair of the House Armed Services Committee, Representative Buck McKeon, and to the chair of the Tactical Air and Land Forces Subcommitte Representative Roscoe Bartlett (R-MD). They teamed up with Representative Sylvester Reyes (D-TX) to oppose any cuts in the White House's 2012 defense budget. Representative Reyes is also high on Lockheed Martin's support program.

Why are we even building this plane? In 2001, the Pentagon wanted a relatively inexpensive tactical fighter plane with stealth technology to replace several fighter aircraft in the inventory. The F-35 program, the biggest program in the history of weapons acquisition, was justified as a replacement for several jet fighters, including the F-22 and the F-16. The Pentagon also said that configuring the Air Force on one fighter aircraft, and not several, would bring great savings in operations and maintenance. The Air Force eventually ordered an end to the production of F-22s, but the savings proved illusory because they are being used to meet the rising cost of the stealthy F-35.

More than 3,400 F-35s were originally scheduled to be built, 600 of them for foreign sales, thus easing the cost to the United States Air Force. (The Clinton administration audaciously took credit for cutting the F-35 program from 2,978 to 2,852 aircraft, a 2 percent reduction.) The first deliveries originally were scheduled for 2010; now the first delivery is scheduled for 2017. In 2002, the Pentagon projected that each F-35 would cost $70 million; current estimates have nearly doubled the cost—to $133 million. The head of the Pentagon's cost-assessment office, Christine Fox, told the Senate in May 2011 that the F-35 will be one-third more expensive to operate than the aircraft it will replace.[25] Each service (Air Force, Navy, and Marines) will have its own version of the F-35, bringing the total cost of the program to more than $400 billion by 2016, begging the question of why, given our dominant Air Force, the separate services need their own aircraft.[26]

The latest Pentagon forecast demonstrated that the total cost of building and operating the F-35 fleet over a fifty-year period could exceed $1 trillion, a figure that even Senator McCain referred to as "jaw-dropping." McCain, who has rarely met a weapons system that he didn't love, referred to the program as a "train wreck." Tom Burbage, who manages the F-35 program for Lockheed Martin Corporation, acknowledged that the "t" word (i.e., trillion) "causes a sensational reaction because no one's ever dealt with 't's' before in a program."[27] The Pentagon's procurement chief, Ashton Carter, conceded in a Senate hearing that the projected cost of the F-35 was on top of an "unacceptably large" procurement bill.

Air Force planners have disclosed significant problems with the F-35, including technical problems associated with the weight of the aircraft and the fact that it is clearly not as stealthy as advertised. Initial flight tests have found cracks associated with the composite materials on new fighter aircraft. The dirty secret with fighter aircraft and bomber programs, however, is that operating and support costs tend to double the initial costs of production and procurement. Even worse is the fact that ninety planes have been purchased, but only 20 percent of the testing has been completed, and the software will not be finalized until 2016.

The courageous and smart decision would be to abandon the entire F-35 program, which would bring a savings of $480 billion after allocations for upgrading F-16s and F/A-18s. The United States has complete domination of the air and has not been threatened from the air for the past six decades. The United States could update its current fighter aircraft and remain in a superior position. The technological advantages of the F-35 could be applied to fighter aircraft already in the U.S. inventory, which would save hundreds of billions of dollars. At the very least, the order for more than 2,440 F-35 aircraft should be halved, and the variants for the Navy and Marines eliminated in view of the costly technological problems for both. The United States cannot afford thousands of these aircraft, and there is no realistic scenario for their use.

The next generation of pilotless armed drones as well as hypersonic cruise missiles have more uses than several thousand sophisticated fighter aircraft. The Air Force had to be ordered to commit several billion dollars for unmanned aerial vehicles, which are currently more effective than fighter aircraft. The Air Force did announce the cancellation of the Northrop Grumman Global Hawk, a surveillance drone that flies at an altitude of 60,000 feet and was intended to replace the piloted U-2 program, which gained fame for flying over the Soviet Union during the Cold War. The drone presents the same sort of problem for the Air Force (no pilots) that Admiral Hyman Rickover's strategic submarines presented for the Navy (smaller crews, fewer officers).

Reducing the Army

The Army, which will lose 57,000 forces by 2017, could save $200 billion over the next ten years by cutting back to a force of 360,000. Fewer forces should be stationed overseas and, in view of U.S. setbacks in Iraq and Afghanistan, far less attention should be given to large-scale counterinsurgency (COIN) wars. The United States lacks the technology and the personnel to fight such wars, and there are too many examples of using the COIN capability to encourage regime change and nation-building.

The current plan governing U.S. deployment is based on brigade combat teams, which are smaller integrated units that include infantry, armor, artillery, and engineers. There are now forty-five active brigade-combat teams (BCTs), and this number could easily be reduced to forty without any lost of combat capability. The commander of the U.S. Army in Europe, Lieutenant General Mark Hertling, referred to these brigades as "mini-divisions" that can be "maneuvered with significant effectiveness." There are currently four BCTs in Europe, three in Germany and one in Italy, each with about 5,000 troops; two of these teams were scheduled to return to the United States in 2012. Other than training with other NATO units, it is difficult to imagine a mission for these troops.

The German-based U.S. 1st Armored Division lowered its flag in May 2011 in order to return to the United States, marking the last Army division to leave Europe. This move was particularly symbolic because the tanks of this particular division first rumbled onto the continent through Italy in World War II. Instead of a transformation that should have marked the recognition of the end of the Cold War and the need to reduce the U.S. footprint in Europe, the withdrawal of this particular division marked the transition of a heavy armor-based unit to smaller and lighter units that, according to the Pentagon, are better able to meet "today's threats." But what are today's threats in Europe?

Over the past fifteen years, the U.S. Army has canceled more than twenty systems that cost several hundred billion dollars. When the so-called Future Combat Systems (FCS), the Army's most important and most sophisticated modernization initiative, was canceled, it had already cost nearly $20 billion, the greatest single procurement loss the Army ever incurred. The FCS was a particularly complex series of systems that included a range of manned systems, a group of unmanned air and ground systems, and sophisticated radios, all tied to a single network to view the battlefield.

The Army's Comanche helicopter was perceived in 2000 as the "quarterback of the digital battlefield" that could operate at night and in bad weather as well as fly farther than any other helicopter.[28] Four years later, the Comanche, dubbed "The Duke" in tribute to actor John Wayne, was canceled after nearly two decades of weapons design and testing and an expenditure of more than $6 billion. With the cancellation of the Comanche, the Army took the $15 billion that had been allocated but not spent, and invested it in tried and tested helicopters in the inventory, such as the Apache and Black Hawk, as well as unmanned drones. The cancellation of the Comanche led to the cancellation of its follow-up helicopter, the Armed Reconnaissance Helicopter, which had rung up $600 million in research and development.

Reducing the Navy

As with the Air Force and its dominance of the skies, the Navy has had total dominance at sea for the past six decades. Chief of Naval Operations Admiral Gary Roughhead concedes that the United States enjoys a "degree of overmatch [with any potential adversary] that is extraordinary." U.S. naval ships are deployed in too many areas with too many missions. The Navy has its own air force, its own army, and its own strategic weapons. It is equal in size to all the navies of the world combined and has a subordinate organization, the Coast Guard, which represents the world's seventh-largest fleet. The Navy must reexamine its need for additional littoral combat ships, which operate in shallow waters in support of ground combat. The littoral combat ships cost more than $600 million each, and each destroyer costs more than $3 billion. The United States has a significant capability to support ground operations with sea-based air power. Littoral combat ships would not be effective against serious military opposition, and are hardly necessary in military operations against weak nations.

Nevertheless, the Navy is merely being asked to retire seven aging cruisers earlier than expected and to cut back production of two littoral combat ships and eight joint high-speed vessels. There will also be delayed construction of one Virginia-class attack submarine, two coastal combat ships, and a large amphibious ship, which represents an extremely modest reduction in force.

The Navy has far too many platforms for the geopolitical and military challenges that exist for the United States in the near future. Tens of billions of dollars could be saved by cutting naval platforms without any risk to U.S. national security. The Navy has far too many tactical and strategic submarines, and $40 billion could be saved between 2012 and 2020 by reducing the projected number of strategic submarines from fourteen to seven and slowing the procurement of tactical submarines by deploying one per year and not two. There would be associated savings in personnel and maintenance costs as well.

The United States doesn't need the DDG-1000 Zumwalt-class destroyer, a naval combatant designed to fight mid-ocean battles that no other nation is preparing to initiate or fight. The existing DDG-51 Arleigh Burke–class destroyer, with its highly sophisticated Aegis combat system, is equipped to track and destroy multiple air, ship, and submarine targets. The Navy lost interest in the Zumwalt, reducing the number on order from thirty-two to two. The end to all production would save $5 billion to $6 billion.

Reducing the number of ships in the U.S. Navy would save $55 billion over ten years, with the cancellation of five amphibious ships, the retirement of six Ticonderoga-class cruisers, and reduced purchases of Virginia-class submarines and littoral combat ships.

The Navy's version of the F-35 is questionable because it will be based on a difficult platform—aircraft carriers. The United States has far too many aircraft carriers for any reasonable scenario, and no other countries are contemplating developing large-scale carrier fleets. If there is any threat to a strategic U.S. platform it would be Chinese development of accurate anti-ship missiles that would force U.S. carriers to deploy farther out in the western Pacific Ocean to get out of range of the Chinese missiles, which would create problems for carrier-based aircraft with limited range. The U.S. Navy is committed to eleven aircraft carrier battle groups; these were "structured to fight the Imperial Japanese Navy."[29] In view of recent advances in Chinese surface-to-surface missiles, it would make more sense to rely on small attack submarines than vulnerable aircraft carriers. The United States already has a significant capability to support ground operations with its sea-based air power.

Second only to the F-35 nightmare is the worst-case costs for the next generation of aircraft carriers. The USS *Gerald R. Ford*, the Navy's most expensive warship, may now be running more than $1 billion in cost overruns under a contract that obligates the U.S. Navy for nearly 90 percent of the cost of the overruns. The original estimated cost for the carrier, scheduled for completion in 2016, was over $5 billion; the current estimated cost is over $6 billion; the projected cost could reach

$14 billion if historical projects are any guide. Navy spokesmen have refused to discuss these overruns publicly, and instead have merely offered to delay construction of the second Ford-class carrier (USS *John F. Kennedy*) by two years. In view of the limited strategic utility of aircraft carriers and the Chinese success in developing anti-ship missiles, the debate should be about the desirability of these floating arsenals and not the production schedule. Unfortunately, the military-industrial complex is more enamored with "first-of-a-kind" naval vessels than with strategic utility.

The Virginia-class submarine was another weapons system designed to counter a Soviet naval system that never got out of the design stage. Like the Cold War–era Seawolf, the Virginia was designed to counter Soviet attack and nuclear-launch submarines. There is no longer a strategic threat from submarines for the United States; the Russian program is virtually moribund, and the Chinese program is technologically inferior. By extending the operating life of the existing fleet of Los Angeles–class fast-attack submarines, the United States could save as much as $5 billion for each Virginia-class submarine it scrubs. Ten of these submarines have already been built, and an end to production would encounter stiff resistance from many congressmen, particularly in Virginia and Connecticut, who view naval construction as public works projects for their states.

Reducing the Marines
The U.S. Marines have more planes, ships, armored vehicles, and personnel in uniform than the entire British military. As in the case of the U.S. Army, the Marine Corps could be cut to a force of 140,000, rather than 182,000, with no serious loss of firepower. A report from the Sustainable Defense Task Force suggested that these cuts could occur over a ten-year period, which would amount to an annual 3.5 percent reduction.[30]

The very existence of the Marine Corps is questionable. The Marines have not conducted an amphibious landing since the Korean War, more than sixty years ago, and this was the only amphibious landing since World War II. There is no other nation in the world that has such a Corps in terms of numbers and capabilities. Critics of the Marine Corps acknowledge that the Army's political missteps have insured the life of the Marines and that, "if the Army were to become politically more astute, the Marine Corps would have a much less successful bureaucratic life."[31]

There is virtually no chance that Congress would allow any reduction in the size or capabilities of the Corps. During the Korean War, when the Army tried to exercise control over the missions of the Corps, the House passed the Douglas Mansfield Act that mandated at least three active Marine divisions and three air wings. This Act provided the Marines with observers on the Joint Chiefs of Staff. Over time, the Marines gained full representation on the Joint Chiefs, and Marine officers have served as chairman and vice chairman of the Joint Chiefs. In 2009, President Obama even appointed a retired Marine Corps general, James Jones, as national security adviser, but Jones was a poor fit and was forced to retire within two years.

The Marines should stop procurement of its V-22 Osprey, a futuristic vertical takeoff and landing hybrid aircraft that has taken up a quarter-century of research, development, and production and still is neither reliable nor safe. The Marines have been developing this system for more than two decades and have built more than eighty of the aircraft, which is far more than enough. Nonetheless, an additional 400 are scheduled to be built, which goes beyond good judgment or planning. The Osprey is more than 150 percent over its original unit cost, with current costs running over $100 million per aircraft. Instead of adding 400 or more Ospreys, the Marines could rely on the proven H-92 and CH-53 helicopters; doing so would save the nation approximately $15 billion.

President George H.W. Bush and Secretary of Defense Cheney tried to kill the Osprey program twenty years ago, when it was projected to cost $27 billion for 682 aircraft. The author of the definitive book on the Osprey, Richard Whittle, noted that the Marine campaign to save the Osprey "bordered on insubordination."[32] Currently, 300 Ospreys are in service or in production, and $36 billion has been spent out of a projected $54 billion. The total number of Ospreys has been reduced from 682 to 458 aircraft, but the overall cost has doubled.

The Osprey's speed permits rapid maneuver from sea-based platforms, but the craft is less stable than other systems, and its slow descent makes it highly vulnerable to ground fire. The GAO gave it high marks for operating in Iraq, a "low-threat theater of operations," but raised serious questions about its ability to operate in "high-threat operations."[33] The Osprey has already claimed more than thirty lives in flight tests.

The Marines are operating a public relations campaign to retain the aircraft. In November 2011, Secretary of Defense Panetta flew from Washington, DC, to New York City on the $70 million aircraft in order to advertise its safety. The congressional fight to save the Osprey is being led by Representative William M. Thornberry (R-TX), whose district is home for the Osprey's assembly lines. This is one more example of the difficulty of trying to cancel or even limit billion-dollar Pentagon programs, even one that has faced repeated safety problems, years of delays, ballooning costs, and tough questions about its utility.[34]

The Marines are good at this kind of aggressive marketing strategy. They never forgot the serious efforts that Secretary of Defense Cheney made in the late 1980s and early 1990s to kill the Osprey program. Every year, Cheney would knock the Osprey funding out of the defense budget, and the Congress would predictably reintroduce it. So, years later, when Cheney was vice president and visiting a base in Jacksonville, North Carolina, that housed a large contingent of Ospreys, two of the aircraft flew low and slow over Vice President Cheney's head as he disembarked from his plane.[35] Just a reminder that the Marines had prevailed.

Like Lockheed Martin, which produces the F-35 in forty-eight states, the makers of the Osprey, Boeing and Bell Helicopter, have built the helicopter in numerous states, guaranteeing support from senators and representatives. Congressmembers manipulate hearings to celebrate the building of these high-end weapons systems, making sure that the Pentagon's congressional liaison officers provide appropriate testimony. The Pentagon is the only government institution that gets to house its liaison officers in the Senate and House office buildings, where they develop strong and lasting relationships with key congresspeople.

The Marine version of the F-35 joint strike fighter is particularly expensive because it will have a take-off and landing capability that resembles that of a helicopter. The program should be canceled or seriously delayed. The F-35 could be replaced on amphibious assault ships with either unmanned aerial vehicles or attack helicopters with no decline in Marine capabilities. According to Winslow T. Wheeler of the Center for Defense Information, the Marine version of the aircraft was "so problematic that I cannot believe the two-year probation was anything other than Gates kicking the can to his successor to kill the thing."[36] Secretary of Defense Panetta, who was a budget hawk when he led the Office of Management and Budget, announced in January 2012 that the Marines' F-35 would resume production. He has shown no interest in canceling any weapons system.

The Expeditionary Fighting Vehicle (EFV), a landing vehicle for the Marine Corps, should be canceled. More than $3 billion has already been spent on research and development for a system that was conceived in the late 1980s. The new vehicle, a thirty-eight-ton landing craft—a tank that swims—is designed to give the Marines a new way to storm a beach, although there is little likelihood in the future of such an expensive and risky venture. It is operated by a three-man crew and can carry seventeen combat-ready Marines at twenty knots on the sea up to twenty-five miles from shore, and as much as forty-five miles per hour on land. The vehicle is designed to replace a slower and older amphibious assault vehicle that carries twenty-one Marines with its crew of three.

There are many reasons for challenging a military program that will eventually cost more than $15 billion and has been plagued by delays and cost overruns. The EFV has cost more than $3 billion to develop, and as costs have skyrocketed, the Pentagon has already reduced the procurement order from 1,025 to 575. Tests thus far have produced numerous failures and critical breakdowns, with every hour of operation requiring more than three hours of maintenance.

Congressional leaders predictably campaign against efforts to kill the program. The chairman of the House Armed Forces subcommittee on Sea Power and Expeditionary Forces, Todd Akin (R-MO), exclaimed that the need to protect the "core capability of the Marines," (i.e., to attack on land from the sea) "has not gone away."[37]

Reducing Nuclear Forces

Nothing has been said about reducing nuclear forces. One of the best-kept defense secrets of the past sixty years has been the high cost of producing and maintaining nuclear weapons, somewhere between $5 trillion to $6 trillion, which represents one-fourth to one-third of overall defense spending. The total is roughly equivalent to the total amount of money spent on the Army or the Navy since WWII; it covers research and development, security, communications and control systems, and environmental cleanup. The staggering cost of maintaining bloated nuclear-related programs over the next decade will amount to $600 billion.

Some of this money is in the budget for the Department of Energy. The total does not include the considerable investment in tactical nuclear weapons, but it does include the huge investment in failed nuclear projects such as a nuclear-powered airplane ($6 billion), nuclear-powered rocket engine ($3 billion), the Midgetman missile ($4 billion), and the Safeguard anti-ballistic missile system ($25 billion). The costs of weapons systems such as the B-52 bomber is doubled when the costs of the nuclear-tipped weapons they carry are included.

When the United States initially began to develop and deploy nuclear weapons, the military-industrial complex stressed that the huge investment in nuclear systems would be an overall savings because it would allow a smaller army and navy. The United States has built more than 70,000 nuclear weapons since the end of WWII and, at its peak in 1967, there were more than 32,000 weapons in the stockpile. Even in the post–Cold War era, the cost of maintaining and deploying nuclear weapons is more than $25 billion a year. At the same time, contrary to the military's promise, our army and navy have gotten larger and costlier for taxpayers.

Two decades after the end of the Cold War, the United States still has 2,500 deployed nuclear weapons as well as 2,600 nuclear weapons in its inventory, along with thousands of warheads held in reserve. In 2011, two U.S. Air Force officers wrote an authoritative essay that pointed specifically to 331 nuclear weapons as providing an assured deterrence capability. Other important nuclear powers such as Britain, France, and China appear to agree, believing that 200 to 300 nuclear weapons are sufficient for deterrence, and the key non-signatories of the Non-Proliferation Treaty (Israel, India, and Pakistan) have focused on 200 nuclear weapons as the appropriate size for deterrence.

The United States should consider ending its dependence on the nuclear triad, which consists of intercontinental ballistic missiles (ICBMs), submarine-launched ballistic missiles (SLBMs), and strategic bombers. The elimination of nuclear weapons from strategic bombers would reduce the nuclear deterrent triad to a more than sufficient dyad, and would bring savings of $40 billion. At the same time, the current fleet of fourteen nuclear-armed submarines could be cut in half, which would still leave the United States with 875 nuclear warheads at sea. An end to production of the D5 SLBM and the retirement of hundreds of Minuteman ICBM missiles would bring huge savings in operating and refurbishing costs.

In order to get Republican support for the nuclear arms treaty of 2010, the Obama administration capitulated to Senator Jon Kyl (R-AZ) and agreed to an unnecessarily large increase of $85 billion for the modernization of our nuclear weapons industry, particularly the expensive complex of nuclear labs and production facilities. The United States has two weapons-design laboratories at Los Alamos, New Mexico, and Livermore, California; one laboratory would suffice. Nuclear weapons research is also conducted at the Sandia National Laboratory in New Mexico.

The Pentagon, which lobbied for $100 billion to upgrade nuclear forces in 2011–2012, plans to build a new plutonium storage facility at Los Alamos National Laboratory that is along a fault line and near an active volcano. The modernization includes the overhaul of thousands of older bombs that should be retired. The modernization of B61 tactical nuclear bombs in Europe is an unnecessary expense in view of the impossibility of conducting operations on a European battlefield that has suffered from the use of tactical nuclear weapons. These tactical nuclear bombs should be dismantled. The Pentagon's modernization plans would add $600 billion to U.S. defense spending over the next decade.

There are other reductions in the nuclear field as well. If the United States reduced its intercontinental ballistic missiles from 500 to 300, the United States could save $80 billion over the next ten years. Senator Tom Coburn (R-TX) supports such reductions as well as delaying the purchase of additional strategic bombers for another decade. In July 2011, General Cartwright, then deputy chairman of the Joint Chiefs of Staff, favored reassessing the role of nuclear weapons, including strategic bombers, in today's international environment. President Obama wanted to appoint General Cartwright as chairman of the Joint Chiefs, but Secretary of Defense Gates blocked the appointment and lobbied for CIA director Panetta, who opposes nuclear reductions.

The New START Treaty could become a stepping stone to a round of still deeper cuts in the U.S. and Russian arsenals as well as to serious negotiations with other nuclear powers, particularly China, Britain, and France. These powers must also deal with the nuclear inventories of India, Israel, and Pakistan, non-signatories of the NPT. Pakistan is especially disquieting because of its unstable civilian government, a powerful military and intelligence corps, and an extremist threat that continues to grow. In the past, Pakistan has been a particular worry because its scientists have been involved in sharing and selling nuclear technology to Iran, Libya, North Korea, and Syria. Because Pakistan fears that the United States might use military force to seize its nuclear weapons, the Pakistanis conduct secret movements of their nuclear weapons so that their locations remain secret—a dangerous practice. Thus far, the United States and its allies have not found an answer to Iran's nuclear program, which appears to be several technical steps away from developing nuclear weapons.

Reducing Military Assistance

Special attention must be given to significantly cutting military aid, including the heavy investment in training and equipping Iraqi and Afghan military forces. The United States dominates the sale of weapons overseas, which represents one more aspect of the military-industrial-congressional complex. In 2011, the United States was responsible for three-quarters of the total arms market globally, which was valued at $85 billion; Russia was a distant second, with $4.8 billion in deals.[38] Total U.S. sales of $66 billion in 2011 marked an extraordinary increase over the $21 billion in deals in the previous year, and more than doubled the previous record year for sales in 2009. The major buyers of U.S. weapons systems are in the Persian Gulf, where Saudi Arabia, the United Arab Emirates, and Oman appear to be responding to the bellicose statements and actions of Iran.

The Pentagon will oppose such cuts, arguing that military assistance contributes to regional defense as well as self-defense, thus reducing the U.S. military burden among developing nations. Secretary of Defense Panetta has campaigned for more support, particularly training and equipment, for military aid projects, and the Defense Department's Quadrennial Defense Review in 2011 endorsed more resources to bolster the military capacity of U.S. allies and partners.

In addition to the DoD, which manages most military aid to Iraq and Afghanistan, the State Department manages military assistance for more than eighty countries through the Foreign Military Financing (FMF) program. The Near East receives the greatest amount of FMF assistance, with Israel and Egypt accounting for $4.3 billion of the $5.5 billion requested for 2011. In addition to Israel and Egypt, Jordan, Pakistan, and Lebanon receive an additional $700 million in assistance, leaving small amounts that total $500 million for the remaining seventy-five countries. In addition to FMF, the U.S. Agency for International Development awards another $7.5 billion in grants for infrastructure assistance, which allows the recipient countries to use their own money for military purposes. The International Military Education and Training program is a modest one that allows the Department of State to provide $110 million to more than 135 countries, with Pakistan the number one beneficiary.

The United States gives assistance to numerous countries that do not need it or do not deserve it because of serious human rights violations. The first category includes Eastern European countries that are sufficiently stable and do not need modern military technology. They receive over $90 million in FMF funding. In the second category is Indonesia, a country with numerous human rights violations that receives $20 million in military assistance. Israel gets military assistance, although it has military superiority in the region as well as its own burgeoning weapons industry. One of the purposes of military assistance should be its contribution to regional stability. It would be difficult to argue that military assistance contributes to regional stability in the Middle East or Eastern Europe.

The United States has been unwilling to cut off military aid and arms sales even in response to well-documented government repression of nonviolent, pro-democracy activists. While condemning Russian arms sales to the Syrian government, for example, the United States continues to provide arms to the al-Khalifa dictatorship of Bahrain, which has systematically killed and tortured nonviolent protestors. This inconsistency inhibited the United States' ability to use diplomatic pressure to encourage Russia to stop selling arms to the Assad regime in Syria.

Military assistance has been particularly ineffective in fighting the war against terror. The best example of failure is Pakistan, where military assistance has had little impact on efforts to garner greater Pakistani assistance in the war against the Afghan Taliban and al-Qaeda. Osama bin Laden's long-term use of a sanctuary in Abbottabad, a military enclave near the Pakistani capital, raised serious questions about the knowledge and perhaps complicity of the Pakistani national security community regarding the top al-Qaeda leadership. Military aid to Yemen and Somalia has not produced favorable results, judging from the instability in both countries and the inability to ensure that military aid gets in the hands of the right forces. The so-called African coalition to fight piracy in the Gulf of Aden has been ineffective.

Congress and the Scandal of Waste

There are too many defense issues that Congress ignores. It should make the Pentagon justify the number of troops in the active-duty force, particularly in the Army and Marine Corps; the number of air wings and aircraft carrier platforms; and the need for national missile defense. There are members of Congress who want to reduce the defense budget, but they represent a small minority and their efforts have led to few reductions.

There was pressure in 2011 to reduce federal spending and to address serious deficit problems. Defense spending was never part of the hard bargaining. Sensitive entitlement issues such as Social Security and Medicare were on the table, even tax issues were on the table; but President Obama declared the defense budget sacrosanct in his State of the Union speeches in 2010 and 2011. In a volte-face, however, the Obama administration suddenly endorsed cutting $460 billion from defense, national security, and intelligence spending over the next 12 years. It did not provide specifics regarding cuts or guidance to the Senate Armed Forces Committee regarding the kinds of cuts that the administration favored. The OMB was similarly unwilling to provide specifics and guidance to the committee.

The Democratic Party has not wanted to appear weak on

defense issues, particularly in the wake of 9/11, and the Republican Party has been at the center of the military-industrial-congressional complex driving defense spending. As a result, during the congressional debates in 2011, the only significant cut came from the vote in the House of Representatives by a margin of 226 to 199 to reduce spending on military bands by $125 million.[39]

Virtually every other House amendment for reducing the 2012 defense budget was defeated. Amendments to require President Obama to submit a timetable for an accelerated transfer of military operations in Afghanistan from U.S. forces to Afghan forces and to withdraw U.S. ground troops were defeated, although they attracted more support than in recent years. Efforts to reduce the number of civilian employees at the Department of Defense by 5 percent over the next five years, and to freeze the defense budget at current levels (except for war costs, personnel costs, and wounded warrior programs) until the Department of Defense can pass an audit were roundly defeated. (The Pentagon has never passed an audit.) Efforts to reduce the number of U.S. forces in Europe as well as to reduce the funds authorized for ballistic missile defense were also defeated.

Defense budgets contribute significantly to big budget items, such as the F-35 Joint Strike Fighter or the Virginia-class submarine, but they do not necessarily create numerous jobs, as is frequently claimed by supporters. In a congressional briefing in May 2011, it was learned that less than 2 percent of the cost of each F-35 pays for labor costs in "manufacturing, fabrication, and assembly" work at the plane's main production facility in Fort Worth, Texas.[40] Conversely, more than 85 percent of the F-35 costs go for overhead, which has nothing to do with jobs that fabricate and assemble the aircraft.[41]

As defense analyst William Hartung notes, the question is not "whether military spending creates jobs—it is whether more jobs could be created by the same amount of money invested in other ways."[42] Many economists believe that a billion dollars spent for military purposes creates 25 percent fewer jobs than a tax cut; one and one-half times fewer jobs than spending on cleaner energy; and two and one-half times fewer jobs than spending on education.[43] The average overall compensation is higher for military jobs than the others, but other types of expenditure create more decent-paying jobs (those paying $64,000 per year or more) than military spending does.[44] A greater share of military spending, moreover, is spent either overseas or on imported goods. Conversely, most of the money generated by spending in areas such as cleaner energy and education is spent in the United States. President Eisenhower warned that the more we spend on unneeded weapons programs, the more layoffs there will be of police officers, firefighters, teachers, and other workers whose jobs are funded directly or indirectly by federal spending. But hypocrisy on this issue reigns supreme. Representative Norm Dicks (D-WA), who says he favors savings, won't let a penny be taken out of the F-35 fighter aircraft built in his district.

For the first time since 9/11, a small congressional group led by Representatives Ron Paul (R-TX), Barney Frank (D-MA), David Obey (D-WI), and Dicks, who is senior minority member on the House Appropriations Defense subcommittee, joined together in 2011 to seek cuts in defense spending. Representative Franks led the way, establishing the bipartisan Sustainable Defense Task Force (SDTF) to find $1 trillion in defense savings over the next ten years. According to the SDTF, a great share of such a reduction would come from reducing the size of the armed forces by 150,000 troops and cutting the number of new ballistic missile submarines and F-35 jet fighters. Unfortunately, Representative Franks, the most imaginative congressman on defense budget savings, announced his retirement in November 2011 following gerrymandering that threatened his reelection.

Other concerned congressmen are Senator Ron Wyden (D-OR) and Representative Walter B. Jones (R-NC).

An end to earmarks would also save billions of dollars on defense spending. President Obama said in the State of the Union message in January 2011 that he would veto legislation containing earmarks. Senator McCain has also been an authoritative voice against earmarks in the defense authorization bill, but he is running into resistance in his own party from the chairman of the House Armed Services Committee, Representative Buck McKeon. The rise of the Tea Party movement could make it easier to establish a more permanent ban on earmarks and to conduct genuine scrutiny of the defense bill, but there is a high level of chauvinism among many leaders of the Tea Party.

The Legacy of Robert M. Gates

Former Secretary of Defense Gates was falsely credited with looking for ways to cut defense spending. Actually, his strategy was one of damage limitation to restrict defense cuts, a strategy that has thus far succeeded. He claimed to want a debate on defense spending, referring to wasteful and unnecessary weapons systems, but consistently dodged the issue, especially when appearing before Congress. He acknowledged that "more and more money is consumed by fewer and fewer platforms that take longer and longer to build." Yet, Gates rarely followed up his rhetoric on savings with operational policies, and he consistently lobbied the Congress for modernization of key systems.

Gates attacked the Pentagon's bureaucracy, ordering cuts in contractors and intelligence agencies as well as the closure of the Joint Forces Command (JFC) in Norfolk. But he bowed to opposition from Virginia's congressional representatives and softened the blow to the JFC by continuing large-scale personnel deployment in the region. Gates's initiatives were responsible for some savings, such as the reduction 50 of the 900 generals and admirals in the military, a number that has grown significantly since 9/11. Gates wanted to cut the staff in his own office and the number of contractors in the Pentagon, since he could not even guess the number of contractors working there. He also wanted to end the practice of beginning full military pensions after twenty years of service.

Secretary of Defense Panetta is moving in the opposite direction, considering granting pensions to servicemen and women who have served less than twelve years, and unwilling to do anything about the bloated officer corps. Gates argued that the huge proportion of general and flag officers has created a Pentagon with the "fine motor skills of a dinosaur." The Department of Defense started dragging its heels on reducing the general staff before Secretary of Defense Gates was out of the building and, by the time Panetta had arrived, began adding four-star generals, undoing a year's worth of Gates's efforts to cut the Pentagon's top brass.[45]

Overall, Gates credited himself with having made $300 billion in reductions after joining the Bush administration in 2006. In fact, most of these so-called savings were shifted to other projects, and the defense budget increased by more than 20 percent in his last two years at the Pentagon. The $300 billion in savings was garnered from eliminated systems such as the F-22 and the Army's Future Combat System, but these "savings" were then invested in other programs. By any measure, Gates's "savings" were a pittance, designed as damage limitation to prevent greater congressional cuts rather than serious attempts to reduce super-inflated defense spending. There were no genuine savings. Gordon Adams, who monitored defense budgets for the Clinton administration in the 1990s, considered Defense Department calculations as "extremely loose at the edges." One of the groups not fooled by Gate's rhetoric was Wall Street; stocks of all major defense companies soared during his stewardship.

Gates also took credit for targeting the "proverbial low-hanging fruit" in the weapons inventory, which he claimed to "pluck . . . stomp on, and crush." In fact, the number of weapons programs increased under Secretary of Defense Gates, according to the Pentagon's Selected Acquisition Reports (SARs). There were increases in both the programs and the costs of the programs. When Gates was asked to remain as secretary of defense in 2009, there were 91 major defense acquisition programs that were projected to cost $16 billion. But the SAR in 2010 noted an increase in the number of acquisition programs to 94 with an increased cost of $1.8 billion. The most recent SAR (December 2010) revealed another increase to 95 programs costing an additional $1.9 billion. Five of the weapons programs canceled in 2010 were relaunched in 2011 or remain in the planning stage. These programs include the Air Force's Combat Search-and-Rescue Helicopter, part of the Army's Future Combat System and Armed Reconnaissance Helicopter, and the Marine Corps' Presidential Helicopter.

The Pentagon's chief weapons buyer, Ashton Carter, favored changing the rules for funding weapons systems by turning to fixed-price contracts; incentive bonuses for good performance; and an end to cost-plus contracts, which have the Pentagon covering all expenses of weapons system in order to assure a guaranteed profit for the contractor. Carter's steps were designed to protect the production of such controversial systems as a new ballistic missile submarine; long-range aerial strike systems; an advanced combat vehicle for the Army; and even a presidential helicopter. Secretary of Defense Panetta, meanwhile, has not addressed the possibility of cuts in weapons systems, air wings, or carrier task forces.

Gates, who received the highest civilian award—the Presidential Medal of Freedom—from the president himself at a farewell ceremony on the Pentagon's parade field in June 2011, was duplicitous in discussing defense savings. On the one hand, he was the first secretary of defense to acknowledge publicly that the United States was spending too much on the military and needed to spend more on diplomacy. Soon after, however, in congressional testimony, he gave a blunt "no" to the idea of transferring funds from the budget of the Defense Department to the budget of the State Department, which is less than one-tenth the size of the defense budget.

Gates's strategy found him repudiating himself over and over again. He asked the annual Navy League convention in 2010 why the Navy needed eleven carrier battle groups, which garnered numerous headlines in the mainstream media, but gave an emphatic "no" in congressional testimony to the possibility of eliminating even one carrier battle group.

In a speech in May 2010 in his home state of Kansas and in testimony to the Senate Appropriations subcommittee on Defense in June, Gates outlined proposals that were an example of damage limitation, designed to create the impression that the Pentagon was dealing with its budgets and didn't require more extensive cuts from the White House or Congress. At the Eisenhower Library in May 2010, he proclaimed that the massive federal deficit required an examination of the "gusher" of defense spending. Gates was looking for a grand bargain with conservatives from both parties, offering reductions in overhead to allow reinvestment of savings elsewhere in the defense budget. The strategy worked; the Pentagon escaped the OMB's mandate on all agencies to cut 5 percent from their budgets.

In 2011, at the American Enterprise Institute, Gates emphasized that defense spending did not contribute to the deficit and should not be a part of any deficit-reduction program. He told his audience, "We're not going to see a return to Cold War defense budgets." The fact is that the United States is spending far more for defense than it did during the worst days of the Cold War. A return to Cold War spending would save the United States around $100 billion annually. Even if there were $1 trillion in defense cuts over the next ten years, defense spending would still be the same in inflation-adjusted terms as the budget in 2007.

During his farewell tour in 2011, Gates inadvertently offered the best reason for reducing defense spending and military missions: "A smaller military will be able to go fewer places and do fewer things." A smaller military also would permit greater control over the spiraling debt crisis and greater spending on dire domestic needs. The government should stop issuing blank checks to the Pentagon in order to stop the planning and procurement of costly and unneeded weapons systems.

Gates argued successfully every year during his five-year tenure as defense secretary for increases in defense spending, and defense spending climbed from $350 billion to $680 billion during his tenure. Gates never mentioned that the defense budget was more than $100 billion greater than the United States spent on average during the Cold War, including the peak of spending during the Reagan administration in the early 1980s. As defense strategist Anthony Cordesman noted, "Gates never really came to grips with the challenge of tying strategy to force plans and procurement plans or shaping U.S. deployment to available resources."

Even in the budget compromise in April 2011 that kept the government open, Gates received assurances that the Defense Department would receive increased funding of more than $5 billion, while the Department of State lost more than $8 billion.[46] The Pentagon was one of very few government agencies that received a boost in spending, which allowed full funding for 1.43 million active-duty and 846,000 reserve troops. The cuts for the Department of State would come mostly from foreign aid, which was hit particularly hard. The biggest single loser was the Department's Economic Support Fund, which helps prop up fragile governments from South Asia to Africa. There were significant cuts (hundreds of millions of dollars) from U.S. appropriations for the United Nations, the U.S. Agency for International Development, and the Millennium challenge Corporation. The cuts to the Millennium fund marked the Obama administration's reneging on its pledge to spur economic development and reform in the Middle East. All of these cuts have hurt long-term U.S. national security interests.

In his memoir, Vice President Cheney accused Gates of often speaking "for himself and not reflecting U.S. policy."[47] An example of that took place on Gates's farewell tour of college campuses and right-wing think tanks in the summer of 2011, when he emphatically warned against reducing defense spending to the levels recommended by President Obama and his deficit commission.[48] As defense theorist Larry Korb pointed out, Gates made "false comparisons" to reductions made after the Korean and Vietnam Wars as well as the end of the Cold War, without addressing the inflated costs and troop strength of these wars.[49] Gates did not mention that the so-called "hollow force" at the end of the Cold War managed to win the Gulf War in 1991 in less than three weeks, and displaced the Taliban from power in Afghanistan in 2001 in less than a month.

Changing the Pentagon's Culture

No one has described the social costs of defense spending better than President Eisenhower:

> Every gun that is made, every warship launched, every rocket fired signifies . . . a theft from those who hunger and are not fed, those who are cold and not clothed. The world in arms is not spending money alone. It is spending the sweat of its laborers, the

genius of its scientists, the hopes of its children. The cost of one modern bomber is this: a modern brick school in more than 60 cities . . . two electric power plants, each serving a town of 60,000 . . . two fine, fully equipped hospitals. This is not a way of life at all . . . . It is humanity hanging from a cross of iron.[50]

Whenever the question of reducing the defense budget is raised, the typical response is that we cannot risk diminishing "our ability or our determination to deal with the threats and challenges on the horizon." These were, in fact, the words of Secretary of Defense Gates in his warnings to both the graduates of Notre Dame University and the neoconservatives of the American Enterprise Institute in May 2011. His successor, Panetta, has argued that U.S. military might is the essential safeguard of global stability and that any cuts would compromise Washington's global leadership. Just the opposite could be argued in view of the counterproductive use of U.S. military power over the past decade in North Africa, the Middle East, and Southwest Asia. Cutting the defense budget would not be an act of altruism. Rather, it would be a realistic way to begin to reduce the operational tempo of the U.S. military, control the deficit, and reorder U.S. priorities.

The United States, the only country in the world with a serious ability to project power, could continue to do so with far fewer weapons and foreign facilities. Continued overseas deployment of tens of thousands of U.S. servicemen and servicewomen nearly seven decades after the end of WWII and two decades after the collapse of the Soviet Union reveals a United States stuck in the sands of old strategic thinking. There is probably no better example of the insidious nature of the military-industrial-congressional complex than the increased power of the defense industry during a period of a reduced strategic threat to the United States.

Even Princeton University economist Paul Krugman has joined conservative economists in arguing that defense spending is not out of control because it represents less than 5 percent of our gross domestic product, half of what it was at the end of the Korean War six decades ago, when defense spending took up half of the federal budget. But defense spending takes up 20 percent of the federal budget as well as more than half of all discretionary spending. If we could cut spending to 2 percent of the GDP, several hundred billion dollars in savings could contribute to deficit reduction or investment in other national priorities. If we could freeze the national security budget at 2011 levels and hold it at that level until 2017, we would save more than $1.1 trillion. Krugman believes that harder choices must be made in the area of health care, but the deficit cannot be addressed only by targeting the poor and the sick. If we are going to ask for greater discipline in spending on Social Security, Medicare and Medicaid, and discretionary domestic spending, there must be discipline on defense spending.

Defense spending and procurement must be related to actual threats that the United States faces or is likely to face. The key challenges at the current time are ethnic violence, terrorism, and the proliferation of WMD, which will not be solved by spending huge amounts of treasure on large-scale platforms from the Cold War. Just as we magnified the Soviet threat during the Cold War, we are now magnifying the Chinese threat to build more missiles, ships, and aircraft. President Obama traveled to Australia in November 2011 and announced that 2,500 U.S. Marines would be stationed in Darwin to conduct amphibious training, a gratuitous threat aimed at China. What is the likelihood that we will end up in a shooting war with China that will lead to a confrontation at sea and in the air? Or that China would exploit a U.S. withdrawal by conducting military operations against Taiwan or its rivals in the South China

Sea? Until the defense budget is connected to the genuine missions of the military as well as the economic constraints on all federal spending, there will be no opportunity for significant reductions. If the United States is serious about dealing with the deficit issue, then the defense budget must be cut and U.S. military missions reduced.

There is one area of the defense budget that should be protected, however, and that is funding for research and development. One of the great little-known aspects of defense technology is the contribution of military innovation to the U.S. economy, particularly some of the biggest U.S. export industries: computers, commercial aircraft, and military aircraft. The Internet was created by the Pentagon's Defense Advanced Research Projects Agency (DARPA), which continued to operate it until 1990. Fairchild Semiconductor and Texas Instruments, which led the way in developing the modern computer industry, particularly the silicon transistor, were military contractors. The Boeing 747 and other modern jetliners were developed from military designs. DoD is an indispensable client for major manufacturers such as Lockheed Martin, General Electric, and Honeywell, although the government has done a poor job of monitoring the huge procurement scandals between the Pentagon and its largest defense contractors.

The Pentagon is responsible for more than half of all federal spending on research and development, and this investment typically accounts for 10 percent of the military budget. This spending fostered the cluster of technology companies that have blossomed in California's Silicon Valley; Massachusetts's Route 128 corridor; and North Carolina's Research Triangle, where the Army opened its Research Office in 1958. The Pentagon is investing in these companies for clean-air technology in order to reduce one of the military's largest budget items, energy costs. The clients of the U.S. Navy, which began budgeting for research in 1946, include 59 Nobel laureates, among them Charles Townes, whose pioneering work in lasers laid the groundwork for laser eye surgery and compact discs.[51]

Changing the Pentagon's Culture

Ironically, two of the men with the most to say about the Pentagon and the military-industrial complex, Senators Levin and McCain, appear to be switching roles, with Levin moving to the right and McCain to the left. Levin seems to have run out of energy for tackling the large problems of national security that he was previously known for. McCain, on the other hand, has begun to campaign for changing the Pentagon culture, suggesting a challenge to the military-industrial-congressional complex. He has argued that "senior Defense management has been inclined to lose sight of affordability as a goal and has just reached for more money as a solution to most problems."[52] Huge cost overruns on sophisticated weapons systems are a perfect example of this culture, particularly the $1.1 billion overrun on the first F-35 Joint Strike Fighters and the $560 million overrun on the newest nuclear aircraft carrier, the USS *Gerald Ford*. During a sixty-day period in the summer of 2011, according to McCain, the Pentagon requested $10 billion in "reprogramming" costs to cover overruns and asked for "authority to start dozens of new programs never before presented to the Congress." He referred to the Army's procurement study that concluded over $3.3 billion "had been wasted . . . every year since 2004."

Any cultural war against the Pentagon must include the terrible waste in the use of contractors to man national security agencies and to conduct national security missions. The bipartisan Commission on Wartime Contracting reported in a three-year study that $30 billion to $60 billion has been wasted on ill-conceived and poorly overseen contracts in Iraq and Afghanistan. Since the start of the wars in Iraq and Afghanistan, the United States has paid over $200 billion to contractors with very little oversight or accountability and "no benefit" to the American people.[53] Many of these contracts have had little or no competition. Over the past ten years, the Pentagon and the State Department have sent more than 260,000 private workers to Iraq and Afghanistan as President Bush opened the sluice gates to firms outside government. The Commission has documented kickbacks paid to civilian officials and even members of the military, and poor construction work that has led to the death of American troops. There have been contracts in Afghanistan in which 20 percent of the contract has gone to "protection" money to local warlords and even insurgents. The withdrawal of forces from Iraq means there will be additional private contractors for security at the U.S. embassy there. There needs to be tight limits on no-bid contracts, a permanent inspector general, and greater accountability to the Office of Management and Budget.

The use of contractors in the intelligence community presents even greater problems of accountability and oversight. The Director of National Intelligence (DNI) office estimates that one-third of its work force consists of contractors, and nearly half of personnel costs are taken up by contractors. Too many Pentagon contracts are classified and not publicly available. Investigations have also determined that around one-third of all jobs in the $80 billion intelligence industry are occupied by contractors, and that the executive salary for some contractors can reach $750,000, which is nearly two times more than the president's salary and four times the salary of Cabinet secretaries. A recent study by the Project on Government Oversight on government-wide contracting determined that federal salaries were less expensive than contractors.[54]

Although contractors are not supposed to take part in security operations, they have been found to recruit spies; conduct torture and abuse; pay bribes for information; and provide security for CIA directors traveling abroad. One of the most notorious contractors, Academi LLC, formerly known as Blackwater and then Xe Services LLC, has paid huge fines to the State Department and the Justice Department for its violations of arms sales. In 2007, moreover, Blackwater personnel were involved in the killing of seventeen Iraqi civilians in Baghdad. The Senate and House intelligence committees need to address these problems.

Congress needs to examine the revolving door between government and contractors that finds senior officials trading in their sensitive knowledge for high-paying corporate jobs. Retired admiral Mitch McConnell, former director of the National Security Agency and former director of national intelligence, the so-called intelligence tsar, is vice president of Booz Allen Hamilton, a consulting firm that has won hundreds of millions of dollars in contracts to protect government computer networks. Over the past fifteen years, McConnell has gone from the Navy to Booz Allen to the Office of the DNI and now back to Booz Allen, where he now earns over $4 million annually to manage the firm's national security contracts.

Congress must rethink national security strategy in order to reduce the roles and missions of the military. More than sixty-five years after the end of World War II, it is difficult to justify the United States devoting resources to defending Europe at a time when the gross domestic product of the European Union is 10 percent greater than that of the United States. We need to discuss the strategic purposes of NATO for the vital interests of the United States and the justification for defending a Europe that is capable of defending itself. Even European leaders recognize that the United States cannot continue to fund the defense of Europe at current levels. NATO Secretary General Anders Fogh Rasmussen told the Munich Security Conference in 2011 that the growing disparity in defense support to the alliance cannot continue, with the United States currently responsible for nearly 75 percent of spending for Europe's defense.[55] He particularly castigated those Europeans on the left who want the United States to provide the "hard power" for the defense of Europe while the Europeans themselves supply the "soft power."

It has never been explained how increases in defense spending would address current threats that include "nuclear proliferation, terrorism, and Middle East revolutions."[56] Instead of huge weapons platforms with their spiraling costs, the United States needs to invest in diplomacy and conflict resolution. The United States needs something other than a strongly worded message from the White House or the introduction of U.S. Marines. A revitalized Department of State that plays a major role in policy development, along with the creation of authoritative U.S. embassies overseas that speak with one voice representing the president would contribute to such a fix.

Panetta's initial remarks as secretary of defense indicated that he would fight for defense dollars in order to continue building the huge Cold War–era platforms, particularly naval ships and fighter aircraft, that require a geopolitical threat such as China. Panetta seemed wedded to a Cold War vision of the world that commanded the congressional appropriations that the Pentagon desired, which has little to do with the geopolitical arena that exists. As Gordon Adams remarked, the United States is "in an arms race with itself."[57]

Panetta seemed to follow the script of his predecessor, Bob Gates, who believed that the "lessons of history" tell us that we "must not diminish our ability or our determination to deal with the threats and challenges on the horizon." Demonizing China serves the political interests of an incumbent president, the economic interests of the military-industrial complex, and the ideological interests of the right wing, but not the national security interests of the American people. The lessons of history tell us that we cannot squander our finite and scarce resources on an unnecessary expansion of military capabilities that do not begin to address the real issues of the twenty-first century. The United States must resort to diplomacy rather than military force to address geopolitical problems that don't threaten vital national security interests. China should not be perceived as a threat, but as an ally or stakeholder contributing to global stability.

Fifty years after President Eisenhower's warning about the military-industrial complex, the United States must come to terms with its elevation of the role of the military; its cult of military spending that has become sacrosanct; and a cultural of militarism that has placed U.S. bases all over the globe. Eisenhower's warnings about the dangers of the "cross of iron" have never been more apparent or more threatening to the American way of life.

It is not too late for the United States to reexamine its national security commitments in order to match objectives to priorities; reorder the system for weapons development and procurement to avoid redundancy and prevent huge cost overruns; and reduce the U.S. military footprint the world over to stop the wave of anti-Americanism and save scarce resources; and finally stop the misuse of sophisticated technology that is placing great costs on political and economic structures. There will always be the need for some redundancy, because, paraphrasing Winston Churchill, "on no one quality, on no one process, on no one country, on no one route, and on no one field must we be dependent." But as President Obama said, we need to "reform our defense budget so that we're not paying for Cold War–era weapons we don't use."

There cannot be a change in the defense budget, however, until the United States addresses fundamental change in the culture of its defense and intelligence establishments. The military-industrial complex creates huge political and economic pressures on the system; the lack of accountability and verification by the Congress and the decline in internal oversight create obstacles to reform; and the perpetual exaggeration of threats that began with international communism and international terrorism means no end to wasteful spending. President Eisenhower understood this culture; his successors by and large have not.

Finally, the United States must abandon its notion of "exceptionalism," which has led this country to gratuitously deploy military forces overseas to advance U.S. values. Great powers typically feel superior to their competitors, as the British believed in asserting that they bore the "white man's burden" and the French invoked in their *"mission civilisatrice."* The United States has been one of the most expansionist powers in modern history, beginning as thirteen small colonies on the East Coast to expand across North America to the Pacific Ocean, invoking "manifest destiny." In his State of the Union address in January 2012, President Obama echoed Presidents Clinton and Bush in labeling the United States the only "indispensable" nation, which does not augur well for genuine change in U.S. defense policy. Without change, the United States will further weaken its economy at home and its standing abroad, and make further contributions to the arcs of instability that exist in key regions.

NINE

WHAT NEEDS TO BE DONE

War is God's way of teaching Americans geography. —Ambrose Bierce

Wars can be started when you will, but they cannot be ended when you please. —Niccolo Machiavelli

We can't solve problems with the same thinking we used when we created them. —Albert Einstein

We must disenthrall ourselves, and then we shall save our country. —Abraham Lincoln

The Case for Change

Nations underestimate the duration and intensity of the wars they enter. The European nations and the United States were stunned by the length and losses of the First World War. When the United States entered the Korean War in 1950, high-ranking military leaders believed that the motley band of North Korean soldiers would probably turn tail and flee when they found themselves up against the "most powerful nation on earth." Few policymakers believed that China would cross the Yalu River and enter the war against the United States, thus prolonging a military struggle that was fought to a stalemate.

Four U.S presidents committed troops to South Vietnam to

counter an underestimated North Vietnamese force that President Lyndon B. Johnson described as "raggedy-assed." The U.S. bombing campaign dropped more tonnage on North Vietnam than on Germany in WWII without deterring Hanoi. The U.S. eventually inserted half a million soldiers, sailors, airmen, and Marines into Vietnam, but was forced to retreat after twelve years of fighting and the loss of more than 55,000 servicemen and women. Several million American men and women served in Vietnam from 1963 to 1975.

Since the end of WW II, the United States has fought inconclusive wars in Korea, Vietnam, Iraq, and Afghanistan; conducted dubious invasions of Cambodia, Lebanon, Grenada, and Panama; and mounted counterproductive covert operations around the world, including those in the Congo, Chile, El Salvador, and Guatemala. Only Desert Storm in Iraq in 1991 can be termed a success, although it left Saddam Hussein in power and President George H.W. Bush out of power the following year, setting the stage for George W. Bush's use of force against Iraq two decades later. Ironically, the two Iraq wars have enhanced U.S. notions of exceptionalism and unilateralism, and there are few signs that the American public has had sufficient access to the real information necessary to disagree with these notions.

The introduction of hundreds of thousands of U.S. troops in Iraq and Afghanistan has not improved U.S. national security in spite of wars lasting longer than WWII. Presidents Bush and Obama campaigned for moderation in foreign policy, but relied too often on military force and Cold War thinking in selecting national security teams. Bush's invasion of Iraq empowered Iraqi Shia to draw closer to Iran, creating a long-term problem for U.S. strategic interests that will be worse than the challenge posed by Saddam Hussein. Obama's initial escalation of force in Afghanistan in 2009 deepened the stalemate between U.S.-NATO forces and the Taliban. Both administrations gave Israel a free hand in the use of military force against Arab entities, which has compromised the U.S. role in the Middle East. In lesser conflicts, U.S. planners exaggerated the role of air power, which did not bring instant success in Bosnia, Libya, or Serbia.

The United States has paid a terrible price for the terrorist attacks of 9/11, but many of the wounds have been self-inflicted. Nearly 4,500 Americans have died in Iraq; more than 2,000 have died in Afghanistan; there have been hundreds of thousands of deaths of innocent civilians and millions of Iraqi and Afghan refugees. We have already spent more than $1.5 trillion dollars in Iraq and Afghanistan, which has contributed significantly to our own financial crisis at home. Just as President Eisenhower warned more than fifty years ago, there have been too many schools we have not built; too many roads and bridges without repair; too little investment in engineering and education. The militarization of our national security and foreign policies is a big part of the overall price. We have turned the sympathy for the United States in the wake of 9/11 into extreme anti-Americanism around the world.

Historians will have to answer the questions that politicians should have asked, debated, and reconciled over the past two decades. Why did the United States have more than one and a half million men and women in uniform two decades after the end of the Cold War? Why was the end of the Cold War considered a triumph instead of a challenge and an opportunity? Why are so many troops stationed in Europe and Japan more than six decades after the end of the Second World War? Why are so many troops stationed in South Korea sixty years after the end of the Korean War? Why are there still hundreds of U.S. bases and operational facilities in Europe and Asia, particularly in view of the overwhelming U.S. ability to project power? Why did the United States spend more than a trillion dollars on military adventures in Iraq and Afghanistan that cost so much blood and treasure but contributed nothing to American national security? Why has the United States been so quick to project power in areas where its vital national interests have not been at stake? What do the high suicide rates and the surge in domestic violence among soldiers and Marines and their families tell us about the impact of the U.S. misuse of force on the military itself? Are there no plausible alternatives to reliance on military force?

The United States, with its emphasis on power projection, has created a global system of more than 700 military bases and facilities. There was no strategic planning for creation of this network; we did it because we could, and never bothered to examine the consequences or the costs. Military bases dot the Middle East and the Persian Gulf and encircle China. There are more than 100 U.S. military sites in Japan; almost 80 in South Korea; and even a few in Central Asia, where the United States does not require a military presence. There are more than 50,000 troops stationed in East Asia and the Pacific, and more than 100,000 in Southwest Asia. This is in addition to our huge and unchallenged naval presence around the world. Osama bin Laden claimed that the bases in the sacred territories of Saudi Arabia were a "blasphemy" that provoked the 9/11 attacks.[1]

The U.S. military presence overseas, designed to strengthen our security, has proved counterproductive. On the one hand, it cannot be coincidental that, in the survey conducted annually by *Foreign Policy* magazine and the Fund for Peace, those countries that have endured U.S. military intervention are among the most volatile on earth. Somalia ranks number one on the failed-state index, despite or because of interventions by the Clinton, Bush, and Obama administrations over the past two decades. Iraq and Afghanistan rank in the top ten, and Pakistan and Yemen are close behind. U.S. special operations forces are deployed in at least sixty and as many as seventy-five countries from South America to Central Asia. The Obama administration has dropped the use of the term "global war on terror," but it is obviously still fighting one.

On the other hand, the continued presence of American forces in Islamic countries will ensure continued anti-Americanism in the Middle East. A National Intelligence Estimate (NIE) issued in April 2006 ("Trends in Global Terrorism") concluded that the war in Iraq was "breeding deep resentment of U.S. involvement in the Muslim world and cultivating supporters for the global jihadist movement." The NIE argued that "activists identifying themselves as jihadists, although a small percentage of Muslims, are increasing in both number and geographic dispersion." It warned that the "operational threat from self-radicalized cells will grow in importance, particularly abroad but also at home."

Over the past decade, the heavy-handed U.S. military presence in Iraq and Afghanistan as well as the increased use of Predator and Reaper drones have provided stimulus for recruiting terrorists. The former chief of the CIA's counterterrorism center, Robert Grenier, argued that these wars have "convinced many Muslims that the United States is the enemy of Islam, and they have become jihadists as a result of their experience in Iraq." U.S. raids in Afghanistan and Iraq have produced an unacceptable number of civilian fatalities, injuries, and property destruction, and remain a major sticking point in U.S.-Afghan relations. Raids that often targeted the wrong individuals have generated a special hatred for the United States. The overuse of the drone in Yemen has become a recruitment tool for terrorists and insurgents, and helps to explain how al-Qaeda in the Arabian Peninsula has grown from a few hundred members in 2009 to at least a thousand members in 2012.

The growing network of U.S. bases has been accompanied

by the increased power and influence of U.S. military commanders, the so-called "commanders-in-chief," who have become the stewards of U.S. foreign policy. These commanders-in-chief (CINCs) have become more powerful than U.S. ambassadors who represent the president, or the assistant secretaries of state who represent the State Department. When Marine General Anthony Zinni was the CINC for the U.S. Central Command, his visits to key countries in the Middle East and the Persian Gulf were treated more seriously by the host countries than those of his State Department counterparts. When General Petraeus was the CINC of the Central Command, he was treated like royalty during his foreign visits—and during his briefings to Congress as well. Secretary of Defense Rumsfeld tried to lower the visibility and importance of the visits, even dropping use of the term CINC, but this had no real impact.

The steady expansion of U.S. military power has contributed to challenges at home and abroad at a time of national malaise and government dysfunction. U.S. defense spending and the internationalization of the U.S. military presence have contributed to a decline in U.S. influence abroad and to economic problems at home. Executive heel-dragging and legislative gridlock have worsened the problem of mounting U.S. debts and deficits. There is a banking and housing crisis in the nation that threatens nearly every state in the Union. The financial and economic crisis, combined with geopolitical realities, demands a reexamination of our national strategy. The United States needs to substantially cut defense spending, increase taxes, introduce tax reform, limit entitlements, and invest in education and innovation.

The tepid economic "recovery" during President Obama's first term has created a greater urgency for reducing defense spending as well as the overall size of the U.S. military. There are more than 46 million Americans living in poverty;

unemployment rates have remained at unacceptably high levels; the home mortgage crisis needs to be addressed; and the economic concerns of the middle class have not been abated. The income gap between the wealthiest Americans and the rest of the country continues to grow sharply. Millions of American have learned that their primary assets—their homes—have become a liability. There is greater unemployment than when President Obama took office in 2009, and the national debt is $5 trillion greater. Savings in defense spending could be applied to our real needs in the areas of health care, education, and the environment.

The election of Mitt Romney would have worsened all of these problems, because he was committed to weakening economic and social programs that benefit the disadvantaged and was prepared to throw greater investment at a military that has been given a blank check for nearly all of the past decade. Romney even opposed the bipartisan agreement to cut defense spending over the next ten years. The base budget for the military is projected at $525 billion, not included war-related costs, but Romney's plan called for increasing annual spending on defense to $986 billion over the next ten years. Romney promised to spend at least 4 percent of gross domestic product on defense, which is a bizarre way to plan for national defense. His bellicose statements on foreign policy interests suggested that he would actually look for new ways to deploy the military.

Unlike Obama, who has pledged to reduce U.S. troop levels by 100,000 over the next five years, Romney wanted to increase troop levels by 100,000, which would cost $200 billion over the next ten years. Romney also wanted to increase shipbuilding for the U.S. Navy to fifteen vessels a year, while Obama favors limiting Navy shipbuilding to the current pace of nine ships a year. Romney's plan would have increased defense spending by $120 billion over the next ten years. He even favored reopening the production line for the F-22 fighter plane, which has already cost the United States nearly $80 billion.

The Obstacles to Change

The United States comprises only 5 percent of the world's population and just under a quarter of the world's economic output, but we account for more than half of the world's military expenditures. Our share is greater than the geopolitical environment demands and greater than our economy allows. Since there is more awareness of the need for reducing the defense budget than ever before, it is essential that the United States examine its global commitments and reduce the size of its footprint. Reforming national security policy would permit the United States to reduce its defense budget, which registered twenty consecutive years of uninterrupted growth from 1998 to 2008.

There will not be significant changes in U.S. defense spending, however, without significant changes in U.S. policies that recognize the decline in U.S. military and economic power. The prospect of significant change faces numerous obstacles, however: the dominance of the military-industrial-congressional complex; the militarization of our national security institutions; a culture of veneration for the military; belief in U.S. exceptionalism; a weakening of our diplomatic institutions; and a dearth of new strategic thinking.

Cultural change is the most difficult of all, and it is the culture of U.S. decision-making that must be revolutionized. Only the United States uses it military to conduct foreign policy, not merely to defend the nation's sovereignty, its borders, and—above all—its people. The world has changed radically over the past two decades, but the United States continues to rely on huge military forces and defense budgets. No significant change has been introduced to the policy process despite new geopolitical realities. The collapse of the Berlin Wall and the Soviet empire in Eastern Europe; and even the Soviet Union itself between 1989 and 1991 should have brought major change, but the United States has remained frozen in place.

More recently, the weakening of the European Union and the Eurozone, particularly the crisis in Greece, are threatening European stability, which will have political and economic consequences for the United States. The incredible events of the Arab Spring, which challenged dictatorships throughout the Middle East and the Persian Gulf and fostered great optimism, have come and gone without a United States response, except for the modest U.S. role in Libya. The violent attack against the U.S. consulate in Benghazi in September 2012 points to the vulnerability of the U.S. presence in North Africa, which remains in disarray. Tensions are rising between Turkey, Cyprus, and Israel, and all three have domestic problems. The threat of Israeli use of force against Iran remains unabated. U.S. relations with three key Muslim states in the Middle East (Egypt, Saudi Arabia, and Turkey) have declined in the past several years.

The old models of military force and military dictatorships have become dysfunctional; even North Korea and Iran have sent subtle signals of interest in change, including contacts with the United States. There have been signs of change in Cuba without any meaningful U.S. response; Washington remains the only capital in North and South America without diplomatic relations with Cuba. U.S. diplomacy remains lacking the world over.

Change will be particularly difficult for the United States because it comes at a time of decline in U.S. power and influence, which has led to conservative opposition to reducing the U.S. global footprint. The military-industrial-congressional complex opposes reductions in defense spending and the U.S. global presence. The Congress has not pressed for significant changes in defense policy, and the mainstream media have adhered to conventional wisdom on national security issues.

Then there is the cumbersome nature of the Pentagon's bureaucracy itself, which prevents "new thinking." The Pentagon has simply grown to unmanageable proportions, spending nearly $1 trillion a year on defense, counting the war in Afghanistan and military action elsewhere, and outspending the rest of the world on defense. The spending on the intelligence community, which has become a Pentagon stepchild, and the Department of Homeland Security, also tied to the military, is out of control, with no one offering good ideas to contain a reliance on military force, intelligence operations, and domestic security.

What Needs to Be Done

The United States will not be able to ensure significant savings in defense spending until it changes its approach to the use of military power. Future production of defense assets must reflect a balance between available security instruments and the effectiveness of these instruments in unpredictable and chaotic international arenas. In 2012, the government poured billions of dollars into large platforms, such as aircraft carriers, that will become available in 2022; by then, the United States will be facing an entirely different geopolitical arena.

With a decline in U.S. power, the United States will have less influence in the international arena and will have to resort to diplomatic initiatives to shape international developments. When the nation was militarily and economically powerful, the United States was in a position to dominate and dictate. With a decline in power, the United States must accept the necessity of negotiation and compromise abroad as well as the enhancement of civilian influence—democracy—in the national security process at home.

Demilitarizing National Security Policy at Home and Abroad

There is probably no better example of President Eisenhower's warning regarding the military-industrial complex than the sales of military equipment to countries that lack political stability. Any effort to demilitarize U.S. national security policy must include a significant reduction in military assistance, which has failed to create leverage or credibility for the United States. There is a misplaced confidence in U.S. reliance on military policy to improve ties to allies in the Third World.

In addition to substantial reductions in military spending and military personnel, discussed in Chapter VIII, the United States must end its reliance on the military instrument in the policy process. Over the past several decades, the United States has supported military regimes in Brazil, Chile, Indonesia, Pakistan, the Philippines, South Korea, and Libya with huge amounts of military assistance. These regimes have eventually been forced to reform or have had to return power to a civilian leadership. Violence typically accompanies these transitions, and there remains the threat of restoration of repressive rule. Limiting the scope of our military activities is the key to reducing the size of our military forces and our procurement and deployment policies.

Military policy has been the major instrument in U.S. foreign policy, and military policy has largely failed. American national security policy would be well served by encouraging demilitarization at home and abroad; strategic and conventional arms control; the strengthening of civilian institutions; and regional dialogue to reduce instability among developing nations. The United States cannot afford the operational military tempo of the past decades, and must reverse course. The rise of militarism must end.

But the United States has no policy for supporting challenges to authoritarian rule or the regressive steps that have prevented political and social progress. The great promise that accompanied the dissolution of the Soviet Union, which should have been an opportunity for "anchoring" Russia to the Western security and economic architecture, was never fulfilled. Instead, the United States exploited the dissolution of the Soviet empire and the Warsaw Pact by inviting the newly liberated states to join NATO, the West's political and military alliance, which took too much credit for winning the Cold War. Twenty years later, there was no U.S. policy response to the hopeful developments of the Arab Spring throughout North Africa and the Middle East.

The best example of the futility of U.S. military power had been the use of force in the Middle East and Southwest Asia. There are two major problems for U.S. interests in these areas: Iran in the Middle East and the Persian Gulf; Pakistan in Southwest Asia. But a decade of U.S. military deployments in Iraq and Afghanistan has strengthened Iran's national security situation, opening up opportunities for Tehran in Iraq and Afghanistan; and jeopardizing the national security of Pakistan, which must deal with a challenge from indigenous extremists and fundamentalists as well as terrorists who have migrated from Afghanistan. The opportunity costs of these deployments have been enormous, jeopardizing U.S. credibility throughout the region and weakening the U.S. economy. In Afghanistan, Pakistan, and Libya, the United States has had to follow up its military aid programs with costly efforts to regain lethal weapons previously provided to clients, including surface-to-air missiles that could threaten U.S. aircraft.

Military aid itself must be re-examined, particularly the conventional wisdom that U.S. grant aid creates U.S. influence among its beneficiaries. The top six recipients of U.S. military assistance (Israel, Afghanistan, Pakistan, Egypt, Iraq, and Turkey) provide little return, let alone leverage, to the United

States for this munificence. Israel has military dominance in the Middle East and doesn't require military assistance. The United States is constantly and deliberately embarrassed by the Israeli government despite the huge amounts of military and economic aid that Israel has received over past decades. The Benjamin Netanyahu government has often timed announcements of settlement expansion to do the most harm to U.S. interests in the region. Settlement activity was announced during a visit by Vice President Joe Biden in 2010, immediately prior to a visit by Secretary of State Clinton in 2011, and on the eve of Netanyahu's summit meeting with President Obama in May 2011. The latter announcement called for an additional 1,550 housing units for southern Jerusalem as well as nearly 300 new units for the Beitar Ilit settlement west of Bethlehem. The Israelis also announced the construction of several new outposts east of Jerusalem in violation of promises made to both the Bush and Obama administrations. In September 2012, eight weeks before the U.S. election, Netanyahu deliberately chose to confront the Obama administration over the issue of Iran's nuclear programs.

Egypt is another case in point, having received more than $60 billion in aid over the past three decades with no indication that Egyptian policy was susceptible to U.S. influence. There is a myth that U.S. military aid played a major role in minimizing the violence that toppled President Hosni Mubarak in February 2011. Pentagon sources suggested that close ties between U.S. and Egyptian armed forces helped the new Egyptian military council become a force for social cohesion rather than repression.[2] Many senior U.S. military officers believe that the presence of large numbers of the best and brightest Egyptian military officers at the National War College and the Army War College has suffused the Egyptian army with U.S. values. A retired commandant of the U.S. Army War College, Major General Robert Scales, has argued that "they learn our way of war . . . but they also learn our philosophies of civil-military relations."[3] If only this were true.

Grant military aid requirements usually include mandatory purchase of U.S. weaponry, which means that U.S. defense contractors are the major beneficiaries of U.S. largesse. Congress requires Egypt to spend on American military hardware such as helicopter engines from GE Aviation, transmitters for Egypt's navy from Raytheon, and Black Hawk helicopters from companies in Connecticut.[4] Tanks come from companies in Michigan; high-speed boats from Mississippi; and Hellfire missiles from Florida.

The cornerstone of U.S.-Egyptian relations has been the $1.3 billion in annual military financing that Egypt has received in "untouchable compensation" for Cairo's willingness to conclude a peace treaty with Israel. As a result, Egyptian armed forces have replaced Soviet weapons with first-rate U.S. weapons such as F-16 fighter planes and M1 tanks. It is debatable, however, whether military assistance buys actual influence in Egypt, particularly since it was in Cairo's own interest to cut its ties to the Soviet Union in the 1970s, stabilize its relations with Israel, and solidify its contacts with the United States. It is similarly debatable whether U.S. influence played a role in the conciliatory posture of the Egyptian military during the Arab Spring, since it was in Egypt's interest to avoid greater violence and instability.

Once again, the Egyptian military has rapidly emerged as the dominant political force in Cairo, and there is no sign of any U.S. influence over the situation. If the United States were to cut military aid to Egypt, it would allow Washington to re-examine its heavy commitment to Israel, which requires far less than the $1.6 billion in annual military aid that it receives. Such measures would send a necessary signal to U.S. allies and clients that military aid will not dominate the implementation of U.S. foreign policy.

Nevertheless, the Department of Defense played a greater diplomatic role than the Department of State in Egypt during the Arab Spring, another indicator of the Pentagon's increased influence as well as the limited influence derived from military aid. There were far more U.S.-Egyptian military-to-military contacts than there were diplomatic contacts during the Arab Spring. In addition to numerous exchanges between Secretary of Defense Gates and his Egyptian counterpart, Field Marshal Muhammad Tantawi, there were frequent exchanges between the chairman of the Joint Chiefs, Admiral Mike Mullen, and the Egyptian army chief, Lieutenant General Sami Enan. Secretary of State Clinton played a minor role, due in part to the fact that there were three different Egyptian foreign ministers (Ahmed Maher, Nabil al-Arabi, and Molhamed El-Drali) during a transition period between January and June 2011, but also due to the weakened role of U.S. diplomacy. Military aid provided no leverage for the United States as Egyptian military commanders played their own hand, accumulated political power, and ignored démarches from U.S. counterparts.

Despite the uncertainties associated with recent developments in the Middle East, there are still defense experts who want to increase military aid to Muslim states, particularly Egypt. Michael Mandelbaum, the Christian A. Herter Professor of American Foreign Policy at Johns Hopkins University, believes that the "uncertainty of the post-Mubarak era means that America's annual aid package to Egypt should continue and perhaps even increase, because it gives Washington some influence over the institution that will have a major say in the country's future—the Egyptian army."[5] If anything, the United States received a lesson in its inability to influence Egypt, notwithstanding our huge military aid package. The Egyptian military is one of the richest (and most corrupt) institutions in the country, and hardly needs foreign largesse. There is no security threat to Egypt that requires the huge weapons platforms that the military desires.

History is repeating itself in Iraq. No sooner had U.S. forces withdrawn from Iraq than the Obama administration announced multibillion-dollar arms sales packages to Iraq, including advanced fighter aircraft, tanks, and helicopters. The government of Prime Minister Nuri Kamal al-Maliki will be receiving the same kind of equipment (i.e., battle tanks, cannons, and armored personnel carriers) that Saddam Hussein once used against Iraqi Kurds and Shiites. In view of al-Maliki's efforts to consolidate authority, create a one-party Shiite-dominated state, and abandon the U.S.-backed power-sharing government, the timing of the arms sale is questionable. U.S. defense planners are obviously trying to justify the nearly nine-year war with Iraq by creating a client for $11 billion in sales of U.S. weapons. This is a dubious achievement that only benefits the military-industrial complex and raises the prospect that U.S. forces in the Persian Gulf could encounter U.S. weaponry in a future confrontation.

The timing of the U.S. sale of $30 billion in arms to Saudi Arabia is also dubious in view of the recent use of Saudi arms to suppress demonstrations for reform in Bahrain. The deal comes at a time when the Pentagon is considering the supply of "bunker-buster" bombs and other munitions to another key Gulf ally, the United Arab Emirates. In view of the increased tensions between the United States and Iran, the United States appears to be using military aid as a form of containment against Iran, which will complicate even further the possibility of a diplomatic solution between Iran and the West. The fact that protestors in the Arab Spring were the targets of tear gas canisters marked MADE IN THE USA will not be soon forgotten.

Afghanistan is unable to use effectively the assistance that it receives, and thus far has been unable to create a military and police force effective against the Taliban threat. These Afghan forces are so ineffective that President Hamid Karzai cannot disband corrupt private security firms that protect the president and Afghan aid projects. Ten years into our invasion and occupation of Afghanistan, the United States is still allocating tens of millions of dollars to finance task forces to study the problem of training sufficient guard forces. Meanwhile, there has been a surge in recent years in incidents of Afghan soldiers and police killing U.S. and European military personnel, which led France to suspend its training and assistance efforts with Afghan forces in January 2012. The United States is currently fighting an insurgent force that was supplied with U.S. weaponry in the 1980s; in the future, we may be fighting an Afghan force that was similarly supplied with U.S. military equipment.

Even though the U.S. withdrawal from Afghanistan began in 2011, and there is speculation regarding an end to the primary U.S. combat role one year before the completion of the U.S. withdrawal in 2014, there is discussion of continued U.S. military aid for the next decade. The Afghan government contends that it will require $4 billion annually for its military and police forces, which number 300,000, and most of this money will come from the United States. U.S. congressional leaders and diplomats such as the most recent U.S. ambassadors to Afghanistan are already building a firewall to make sure that U.S. forces continue to supply air support, artillery, and combat logistics to Afghan forces in a so-called indeterminate transition period.[6] There is no serious planning under way for U.S. policy in Afghanistan in the wake of the withdrawal of U.S. combat forces.

The most futile example of a U.S. military aid program is the case of Pakistan. President Reagan sent more than $3 billion to the Pakistan mujahideen to fight in Afghanistan in the 1980s as well as additional billions in grant aid to Pakistan's military. Much of the aid to the mujahideen went to the very fundamentalist groups, such as the Haqqani network and al-Qaeda, that are fighting the U.S. presence in Afghanistan. At the same time, the Reagan administration ignored Pakistan's nuclear program in violation of U.S. law.

U.S. support dwindled in the 1990s because of Pakistan's support for the Taliban government in Afghanistan, but in the wake of 9/11 U.S. support resumed. The Bush administration sent $11 billion to Pakistan, including $8 billion directly to the Pakistani army for "security." The Obama administration followed the same course, with Secretary of State Clinton promising billions of dollars in aid as well as support for the 2009 Kerry-Lugar bill that appropriated $7.5 billion to economic development over the next five years. The United States has never used its limited influence to promote democracy in Pakistan, and Pakistan has never stopped its double dealing on pledges to fight the Afghan Taliban. The incompetence and corruption of the Pakistani government continues, but there is no indication that the United States is making reform a trade-off for its military and economic aid. A lower U.S. profile is needed in Pakistan; the U.S. military presence, even its efforts at assistance, merely contribute to militant anti-Americanism.

Over the years, members of the U.S. Joint Chiefs of Staff worked assiduously—and unsuccessfully—to forge links with Pakistan following the tensions in U.S.-Pakistani relations due to Pakistan's secret nuclear program and Pakistani cooperation with the nuclear programs of such "rogue states" as Iran, Libya, and North Korea. More recently, as chairman of the Joint Chiefs over a three-year period, Admiral Mullen flew to Pakistan more than twenty times for meetings with the chief of the Army, General Ashfaq Kayani, to build a personal rapport with the man widely seen as more influential than the president and prime minister of the country. But Kayani's ties to the United States have only embarrassed him in the eyes of the senior Pakistani military leadership, particularly in the wake of the U.S. killing of bin Laden in Pakistan in May 2011, when Pakistan received no early warning.

The deaths of twenty-four Pakistani soldiers caused by U.S. and NATO forces in November 2011 brought a new wave of Pakistani anti-Americanism. There is no better example of the decline of the State Department and the power of the Pentagon than the presidential handling of the accidental killing of the Pakistani soldiers. The State Department wanted an apology or at least a strong statement of remorse. The Pentagon wanted nothing said. It took President Obama several days to make any statement, and the perfunctory condolence statement with no apology took more than a week. Eventually Secretary of State Clinton issued an apology eight months later in order to get a resumption of NATO supply trucks through the Afghan-Pakistan border.

Domestic Demilitarization
Reducing the influence of the Pentagon must include a lesser role for the Pentagon in national security affairs, where it plays an outsize role in the implementation of U.S. foreign policy and an expanded role in gathering intelligence, both abroad and even within the United States. Congress has granted the Department of Defense greater legal authority to conduct domestic security activities in the name of post-9/11 surveillance.[7] The Pentagon received reports from intelligence and law enforcement agencies in violation of the U.S. Privacy Act of 1974 , which orders the purge of all information after ninety days if not part of an ongoing investigation.[8] In 2003, the department created a little known agency, Counterintelligence Field Activity (CIFA), to "maintain a domestic law enforcement database that includes information related to potential terrorist threats." CIFA, with a thousand employees and a secret budget, sought authority to

investigate crimes within the United States such as treason, foreign sabotage, and economic espionage.

Deputy defense secretary Paul Wolfowitz established a reporting mechanism known as TALON (Threat and Local Observation Notice) in 2003, which collected domestic intelligence that was stored in a CIFA database. CIFA, in turn, awarded $33 million in contracts to Lockheed Martin, Unisys Corporation, and Northrop Grumman to develop databases that comb through commercial information and Internet chatter to collect information on "persons of interest."[9] Thus, the military has been deputized to spy on law-abiding American citizens, with military officers attending antiwar and peace rallies, and staff sergeants seconded to the National Security Agency engaged in warrantless eavesdropping on U.S. citizens.

In addition to the use of military techniques in the implementation of domestic security policy, there has been intelligence surveillance on the local level. Since 2003, the New York City police department has conducted covert surveillance of people protesting the Iraq war, even bicycle riders taking part in mass rallies and mourners at a street vigil for a cyclist killed in an accident.[10] Covert surveillance has been conducted throughout the United States, Canada, and Europe, with law enforcement employees and informants infiltrating meetings of political groups, posing as sympathizers or fellow activists. The police department's Intelligence Division created files on members of social movements like Occupy Wall Street, as well as street theater companies, church groups, antiwar organizations, environmentalists, and people opposed to the death penalty. The information from this activity was shared with other police departments. There is no evidence that Congress has been briefed on the full extent of this activity.

New York's deputy policy commissioner for intelligence, David Cohen, a former deputy director for operations at the CIA, initiated police surveillance of public events. In September

2002, Cohen wrote in an affidavit that the police department should not be required to have a "specific indication" of a crime before investigating.[11] "In the case of terrorism," Cohen wrote, "to wait for an indication of crime before investigating is to wait for too long." Cohen was thinking like the intelligence officer he used to be, and not like a policy official with respect for law and civil liberty. In granting the city's surveillance requests, a federal judge in Manhattan ruled that the dangers of terrorism were "perils sufficient to outweigh any First Amendment cost." As a result, the police department was authorized to conduct investigations of political, social, and religious groups.

The New York police department has monitored Muslim students far beyond the city limits, including at Ivy League colleges, with names recorded in reports for Police Commissioner Raymond Kelly, despite no evidence of wrongdoing. The New York police also monitored student websites, an obvious violation of civil rights, which apparently exceeds the activities of the Federal Bureau of Investigation. The New York police department also placed informants or undercover officers in Muslim student associations at numerous New York colleges and universities.[12]

The U.S. Army issued a new directive in January 2012 that allows domestic police to request the assistance of unmanned drone aircraft for "domestic operations." According to an Army memorandum, drones "represent emerging technology" requiring "access to the National Airspace System."[13] Such access presents a challenge to the post-Reconstruction Posse Comitatus Act of 1877, which bars the military from engaging in domestic law enforcement. According to the *New York Times* and the *New York Post*, the CIA was involved in training the New York police in counterintelligence activities, which violated the CIA charter against domestic activities.[14]

The National Defense Authorization Act (NDAA) for 2012, which the Congress approved in December 2011, allows the Pentagon to indefinitely detain U.S. citizens apprehended on U.S. soil without any charge. It also mandates military custody for any person who supports or aids "belligerent" acts against the United States, another violation of the Posse Comitatus Act. In other words, if the Defense Department suspects someone, then there would be no presumption of innocence and no Fifth Amendment right to remain silent.

In the NDAA, a suspect's seizure is a "requirement" if the suspect is deemed to have been "substantially supporting" al-Qaeda or "associated forces." Anyone in military custody could be held indefinitely, without charge and without access to civilian courts, thus eliminating the role of federal courts in terrorism cases. Finally, the Defense Authorization Act would extend the ban on transfers from Guantánamo, making it impossible to transfer the eighty-eight prisoners there who are cleared for release. As two four-star Marine generals have noted, the Act "undermines our ideals in the name of fighting terrorism."[15]

New Thinking in U.S. Foreign Policy
There needs to be a radical restructuring of U.S. foreign policy that places greater reliance on diplomacy and negotiation; arms control and disarmament; and international organizations and multilateralism. Our goals must take into account our more limited global influence and must recognize that a stronger domestic economic base is needed for an effective international presence. There are too many variables in the international arena to permit any single strategic doctrine such as the 1951 National Security document 68 in 1951 that depended on military power; the Flexible Response doctrine of the 1960s that led to regional intervention; or the more recent preemption doctrine that cost the loss of American blood and treasure in the Middle East. The United States needs more flexible diplomatic instruments of influence that will facilitate a more robust international role.

Middle East Quicksand

The independent variables that govern the political dynamics in the Middle East add to the difficulty of developing a single strategic policy toward the region. There are many reasons for the instability throughout the Islamic community, and each nation has its own causes for the current turmoil. In Egypt, there are serious conflicts between Muslims and Christians; in Tunisia, a growing problem of fundamentalism; in Syria, an authoritarian government that ignores the demands of majority Sunnis vis-à-vis the minority Alawite; in Bahrain an authoritarian minority Sunni government ignoring the majority Shia; and in Libya, greater tribal and clan violence following the killing of Qadhafi. Solving the Israeli-Palestinian problem is essential, but it would not resolve any of these national and sectarian issues. Spiraling tensions between Israel and Iran involve the United States.

The United States claims to support democratization in the Middle East, although the United States would not benefit from democratization. Elections in Gaza in 2007 led to a ruling role for Hamas, a hardline movement. Elections in Lebanon did the same for the Iran-backed Hezbollah party, which joined the coalition government in 2008 and then forced the collapse of that government in 2011. It is ironic that the United States has begun the process of political discussions with the Taliban in Afghanistan, but has refused to deal with either Hamas or Hezbollah, which have stronger claims to national standing and nation-building.

In the wake of the Arab Spring, the challenge and even removal of authoritarian leaders has permitted the emergence of extremist groups, particularly in Egypt and Libya, where there have been violent demonstrations against the United States. The opposition movement in Yemen consists of anti-Western Islamists and communists. A weak Yemeni government makes it more difficult to pursue the Yemen-based al-Qaeda faction that is active in terrorist operations against the United States.

President Obama's problem at the outset was the inheritance of two losing or stalemated wars in Iraq and Afghanistan that have alienated the Islamic community and created the highest level of anti-Americanism since the Vietnam War. U.S. counterterrorist and counterinsurgency tactics included torture and abuse in secret prisons, nighttime raids that have led to the deaths of innocent civilians, extraordinary renditions that send innocent victims to foreign prisons for torture and abuse, and a refugee problem that counts more than seven million displaced persons. A reduced military footprint is a sine qua non.

Far too much time, energy, and resources have been devoted to the Middle East and Southwest Asia over the past decade, particularly in view of the larger strategic problems that exist in the Persian Gulf (Iran) and East Asia (North Korea). The potential for conflict in the latter regions outranks the goals and objectives associated with the U.S. presence in Iraq and Afghanistan. The commander of the Joint Readiness Training Center at Fort Polk, Louisiana, Major General Dan Bolger, stated, "There's a belief that the president of the United States can pick up the red phone and order forcible entry operations. But that takes practice, and we don't get a lot of practice."[16] The general's comments reflect the views of many senior officers toward the fool's errands that they have been assigned in Iraq and Afghanistan, which have hurt overall readiness.

The United States will continue to support the survival and viability of Israel, but it must be more supportive of Palestinian statehood and less supportive of the excesses of Israeli use of force and occupation policies. Diplomacy in the Arab world is needed to repair the damage from Israel's reckless use of military power in Gaza in 2008 and a continuing Israeli quarantine that denies Gazans access to reconstruction materials, including cement, irrigation pipes, and glass for windows need to repair the devastation from the use of air power against a defenseless community. The

U.S. failure to condemn Israeli actions merely contributed to a stronger political position for Hamas, the ruling party in Gaza.

The United States also endorsed the Israeli invasion of Lebanon in 2008, which strengthened the position of Iranian-backed Hezbollah, the most powerful political and military force in Lebanon. Hezbollah is now the kingmaker in Lebanon's political arena, and Iran's covert support for Hezbollah has created a greater challenge for Israeli national security. U.S. support for Iraq has not been able to stop the government in Baghdad from assisting Iran's efforts to extend aid to Hezbollah as well as the repressive Syrian government.

Meanwhile, as it continues to build illegal settlements on Palestinian land, Israel refuses to enter a genuine discussion of Palestinian statehood, which has isolated Israel and weakened the credibility of the United States. The recent actions of Hamas and the Palestinian Authority indicate that there is an opportunity for serious negotiations between Israelis and Palestinians toward Palestinian statehood. The United States should play the role of honest broker in arranging these talks. Instead, the Obama administration criticized the reconciliation efforts between Hamas and the West Bank government, making the United States the only member of the Quartet Group (United States, Russia, the UN, and the European Community) to do so.

The Arab Spring in 2011 opened a hopeful chapter in the Middle East and North Africa, but it exposed the Obama administration's lack of any strategy or plan for the region. Washington was caught totally off guard despite decades of demographic change, rampant corruption, political repression, and economic backwardness leading up to the volcano of rage that broke out in Tunisia in December 2010, then spread rapidly to Egypt, Libya, Syria, Yemen, Bahrain, and even Saudi Arabia. The intelligence community failed completely in its mission to provide premonitory intelligence.

The outbreak of massive protests against authoritarian regimes throughout the Middle East gave the Obama administration an excellent window of opportunity to endorse political freedom throughout the region. But President Obama was aggressive when he should have been cautious in dealing with Afghanistan, and cautious when he should have been aggressive in dealing with the "volcano of rage" in the Middle East, North Africa, and the Persian Gulf. The United States needed to recognize the moral and political imperatives to support the freedom revolution that was sweeping the region, but Washington became a spectator and not a participant. U.S. dependence on energy supplies from Saudi Arabia and Libya added to the perception of a United States pursuing mercenary interests in the region.

The United States was hesitant initially in the Libyan situation, despite the fact that it was dealing with a megalomaniac who had no concern for the lives of his own people. As late as 2008, the U.S. embassy in Tripoli cabled Secretary of State Condi Rice that Libya was a "strong partner in the war against terrorism," that we had "excellent" intelligence cooperation, and that Colonel Qadhafi was a strong ally in blocking the return of Libyan militants from Iraq and Afghanistan and blunting the "ideological appeal of radical Islam."[17] The release of thousands of U.S. embassy cables from the Middle East demonstrated a similarly narrow focus on U.S. interests in the region as well as the failure to identify domestic tensions in key Arab capitals. Three decades earlier, the U.S. embassy in Tehran sent similar messages praising the Shah only months before his removal from power in 1979.

The U.S. Embassy was praising Qadhafi despite his responsibility for the murder of dozens of Libyan exiles around the world, including in the United States; the midair terrorist bombing of French and American commercial airliners with the deaths of more than four hundred people, and the deaths of thousands during Libya's repeated interventions in Chad in the 1980s. He ultimately threatened to use his Air Force to kill large numbers of his own people, whom he described as "greasy rats" and "cockroaches." Qadhafi eventually took responsibility for the bombings of the commercial airliners, but the underlying violence of his regime never changed, and Libyans were denied any political role in the country. The U.S. Embassy may have failed to notice these facts, but not even the Western oil companies that did business with Libya pretended that Qadhafi was a "strong partner."

The violent Syrian situation is particularly difficult, because the downfall of Bashar al-Assad would have consequences for all of the major players in the region. In 2011 and 2012, we have watched Tunisia, Egypt, Yemen, and Libya implode; Syria's situation is far different: It could explode. Syria's neighbors (e.g., Israel, Turkey, Iran, Iraq, and Jordan) have strong interests in developments in Damascus and will find ways to exploit the turmoil. The challenge to Assad has already forced Hamas to find a new home for its top leadership. Syria is the conduit for Iranian assistance to Hezbollah; therefore, the Syrian outcome could limit Iran's influence in Syria and Lebanon. Chaos in Syria could lead to restlessness among Syria's Kurdish minority, which would affect Turkish attitudes toward Syria.

The civil war in Syria has worsened a refugee situation in the region that has not recovered from ten-year wars in Iraq and Afghanistan. The United States should be leading the way in the formation of a safe haven in border regions inside and outside Syria in order to save innocent civilians, and providing military support to a rebel group that threatens the worst tyrant in the region. President Obama's lack of engagement in the Syrian crisis and unwillingness to accept any level of risk is worrisome. The United States should have led a coalition of like-minded nations, reached out to the Syrian opposition, and ignored the intransigence of Russia and China. Instead, the Department of State has been mostly silent, and the United States remains an observer, which has left Turkey virtually alone to support the Syrian opposition and assist Syrian refugees.

The sad reality for U.S. policy in the region is that the United States has run out of steam. During and even after the Cold War, we signaled an interest in the region's oil and natural gas supplies and indicated that we favored authoritarian regimes that would protect our access. Our security was lashed to the region's autocrats, and there was no attempt to challenge corrupt governance in the area or to relate to the rights of citizens there, particularly the disadvantaged. The United States has ignored the Arab populace, and, as a result, we were totally surprised by the game-changing power of the grassroots social movements that blossomed into the Arab Spring.

Afghanistan and Pakistan

The greatest need for change in policy concerns Southwest Asia, particularly Afghanistan, where the United States has no vital interest but still retains more than 70,000 troops in a military stalemate. The most difficult aspect of change will be the need to curtail U.S. involvement in Afghanistan, but the greater long-term problem is defining U.S. policy toward Pakistan. Afghanistan has been dysfunctional for most of its history, and Pakistan has been dangerously dysfunctional since its creation seven decades ago. As prospects for U.S.-NATO success fade in Afghanistan, the domestic costs of Afghanistan continue to rise, and the political pressures for withdrawal gain momentum, it is necessary to consider alternatives to the current stalemate. Supporters of the war, including conservatives in both political parties as well as those forces aligned with the Pentagon, will oppose any scenario that involves disengagement on any level and will equate any diminished U.S. role with a strategic defeat. The

U.S. presence in Afghanistan merely increases U.S. dependence on Pakistan, where there is great opposition to a U.S. military presence. A reduced U.S. presence in Afghanistan would permit a reduction in U.S. military aid to Islamabad, thus forcing the Pakistanis to rely more on China for assistance and perhaps to improve bilateral relations with India.

The United States has had little success over the past decade in encouraging Pakistan to support the effort to stabilize Afghanistan, and it has failed to improve relations between Pakistan and India, to gain reassurance regarding the security of Pakistan's growing nuclear arsenal, to foster democracy in Pakistan, or to gain Pakistan's full support for counterterrorism. The emphasis on getting Pakistan's support in Afghanistan has ensured that more important objectives regarding nuclear proliferation and democratization will get less attention.

Fifty-five years ago, President Eisenhower warned against the heavy U.S. military involvement in Pakistan, which he referred to as the "worst kind of a plan and decision we could have made. It was a terrible error, but we now seem hopelessly involved in it." For the past sixty years, we have cooperated with the Pakistani military in order to gain Pakistan's policy support for U-2 flights (1950s); logistic support for the opening to China (1960s and 1970s); assistance for arming the Afghan mujahideen (1980s); or logistic support for the U.S. military occupation in Afghanistan. As a result, the United States has overlooked Pakistan's military dictatorship (1970s and 1990s); its terrorism and support for separatism in Kashmir; its nuclear program (1980s); and its myriad domestic shortcomings. The United States pays too little attention to the double dealing of Pakistan's military and intelligence services.

The United States would have better success in stabilizing Pakistani politics by improving Indian-Pakistani relations and thus reducing Pakistan's fear of Indian objectives in the region.

The U.S. nuclear agreement with India during the Bush administration did not lead to an improved U.S. bilateral relationship with India, but it did lead to greater Pakistani suspicion of U.S. intentions. If Pakistan perceived less of a threat from India, then it is possible that Islamabad would be willing to commit more resources to countering extremists. A coherent set of development priorities in Pakistan could also contribute to the stabilization of U.S.-Pakistani relations.

A smaller U.S. military role in Afghanistan would not only reduce U.S. dependence on logistical support from Pakistan, but it would create less U.S. reliance on Russia for helping the U.S. supply trail to Afghanistan. Every crisis in U.S.-Pakistani relations has led to shutting down supply routes to Afghanistan, and, as a result, half of all non-combat supplies to U.S. and NATO forces now traverse Russia, Central Asia, and the Caucasus. More than 200,000 Americans have traveled through Russian airspace on more than 1,500 military flights in the past several years. A disengagement process, according to Selig Harrison of the Center for International Policy, could set in motion UN-brokered peace negotiations resembling the Dayton process of the 1990s that reduced tensions in the Balkans.[18]

There were members of the Obama administration, the late Richard Holbrooke being the most prominent, who believed that it was time to talk to the Taliban, but Secretary of State Clinton and Secretary of Defense Gates were opposed. There have been secret contacts at an exploratory level with low-level members of the Taliban, but no sign that peace negotiations are about to break out. Secretary of State Clinton's declaration in October 2011 of a policy in Afghanistan that turns on "Fight, Talk, and Build" has no support in the Congress and makes little sense to our so-called allies in Afghanistan and Pakistan. Nevertheless, there needs to be a start to talks at some level. As long as military and intelligence operations dominate U.S. policy toward

Afghanistan, however, there is no hope for developing a political strategy, however protracted, that will end the U.S. role there.

The Pentagon is putting the best face possible on the U.S. role in Afghanistan, but the simple fact is that the situation is a stalemate and an unwinnable nightmare. The Taliban cannot be defeated as long as it has a sanctuary in Pakistan; no counter-insurgency has ever been successful when insurgents have had such a sanctuary. The key urban areas are relatively stable with reasonable security, which the Taliban cannot threaten as long as 75,000 U.S. and NATO forces remain there; conversely, the ethnic and tribal militias as well as criminal gangs control the countryside. For the U.S., there is no military solution.

Iraq and Iran

There has been no better example of the misuse of U.S. military power than the invasion and nearly nine-year occupation of Iraq. President Obama kept his campaign pledge to end U.S. combat in Iraq, completing the withdrawal of combat forces in December 2011, thus leaving Iran as the major outside influence in an Iraq on the brink of disaster. Nevertheless, the United States has built its largest embassy in the world in Baghdad and is leaving behind thousands of U.S. military forces that will remain in harm's way while ostensibly engaging in training missions. The U.S. public was told that the goal of the U.S. invasion in 2003 was the removal of Saddam Hussein, the creation of a functioning government in Baghdad, and the end to sectarian fighting in Iraq. One out of three isn't good enough, as Iraq is headed toward a sectarian autocracy under Shiite leadership, a possible civil war between Sunnis and Shia, and the creation of a separate Kurdish state in northern Iraq. The Obama administration, like the previous Bush administration, believes that military aid will provide some leverage over the government of Prime Minister Nuri Kamal al-Maliki, but this is unlikely.

As in the case of Egypt in the wake of the Arab Spring, there is an erosion of judicial independence in Iraq, the intimidation of political opposition, and the dismantling of independent institutions to prevent corruption. The Iraqi military doesn't boast the power and influence of its Egyptian counterpart, and there is far greater opportunity for sectarian violence in Iraq than in Egypt. In Egypt, the military leadership is searching for ways to compromise the election victory of the Muslim Brotherhood; in Iraq, the Shiites having successfully prevented the implementation of the 2010 election victory of a political coalition committed to resolving sectarian strife.

Instead of moving the Maliki government toward a power-sharing arrangement, the United States is using its embassy to guide funding to Iraq's military, police, and intelligence services —which are responsive to the Shiites' Dawa Party—and is shying away from a commitment to a unity government. The Iraq economy is in shambles: The agricultural system has effectively collapsed, and the regime is hostage to the price of oil. Thus far, the United States is merely offering sales of fighter aircraft and armored vehicles to the Iraqi military instead of creating a diplomatic dialogue that includes Turkey and particularly Iran to assure some geopolitical stability for a vulnerable Iraqi state. Instead of stemming the threat of terrorism, the impact of U.S. military attacks and occupation has led to the outbreak and spread of terrorism throughout the country, and there is no indication that the Baghdad government is prepared to deal effectively with continued violence. The U.S. invasion also fostered close relations between Iran and Iraq, which has been harmful to U.S. interests in the region.

The U.S. embassy will permit the United States to maintain a large CIA mission in Baghdad, a strong counterterrorism presence, and a headquarters for joint U.S.-Iraqi military operations. U.S. forces will not be permanently stationed in Iraq, but there will be a military and intelligence presence to manage training, exchange programs, and tactical exercises as well as surveillance and reconnaissance operations. Some sensitive operations may have to be moved to Turkey or Kuwait because of the dicey conditions in Iraq, particularly in Anbar, the western Iraqi desert province that produced al-Qaeda in Iraq; Basra, a hub for Iran's Revolutionary Guard; and Najaf, the capital for Shia activism. The need to maintain Iraq as a hub for clandestine activities against Syria and Iran will also require a large complement in Baghdad.

Iran is a particularly difficult problem because of the absence of diplomatic relations since 1979 and the hardening of positions in both Tehran and Washington. The Clinton administration had an opportunity to participate in oil extraction in Iran in 1994, but President Clinton lost his nerve regarding commercial ties with Iran. The Bush administration had an opportunity to work secretly with Iran to stabilize events in Afghanistan, but President Bush inexplicably preferred to brand Tehran as part of the "axis of evil." The Obama administration, soon after the inauguration, extended a diplomatic hand to Tehran, but it was unfortunately met with a clenched fist. President Obama must find a way to pursue both diplomacy and pressure simultaneously, but his administration has never demonstrated the ability to pursue seemingly contradictory objectives.

Iran may be more isolated than ever due to Obama's tactics, but there has been no progress in stopping Iran from gaining the wherewithal to develop nuclear weapons. The Obama administration is creating a ballistic missile defense against Tehran, and the U.S. Navy announced in January 2012 that it was converting an amphibious transport and docking ship to serve as a floating base for military operations in the Persian Gulf and the Middle East. The staging base would allow commandos, helicopters, speedboats, and even aircraft with short take-off capability to operate in areas where the United States chooses to deploy secret commando missions offshore. Such a staging base would be particularly valuable in the event that Iran follows through on threats to close the Strait of Hormuz.

The potential for compromise seems apparent, but neither Washington nor Tehran appears ready. Turkey and Brazil have demonstrated that Iran will hold talks on shipping Iran's enriched uranium abroad for further refinement, but the United States was not supportive, having committed itself to a hard-nosed sanctions resolution in the UN Security Council rather than a full-court diplomatic press. More recently, Iran stated its willingness to pursue Russia's proposal to defuse the nuclear standoff, which was similar to the Turkish-Brazilian solution. Iran has demonstrated the ability in the past to change course in a moderate direction, particularly in 1988 to end the war with Iraq, in 1993 to stop the assassinations of Iranian dissidents in Europe, and in 2003 to suspend uranium enrichment, which was a signal to the Bush administration that went unanswered.

The stalemate allows Israel to pursue pressure tactics against Iran, which include the threat of attack as well as the assassination of Iranian nuclear and chemical engineers. Israel's hardline tactics make it difficult for the United States to pursue a diplomatic solution. The use of military power against Iran's nuclear sites would be both futile and dangerous, as Secretaries of Defense Gates and Panetta affirmed, but the war hawks in the United States echo the Israeli government in calling Iran an "existential threat." Iran's political instability and the U.S. presidential election make it difficult for both Tehran and Washington to pursue a nuclear compromise. In the absence of diplomatic activity, the current bellicosity between Iran, Israel, and the United States could lead to serious escalation of the conflict.

The United States and Europe: Separate Tables

U.S. leaders should recognize that the United States and Europe have a great deal in common. On the domestic front, both face mounting debt, weak economies, political gridlock, and general insecurity about the future. The U.S. struggle to control the costs of Social Security and Medicare is very familiar to European leaders' struggles to change pension laws, retirement ages, and medical costs. However, the two sides differ on access to guns, comprehensive health care, and the use of capital punishment as well as their approaches to national security challenges.

The United States and the Western European members of NATO have moved in different directions in their approaches to their challenges. These differences are reflected in their approaches to defense spending, the use of force, and the role of law enforcement in countering terrorism. The United States would benefit from recognizing that European reductions in military spending have not had an adverse impact on their national security.

President Obama's visit to Poland in May 2011 pointed to many of the differences. In addition to cooperative steps on regional missile defense, the Obama administration announced that it would be basing U.S. fighter jets in Poland. As with the Clinton and Bush administrations, the Obama administration is ignoring the verbal commitment that Secretary of State James Baker made to the Soviet Union in 1990, when he said that the United States would not "leapfrog" over a united Germany in order to incorporate the Eastern European states in an anti-Russian NATO alliance.

President Obama has received some credit for pushing the "reset" button in relations with Russia, but much progress is needed to institutionalize bilateral relations. There needs to be an end to the expansion of NATO and to the Jackson-Vanik Bill restricting trade with Russia; it should not have taken two decades to gain Russian membership in the World Trade Organization; and more aggressive disarmament measures to reduce the strategic arsenals of both states are needed. The Western European members of NATO are more open to conciliatory steps toward Russia than the United States has been.

For the first time since the end of WWII, the United States appears to lack influence in European decision-making. When U.S. Secretary of the Treasury Tim Geithner used a meeting of the European Community in 2011 to suggest changes in European economic policy, he was actually met with a chorus of hisses. Meanwhile, U.S. economic policies appear to be hostage to Europe's solution to its own more serious financial crisis, particularly the currency problems of the euro. When the U.S. economy was a dynamic jobs creator in the 1990s, the Europeans paid attention to U.S. counsel. With U.S. unemployment still over eight percent, Europeans are no longer paying attention.

The economic situation in Greece points to the decline in U.S. influence in Europe. At the end of WWII, when Greece was threatened with political and economic disarray, the United States announced the Truman Doctrine to bail out the Greek economy and help stabilize Greece's political situation. More recently, with Greece facing an economic crisis that threatens the entire European Community as well as the United States, there are no initiatives from the Obama administration.

The Obama administration's decision to remove two of the remaining four Army brigades in Europe is a recognition of the need for cost-cutting and the absence of a geopolitical threat on the continent. The reduction of 10,000 to 15,000 soldiers will be an important down payment on the effort to reduce the Army from 560,000 soldiers to at most 490,000. This move will also leave the United States with less than 65,000 soldiers and airmen in Europe, including a cavalry brigade in Germany and an airborne brigade in Italy. During the height of the Cold War, the Army reached a peak of 280,000 troops on the Continent.

The United States and the Western European members of NATO differ on the role of NATO expansion, the integration of former Soviet republics into NATO's military exercises, and the need for regional missile defense in Eastern Europe. In June 2011, the United States gratuitously sent the USS *Monterey* into the Black Sea as part of an annual joint military exercise conducted by NATO and Ukraine, which offended Moscow. The United States regularly sent warships into the Black Sea as part of its defense of freedom of the seas during the Cold War, and these exercises typically led to Soviet-American frictions. In the post–Cold War era, Russia has reasonably questioned NATO membership for Ukraine as well as Ukraine's participation in NATO maneuvers.

The USS *Monterey* is particularly objectionable to the Russians because its capabilities represent the first part of a plan to create a European missile shield, which is also anathema. The shield calls for placing land- and sea-based radars and interceptors in several Eastern European states that are NATO members, a more extensive missile defense system than that envisaged by the Bush administration. Both the Bush and Obama administrations maintained that the system was designed to guard against Iranian missile launches against Europe, which appears far-fetched on the face of it. Russia has never bought into the logic of a defensive system against Iran and assumes that the shield is designed to threaten its own nuclear forces and thus undermine Russia's deterrent capabilities.

Exit Europe/Enter China

The United States should have learned lessons from a Cold War that lasted in Europe for more than four decades as well as from the huge expense of deploying forces to Iraq and Afghanistan for another decade. But no sooner had the United States handed over its largest base in Iraq, the ironically named "Camp Victory," than U.S. decision-makers were talking about a new focus on military planning: China, our largest foreign creditor. High-level U.S. officials are using various euphemisms to describe this move, such as the "rebalancing" of U.S. forces or the "pivoting" of U.S. power from the Middle East to Asia. The word they do not use is "containment," the word that comes to mind in Beijing to describe U.S. relations with Southeast Asian countries that have territorial disputes with China.

In the spring of 2001, Secretary of Defense Rumsfeld completed a strategic review of global military policy that marked China as the principal threat to U.S. global dominance. U.S. wars in Iraq and Afghanistan got in the way of operational changes in the Pacific, but, now that we have withdrawn from Iraq and have begun withdrawal from Afghanistan, the Obama administration for no good reason has set its sights on "containment" of China, even if it doesn't use the word. In November 2011, President Obama traveled to Australia and declared that the United States would now "allocate the resources necessary to maintain our strong military presence in this region."[19] He announced that as many as 2,500 Marines will eventually be deployed to an air base in Darwin, Australia, in order to conduct amphibious training; Obama failed to mention that the last Marine amphibious landing took place in 1951. He seemed to have no doubt that China would continue lending currency to the United States to fund this military expansion.

In November 2011, the White House also announced the sale of twenty-four F-16 fighter aircraft to Indonesia; the Pentagon announced it would be basing naval warships in Singapore; and Secretary of State Clinton made an unusual trip to Myanmar, a longtime Chinese ally, the first such trip by a U.S. secretary of state in five decades. Since then, Secretary of Defense Panetta has referred to enhanced military ties with Singapore, Thailand, and Vietnam, countries that are important to China's commercial relations in the region. The coordinated actions of Obama, Clinton, and Panetta demonstrate a policy focus that will draw on the same instruments of containment that were used against the Soviet Union until the collapse of the Berlin Wall in 1989.

Two decades after the Philippines kicked the U.S. military out of its sprawling naval base at Subic Bay and the United States abandoned Clark Air Base due to a nearby volcanic eruption, the two countries began secret talks to expand their military ties. Currently, the United States has approximately six hundred special operations troops in the Philippines to assist in the struggle against local rebels sympathetic to the al-Qaeda movement. Washington is looking for ways to deploy more troops and ships in a rotational mode, including the renewed use of Subic Bay. In return, the Philippines seeks the acquisition of additional U.S. military platforms, particularly F-16 fighter aircraft and naval ships.

The renewed U.S. interest in Vietnam is the most dramatic aspect of the U.S. "pivot" to Asia. Last summer, for the first time in thirty-eight years, a U.S. naval ship visited the Vietnamese naval base at Cam Ranh Bay, which was one of the largest U.S. facilities during the Vietnam War. Since 2009, Vietnam has been opening its bases to the U.S. Navy for port visits and ship repairs. China is paying close attention to these developments.

Once again, a U.S. administration is using its military forces to conduct foreign policy—sending a signal to China—instead of resorting to diplomatic instruments to enhance the U.S. position. The United States and China, after all, share important concerns, including the political disarray in North Korea; the serious proliferation possibilities that Pyongyang's nuclear program represents; terrorism and the danger of the transfer of weapons of mass destruction to a terrorist organization or other non-state entity; and various maritime disputes in the South China Sea. The Chinese military is no match for its U.S. counterpart, particularly in terms of nuclear, air, naval, and power projection forces, and there is no reason to believe that China will match U.S. capabilities in the next decade or two.

If the United States were genuinely looking for significant reductions in the defense budget, it would not be gratuitously looking for competition in the Pacific with China. Beijing's agenda emphasizes domestic investment; it has worked to improve relations with Taiwan; and China's neighbors, particularly the relatively weak states of Southeast Asia, do not seem unduly concerned with China. Beijing's leaders did not use the U.S. bombing of the Chinese Embassy in Belgrade in 1999 to pick a fight with the United States; similarly, China did not use an imbroglio over a U.S. spy plane in 2001 to worsen relations. Certainly, as the Chinese grow stronger, they will look for ways to enhance their international position, but there is no sign of a Chinese threat to American interests and no sign of an existential threat from China to it's neighbors. To avoid an unwanted imbroglio, the Obama administration needs to temper its language—on its current course it risks creating a self-fulfilling prophecy.

Changing the Home Front

Congress and the courts have contributed to U.S. militarism by their unwillingness to engage the national security process. Congress needs more effective legislative tools in the decision-making process, and the courts must stop bowing to the principle of state security by waiving their responsibility in cases that involve national security. In an effort to restore congressional powers over issues of war and peace, Congress passed the War Powers Resolution (WPR) in 1973 to provide for "collective judgment" before U.S. troops were sent into combat. The WPR was passed over President Nixon's veto; successive presidents have refused to acknowledge the resolution; and the judicial branch has not acknowledged the role of the WPR in the national security process. There has been an all-around absence of political will on these issues as the Congress and the courts fail to protect their institutional interests.

In the mid-1980s, the Iran-Contra affair, which marked the confluence of two politically controversial and illegal foreign policies (arming the Nicaraguan counterrevolutionaries and selling weapons to Iran), exposed the problem of an unbalanced institutional participation between the executive and legislative branches. The Reagan White House simply ignored the Constitution and the laws of the land, creating the greatest U.S. political scandal since Watergate. As a result, there were calls for a redefinition of the terrain of national security law, including a rewriting of the National Security Act of 1947. In the wake of the affair, Congress and President George H.W. Bush battled over reforms to the Intelligence Reform Act, which eventually produced a statutory Inspector General (IG) for the CIA. Presidents George W. Bush and Barack Obama ensured that the CIA IG has little oversight power, thus further weakening civilian control and contributing to the militarization of the intelligence community.

In the last four decades, there have been too many examples of White House use of force unaccompanied by congressional consultation. In the Ford administration, the Mayaguez rescue effort didn't involve congressional consultation; in the Carter administration, the Iran rescue operation was considered too sensitive for any consultation; in the Reagan administration, the invasion of Grenada, the bombing of Libya, and the air campaign against Iran were accomplished without congressional review; and in the Bush I administration, the same was true for the use of force in the Philippines, Panama, and El Salvador. The Bush II and Obama administrations also observed the WPR in the breach. There needs to be a political definition of the word "hostilities" so that military operations, such as those conducted by the U.S. in Libya in 2011, can't be conducted under the political radar.

The United States needs a political dialogue on the role of U.S. military power in the twenty-first century in order to understand the costs and benefits of huge defense outlays that don't advance the U.S. strategic position. The occupations of Iraq and Afghanistan did not contribute to U.S. security, have created greater regional tensions, and have fostered instability in both countries. The United States needs to step aside and use such multilateral organizations as the United Nations or key regional actors to address global security problems, particularly in less vital regions such as South America and Africa. The United States needs to move in the direction of compromise and negotiation and drop the ambitious goals connected with military force and nation-building.

U.S. leverage is not what it once was, and the United States cannot write checks the way it once did. In the European financial crisis, the United States is not playing a supporting role, even though China stepped up to the plate and promised $150 billion in bail-out assistance to the European banks. In the aftermath of the end of the Cold War, the Clinton administration ignored conservative criticism to orchestrate billion-dollar rescue packages for Mexico and some Asian states. Of course, there is no comparison to the post-WWII period, when the United States instituted and financed the Marshall Plan on behalf of downtrodden European governments. The United States spent 5 percent of its gross domestic product on the Marshall Plan and the Truman Doctrine, the kind of investment that is no longer feasible in light of the nation's staggering debt.

U.S. unilateralism and triumphalism have been a costly self-perception that we can no longer afford. It is time for substantial cuts in military forces, military bases, and military assistance. We are no longer the world's policeman and no longer the world's financier. Most of the problems associated with ethnic and religious conflicts are not U.S. problems. There must be greater support for international organizations and cooperation, not merely the activities of the UN, but those of regional institutions such as the Organization of American States, the Organization of African Unity, and the Association of Southeast Asian Nations. The United States should no longer remain apart from major disarmament treaties such as the Comprehensive Test Ban Treaty and the Landmines Ban or multilateral associations such as the International Criminal Court.

The certainty that there would be at least $485 billion removed from defense budgets over the next ten years has brought out the Cassandras and war hawks warning against further cuts; they must be challenged. The historian Robert Kagan of the Carnegie Endowment for International Peace warned that a "reduction in defense spending . . . would unnerve American allies and undercut efforts to gain great cooperation."[20] The journalist Robert Kaplan apocalyptically warned that "lessening [the United States'] engagement with the world would have devastating consequences for humanity." The most ludicrous warning came from Secretary of Defense Panetta, who told the National Guard in November 2011 that further cuts in defense spending would imperil U.S. national security by "inviting aggression."[21] Panetta and others argue that further cuts would turn the military into a "hollow force," although it was such a hollow force that completed Desert Storm in 100 hours.

The reliance on military instruments of power to implement foreign policy has increased the Pentagon's influence and decreased the State Department's influence; this trend must be reversed. The State Department budget is less than one-tenth of the defense budget and smaller than the budget of the intelligence community. The decline of the Agency for International Development and dissolution of the Arms Control and Disarmament Agency and the United States Information Service (USIS) have contributed to the decline of civilian influence in making policy. The United States has weakened its ability to conduct foreign policy at the very time when it is in a weaker strategic position and, as a result, has become insufficiently innovative in using diplomacy and conflict resolution to enhance its geopolitical position.

The Pentagon's Defense Science Board recommended in the wake of 9/11 that the United States needed to create "strategic communications" operations with the Muslim world in the wake of 9/11.[22] President Clinton erred when he capitulated to right-wing pressure and abolished the USIS, the one government agency that could conduct strategic communications around the world. The Defense Science Board correctly noted that an information campaign was needed to "separate the vast majority of nonviolent Muslims from the radical-militant Islamist-Jihadists." The Board's report courageously challenged President Bush's argument that the Muslims "hate our freedom," noting that Muslim hatred was reserved for U.S. policies, particularly the one-sided support of Israel, the failure to support Palestinian rights, and the support for "tyrannies, most notably Egypt, Saudi Arabia, Jordan, Pakistan, and the Gulf states."

Senior military officers, including those who served in Iraq and Afghanistan, have little knowledge of Islam or Islamic culture or understanding of the difference between Islam and Islamic extremism. There is little military training on linguistic and cultural issues in the Middle East or any other region, for that matter. Our civilian educational institutions pay insufficient attention to the religion, language, and culture of the Middle East. Our news media divide Muslims into secularists and extremists, and there is little understanding of the difference between the devout and the radical or the sympathizer and the opportunist. The Cold War, particularly the Soviet launch of Sputnik in 1957, led to the National Defense Education Act and the encouragement of Soviet studies, but two decades of involvement in the Middle East have had no similar impact. We have a superficial understanding of al-Qaeda, and virtually no familiarity with terrorist organizations such as al-Shabab in Somalia or Jemaah Islamiah in Southeast Asia.

In view of America's ignorance of the Middle East generally, let alone al-Qaeda, Islam, and ethnic nationalism and violence, it is particularly deplorable that nothing has been done in Congress or academe to improve our linguistic and cultural studies. The terrorist attacks in New York City in 1993 and 2001 should have had such an impact, but when a group of interested Arab Americans merely wanted to build a mosque and Islamic cultural center in New York, Americans of all political persuasions were opposed, proudly displaying their ignorance of Islamic culture and the meaning of the Koran. Unfortunately, President Obama catered to this thinking when he failed to endorse the building of a mosque in New York City.

When Franklin D. Roosevelt assumed the presidency in 1933, he told a small group of close advisers that the United States needed a new vision of domestic security, that we were "trapped in the ice of our own indifference."[23] Now we need a new vision of international security; once again we are trapped in the ice of our own lack of imagination. Sadly, there is no political figure willing to challenge the conventional wisdom on U.S. security and the domination of the military. President Eisenhower outlined the problem in his farewell address in 1961, but he made no comprehensive attempt during his eight-year stewardship to educate the American people regarding the need for change. Eisenhower's prophecy has never been more apparent: the defense, intelligence, and homeland security components of the U.S. budget are some of the most important parts of the U.S. economy; these components have unchecked influence and power in the U.S. Congress. It has been said that Prussia was a state owned by its army.[24] Will the same be said for the United States?

The late George F. Kennan, the author of the Cold War containment strategy against the Soviet Union, warned in 1999 about the dangers of war and the reliance on the military instrument, and the nation should pay close attention to his warning:

> This whole tendency to see ourselves as the center of political enlightenment and as teachers to a great part of the rest of the world strikes me as not thought through, vainglorious, and undesirable. If you think that our life here at home has meritorious aspects worthy of emulation by peoples elsewhere, the best way to recommend them is, as John Quincy Adams maintained, not by preaching at others but by the force of example.

There is some good news in the overall picture. President Obama has correctly responded to the Bush administration's misuse of unilateral military power by limiting U.S. global involvement and recognizing that the United States cannot deploy troops the way it once did. U.S. combat in Iraq has ended, which might not have happened if Obama lost the election; a limited withdrawal from Afghanistan is on schedule; and there is the possibility of additional withdrawals over the next several years as well as an end to large-scale military operations in Afghanistan in 2013, a year before schedule. The United States played only a supporting role in the Libyan operation, letting the British and the French take the lead and avoiding the use of U.S. ground forces. The neoconservatives attacked Obama when one of his advisers proclaimed that the president was leading in Libya "from behind," but that is exactly what the United States needed to do.

President Obama may not have a grand strategy for American foreign policy, but he does understand that the United States is far less exceptional than his domestic opponents believe, that the United States has to reduce its military footprint, and that both European and Asian powers—particularly the Western European members of NATO as well as China and India—have to assume more of the international burden. Stalemates such as the Israeli-Palestinian conflict and the Afghan Civil War can only be resolved at the negotiating table; even the Iranian nuclear stalemate is susceptible to negotiation. Military force will not work in these situations. Just as former Secretary of State Henry Kissinger shuttled successfully between Jerusalem, Cairo, and Damascus to arrange for Israeli troop withdrawals in the 1970s, it will be necessary to shuttle between Israelis and Palestinians as well as between the Karzai government in Kabul and the Afghan Taliban to end hostilities.

A serious diplomatic shuttle would restore the State Department to a central position in U.S. policy and relegate the Pentagon to the "wingman's" role that it should occupy. In the name of the Global War on Terror, the military has been given too much power over national security and foreign policy, with the Pentagon's reach extending to covert operations, intelligence collection, and nation-building. Sadly, the most recent secretaries of state—Condi Rice and Hillary Clinton—have been roving ambassadors rather than serious stateswomen, and this must be corrected. The misuse of U.S. military power in Iraq and Afghanistan over the past decade has ensured violence and chaos in these regions for years to come, and reminds us that the age of the superpower is over. Building peace is an enormous enterprise, but it is the only way to stop costly conflicts that have weakened the United States and the societies that are caught up in these conflicts. As Winston Churchill once said, "Jaw jaw is better than war war."

In 1955, Bertrand Russell and Albert Einstein issued a manifesto that in our times is more prophetic than ever: "We have to learn to think in a new way. We have to learn to ask ourselves, not what steps can be taken to give military victory to whatever group we prefer, for there no longer are such steps; the question we have to ask ourselves is: what steps can be taken to prevent a military contest that will be disastrous to all parties?"[25]

Endnotes

INTRODUCTION

1. Craig Whitlock and Greg Miller, "U.S. creating a ring of secret drone bases," *Washington Post*, September 21, 2011, p. 1.
2. Nick Turse, "Obama's Arc of Instability: Destabilizing the World One Region at a Time," www.tomdispatch.com/dialogs/print/?id=175442.
3. John Tirman, "The Forgotten Wages of War, *New York Times*, December 30, 2011, p. 19.
4. Eric Schmitt, Mark Mazzetti, and Thom Shanker, "Admiral Pushing For Freer Hand With Commandos," *New York Times*, February 13, 2012, p. 1.
5. Daniel Yergin, *Shattered Peace: The Origins of the Cold War and the National Security State*, Boston: Houghton Mifflin, 1977, p. 196.
6. Robert Scheer, *The Pornography of Power: How Defense Hawks Hijacked 9/11 and Weakened America*, New York: Hachette Book Group, 2008, p. 192.
7. Robert Kagan, *The World America Made*, New York: Alfred A. Knopf, 2012, p. 18.
8. *New York Times*, February 10, 2002, p. 11.

CHAPTER ONE

1. Craig Whitlock, "Panetta Institute honors co-founder's predecessor, Gates," *Washington Post*, November 5, 2011, p. 2.
2. David A. Nichols, *Eisenhower 1956: The President's Year of Crisis/Suez and the Brink of War*, New York: Simon & Schuster, 2011, p. 65.
3. See Jonathan Turley, "Ten reasons we're no longer the land of the free," *Washington Post*, January 15, 2012, p. 1, for an excellent comparison of the loss of freedoms in the United States that compare with so-called repressive regimes around the world.
4. James Ledbetter, *Unwarranted Influence: Dwight D. Eisenhower and the Military-Industrial Complex*, New Haven, CT: Yale University Press, September 20, 2011.
5. Susan Eisenhower, "50 years later, we're still ignoring Ike's warning," *Washington Post*, January 16, 2011, p. B3.
6. Gaither Report was titled "Deterrence and Survival in the Nuclear Age." It exaggerated the capabilities of Soviet strategic aircraft and missiles in order to demand an urgent U.S. military buildup.
7. NSC-68 was a secret review of Soviet policies that exaggerated Soviet capabilities and even anticipated that, once it could, Moscow would launch a surprise nuclear attack against the United States.
8. Dwight D. Eisenhower, *The White House Years: Mandate for Change, 1953-1956*, Garden City, NY: Doubleday, 1965, pp. 20–23.
9. "Report of the Special Study Group (Doolittle Committee) on the Covert Activities of the Central Intelligence Agency" (September 30, 1954), in William M. Leary (ed.), *The Central Intelligence Agency: History and Documents*, Tuscaloosa, AL: University of Alabama Press, 1984, p. 144.

10. See Nicholas Cullather, *The CIA's Secret History of Its Guatemalan Coup* (Stanford, CA: Stanford University Press, 1998), which benefited from access to CIA files on the Arbenz coup code-named *Operation PBSUCCESS*.

11. Peter W. Singer, "Do Drones Undermine Democracy?," *New York Times*, January 22, 2012, p. 5; Juan Cole, "The Age of American Shadow Power," *The Nation*, April 30, 2012, p. 26.

12. President Jacobo Arbenz died a broken man in Mexico in 1971, leaving his family to fight unsuccessfully in the Guatemalan courts to restore his reputation and their confiscated property. In 1999, the family went to the Inter-American Commission on Human Rights in Washington, which accepted the complaint in 2006, resulting in five years of negotiation. Finally, in May 2011, nearly sixty years after the coup, the Arbenz family received monetary reparations, and the Guatemalan government—led by a leftist president for the first time since Arbenz was head of state—agreed to hold a public ceremony to admit the state's role in the coup as well as proffer a letter of apology to the family.

13. See Noam Chomsky, *Year 501: The Conquest Continues*, Boston: South End Press, 1993, p. 121.

14. Derek Leebaert, *The Fifty-Year Wound: The True Price of America's Cold War Victory*, Boston: Little, Brown and Company, 2002, p. 327.

15. James Strodes, *Allen Dulles: Master of Spies*, Washington, DC: Regnery Publishers, 1999, p. 494.

16. Leebaert, *The Fifty-Year Wound*, p. 327.

17. Martin Kettle, "President 'ordered murder' of Congo leader," August 10, 2000, http://www.guardianunlimited.co.uk/Archive/Article/html.

18. Ibid., p. 10.

19. Alex Shoumatoff, "Mobutu's Final Days," *Vanity Fair*, August 1997, p. 97.

20. Church Committee, *Alleged Assassination Plots Involving Foreign Leaders*, New York: W.W. Norton, 1974, pp. 79–83.

21. Tim Weiner, "CIA Bares Its Bungling in Report on Bay of Pigs Invasion," *New York Times*, February 22, 1998, p. 6.

22. Pat M. Holt, *Secret Intelligence and Public Policy: A Dilemma of Democracy*, Washington, DC: Congressional Quarterly Press, 1995, p. 162.

23. Stanley Karnow, "Spook," *New York Times Magazine*, January 3, 1999, p. 34.

24. Gregory Treverton, *Covert Action*, New York: Basic Books, 1987, p. 11.

25. Elisabeth Malkin, "Guatemala to Restore Legacy of a President the U.S. Helped Depose," *New York Times*, May 27, 2011, p. 11.

26. Robert M. Gates, *From the Shadows: The Ultimate Insider's Story of Five Presidents and How They Won the Cold War*, New York: Simon & Schuster, 1996, p. 32.

27. House Permanent Select Committee on Intelligence, *IC 21: The Intelligence Community in the 21st Century*, Washington, DC: Government Printing Office, April 9, 1996, p. 205

28. Commission on the Roles and Capabilities of the United State Intelligence Community, *Preparing for the 21st Century: An Appraisal of U.S. Intelligence*, Washington, DC: Government Printing Office, March 1, 1996; and Council on Foreign Relations, *Making Intelligence Smarter: The Future of U.S. Intelligence*, New York: Council on Foreign Relations, 1996, p. 21.

29. *New York Times*, September 13, 1998, p. 7; February 26, 1999, p. 9.

30. Gates, *From the Shadows*, p. 51.

31. *The Need to Know: The Report of the Twentieth Century Fund Task Force on Covert Action and American Democracy*, New York: Twentieth Century Fund Press, 1992, pp. 21–23.

CHAPTER TWO

1. Daniel Patrick Moynihan, *Daniel Patrick Moynihan: A Portrait in Letters of an American Visionary*, edited by Steven R. Weisman, New York: Public Affairs, 2010, p. 549.

2. Dispatch, Vol. 5, No. 8, February 21, 1994, Washington, DC: U.S. Department of State, Bureau of Public Affairs, p. 96.

3. Walter LaFeber, *America, Russia, and the Cold War*, New York: McGraw-Hill, 2002, p. 348.

4. NIE 11-3/8-66, "Soviet Strategic Capabilities and Objectives".

5. Michael Getler, "General Relieved of NSC Job After Unauthorized Speech," *Washington Post*, October 21, 1981, p. 7.

6. Sidney Blumenthal, *Pledging Allegiance: The Last Campaign of the Cold War*, New York: Harper Collins, 1990, pp. 322–323; Jack Beatty, "Reagan's Gift," *The Atlantic*, February 1989, pp. 45–46.

7. Admiral Stansfield Turner, *Burn Before Reading: Presidents, CIA Directors, and Secret Intelligence*, New York: Hyperion, 2005, p. 210.

8. Blumenthal, *Pledging Allegiance*, p. 323.

9. Owen Ullman, "Bush White House Attacks Reagan," *Bergen Record* (New Jersey), March 24, 1989, p. 5.

10. See George P. Shultz, *Turmoil and Triumph: My Years as Secretary of State*, New York: Charles Scribner's Sons, 1993; and Jack Matlock, *Anatomy on an Empire: The American Ambassador's Account of the Collapse of the Soviet Union*, New York: Random House, 1995. Shultz's memoir is the most candid and hardest-hitting assessment of the State Department and the politics of U.S. foreign policy ever written by a secretary of state. Matlock, a former Foreign Service Officer and a senior Kremlinologist, produced a valuable but pedestrian account of a tense period.

11. George H.W. Bush, "Address at the Hofburg, Vienna, September 21, 1983," *Department of State Bulletin*, November 1983, Vol. 83, pp. 20–23.

12. Ibid.

13. Raymond L. Garthoff, *The Great Transition: American-Soviet Relations and the End of the Cold War*, Washington, DC: The Brookings Institution, 1994, p. 129.

14. Don Oberdorfer, "Strategy for Solo Superpower: Pentagon Looks to 'Regional Contingencies,'" *Washington Post*, May 19, 1991, p. 1.

15. James A. Baker III, *The Politics of Diplomacy*, New York: G.P. Putnam's Sons, 1995, pp. 21–22.

16. Bob Woodward, *The Commanders*, New York: Simon & Schuster, 1991, p. 93.

17. Lawrence Freedman and Efraim Karsh, *The Gulf Conflict, 1990-1991*, Princeton, NJ: Princeton University Press, 1993, p. 413.

18. Bob Woodward, *The Commanders*, New York: Simon & Schuster, 1991, p. 108.

19. Blumenthal, *Pledging Alliances*, p. 277.

20. Baker, *Politics of Diplomacy*, p. 93.

21. Ibid., p. 93.

22. Ibid., p. 68.

23. Michael Beschloss and Strobe Talbott, *At the Highest Levels: The Inside Story of the End of the Cold War*, Boston: Little, Brown and Company, 1993, p. 442.

24. "Address Before a Joint Session of Congress on the Crisis in the Persian Gulf and the Federal Budget Deficit," September 11, 1990, *Public Papers of the Presidents of the United States: George Bush, 1990*.

25. Interview with General Brent Scowcroft, National War College, Washington, DC, September 27, 2000.

26. George F. Kennan, "The Kennan 'Long Telegram,' " in *Origins of the Cold War*, Kenneth M. Jensen (ed.), Washington, DC: United States Institute of Peace, 1991, pp. 17–31.

27. Zbigniew Brzezinski, "The Premature Partnership," *Foreign Affairs*, Vol. 73, No. 3, May-June 1994, pp. 67–82.

28. John H. McNeill, "Military-to-Military Arrangements for the Prevention of U.S.-Russian Conflict," *Naval War College Review*, Spring 1994, pp. 23–29.

29. Beschloss and Talbott, *At the Highest Levels*, p. 170. The following year, Gorbachev put the question directly to congressional officials when they raised the issue of Soviet force in Lithuania: "Why did you let your administration intervene in Panama if you love freedom so much?"

30. Bob Woodward, *The Commanders*, New York: Simon & Schuster, 1991, p. 89.

31. Michael R. Gordon, "Hussein Wanted Soviets to Head Off U.S. in 1991," *New York Times*, January 21, 2011, p. 10.

32. Andrew Bacevich, "A Less than Splendid Little War," *Wilson Quarterly*, Winter 2001, p. 84.

33. The details of the discussions between Tariq Aziz and Mikhail Gorbachev; Aziz and Saddam Hussein; and Hussein and Gorbachev are now available in the form of official government transcripts that were released on January 17, 2011, the 20th anniversary of the air campaign that began on January 1, 1991. The full archive is stored in digital form at the National Defense University in Washington, DC, which has released a very small portion of the collection.

34. Gordon, "Hussein Wanted Soviets to…," p. 10.

35. Iraqi Diplomatic Archives, National Defense University, Washington, DC.

36. Gordon, "Hussein Wanted Soviets to…," p. 10.

37. See George Bush and Brent Scowcroft, *A World Transformed: The Collapse of the Soviet Empire, the Unification of Germany, Tiananmen Square, and the Gulf War* (New York: Alfred A. Knopf, 1998), an unusual and unprecedented memoir that was jointly crafted by a president and a national security adviser.

38. Leebaert, *The Fifty-Year Wound*, p. 609.

39. William S. Cohen and George J. Mitchell, *Men of Zeal*, New York: Viking Press, 1988, pp. 264–272.

40. Ibid., p. 285.

41. Theodore Draper, *A Very Thin Line: the Iran-Contra Affairs*, New York: Hill and Wang, 1991, pp. 573–574.

42. Cohen and Mitchell, *Men of Zeal*, p. 271.

43. *New York Times*, January 29, 1988, p. 11.
44. Lawrence E. Walsh, *Firewall: The Iran-Contra Conspiracy and Cover-Up*, New York: W.W. Norton & Company, 1997, pp. 452–453.
45. Walsh, *Firewall*, p. 494.
46. *New York Times*, January 23, 1992, p. 1.
47. General Accounting Office, January 26, 1995.
48. The Virginia-class submarine is built by Electric Boat, which is based (no surprise) in Connecticut. Electric Boat also has received billions of dollars to upgrade older nuclear-missile-carrying submarines. Another Connecticut-based manufacturer, Sikorsky, benefited from Senator Lieberman's largesse on behalf of helicopter construction. Connecticut is also the home of Pratt & Whitney, whose airplane engines go into Lockheed's F-22 and F-35 Raptor fighters. See Robert Scheer, *The Pornography of Power: How Defense Hawks Hijacked 9/11 and Weakened America*, New York: Grand Central Publishing, 2008.
49. The Virginia-class submarine carries both torpedoes and Tomahawk missiles and has a torpedo room that can be reconfigured to hold Navy SEALS.
50. *New York Times*, February 10, 2002, p. 11.

CHAPTER THREE

1. Patrick E. Tyler, "U.S. Civilians Not Told of Raid on Palestinians," *New York Times*, May 31, 2003, p. 6.
2. John F. Harris, *The Survivor: Bill Clinton in the White House*, New York: Random House, 2005, p. 17.
3. *Washington Post*, September 19, 2010, p. B3, "Five Myths about 'don't ask, don't tell.' "
4. Harris, *The Survivor*, p. 51.
5. GAO Report, January 26, 1995. See Robert Scheer, *The Pornography of Power*, p. 93.
6. Douglas Garthoff, *Directors of Central Intelligence as Leaders of the U.S. Intelligence Community, 1946-2005*, Washington, DC: Center for the Study of Intelligence, Central Intelligence Agency, 2005, p. 225.
7. Peter Galbraith was involved in a second imbroglio, this time in Iraq, where he served in various U.N. capacities, until he was found to be filling his own coffers with oil production profits in Kurdistan at the same time he was lobbying for an independent Kurdish state or at least U.S. occupation of Kurdistan.
8. Harris, *The Survivor*, p. 164. According to Harris, Clinton liked advisers who understood the political and practical realities of key issues, having no patience for "moralistic arguments that were blind to practical realities."
9. Leebaert, *The Fifty-Year Wound*, p. 612.
10. David Scheffer, *All the Missing Souls: A Personal History of the War Crimes Tribunals*, New Jersey: Princeton University Press, 2012, p. 117. Mr. Scheffer was the Clinton administration's point man on international justice. His book details the difficulty of getting the defense and intelligence communities to share evidence of war crimes in the Balkans.
11. See Richard Holbrooke, *To End a War*, New York: Random House, 1998.
12. See Colin L. Powell, *An American Journey*, New York: Random House, 1995.
13. Bob Fehribach, "Using Landmines Offers No Benefits to U.S. Military," *Lansing State Journal*, January 14, 2003.

14. Bill Clinton, *My Life*, New York: Vintage Books, 2005, p. 765.
15. Terry L. Deibel, "The Death of a Treaty," *Foreign Affairs*, Vol. 81, No. 5, p. 142.
16. Ibid., p. 154.
17. The funding for the national missile defense system that is now being deployed in Alaska and California is the largest line item for a weapons system in the current military budget. Although the system has not proved workable in its various tests, it receives over $10 billion a year; the Pentagon, moreover, has not shared sensitive testing data with the Senate Armed Forces Committee as required by law.
18. These reductions were announced by Secretary of Defense William Cohen as part of the Quadrennial Defense Review.
19. Congressional Budget Office, "A Look at Tomorrow's Tactical Air Forces," January 7, 1997, p. xii.
20. Harris, *The Survivor*, p. 370.

CHAPTER FOUR

1. See George W. Bush, *Decision Points*, New York: Crown Publishers, 2010; Dick Cheney, *In My Time: A Personal and Political Memoir*, New York: Threshold Editions, 2011; Donald Rumsfeld, *Known and Unknown: A Memoir*, New York: Sentinel, 2011; Condoleezza Rice, *No Higher Honor: A Memoir of My Years in Washington*, New York: Crown Publishers, 2011.
2. Rumsfeld, *Known and Unknown*, 2011, p. 418.
3. Paul Krugman, "Osama, Saddam and the Ports," *New York Times*, February 24, 2006, p. 27. Krugman used notes that were released after a Freedom of Information Act request.
4. Richard A. Clarke, *Against All Enemies: Inside America's War on Terror*, New York: Free Press, 2004, p. 78.
5. Cheney, *In My Time*, p. 413.
6. Bush, *Decision Points*, p. 498.
7. Bob Woodward, *Plan of Attack*, New York: Simon & Schuster, 2004, p. 117.
8. All of these documents are available on the White House and State Department websites at www.whitehouse.gov.news/releases and www.state.gov/secretary/former/Powell/remarks/2003.
9. Bush, *Decision Points*, p. 92.
10. Rice, *No Higher Honor*, p. 319.
11. See Woodward, *Plan of Attack*.
12. Scott Shane, "Doubts Cast on Vietnam Incident, but Secret Study Stays Classified," *New York Times*, October 31, 2005, p. 1.
13. Barton Gellman and Walter Pincus, "Depiction of Threat Outgrew Supporting Evidence," *Washington Post*, August 10, 2003, p. 1.
14. CNN, September 8, 2002; *New York Times*, September 8, 2002, p. 1.
15. Elisabeth Bumiller, "Traces of Terror: The Strategy," *New York Times*, September 7, 2002, p. 1.
16. Ibid., p. 1.
17. Greg Miller, "CIA Corrects Itself on Arms," *Los Angeles Times*, February 1, 2005, p. 1.

18. Joseph Cirincione, "Gold Medal Inspector," Carnegie Endowment for International Peace monograph, October 20, 2005, p.11.
19. "Iraq's Continuing Programs for Weapons of Mass Destruction," cited in the Robb-Silberman Report ("Final Report on Intelligence Capabilities of the United States Regarding Weapons of Mass Destruction"), p. 227.
20. Ibid., p. 236.
21. President George Bush, Remarks in Meeting with President Alvaro Uribe of Colombia, September 25, 2002. See www.whitehouse.gov/news/releases/2002/09/20020925-1.html.; *Washington Post*, December 22, 2005, p. 17.
22. Eric Schmitt, "Rumsfeld Says U.S. Has 'Bulletproof' Evidence of Iraq's Links to al Qaeda," *New York Times*, September 28, 2002, p. 9; John B. Judis and Spencer Ackerman, "The First Casualty," *New Republic*, June 30, 2003, p. 24.
23. President George W. Bush, "World Can Rise to This Moment," Speech, February 6, 2003.
24. President Bush, Statement after Cabinet Meeting, June 17, 2004.
25. Central Intelligence Agency, "Iraq and al-Qa'ida: Interpreting a Murky Relationship," June 21, 2002.
26. Secretary of State Colin Powell, Speech to the UN Security Council, February 5, 2003.
27. Secretary of Defense Donald Rumsfeld, Defense Department Briefings, February 4, 2003.
28. National security adviser Condoleezza Rice, interviews on *Face the Nation* and *Fox News Sunday*, March 9, 2003 and September 7, 2003.
29. Richard A. Clarke, *Your Government Failed You: Breaking the Cycle of National Security Disasters*, New York: Harper Collins Publishers, 2008, p. 52.
30. Central Intelligence Agency, National Intelligence Estimate on Iraq's Continuing WMD Programs, October 2, 2002, p. 13.
31. Central Intelligence Agency, "Iraqi Support for Terrorism," January 29, 2003.
32. Cheney, *In My Time*, pp. 415–416.
33. *Meet the Press: Interview with Vice President Cheney*, NBC television broadcast, December 9, 2001.
34. CIA, "Iraqi Support for Terrorism," January 29, 2003.
35. Bob Drogin and John Goetz, "How U.S. Fell Under the Spell of 'Curveball,' " *Los Angeles Times*, November 20, 2005, p. 1.
36. Ibid.
37. Ibid.
38. James Risen, *State of War: The Secret History of the CIA and the Bush Administration*, New York: Free Press, 2006, p. 117.
39. Drogin and Goetz, "The Spell of 'Curveball,' " p. 1.
40. Craig Unger, "The War They Wanted, the Lies They Needed," *Vanity Fair*, March 2007, p. 179.
41. Jay Solomon and Gabriel Kahn, "The Italian Job: How Fake Iraq Memos Tripped up Ex-Spy," *Wall Street Journal*, February 24, 2006, p. 1.
42. Tim Phelps and Knut Royce, *Long Island Newsday*, July 22, 2003; and David Ensor, CNN, July 13, 2004, as cited in Larry Johnson, "An Updated Plamegate Timeline," noquarter.typepad.com, April 11, 2006.

43. Larry Johnson, "An Updated Plamegate Timeline, noquarter.typepad.com, April 11, 2006.

44. Ibid.

45. Dafna Linzer, "Prosecutor in CIA Leak Case Corrects Part of Court Filing," *Washington Post*, April 12, 2006, p. 8.

46. Condoleezza Rice, *No Higher Honor: A Memoir of My Years in Washington*, New York: Crown Publishers, 2011, p. 372.

47. Joby Warrick, "Lacking Biolabs, Trailers Carried Cast for War," *Washington Post*, April 12, 2006, p. 1.

48. James Risen, "Intelligence Points to Iraqi Biological Weapons," *New York Times*, May 22, 2003, p. 16.

49. Warrick, "Lacking Biolabs," p. 22.

50. Paul Pillar, "Intelligence, Policy, and the War in Iraq," *Foreign Affairs*, March/April 2006, p. 62.

51. Scot Lehigh, "Revealing the Road to 'The Dark Side,' " *Boston.com*, July 13, 2006.

52. "Decoding Mr. Bush's Denials," editorial, *New York Times*, November 15, 2005, p. 28.

53. Richard Kerr, Thomas Wolfe, Rebecca Donegan, and Aris Pappas, "Collection and Analysis on Iraq: Issues for the U.S. Intelligence Community," *Studies in Intelligence*, Vol. 49, No. 3, 2005, p. 53.

54. Paul Pillar, "An Oversight Hearing on Pre-War Intelligence Relating to Iraq," Senate Democratic Policy Committee Hearing, June 26, 2006.

55. Thomas S. Blanton, ForeignPolicy.com, September 5, 2012.

56. The NIE on Iraqi WMD and the unclassified White Paper were excellent examples of the 2002 Downing Street memorandum accusing the United States of "fixing intelligence to policy."

57. Rice, *No Higher Honor*, p. 417.

58. President Obama's selection of Shinseki to head the Department of Veterans Administration in December 2008 was an attempt to apologize to the general for his shabby treatment at the hands of Secretary of Defense Rumsfeld.

59. Kerr, Wolfe, Donegan, and Pappas, "Collection and Analysis on Iraq," p. 48; Risen, *State of War*, p. 175.

60. Walter Pincus, "Tenet Defends Iraq Intelligence," *Washington Post*, May 31, 2003, p. 1.

61. Michael Eisenstadt, "Understanding Saddam," *The National Interest*, Fall 2005, p. 121.

62. Adam Liptak, "Justices Reject GPS Tracking In a Drug Case," *New York Times*, January 24, 2012, p. 1.

63. Ken Dilanian, "A Key Sept. 11 legacy: more domestic surveillance," www.LATimes.com, August 29, 2011.

64. Ibid.

65. Pat Towell, "Defense Bill Wins Solid House Passage," *Congressional Quarterly Weekly Report*, September 29, 2001, p. 2,278.

66. The figures for the military budget come from the Office of Management and Budget and the Congressional Budget Office.

67. Rice, *No Higher Honor*, p. 319.

CHAPTER FIVE

1. Thom Shanker, "Robert Gates Warns NATO of 'Dim' Future," *New York Times*, June 10, 2011, p. 1.

2. Peter Spiegel, "Gates Raps NATO laggards over air war," *Financial Times*, June 10, 2011, p. 2.

3. Greg Jaffe and Michael Birnbaum, "In harsh speech, Gates presses allies to spend on defense," *Washington Post*, June 10, 2011, p. 1.

4. Scott Shane, "Director Petraeus to Face Different Culture at C.I.A.," *New York Times*, April 28, 2011, p. 9.

5. Elisabeth Bumiller, "Panetta Pleads for More Cash," *New York Times*, August 5, 2011, p. 7; Greg Jaffe and Jason Ukman, "Panetta warns against additional cuts in Pentagon's budget," *Washington Post*, August 5, 2011, p. 5.

6. Greg Jaffe, "Pentagon's No. 2 civilian plans to resign," *Washington Post*, July 8, 2011, p. 3.

7. Jim Hightower, "The Unanswered Question in Afghanistan Is, Why?" June 29, 2011, *www.truthout.org*.

8. Matthew Sherman, "What the Afghan war is missing: A sense of desperation," *Washington Post*, Outlook Section, June 26, 2011, p. 1.

9. Dexter Filkins, "Comment: Endgame," *The New Yorker*, July 4, 2011, p. 18.

10. Rajiv, Chandrasekaran, "Afghan war cost to be big factor in troop drawdown," *Washington Post*, May 31, 2011, p. 10.

11. See Jonathan Altar, *The Promise: President Obama, Year One*, New York: Simon & Schuster, 2011.

12. Alissa J. Rubin, "U.S. General in Afghanistan Says Troops May Stay Past 2014," *New York Times*, January 9, 2012, p.9.

13. Robert Burns, "Ex-Commander: US Started War," Associated Press, October 6, 2011.

14. Helene Cooper, "Obama Sets Goal of Economy Built for the Long Run," *New York Times*, January 25, 2012, p. 19.

15. United Nations Security Council Resolution, March 17, 2011, UNSC Resolution 1973.

16. Unfortunately, President Obama is prone to this type of mistake. In addition to saying that Qadhafi "must go" in March 2011, he proclaimed on May 19, 2011, that Syrian President Bashir Assad "can lead the transition, or get out of the way." Similarly in February 2011, the president issued an imperial commandment for Egypt, in which he said the "transition must begin now." Fortunately for President Obama, the transition soon began . . . and continues.

17. *New York Times*, March 23, 2011, p. 11.

18. *Washington Post*, March 23, 2011, p. 14.

19. Frank Oliveri, "Top Officer Says 'No-Fly' Zone Over Libya Might Not Help Rebels," *Congressional Quarterly Today Online*, March 17, 2011.

20. *The New Yorker*, September 5, 2011, p. 19.

21. Herbert Hongju Koh, *The National Security Constitution: Sharing Power After the Iran-Contra Affair*, New Haven, CT: Yale University Press, 1990, p. 39.

22. Secretary of Defense William Cohen, Graduation Speech, Yale University, June 5, 1997.

23. Daniel W. Drezner, "Does Obama Have a Grand Strategy?," *Foreign Affairs*, July/August 2011, Vol. 90, No. 4, pp. 57ff.

24. It is noteworthy that one of the criticisms of the speech concerned its length (a mere 13 minutes), cited in a *New York Times* editorial as a major flaw in the announcement. See *New York Times*, June 23, 2011, p. 22.

25. Eric Alterman, "Obama's Failures . . . and Ours," *The Nation*, December 6, 2010, p. 9.

CHAPTER SIX

1. Louis G. Sarris, "McNamara's War on the Facts," *New York Times*, September 8, 1995, p. 11.

2. Scott Shane, "Doubts Cast on Vietnam Incident, But Secret Study Stays Classified," *New York Times*, October 31, 2005, p. 1.

3. Robert M. Gates, "The CIA and American Foreign Policy," *Foreign Affairs*, Vol. 66, Winter 1987–1988, p. 227.

4. Richard Helms and William Hood, *A Look Over My Shoulder: A Life in the Central Intelligence Agency*, New York: Simon & Schuster, 2001, p. 410.

5. Richard Reeves, *President Nixon: Alone in the White House*, New York: Simon & Schuster, 2001, p. 483.

6. Helms and Hood, *A Look Over My Shoulder*, p. 410.

7. John Prados, *Lost Crusader: The Secret Wars of CIA Director William Colby*, New York: Oxford University Press, 2002, p. 276.

8. Douglas Jehl, "Chief of CIA Tells His Staff to Back Bush," *New York Times*, November 17, 2004, p. 15.

9. Robert E. White, "Renewal in El Salvador," *Washington Post*, January 16, 1992, p. 17.

10. Robert Parry, *Secrecy and Privilege: Rise of the Bush Dynasty from Watergate to Iraq*, Arlington, VA: Media Consortium, 2004.

11. Frances Fitzgerald, *Way Out There in the Blue: Reagan, Star Wars and the End of the Cold War*, New York: Simon & Schuster, 2000, p. 330.

12. Ibid., p. 330.

13. Noel E. Firth and James Noren, *Soviet Defense Spending: A History of CIA Estimates, 1950–1990*, College Station, TX: Texas A&M University Press, 1998, p. 94.

14. Senate Foreign Relations Committee, "Estimating the Size and Growth of the Soviet Economy," Senate Hearing 101-1112, 101st Congress, 2nd session, 1990, p. 4.

15. "Intelligence Forecasts of Soviet Intercontinental Attack Forces: An Evaluation of the Record," CIA Directorate of Intelligence Research Paper, April 1989 (declassified in October 1993), p. 5.

16. Seymour Hersh, *The New Yorker*, March 29, 1993, p. 33.

17. David Ignatius, "Reshaping the rules of war," *Washington Post*, June 2, 2011, p. 17.

18. Ibid.

19. Ibid.

20. Matt Renner, "Pentagon Officer Created Phony Intelligence on Iraq/al Qaeda Link," www.truthout.org, April 6, 2007. p. 2.

21. Walter Pincus and Jeffrey Smith, "Official's key report on Iraq is faulted," *Washington Post*, February 9, 2007, p.7.

22. Michael Isikoff, "The Other Big Brother," *Newsweek*, January 22, 2006, p. 15.

23. See Alex Strick van Linschoten and Felix Kuehn, *An Enemy We Created: The Myth of the Taliban/Al Qaeda Merger*, London: Hirst & Company, 2012.

24. Paul Pillar, "Intelligence, Policy, and the War," pp. 15-27.

25. Ibid., p. 24.

26. James Risen and Eric Lichtblau, "Bush Lets U.S. Spy on Callers Without Courts," *New York Times*, December 15, 2005, p. 1.

27. Lowell Bergman, Eric Lichtblau, Scott Shane, and Don Van Natta Jr., "Spy Agency Data after Sept. 11 Led FBI to Dead Ends," *New York Times*, January 17, 2006, p. 1.

28. Ibid.

29. Walter Pincus, "For Petraeus, first impressions at CIA will be critical," *Washington Post*, April 29, 2011, p. 2.

30. Walter Pincus, "Petraeus would lead a militarized CIA," *Washington Post*, April 28, 2011, p. 4.

31. Pincus, "For Petraeus, first impressions," p. 2.

32. Pincus, "Petraeus would lead,"p. 4.

CHAPTER SEVEN

1. John Arquilla and Fogelson-Lubliner, "The Pentagon's Biggest Boondoggles," *New York Times*, March 13, 2011, p. 12. (Arquilla is the author of *Worst Enemy: The Reluctant Transformation of the American Military*, New York: Prometheus Books, 2009.

2. Websites that provide useful up-to-date information on national missile defense include those of the Union of Concerned Scientists, the Federation of American Scientists, the Council for a Livable World, the Non-Proliferation Project of the Carnegie Endowment for International Peace, and the Coalition to Reduce Nuclear Dangers.

3. Henry A. Kissinger, *White House Years*, Boston: Little, Brown and Company, 1979, p. 539.

4. Lou Cannon, *President Reagan*, New York: Prometheus Books, 2009, p. 333.

5. Ibid.

6. Raymond Garthoff, "The Great Transition: American-Soviet Relations and the End of the Cold War," Washington: The Brookings Institution, 1994, p. 516.

7. Frances Fitzgerald, *Way Out there in the Blue: Reagan, Star Wars and the End of the Cold War*, New York: Simon & Schuster, 2000, p. 128.

8. As late as October 1988, three years after Soviet Communist Party leader Mikhail Gorbachev had begun the revolution that eventually cost him his country and his job, Gates warned in a speech, "The dictatorship of the Communist Party remains untouched and untouchable . . . . A long, competitive struggle with the Soviet Union still lies before us." Over the next three years, the Berlin Wall, the Warsaw Pact, and even the Soviet Union itself collapsed

9. Noel E. Firth and James H. Noren, *Soviet Defense Spending: A History of CIA Estimates, 1950–1990*, College Station, TX: Texas A&M University Press, 1998,

10. George Ball, *The New York Review of Books*, April 11, 1985, pp. 38–44.

11. Fitzgerald, *Way Out There*, p. 371.

12. Ibid.

13. Ibid., p. 167.

14. Larence T. DiRita, Baker Spring, and John Luddy, "Thumbs Down to the Bottom-up Review," Backgrounder #957, Heritage Foundation, September 14, 1993.

15. *New York Times*, September 26, 1988, p. 11.

16. Seymour Hersh, "Missile Wars," *The New Yorker*, September 26, 1994, p. 91. Seventeen years later, writing in the *New Yorker*, Hersh deflated the wild claims of the military-industrial-congressional complex regarding Iran's missile capabilities that have been cited to justify deployment of a regional missile defense in Eastern Europe.

17. George Tenet is best known for his remark to President George Bush in December 2002 ("It's a slam dunk, Mr. President"), when the White House wanted intelligence tailored to make the public case for war against Iraq.

18. There are unclassified versions of both the 1998 Report of the Commission to Assess the Ballistic Missile Threat to the United States (also known as "The Rumsfeld Report"), and the 1999 National Intelligence Estimate ("Foreign Missile Developments and the Ballistic Missile Threat to the United States Through 2015." The Rumsfeld Report played a major role in worsening the perception of the ballistic missile threat, and the National Intelligence Council estimate incorporated a number of the Rumsfeld Report's recommendations. These versions can be found on the website of the Federation of American Scientists. Also see Richard L. Garwin's "The Rumsfeld Report: What We Did," *Bulletin of the Atomic Scientists*, November/December 1998.

19. Fitzgerald, *Way Out There in the Blue*, pp. 167–168.

20. *New York Times*, January 12, 2001, p. 11.

21. Rumsfeld, *Known and Unknown*, p. 308.

22. "What the G.O.P. Missed," editorial, *New York Times*, November 28, 2010, p. 22.

23. Chris Strohm and David Lerman, "Defense contractors beef up cybersecurity, space programs," *Washington Post*, January 16, 2012, p. 17.

24. Ignatius, "Reshaping the rules of war," p. 15.

25. David Ignatius, "Ike was right: Cut defense," *Washington Post*, January 26, 2011, p. A23.

26. Short-range missiles are capable of reaching targets within approximately 621 miles (1,000 km).

27. William Broad, "U.S. Missile Defense Strategy is Flawed, Panel Finds," *New York Times*, September 12, 2012, p. 3.

CHAPTER EIGHT

1. Daniel Wirls, *Irrational Security: The Politics of Defense from Reagan to Obama*, Baltimore, MD: Johns Hopkins University Press, 2010, pp. 134-135.

2. It's important to keep in mind that there are risks to force protection in any withdrawal scheme. The month of June 2011, for example, saw the deaths of fourteen U.S. servicemen, marking the worst month for U.S. fatalities in three years.

3. Richard Betts, "A Disciplined Defense: How to Regain Strategic Solvency," *Foreign Affairs*, November-December 2007, p. 87.

4. Thom Shanker, "Economics Crash Course for New Military Chief," *New York Times*, October 3, 2011, p. 8.
5. Tom Vanden Brook and Ray Locker, "Mentor's Role Led to Altered Exercise: Air Force retiree also a Boeing exec," *USA Today*, November 29, 2011, p. 1.
6. David Barstow, "Pentagon Finds No Fault in Ties to TV Analysts," *New York Times*, December 25, 2011, p. 18.
7. Craig Whitlock, "Defense budget a target for cuts," *Washington Post*, January 27, 2011, p. 18.
8. Marcus Weisgerber, "Pentagon's Phantom Savings: $330 Billion Claim Erodes as Programs Reappear," *Defense News*, May 16, 2011, p. 1.
9. The section has benefited from the excellent work in the area of reducing defense spending that has been done by the Bipartisan Policy Center, Center for a New American Security, Congressional Budget Office, the Sustainable Defense Task Force, and the National Commission on Fiscal Responsibility and Reform.
10. "National Defense Budget Estimates for FY 2011 (Green Book)," Department of Defense, Table 7-5.
11. "Defense Manpower Requirements Report for FY 2011," Defense Department, Table 2-1.
12. "Debts, Deficits, and Defense: A Way Forward," Report of the Sustainable Defense Task Force, 2011, p. 25.
13. Amy Belasco, "The Cost of Iraq, Afghanistan, and Other Global War on Terror Operations Since 9/11," Washington, DC: Congressional Research Service, 2011, p. 33.
14. Congressional Budget Office, June 30, 2011. (Walter Pincus, "Pentagon costs are rising quickly, CBO warns," *Washington Post*, July 1, 2011, p. 2.)
15. Secretary of Defense Robert Gates, Speech to the American Enterprise Institute, May 27, 2011.
16. Ellen Nakashima, "New Post Proposed at Pentagon," *Washington Post*, March 29, 2009, p. 3.
17. Http://www.defense.gov/news/newsarticle.aspx?id=60360.
18. Elisabeth Bumiller and Thom Shanker, "Pentagon Says Cuts Would Affect Raises, Health Plan and Base Closings," *New York Times*, January 27, 2012, p. 11.
19. Even Department of Defense studies acknowledge that there are a significant number of troops in areas that do not require a U.S. military presence. See http://militarybases.com and http://siadapp.dmdc.osd.mil/personnel/military/history/hst1012.pdf.
20. Belasco, "Cost of Iraq, Afghanistan, and Other Global War on Terror Operations," pp. 37–38.
21. Commission on Wartime Contracting in Iraq and Afghanistan, "Special Report on Contractor Business Systems," September 29, 2009, www.wartimecontracting.gov/docs/CWC_SRI_business-systems_2009-09-21.pdf.
22. Ronald O'Rourke, "Air Force F-22 Fighter Program: Background and Issues for Congress," September 11, 2009, Washington, DC: Congressional Research Service, 2009, p. 8.
23. Pat Towell, "House Puts Pentagon on Notice with Move to Hold Up F-22," *Congressional Quarterly Weekly*, July 24, 1999, pp. 1803–04.

24. Christopher Bolkcom, "F/A Raptor," January 6, 2005, Washington, DC: Congressional Research Service, p. 6.
25. Ibid.
26. Christopher Drew, "New Details On Troubled F-35 Fighter," *New York Times*, January 26, 2011, p. B1.
27. Nathan Hodge, "The $1 Trillion Fighter-Jet Fleet," *Wall Street Journal*, May 26, 2011, p. 3.
28. Marjorie Censer, "Go big or go to war with the weapons you have," *Washington Post*, May 29, 2011, p. 1.
29. William Pfaff, "Manufacturing Insecurity: How Militarism Endangers Americans," *Foreign Affairs*, Vol. 89, No. 6, November/December 2010, p. 138.
30. "Debts, Deficits, and Defense: A Way Forward," A Report of the Sustainable Defense Task Force, June 2010, p. 31.
31. See Harvey M. Sapolsky, Eugene Gholz, and Caitlin Talmadge, *US Defense Politics: The Origins of Security Policy*, New York: Routledge, 2009, p. 111.
32. Richard Whittle, *The Dream Machine: The Untold History of the Notorious V-22 Osprey*, cited in Elisabeth Bumiller, "Costly Aircraft Suggests Cuts Won't Be Easy," *New York Times*, November 20, 2011, p. 24.
33. Michael J. Sullivan, "V-22 Osprey Aircraft: Assessments Needed to Address Operational and Cost Concerns to Define Future Investments," Washington, DC: General Accounting Office, 2009.
34. An Osprey crashed in Afghanistan in 2011, killing four of the twenty-two aboard the aircraft. The cause of the crash has never been determined.
35. Cheney, *In My Time*, p. 166.
36. Drew, "Troubled F-35 Fighter," B1.
37. Walter Pincus, "Lawmakers will fight Gates's plan to cancel Marine vehicle," *Washington Post*, January 16, 2011, p. A6.
38. *New York Times*, September 1, 2012, p. 12.
39. Walter Pincus, "House votes to cut $125 million in spending on military bands," *Washington Post*, July 7, 2011, p. 3.
40. U.S. Committee on Armed Services, "Hearing to Receive Testimony on the F-35 Joint Strike Fighter Program in Review of the Defense Authorization Request for Fiscal Year 2012 and Future Years Defense Program," May 19, 2011, p. 14.
41. Andrea Shalal-Esa, "Lockheed, Pentagon Vow to Attack F-35 Costs," Reuters.com, May 12, 2011.
42. William D. Hartung, "Military Spending: A Poor Job Creator," Washington, DC: Center for International Policy, August 2011, p. 2.
43. Robert Pollin and Heidi Garrett-Peltier, "The U.S. Employment Effects of Military and Domestic Spending Priorities," Department of Economics and Political Economy Research Institute, October 2009.
44. See "What Kinds of Federal Spending Create the Most Good Jobs," http://www.wand.org/wp-content/uploads/2010/08/fact-jobs-08.pdf.
45. Ben Freeman, National Security Fellow at Project on Government Oversight, Washington, DC, December 12, 2011.
46. The increased military spending equals the cuts that were sustained by the

Department of Education ($1.3 billion); the Department of Labor ($870 million); the Environmental Protection Agency ($1.35 billion); Housing and Urban Development ($942 million); and the Department of Agriculture's Women, Infants and Children program ($504 million), which provides food and baby formula to low-income families. *Washington Post*, April 13, 2011, p. 3: "Budget cuts spread the pain." The ironic title of this article conveys the message that the mainstream media often extend to the budget process.

47. Dick Cheney with Liz Cheney, *In My Time: A Personal and Political Memoir*, New York: Threshold Editions, 2011.

48. Secretary of Defense Gates, Commencement Address to Notre Dame University, May 22, 2011.

49. Larry Korb, "The Myth of Robert Gates," *National Interest*, May 27, 2011, www.nationalinterest.org.

50. *Public Papers*, Eisenhower, Item 50: "The Chance for Peace," delivered before the American Society of Newspaper Editors, April 16, 1956, p. 182.

51. Binyamin Appelbaum, "Neighbors May Suffer as the Military Shrinks," *New York Times*, January 7, 2012, p. 3.

52. Walter Pincus, "The Pentagon and its spending culture," *Washington Post*, September 20, 2011, p. 15.

53. See "Transforming Wartime Contracting: Controlling costs, reducing risks," Commission on Wartime Contracting in Iraq and Afghanistan, Washington, DC: US Government Printing Office, August 2011.

54. Joe Davidson, "Intelligence contractors' pay, numbers raise concerns," *Washington Post*, September 21, 2011, p. B4

55. "US military forges ahead with European force cuts," Associated Press/AP Online, May 21, 2011.

56. Phil Steward, "Gates calls Pentagon cuts a threat to global stability," *Washington Post*, May 23, 2011, p. 17.

57. *New York Times*, January 3, 2012, p. 1.

CHAPTER NINE

1. William Pfaff, "Manufacturing Insecurity: How Militarism Endangers America," *Foreign Affairs*, Vol. 89, No. 6, November-December 2010, p. 133.

2. "Military-to-Military Relationships: The ties that bind," *The Economist*, February 26, 2011, p. 65.

3. Ibid.

4. Farah Stockman, "Critics Question Billions in Aid Routed Back to US Contractors," *Boston Globe*, February 3, 2011, p. 1.

5 Michael Mandelbaum, "Superpower on the Cheap," *Washington Post*, February 20, 2011, p. 4.

6. Ronald E. Neumann, "A continued U.S. deployment in Afghanistan," *Washington Post*, February 20, 2012, p. 19.

7. Walter Pincus, "Pentagon Expanding its Domestic Surveillance Activity," *Washington Post*, November 27, 2005, p. 1.

8. William Arkin, "The Pentagon Breaks the Law," *Washington Post*, December 22, 2005, p.

9. Ibid.

10. Jim Dwyer, "New York Police Covertly Join In at Protest Rallies," *New York Times*, December 22, 2005, p. 1.

11. Ibid., p. 28.

12. Chris Hawley, "NYPD monitored Muslim students," *Washington Post*, February 19, 2012, p. 14.

13. U.S. Army Memorandum cited in "Secrecy News" of the Project on Government Secrecy, edited by Steven Aftergood, January 19, 2012.

14. WNYC.org, August 24, 2011, "Report on NYPD-CIA Collaboration Sparks Calls of Oversight and NYPD Denial," Associated Press, August 24, 2011.

15. Charles C. Krulak and Joseph P. Hoar, "Guantánamo Forever?," *New York Times*, December 13, 2011, p. 29.

16. David Wood, "Busy With Afghanistan, the U.S. Military Has No Time to Train for Big Wars," www.politicsdaily.com, December 27, 2010.

17. *New York Times*, February 28, 2011, p. 9

18. Selig Harrison, "How to Leave Afghanistan Without Losing," *Foreign Policy*, August 24, 2010, p. 47.

19. *Washington Post*, November 18, 2011, p. 11.

20. Joseph M. Parent and Paul K. MacDonald, "The Wisdom of Retrenchment: America Must Cut Back to Move Forward," *Foreign Affairs*, November/December 2011, Vol. 9, No. 6, p. 37.

21. Yochi J. Dreazen, "Panetta Plays Last Card, Warns Defense Cuts Harm the U.S.," *National Journal*, November 10, 2011.

22. The report was completed in 2004, but kept out of circulation until after the presidential elections of November 2004; it can be found on the website of the Federation of American Scientists.

23. Jonathan Alter, *The Defining Moment: FDR's Hundred Days and the Triumph of Hope*, New York: Simon & Schuster, 2006. p. 336.

24. William Pfaff, "Managing Insecurity: How Militarism Endangers America," *Foreign Affairs*, Vol. 89, No. 6, November/December 2010, p. 140.

25. Matthew Evangelista, *Unarmed Forces: The Transnational Movement to End the Cold War*, Ithaca, NY: Cornell University Press, 1999, p. 3.

Index

433

and Obama administration, 201
preemptive use of force and "Defense Policy Guidance", 19
and the "surge", 211–12
and U.S. foreign policies, 399–400
and U.S. military aid, 384
and weapons of mass destruction (WMD), 156–62
Iraq Study Group, 191
Iraq Survey Group, 165, 171
Iron Curtain, 66–67
"iron triangle", 189–90
Islamic culture, 412–13
"Islamoterrorism", 315–16, 373
Islarnbouli, Muhammad Shawqi, 57
Israel
    and ABM systems, 291
    and ballistic missiles, 310–11
    and Clinton administration, 141–42
    and Egypt, 382
    and Nuclear Non-Proliferation Treaty, 224, 345, 347
    and Obama administration, 237
    and U.S. foreign policies, –3, 198, 370–71, 377, 391, 392
    and U.S. military aid, 348, 349, 381

Jackson, Henry "Scoop", 25, 281
Jackson-Vanik Bill, 403
Jeffrey, James F., 92
Johns Hopkins University, 31–32, 383
Johnson, Hiram, 239
Johnson, Lyndon B., 24, 33–34, 36, 51, 82, 85, 152, 240, 242, 272–73, 287, 369–70
Johnson, Robert, 47
Johnston, J. Bennett, 288
Joint Chiefs of Staff (JCS), 103, 105–6, 110, 166–67, 190, 218, 228, 235, 241, 327, 341, 347, 353
Joint Forces Command (JFC), 353
Joint Readiness Training Center, 392
Jones, James, 195, 215, 266, 269, 341
Jones, Walter B., 353
Jordan, 228, 255, 348

Joseph, Robert, 166
Justice Department, 184, 229–30

"K" group, Guatemala, 45
Kagan, Robert, 22–23, 411
Kamal, Hussein, 176–77
Kaplan, Robert, 411
Karzai, Hamid, 16, 206, 212, 213, 221, 385, 415
Kay, David, 165, 171
Kayani, Ashfaq, 386
Kellog-Briand Pact, 224
Kelly, Raymond, 389
Kemp, Jack, 287
Kennan, George F., 16, 46, 82–83, 109, 136, 414
Kennedy, John F.
    and arms control, 125, 128, 248, 310
    and Bay of Pigs, 24, 33, 49–50, 85
    and inexperience with military bureaucracy, 36
    and national security concerns, 34
    and Vietnam, 50–51, 240, 272–73
Kennedy, Paul, 18
Kerr, Richard, 157, 173–74, 177, 202, 255
Kerry, John F., 104, 143, 226
Kerry-Lugar Bill, 386
Keyworth, George, 304
Khan, A. Q., 254
Khrushchev, Nikita, 251
Khyber Pass, 212, 215
Kim Jong-il, 274
King Ethelbert of Kent, 287
Kinsley, Michael, 155
Kirkpatrick, Jeane, 69
Kissinger, Henry A.
    and ABM systems, 281
    and ABM Treaty, 34
    and Chile, 52
    and disarmament, 225
    intellect of, 79
    and Iran, 42
    and Israel, 415
    and Nixon administration, 109

Pahlavi, Ashraf, 42
Pahlavi, Mohammed Reza (Shah), 39,
    42–43, 55, 394
Pakistan
    and al-Qaeda, 214
    and ballistic missiles, 310–11
    and covert U.S. actions, 53
    domino effect and Afghanistan, 210
    and lack of U.S. diplomacy, 16
    and Najibullah regime, 95
    and Nuclear Non-Proliferation
        Treaty, 224, 345, 347
    and nuclear weapons, 254–55, 294
    and Obama administration, 205,
        232
    and the Taliban, 209, 210, 211, 212
    and U.S. foreign policies, 396–99
    and U.S. military aid, 348–49,
        385–87
    and U.S. use of force, 16, 192, 256
    and weapons of mass destruction
        (WMD), 282
Palestine, 141–42, 237, 391, 392, 393,
    412
Pan American flight 103, 75–76
Panama, 75, 85–87, 194, 409
Panetta Institute for Public Policy,
    27–28
Panetta, Leon
    and arms control, 347
    and China, 406–7
    and the CIA, 266, 270
    and Clinton administration, 203–4
    and defense spending, 328, 330,
        342, 343, 348, 354, 355, 359,
        365, 411
    and Iran, 402
    and Iraq, 159
    and James Woolsey, 111
    and Obama administration, 195,
        196, 199, 201–4, 215, 217
    and the War on Terror, 256
Panetta, Sylvia, 28
Partial Test Ban Treaty, 125, 310
Patriot missiles, 291
Paul, Ron, 226, 352

Pax Americana, 19, 73
Pax Brittanica, 18
Pearl Harbor attack, 140
the Pentagon
    and 9/11 attacks, 159–60
    and Afghanistan, 207–12
    and Bush II administration, 189–92
    and the CIA, 239–46, 250–52,
        267–69
    and the Comprehensive Test Ban
        Treaty (CTBT), 128–30
    Ford administration and Na-
        tional Intelligence Estimates
        (NIEs), 246–48
    and intelligence militarization, 246,
        261–63
    and the National Security Agency
        (NSA), 263–71
    and national security demilitariza-
        tion, 271–76, 379–87
    Pentagon culture and defense
        spending, 358–67
    Reagan administration and Bill
        Casey, 248–50
    and relations with the Clinton
        administration, 103–8, 118
    and satellite imagery, 252–56
    and USS *Cole* bombing, 134–35
    and the War on Terror, 256–61
    See also defense spending; national
        missile defense
Pentagon Papers on Vietnam, 207–8
Peres, Shimon, 98
Perle, Richard, 20–21, 69, 78, 107, 259,
    309–10
Perry, William, 110–11, 136, 138, 225
Persian Gulf and Bush I administration,
    87–93
Petraeus, David
    and Afghanistan, 205–6, 215–17,
        218, 220, 267, 268–69
    and Central Command, 374
    and the CIA, 268–71
    and Iraq, 268
    and Obama administration, 196,
        199–201, 216–17, 219, 267

453

About the Author

Melvin A. Goodman was a Soviet analyst at the CIA and the Department of State for twenty-four years and a professor of international relations at the National War College for eighteen years. He served in the U.S. Army in Athens, Greece, for three years, and was intelligence adviser to the SALT delegation from 1971 to 1972. Currently, Goodman is senior fellow at the Center for International Policy in Washington, DC, and adjunct professor of government at Johns Hopkins University. He has authored, co-authored, and edited seven books, including *Gorbachev's Retreat: The Third World*; *The Wars of Eduard Shevardnadze*; *The Phantom Defense: America's Pursuit of the Star Wars Illusion*; *Bush League Diplomacy: How the Neoconservatives are Putting the World at Risk*; and *Failure of Intelligence: The Decline and Fall of the CIA*. His articles and op-eds have appeared in numerous publications, including the *New York Times*, *Harper's*, *Foreign Policy*, *Foreign Service Journal*, the *Baltimore Sun*, and the *Washington Post*.